MAKING ENGLAND, 796–1042

Making England, 796–1042 explores the creation and establishment of the kingdom of England and the significant changes that led to it becoming one of the most successful and sophisticated political structures in the western world by the middle of the eleventh century.

At the end of the eighth century when King Offa of Mercia died, England was a long way from being a single kingdom ruled by a single king. This book examines how and why the kingdom of England formed in the way it did and charts the growth of royal power over the following two and a half centuries. Key political and military events are introduced alongside developments within government, the law, the church and wider social and economic changes to provide a detailed picture of England throughout this period. This is also set against a wider European context to demonstrate the influence of external forces on England's development.

With a focus on England's rulers and elites, *Making England, 796–1042* uncovers the type of kingdom England was and analyses its strengths and weaknesses as well as the emerging concept of a specifically English nation. Arranged both chronologically and thematically, and containing a selection of maps and genealogies, it is the ideal introduction to this subject for students of medieval history and of medieval England in particular.

Richard Huscroft is Head of History at Westminster School, London, and is the author of several books on medieval history, including *Ruling England, 1042–1217* (2016) and *Tales from the Long Twelfth Century* (2016).

MAKING ENGLAND, 796–1042

Richard Huscroft

Routledge
Taylor & Francis Group

LONDON AND NEW YORK

First published 2019
by Routledge
2 Park Square, Milton Park, Abingdon, Oxon OX14 4RN

and by Routledge
711 Third Avenue, New York, NY 10017

Routledge is an imprint of the Taylor & Francis Group, an informa business

British Library Cataloguing-in-Publication Data
A catalogue record for this book is available from the British Library

Library of Congress Cataloging-in-Publication Data
A catalog record for this book has been requested

ISBN: 978-1-138-18245-5 (hbk)
ISBN: 978-1-138-18246-2 (pbk)
ISBN: 978-0-429-47025-7 (ebk)

Typeset in Bembo
by Apex CoVantage, LLC

MIX
Paper from
responsible sources
FSC
www.fsc.org   FSC™ C013985

Printed in the United Kingdom
by Henry Ling Limited

CONTENTS

Preface   *ix*
Chronology of main events   *xi*
A note on money   *xvii*
References and abbreviations   *xix*
List of debates   *xxi*
Maps   *xxiii*
Lists and Genealogies   *xxix*

Introduction: England and the English in 796   1

PART I
The origins of a kingdom, 796–899   **15**

1 The events, 796–899   17
    796–839   17
    839–858   21
    858–871   24
    871–878   27
    878–892   31
    893–899   34
    Notes   38

2 Ruling the kingdoms, 796–899   40
    Becoming king   40
    The requirements of kingship   43

'Tools and resources'   46
Ruling at a distance   50
Military organisation   52
The reign of Alfred the Great   54
The kingdom of the Anglo-Saxons   72
Notes   74

3 The kings and the law, 796–899   76
Principles and practice   76
Alfred the Great and the law   82
The limits of the law   89
Notes   90

4 The kings and the church, 796–899   91
The structure of the English Church   91
English kings and the pre-viking church   95
The English Church and the Vikings   98
Alfred the Great and the church   99
Between a viking rock and a royal hard place   104
Notes   105

PART II
The birth of a kingdom, 899–975   **107**

5 The events, 899–975   109
899–902   109
903–918   110
919–924   113
924–939   115
939–946   120
946–955   121
956–959   123
959–975   125
Notes   126

6 Ruling the kingdom, 899–975   128
The bumpy road to a single English kingdom   128
Military power   130
Household government   134
Government by assembly   137
Regional government   142
Mints and coins   145

	Royal wealth	*147*
	Royal power in the north	*148*
	Edgar's English kingdom	*149*
	Notes	*151*
7	The kings and the law, 899–975	153
	Law and government	*153*
	Law codes and their concerns	*155*
	Courts	*161*
	Hearing a case	*163*
	Policing and punishment	*166*
	The longer arm of the law	*168*
	Notes	*170*
8	The kings and the church, 899–975	172
	Royal government and the church	*172*
	Kings and dioceses	*174*
	Monasticism and realpolitik	*178*
	Reform and reality	*186*
	Notes	*188*

PART III
The testing of a kingdom, 975–1042   191

9	The events, 975–1042	193
	975–979	*193*
	979–991	*195*
	992–1005	*197*
	1006–1012	*200*
	1013–1016	*202*
	1016–1035	*207*
	1035–1042	*210*
	Notes	*213*
10	Ruling the kingdom, 975–1042	215
	King and nobility	*215*
	Household government	*221*
	Local government	*227*
	Military organisation	*230*
	Royal finance	*232*
	A kingdom worth fighting for	*236*
	Notes	*238*

11 The kings and the law, 975–1042   240
    Aethelred's laws   *240*
    Cnut's laws   *248*
    Law in action   *250*
    The roots of the common law   *256*
    Notes   *257*

12 The kings and the church, 975–1042   259
    All churches great and small   *259*
    The church and royal power   *260*
    Aethelred II and the church   *261*
    Cnut and the English Church   *265*
    Out of the frying pan . . .   *269*
    Notes   *270*

Glossary of terms   *271*
Suggestions for further reading   *277*
Index   *289*

PREFACE

In 2005, my book *Ruling England, 1042–1217* was published. A somewhat revised second edition was produced in 2016. This book is designed to complement *Ruling England* and, in many ways, serve as a prequel to it. It is overwhelmingly concerned, like its predecessor, with the exercise of political power by the kings of England and with how England's governmental, legal and ecclesiastical structures developed during this earlier period to underpin and strengthen royal authority. It is also subject to the same limitations as *Ruling England* in that it considers events in the rest of the British Isles and (within England) society beyond the political elite only in passing and only where relevant to its main themes. Having said that, there is one big difference between the two books. The Norman and Angevin kings who featured in *Ruling England* ruled over a single English kingdom. Its size and shape were largely settled by 1066, and these remained more or less the same over the next 150 years. By contrast, at the start of the period covered here, a single English kingdom did not exist, and one only came into being during the ninth and tenth centuries. How this happened and why are the major themes of this book.

Like *Ruling England*, this book is divided into three chronological parts, and each part is subdivided into four chapters. The first chapter in each part contains an outline of the principal political and military events. The other three chapters in each part deal in turn with developments in government, law and the kings' relationship with the English Church during the periods in question. From time to time, I have also included discrete, short 'debates' on particular topics. But it needs to be stressed that this book is only an introduction to the areas it covers. Far more involved, detailed and ground-breaking work has been done by the dozens of scholars on whose research and ideas I have almost entirely depended. A brief idea of how much more there is to consider is provided by the Suggestions for further reading section at the end of the book.

I have depended on the generosity of others, too, as well as their work. I am deeply grateful to the Governors of Westminster School who granted me a sabbatical in Play Term 2016 in order to write this book; to the Head Master, Patrick Derham, who put my case to them with such whole-hearted enthusiasm, and to my colleagues in the History Department who covered my absence and supported my plan so selflessly. Inevitably, being away from work meant spending more time at home, where my family tolerated and indulged my passing preoccupation with all things Anglo-Saxon. Writing is ultimately a solitary business, but it is much easier when those close by are both encouraging and yet still grounded in the real world. I dedicated *Ruling England* to my queen and my princess in 2005, and I do the same now. Without them, neither of these books would ever have been written.

CHRONOLOGY OF MAIN EVENTS

758–96	Offa, king of Mercia
768	Charlemagne, king of the Franks
786–802	Beornwulf, king of Wessex
787	Ecgfrith, son of Offa, consecrated king of the Mercians
789	Beornwulf marries Eadburh, Offa's daughter
	Viking raid on Portland, Dorset
793	Vikings sack Lindisfarne, Northumbria
796	Deaths of Offa and Ecgfrith
	Eardwulf consecrated king of Northumbria
796–821	Cenwulf, king of Mercia
800	Charlemagne crowned emperor
802–39	Ecgberht, king of Wessex
814	Death of Charlemagne
814–40	Louis the Pious, emperor and king of the Franks
821–3	Ceolwulf I, king of Mercia
823	Ceolwulf I deposed
823–6	Beornwulf, king of Mercia
825	Battle of *Ellendun* (Wroughton): Ecgberht defeats Beornwulf
826	Death of Beornwulf
826–7	West Saxon conquest of south-east England
	Aethelwulf, son of Ecgberht, king of Kent
827	Death of Ludeca, king of Mercia
827–c.838	Wiglaf, king of Mercia
838	Battle of Hingston Down: Ecgberht defeats Cornish and viking allies
839	Death of Ecgberht
839–58	Aethelwulf, king of Wessex
839–c.852	Aethelstan, son of Aethelwulf, king of Kent

840–52	Beorhtwulf, king of Mercia
843–77	Charles the Bald, king of the Franks
849	Birth of Alfred, son of Aethelwulf, at Wantage, Berkshire
852–74	Burgred, king of Mercia
853	Burgred marries Aethelswith, daughter of Aethelwulf
	Alfred visits Rome
855–6	Aethelwulf's pilgrimage to Rome with Alfred
	Aethelbald, son of Aethelwulf, seizes power in Wessex
	Aethelwulf visits court of Charles the Bald
	Aethelwulf marries Judith, daughter of Charles the Bald
856–8	Aethelwulf and Aethelbald divide power in Wessex
858	Death of Aethelwulf
858–60	Aethelbald, king of Wessex
	Aethelberht, son of Aethelwulf, king of Kent
	Aethelbald marries Judith
860	Death of Aethelbald
860–5	Aethelberht, king of Wessex
865	Death of Aethelberht
865–71	Aethelred I, king of Wessex
865	The 'Great Army' led by Ivarr the Boneless arrives in England
867	Great Army conquers Northumbria
868	Joint Mercian/West Saxon siege of Nottingham
	Alfred marries Ealhswith of Mercia
868–9	Great Army returns to Northumbria
869–70	Great Army conquers East Anglia
869	King Edmund of East Anglia killed by Vikings
870–1	Great Army attacks Wessex
871	Battles of Ashdown and Basing
	Death of Aethelred I
	'Summer Army' led by Guthrum arrives in England
871–99	Alfred, king of Wessex
871	Battle of Wilton: Alfred defeated by Vikings
872	Vikings return to Northumbria
873–4	Vikings conquer Mercia
874	King Burgred of Mercia flees to Rome
874–8/9	Ceolwulf II, king of Mercia
875–7	Vikings attack Wessex
876	Vikings settle southern Northumbria and establish kingdom of York
877	Ceolwulf II and Guthrum partition Mercia
	Vikings leave Wessex (August)
878	Guthrum attacks Chippenham (January)
	Alfred takes refuge on Athelney

	Battle of Edington (May): Alfred defeats Guthrum
	Guthrum baptised
878x90	Treaty between Alfred and Guthrum
879–80	Vikings settle in East Anglia
879–90	Guthrum, king of East Anglia
883	Aethelred, lord of Mercia
886	Alfred 'occupies' London
	? Aethelred of Mercia marries Aethelflaed, daughter of Alfred
892–6	Vikings attack Wessex
892–3?	First version of *Anglo-Saxon Chronicle* completed
	Asser writes *Life* of Alfred
899	Death of Alfred (26 October)
899–924	Edward the Elder, son of Alfred, king of Wessex
899–902	Revolt of Aethelwold atheling, son of Aethelred I
902	Battle of the Holme (December): death of Aethelwold
910	Battle of Tettenhall (August): West Saxons and Mercians defeat Danes of York
911	Death of Aethelred, lord of Mercia
911x919?	Burghal Hidage compiled
911–18	Aethelflaed, Lady of the Mercians
	West Saxon/Mercian conquest of England south of the Humber
918	Death of Aethelflaed
	Edward the Elder takes direct control of Mercia
920	Northumbrians and Strathclyde Welsh submit to Edward
	Sihtric, king of York
924	Death of Edward the Elder (17 July)
	Aethelstan, son of Edward the Elder, king of the Mercians
	Death of Aelfweard, son of Edward the Elder
924–39	Aethelstan, king of the English
926	Sihtric marries Eadgyth, sister of Aethelstan
927	Death of Sihtric
	Aethelstan takes control of Northumbria
	Aethelstan meets British rulers at Eamont, Cumbria (July)
	Welsh and Cornish submit to Aethelstan
933	Death at sea of Edwin atheling, half-brother of Aethelstan
934	Aethelstan campaigns in Scotland
937	Battle of *Brunanburh*: Aethelstan defeats coalition of Scots, Dublin Vikings and Strathclyde Welsh
939	Death of Aethelstan (27 October)
	Olaf Guthfrithson seizes control of York
939–46	Edmund, son of Edward the Elder, king of the English
940	Olaf Guthfrithson sacks Tamworth and seizes the 'Five Boroughs'
	Dunstan abbot of Glastonbury

941	Death of Olaf Guthfrithson
944	Edmund conquers Northumbria
946	Edmund murdered (26 May)
946–55	Eadred, son of Edward the Elder, king of the English
947/8; 952–4	Erik Bloodaxe, king of York
c.954–63	Aethelwold, abbot of Abingdon
954	Erik Bloodaxe, last viking king of York, killed on Stainmore
955	Death of Eadred (23 November)
955–9	Eadwig, son of Edmund, king of the English
957	? Edgar, son of Edmund, king of the Mercians
c.957–9?	Westminster converted into Benedictine monastery by Dunstan, bishop of London
959	Death of Eadwig (1 October)
959–75	Edgar, king of the English
959–88	Dunstan, archbishop of Canterbury
961	Oswald, bishop of Worcester
963–84	Aethelwold, bishop of Winchester
c.963–70	Edgar orders ejection of secular priests from all minsters and replacement by monks and nuns
	Edgar orders establishment of more than forty monasteries
964	Aethelwold, with Edgar's help, expels secular priests from Old Minster, Winchester, and replaces them with Benedictine monks from Abingdon (February)
	Edgar marries Aelfthryth, daughter of Ealdorman Ordgar
c.966–70	? *Regularis Concordia* issued
966	Edgar's charter for the New Minster, Winchester
971–92	Oswald, archbishop of York
c.973	Reform of English coinage by Edgar
973	Coronation of Edgar at Bath (May)
	Edgar meets other British rulers at Chester
975	Death of Edgar (8 July)
975–8	Edward the Martyr, king of the English
978	Edward murdered at Corfe, Dorset (18 March)
978–1016	Aethelred II, king of the English
979	Aethelred II consecrated at Kingston (4 May)
c.985	Aethelred II marries Aelfgifu, ? daughter of Ealdorman Thored of Northumbria
c.987–1014	Swein Forkbeard, king of Denmark
991	Battle of Maldon, Essex (August): Vikings defeat and kill Byrhtnoth, ealdorman of Essex
	First payment of tribute by Aethelred II to Vikings (£10,000)
	Treaty of Aethelred II with Duke Richard I of Normandy (March)
994	Treaty of Aethelred II with Olaf Tryggvason
995–9	Olaf Tryggvason, king of Norway

1002	Aethelred II marries Emma, daughter of Duke Richard II of Normandy
	St Brice's Day Massacre (13 November)
1002–23	Wulfstan, bishop of Worcester and archbishop of York
1006–7	The 'great fleet' led by Tostig ravages in England
1007–17	Eadric Streona, ealdorman of Mercia
1009	Destruction of new English fleet
1009–12	Thorkell the Tall's army in England
1012	Archbishop Aelfheah of Canterbury murdered at Greenwich
1013	Swein Forkbeard invades England (August)
1013–14	Swein Forkbeard, king of the English
	Aethelred II and family flee to Normandy
	? Cnut marries Aelfgifu of Northampton, daughter of Ealdorman Aelfhelm of southern Northumbria
1014	Death of Swein (3 February)
	Danish army chooses Cnut, Swein's son, as his successor
	Return of Aethelred II to England
	Cnut driven out of England and returns to Denmark
	Death of Aethelstan atheling, son of Aethelred II
1015	Murders of Sigeferth and Morcar
	Edmund atheling, son of Aethelred II and Aelfgifu, marries Sigeferth's widow
	Cnut returns to England
1016	Death of Aethelred II (23 April)
	Londoners choose Edmund Ironside as king; others choose Cnut
	Battle of Ashingdon, Essex (18 October): ? Cnut defeats Edmund
	England divided between Edmund and Cnut
	Death of Edmund (29 November)
1016–35	Cnut, king of the English
1017	Consecration of Cnut
	Cnut marries Emma, widow of Aethelred II
	Eadric Streona killed
1018	Agreement at Oxford between English and Danes
1019–35	Cnut, king of Denmark, following death of brother Harald
c.1023	Godwin, earl of Mercia
1023/32	Leofric, earl of Mercia
1026	Battle of the Holy River :? Cnut defeated by Swedes and Norwegians
1027	Cnut's pilgrimage to Rome
1028–30	Norway conquered by Danes
1033	Siward, earl of Northumbria
1035–47	Magnus, king of Norway
1035	Death of Cnut (12 November)
1035–42	Harthacnut, son of Cnut and Emma, king of Denmark

1035–40   Harold I, son of Cnut and Aelfgifu, king of the English
1036   Murder of Alfred atheling, son of Aethelred II and Emma
1040   Death of Harold I (17 March)
1040–2   Harthacnut, king of the English
c.1040/1   Edward atheling, son of Aethelred II and Emma, returns to England
1042   Death of Harthacnut (June)
1042–66   Edward the Confessor, king of the English

A NOTE ON MONEY

During the period covered by this book, there was usually only one coin in circulation, the silver penny. There were 12 pennies in a shilling and 240 pennies (20 shillings) in a pound. However, 'shillings' and 'pounds' were terms used for accounting and descriptive purposes only. There were no coins with those values.

REFERENCES AND ABBREVIATIONS

I have attempted to keep references to a minimum by giving a citation only when a source or secondary work has been quoted or referred to explicitly in the text. The following abbreviations have been used when citing the works which I have referred to most frequently. Full citations for the works listed here are given in the Suggestions for Further Reading section.

ASC (followed by a year)	*Anglo-Saxon Chronicle*, ed. Whitelock
Attenborough, *Laws*	*The Laws of the Earliest English Kings*, ed. Attenborough
BEH	*Bede's Ecclesiastical History of the English People*, ed. Colgrave and Mynors
Chron. Aethelweard	Aethelweard, *Chronicle*, ed. Campbell
EHD, i	*English Historical Documents c. 500–1042*, vol. i, ed. Whitelock
EHR	*English Historical Review*
JW, ii	*The Chronicle of John of Worcester*, vol. ii, ed. McGurk and Darlington
K&L	*Alfred the Great*, ed. Keynes and Lapidge
ODNB	*Oxford Dictionary of National Biography*
RC	*Regularis Concordia*, ed. Symons
Robertson, *Anglo-Saxon Charters*	*Anglo-Saxon Charters*, ed. Robertson
Robertson, *Laws*	*The Laws of the Kings of England from Edmund to Henry I*, ed. Robertson
S (followed by a number)	The designation given to an Anglo-Saxon charter in *Anglo-Saxon Charters*, ed. Sawyer and in The Electronic Sawyer
VSO	*Byrhtferth of Ramsey. The Lives of St Oswald and St Ecgwine*, ed. Lapidge
WJGND, ii	*The Gesta Normannorum Ducum of William of Jumièges*, vol. ii, ed. Van Houts
WMGRA, i	William of Malmesbury, *History of the Kings of England*, vol. i, ed. Mynors, Thomson and Winterbottom
Wormald, *MEL* i or ii	Patrick Wormald, *The Making of English Law*, vols. i and ii.

DEBATES

1 The *Anglo-Saxon Chronicle*: facts or fake news?   20
2 Who were the Vikings?   36
3 How 'Great' was King Alfred?   73
4 Where was *Brunanburh*?   119
5 How Danish was the Danelaw?   169
6 Who killed Edward the Martyr?   194
7 How 'Unready' was Aethelred II?   206
8 How rich was eleventh-century England?   212
9 Where did Anglo-Saxon royal documents come from?   226
10 Was England a nation-state by 1042?   237

MAPS

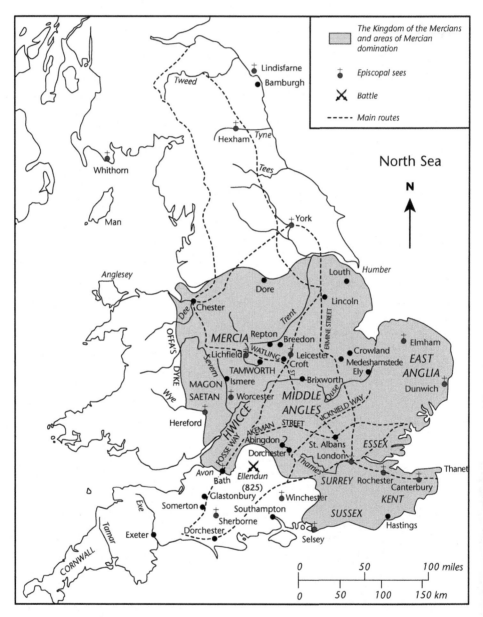

The Kingdom of the Mercians and areas of Mercian domination

† Episcopal sees

✕ Battle

- - - - Main routes

North Sea

N

Lindisfarne
Bamburgh
Tweed
Hexham
Tyne
Tees
Whithorn
Man
Anglesey
York
Louth
Humber
Dore
Lincoln
Chester
Dee
OFFA'S DYKE
MERCIA
Repton
Breedon
Lichfield
Leicester
Croft
ERMINE STREET
Crowland
Elmham
WATLING STREET
Medeshamstede
Ely
EAST ANGLIA
Severn
TAMWORTH
MAGON SAETAN
Ismere
Brixworth
Dunwich
Wye
Worcester
MIDDLE ANGLES
Ouse
Hereford
HWICCE
AKEMAN STREET
ICKNIELD WAY
Abingdon
St. Albans
ESSEX
FOSSE WAY
Dorchester
London
Thanet
Avon
Ellendun (825)
Thames
Rochester
Bath
SURREY
Canterbury
Glastonbury
Winchester
KENT
Somerton
Southampton
SUSSEX
Exe
Sherborne
Hastings
Tamar
Dorchester
Selsey
Exeter
CORNWALL

0   50   100 miles
0   50   100   150 km

MAP 1   England, (*c.*800)

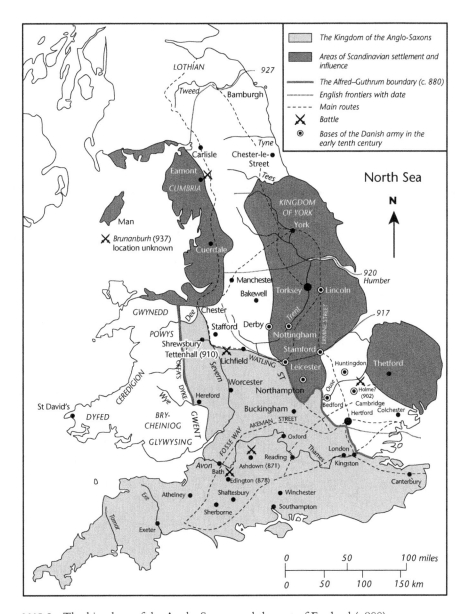

MAP 2 The kingdom of the Anglo-Saxons and the rest of England (*c.*900)

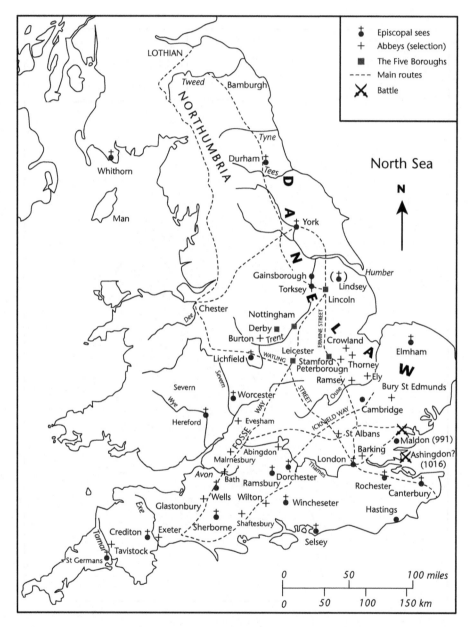

MAP 3 The Kingdom of the English (*c*.1000)

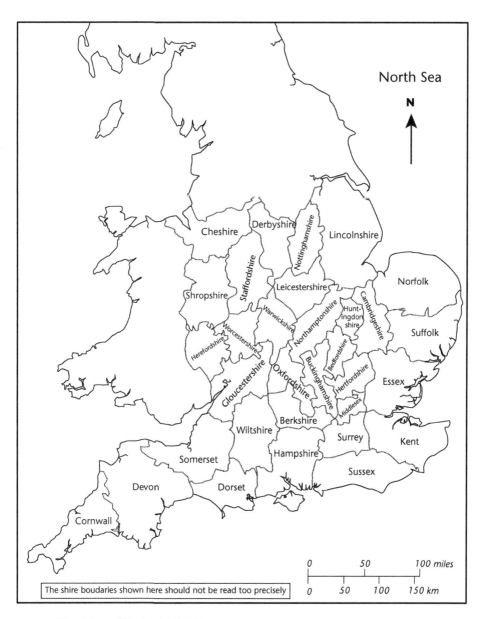

North Sea

N

Cheshire
Derbyshire
Nottinghamshire
Lincolnshire
Norfolk
Shropshire
Staffordshire
Leicestershire
Warwickshire
Northamptonshire
Hunt-
ingdon-
shire
Cambridgeshire
Suffolk
Worcestershire
Herefordshire
Gloucestershire
Oxfordshire
Buckinghamshire
Bedfordshire
Hertfordshire
Essex
Middlesex
Berkshire
Wiltshire
Surrey
Kent
Somerset
Hampshire
Sussex
Devon
Dorset
Cornwall

0   50   100 miles
0   50   100   150 km

The shire boudaries shown here should not be read too precisely

MAP 4 The shires of England (*c.*1050)

LISTS AND GENEALOGIES

Rulers of Northumbria and York to 954

The details given here are frequently speculative and open to question. The relationships between these rulers (familial or otherwise) are also hard to establish conclusively. It seems more helpful in this case simply to list the rulers rather than to try and construct their genealogies.

Kings of the Northumbrians

Aethelred I (790–796)
Osbald (796)
Eardwulf (796–*c*.806)
Aelfwald II (*c*.806–*c*.808)
Eardwulf (again) (808–*c*.810)
Eanred (*c*.810–*c*.848)
Osberht (*c*.848–862/3)
Aelle (*c*.862/3–867)
Osberht (again) (867)
Ecgberht I (867–873)
Ricsige (873–876)
Ecgberht II (876–878)
Aethelwold (son of Aethelred, king of the West Saxons) (*c*.900–902)

Viking rulers of York

Halfdan (brother of Ivarr the Boneless) (*c*.mid-870s–877)
Guthfrith I (878–*c*.895)

Sigfrith (*c*.895–*c*.900)

Cnut (*c*.900–902)

Eowils and Halfdan II, joint rulers (d.910)

Ragnall (son of Sihtric I, king of Dublin, grandson of Ivarr the Boneless) (919–920)

Sihtric II (son of Sihtric I) (920/1–927)

Olaf Sihtricson (son of Sihtric II) (927)

Guthfrith II (son of Sihtric I) (927)

Olaf Guthfrithson (son of Guthfrith II) (939–941)

Olaf Sihtricson (again) (941–944)

Ragnall Guthfrithson (son of Guthfrith II) (943–944)

Erik 'Bloodaxe' (son of Harald 'Fairhair', king of Norway (d.*c*.930)) (947–949)

Olaf Sihtricson (again) (949–952)

Erik 'Bloodaxe' (again) (952–954)

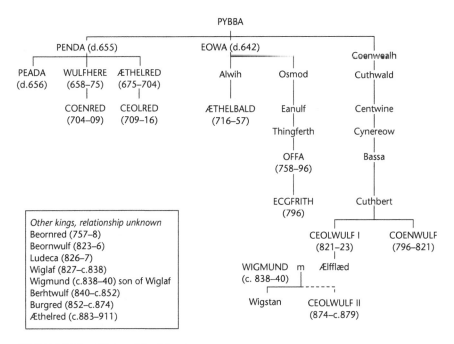

PYBBA

PENDA (d.655)   EOWA (d.642)
                                                      Coenwealh

PEADA   WULFHERE   ÆTHELRED   Alwih   Osmod   Cuthwald
(d.656)   (658–75)   (675–704)

          COENRED   CEOLRED   ÆTHELBALD Eanulf   Centwine
          (704–09)   (709–16)   (716–57)
                                             Thingferth Cynereow

                                             OFFA   Bassa
                                             (758–96)

                                             ECGFRITH   Cuthbert
                                             (796)
Other kings, relationship unknown
Beornred (757–8)   CEOLWULF I   COENWULF
Beornwulf (823–6)   (821–23)   (796–821)
Ludeca (826–7)
Wiglaf (827–c.838)   WIGMUND m   Ælfflæd
Wigmund (c.838–40) son of Wiglaf   (c. 838–40)
Berhtwulf (840–c.852)   Wigstan   CEOLWULF II
Burgred (852–c.874)   (874–c.879)
Æthelred (c.883–911)

GENEALOGY 1   Kings of the Mercians

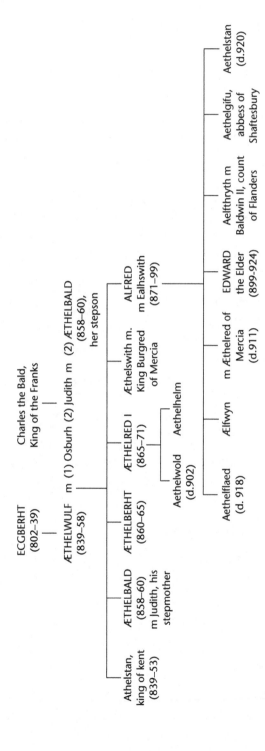

GENEALOGY 2 Kings of Wessex and, from c.880, of the Anglo-Saxons, to 924

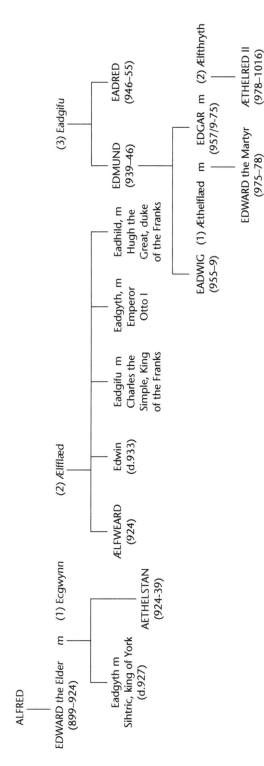

GENEALOGY 3 Kings of the Anglo-Saxons and, from 927, of the English, to 1016

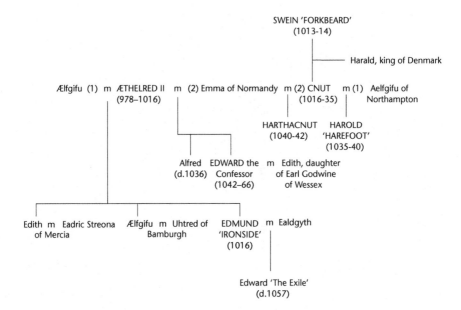

SWEIN 'FORKBEARD'
(1013-14)

———— Harald, king of Denmark

Ælfgifu (1) m ÆTHELRED II m (2) Emma of Normandy m (2) CNUT m (1) Aelfgifu of
(978–1016)   (1016-35)   Northampton

HARTHACNUT   HAROLD
(1040-42)   'HAREFOOT'
(1035-40)

Alfred   EDWARD the m Edith, daughter
(d.1036)   Confessor   of Earl Godwine
(1042–66)   of Wessex

Edith m Eadric Streona   Ælfgifu m Uhtred of   EDMUND m Ealdgyth
of Mercia   Bamburgh   'IRONSIDE'
(1016)

Edward 'The Exile'
(d.1057)

GENEALOGY 4   Kings of the English, to 1066

INTRODUCTION

England and the English in 796

Kings and kingdoms

At the end of the eighth century, that part of the island of Britain which today is called 'England' was divided into several different kingdoms. At least one of these, Dumnonia in the far south-west, was an ancient entity which had existed in some form since pre-Roman times. At its greatest extent, probably in the sixth century, it had incorporated Cornwall, Devon and much of Somerset. Two hundred years later, Cornwall was a kingdom in its own right, whilst other kingdoms, like that of the South Saxons which covered Sussex and parts of Kent and Hampshire, and that of the mysterious *Hwicce* in the west midlands, had already risen and disappeared, swallowed up by their larger, more successful neighbours.

By 796 England was dominated by four major kingdoms, all of which were ruled by the descendants of settlers who had come from northern Europe after the Romans left Britain roughly 400 years before. The smallest of the four was the kingdom of East Anglia, which consisted of what eventually became the counties of Norfolk and Suffolk. South of the river Thames was the kingdom of the West Saxons, or Wessex. Its origins are obscure, but probably lay in the sixth century (when the West Saxons were known as the *Gewisse*) along the upper Thames valley, in what is now Oxfordshire and Berkshire. At the other end of England was the kingdom of Northumbria. It was formed by the union during the seventh century of two separate and often hostile realms: Deira, covering what were to become the East Riding of Yorkshire and Lancashire, and Bernicia, the region north of the Tees where the centre of power was the great fortress rock of Bamburgh in modern Northumberland. By the late 600s one king usually ruled a single kingdom of Northumbria which periodically stretched from the Humber estuary to the Firth of Forth and from the North to the Irish Sea. However, it was the fourth kingdom, Mercia, which, in 796, was the dominant one in England. It took its name from its

position on 'the march' or frontier, presumably the one in the west with the indigenous Britons, and its core area was probably the valley of the river Trent. By the
late eighth century, Mercia encompassed the whole of central England from the
Humber to the Thames and controlled the former kingdoms of the *Hwicce*, Kent,
the East Saxons and the South Saxons. For a short time, too, at the end of the 700s,
the kingdom of East Anglia was also under Mercia's control.

The seeds of Mercian power had been sown by its Kings Wulfhere (658–75) and
Aethelred (675–704), although they ruled at a time when the foremost kingdom
in England was Northumbria. So it was the Mercian kings of the eighth century
who transformed their kingdom's position. Aethelbald (716–57) and Offa (758–96)
were remarkably long-lived rulers and, between them, remarkably successful. When
the Northumbrian monk Bede, who died in 735, described the political situation
in England in 731, he asserted confidently that all the southern kingdoms and their
various kings were subject to Aethelbald at that time. He referred specifically to
the kingdoms of Kent, the East Saxons, the East Angles, the West Saxons, the Mercians, the *Hwicce*, Lindsey (modern Lincolnshire), the people of the Isle of Wight,
and the South Saxons.[1] There was probably some exaggeration in this assessment,
and matters were not quite as simple as Bede made them sound. Aethelbald had
to fight to maintain his dominance, and in the end, he was murdered by his own
bodyguards and a brief civil war ensued. Nevertheless, his eventual successor, Offa,
managed to rebuild and surpass Aethelbald's accomplishments. The kingdoms of
the South Saxons and the *Hwicce* were incorporated into Mercia, and their kings
were deprived of their royal status; Offa was in sole control of the kingdom of
Kent by 785. The kingdoms of the East Saxons and East Anglia retained their own
kings but acknowledged Mercian supremacy. The king of East Anglia, Aethelberht,
remained in place, too, at least until 794 when he was beheaded at Offa's court.
And if Offa did not conquer or suppress the kingdoms of Wessex or Northumbria,
he did manage to assert his influence over them in other ways. In 789 Offa married his daughter, Eadburh, to the West Saxon king Beorhtric (d.802), whilst, three
years later in 792 another daughter, Aelfflaed, married the Northumbrian king,
Aethelred I (d.796). So triumphant within Britain had Offa become by the last
decade of his reign that his reputation had spread abroad. The great Frankish king
Charlemagne (d.814) corresponded with him about trade deals and potential marriage alliances and seems to have regarded Offa, if not as his equal, then as a fellow
ruler worthy of respect.

Early English kingship

The English kings of the sixth and seventh centuries were, before anything else,
successful warlords. This means that they fought battles and conquered the territories of their rivals, but doubtless more routine was the bullying and intimidation
of people and local leaders to extract their submissions and payments of tribute,
which were probably given in food and livestock more than money or treasure.
Typically, a king's core support would have been tribally based (his kindred and

neighbours), but as he prospered, that base widened to include not just those he had grown up with and those whom he had subjected to his rule, but also others who sought him out to serve and fight alongside him in his war-band, the very heart of his power. In return for the loyalty they promised him, the leader pledged to protect those who had accepted his supremacy. Early kingship was not so much about control of territory, therefore, as influence over people: 'it was social relationships, rather than occupation of space, which lay at the heart of kingship formation'.[2]

Household and witan

These social links could be constructed out of more than just military might, although this supported every other strategy. Marriages could establish connections with other tribes or communities and pre-eminence might be negotiated between rulers as much as it was fought for. But the most important relationships a king had were the ones he enjoyed most frequently, those with his close family, his advisors, his spiritual guides and his servants. Every king was surrounded by these people, who together made up what historians might loosely refer to as his household. They met his immediate needs (food, shelter, transport, clothing); provided him with companionship; and counselled him on important business. Sometimes, the group of advisors around the king would expand if there was something particularly significant to deal with. So King Ine of Wessex (688–726) began his law code by acknowledging how he had made it 'with the advice and assistance of my father Cenred, and my bishop Haedde, and my bishop Eorcenwold, along with all my ealdormen and the chief councillors of my people, and also a great assembly of all the people of God'.[3] These were the king's *witan* (this Old English word means 'wise men') who were expected and required to counsel the king. Without their support, he would be unable to rule.

Kings also expressed their authority and forged new relationships by moving around their kingdoms in a more or less regular circuit. They would travel between their own estates and feed off the produce laid up there in anticipation of their arrival. But they would also tour beyond their own lands to visit their leading subjects in their homes. Then the obligation to provide food and accommodation for the ruler and his entourage rested on those who were fortunate enough to receive his visits. This duty was onerous and expensive, but it did ensure regular contact between the king and his important men, give the former the chance to keep abreast of his followers' concerns and the latter an opportunity to take advantage of their close proximity to the king and benefit from his patronage. However, more than anything else, successful military and political leadership was based on rewarding loyal service. A king was expected to be generous and open-handed, favouring individual followers with gifts (magnificent weapons and jewellery, for example) and more broadly providing hospitality in his hall. The royal household in ninth-century Wessex has been described as 'a continuous stage for the operation and renewal of royal lordship'.[4] But inevitably, the ever-pressing need to give gifts only served to renew the imperative for conquest, because the leader's resources came mainly from the spoils of war and the tribute offered by subject peoples.

By the start of the seventh century, some of these war-leaders had attracted enough support, gathered enough resources and acquired enough influence to try and make their achievements more permanent. Various strategies could be used to bolster a king's power and status. This was a time when the transmission of ideas through visual signs and symbols was more important than written communication, so rituals and ceremonial were almost certainly central to the way early English kings transmitted their authority and identified themselves as special. Meetings of the *witan* were probably stage-managed affairs, full of pomp and show. Grants of land by the king were probably public acts, scripted, formal and solemn. When the king progressed through his territories or arrived at his destination, he might have done so magnificently, like King Edwin of Northumbria (d.633): 'So great was his majesty in his realm', Bede says, 'that not only were banners carried before him in battle, but even in time of peace, as he rode about among his cities, estates and kingdoms with his thegns, he always used to be preceded by a standard-bearer'.[5] The aim was to awe those who witnessed such a spectacle, but also in a more mystical way to associate them with the majesty of their king and establish their connection with him.

Genealogies, charters and laws

Nevertheless, stability remained elusive and the achievements of one leader, however great, were always threatened and often destroyed after death removed his charismatic, domineering personality. This made politics fluid and unpredictable, and continuity would only become possible once some kind of institutional framework was put in place to complement and buttress the personal contribution of individual kings. There are some signs that steps were being taken in this direction by the end of the eighth century although they are very hard indeed to interpret conclusively. There were attempts to add a veneer of legal justification to the hard reality of power, for example, and this explains a growing interest in the construction of royal genealogies across the ruling elites. These were family trees which attempted to link individual kings, and thereby their families and potential successors, with distinguished predecessors, often ones who lived (or reputedly lived) before the arrival of the Anglo-Saxons in England. Some of these ancestors were real enough, but the longer the genealogies became the more fictional their contents look. The kings of Kent, whose genealogy seems to date from the eighth century, claimed descent from Hengest, the legendary leader of the Saxons 300 years before, and by the ninth century, the *Anglo-Saxon Chronicle* had perfected the art by extending the ancestry of King Aethelwulf of Wessex back to the family of Noah and, ultimately, Adam.[6] More concretely than this, however, kings also began to utilise documents which articulated their own ideas about the kind of power they exercised. The earliest English royal charters (historians also call them diplomas) survive from late seventh-century Kent, and it has been argued that they were introduced to England by St Augustine.[7] The charter was originally designed to protect the newly established Christian Church by providing clear and unambiguous records of the lands which individual churches received from rulers and the terms upon which those lands were granted, and it is no coincidence that all of the earliest authentic charters were grants to the church in one form or another. The security of tenure it gave was key to the charter's success, as land granted by charter (a *landboc* in Old English), which was known as bookland (*bocland*), was conveyed in perpetuity, free of all but certain specified obligations.

The first charters were typically written by the recipients of the grant themselves or by other churchmen, not by any kind of royal secretariat. Nevertheless, kings were not slow to recognise the benefits charters could bring them. The grants to the church associated them with God's plan for the world and added some spiritual lustre to their image. Soon enough, however, grants were being made to laymen and not just to churches, and charters began to give an added degree of formality and solemnity to the exercise of royal patronage. There were ideological attractions, too: in a grant of 679 by King Hlothere of Kent to Abbot Brihtwold of Reculver, the king would have been pleased to see himself described as 'king of the people of Kent'. However, by 736, King Aethelbald of Mercia felt bold enough to authorise a charter granting land to one of his ealdormen in which he was described first as 'by the gift of God king not only of the Mercians but also of all provinces which are called by the general name 'South English', and second, where he witnesses the charter, as 'king of Britain'.[8] It is easy to think of Bede's list of *imperium*-exercising rulers at this point* and to wonder whether Aethelbald knew of it and saw himself as the latest in that line. Whether he did or not, his claims were aspirational rather than reflections of political reality. But in an age where the opportunities to convey any kind of political message were extremely limited, charters would give the kings of ninth- and tenth-century England a valuable propaganda weapon as well as an effective means of transmitting their power over a considerable distance.

So would the laws that they issued. The making of laws was a sure sign that rulers aspired to control individuals through something more than the exercise or threat of force. The earliest surviving English royal laws are those of Aethelberht of Kent (d.616). They survive only in a twelfth-century copy, but Bede refers to them in the *Ecclesiastical History*, and they were probably issued in the early 600s. It is almost certainly no coincidence that the publication of his *Laws* coincided with Aethelberht's conversion to Christianity at the hands of missionaries form Rome: making laws was what the ancient Romans did, whilst the kings of the Old Testament were lawgivers, too. Their ideological purpose was probably just as important as their content to the kings who put their names to these early laws. King Ine of Wessex (688–726) published his own law code at the end of the seventh century, but he probably did so more to show himself off as a provider of justice and a guarantor of peace than to solve specific legal problems.

---

* Below, p. 19

Tribute, trade and coins

How wide a practical impact early royal genealogies, diplomas and laws actually had is open to question, of course, and kings still had to make efforts to enforce and strengthen their authority with more applied measures. Here control over resources, both human and economic, was vital. The so-called Tribal Hidage is a controversial document which only survives in a copy made around 1000, but it was probably written in the seventh century.[9] Its purpose is obscure, but many historians think it is a list of those peoples or areas required to pay tribute to a king of this period, perhaps Wulfhere of Mercia (658–75). Each name (thirty-four tribes or territories are listed in all) is equated with a specific number of 'hides' (for example, 'Pecsaetna' (probably the Peak District) is equated with 1,200 hides and 'Wihtgara' (probably the Isle of Wight) with 600), a hide originally being the land deemed necessary to support one free man, his family and household. In total, the number of hides in the document comes to over 244,000. But if the hide came into existence as a gauge of social status (the more hides of land you controlled, the richer you were), by the time of the Tribal Hidage, it seems to have been in use principally as a unit for assessing financial and other liabilities to the king. So if the Tribal Hidage is indeed a tribute list, it implies the existence of a sophisticated organisation, even a bureaucracy of some sort, able to calculate fiscal obligations over large expanses of territory. It also implies the existence of a powerful central authority capable of enforcing this system. As does Offa's Dyke, the great fortified earthwork which the kings of Mercia built along their frontier with the Welsh in the eighth century. It was probably built to keep the Welsh out of Mercian territory, but whatever its purpose it cannot have been raised without the labour of perhaps thousands of individuals organised and deployed for its construction.

Control of trade was another way of increasing kingly power, and it is certainly possible to argue that urban life in England began to develop in tandem with royal authority. It was in a king's interest to encourage trade within his kingdom and to facilitate commercial contacts with areas outside his immediate sphere of authority, and rulers took an active interest in the trading centres (historians tend to call them *emporia* or *wics* rather than towns at this point) which emerged in England during the seventh and eighth centuries. Often established on the coast (*Hamwic* in Wessex, for example, near where Southampton was later established) or on navigable rivers (like *Lundenwic* (Aldwych in London) on the Thames in Mercia and *Eoforwic* (York) in Northumbria), they could provide a regular supply of the kind of luxury goods from the continent which the kings needed to satisfy their followers. But they also gave the kings an opportunity to maintain important contacts with rulers and courts on the European mainland and make a profit, either by levying tolls on the merchants who traded in the *emporia* or by granting exemptions from such charges. The eighth-century kings of Kent and Mercia issued numerous charters dealing with such matters.[10]

As economic business became more complex and more important, a new means of exchange was developing by the second half of the seventh century, England's silver currency. This facilitated trade but also provided another opportunity for kings to augment and display their authority. It was the kings who authorised the issuing of minted coins, so their reputation depended to a considerable extent on the way they managed the system and on the quality (mainly the silver content) of their pennies. But Offa of Mercia went further from about 760 when he actually had his name put on the coins he licensed, thus associating himself directly and unequivocally with the need for a sound currency. However, the coinage might enhance royal power in other ways. Across the English Channel, at around the same time as Offa was making his reforms, Charlemagne and then his son Louis the Pious (814–40) were establishing a uniform currency for the whole of their empire and producing coins with more or less standardised designs, silver content and weight. This single currency was intended to encourage trade and make the payment of taxes and tolls easier across diverse and widely spread territories, and it seems that the English kings eventually came to appreciate this and tried to emulate their Carolingian neighbours. There remained significant variety in the appearance and design of English coins during the first half of the ninth century, however, and meaningful steps towards the creation of a common English currency were not taken until the 860s. Nonetheless, already at the end of the eighth century, it seems that foreign merchants arriving in England were expected to change their coins into local money before they could start to trade. This would have to be done at one of the royally licensed mints, most of which were located at commercial centres with continental trading links (Canterbury, Rochester, London, York and Ipswich), and a fee would be charged for reminting, the profits from which would go to the king. So from this point on, coins would become an increasingly important weapon in the English kings' ongoing efforts to make money and, through the coins' rich iconography and the mechanics of the coinage system itself, project their power.

Military power

It was no accident that England's growing prosperity during the eighth and early ninth centuries coincided with the start of the viking raids. Military responses to this new threat had to be developed, albeit ones built on existing systems. The king's war-band or hearth troop remained central to his campaigning. These were the men immediately around the king who routinely hunted and feasted with him and formed the core of his army in wartime. However, beyond this group, the rules might have been less clear. So King Ine of Wessex, in his law code, set out penalties for various degrees of free men (nobles who held land, those who did not, and non-noble free men) who failed to fulfil their military duties.[11] Precisely what these military duties were is much less clear, but at least there is some sense of an organising structure in place here, and of expectations which were based on more than just the king's personal relationship with his followers. This was even more the case in eighth-century Mercia. By the end of Offa's reign, when the king made a grant of bookland, it was increasingly standard practice to stipulate that the recipient was still obliged to serve on royal military expeditions, along with a specified number of men determined by the size (or value) of his estates, and also that he was required to contribute to the maintenance of bridges and fortresses on his land by providing labourers. These three obligations are usually referred to by historians as 'the common burdens', and they were in place in other kingdoms, if not by 800, then certainly by the mid-ninth century. This system would be one of the mainstays of England's military defence until the Norman Conquest and beyond.

England and its neighbours

It was not just in England that kings and kingdoms dominated by 796 – they did so in Wales, Scotland and Ireland, too. In Wales, there were kings of Gwynedd and Powys in the north, and Dyfed and Brycheiniog in the south; in western Scotland, there were kings with ultimately Irish origins in Gaelic-speaking Dalriada and British ones in Strathclyde, whilst Pictish kings controlled much of the east and the south. Meanwhile in Ireland, powerful royal dynasties were starting to develop in Leinster, Connacht and Munster. Perhaps even more than in England, the political situation to the north and west was fluid and volatile, and the powers of these different kings varied and fluctuated widely. However, it is probably fair to say that all the rulers of Britain exercised power, or tried to, in similar ways. They would typically have direct control over land which they had inherited or conquered and the loyalty of their family, neighbours and tribe. But (and this is what made someone a king rather than just another powerful man) they would also claim authority over people, perhaps even other kings, outside their own lands and expect those people to honour them and pay them tribute. Power was maintained by a mixture of exacting measures (battle, ravaging, taking hostages), on the one hand, and more conciliatory ones (feasting with followers and distributing treasure amongst them, for example), on the other.

But although they ruled and were ruled in broadly similar ways, how much contact the kings and peoples of early medieval Britain had with each other is far from clear. Chroniclers tended to be interested only in recording battles between them, although the remains of Offa's Dyke support the notion that relations between the Mercians and their Welsh neighbours were routinely tense if not hostile. On a less confrontational level, there would have been major linguistic barriers to overcome, not to mention differences in cultural habits and social conventions. The peoples of Britain were all Christians by this time, of course, and missionaries from Ireland and western Scotland had contributed enormously to the conversion of the Anglo-Saxons during the seventh century. However, this cannot have been a straightforward process. When, in 635, King Oswald of Northumbria decided to introduce his people to the Christian faith, he sought help from Ireland where he had earlier been baptised during a period of political exile. He was lucky enough to be sent Aidan from the monastery of Iona, 'a man of outstanding gentleness, devotion, and moderation', according to Bede. But Aidan 'was not completely at home in the English tongue', so when he preached, it was King Oswald himself, with his 'perfect knowledge of Irish', who had to translate what he was saying so that others could understand it.[12] Routine communication between ordinary people was probably much more makeshift and difficult than this, although the ships which crossed the Irish Sea and the Bristol Channel must have normalised trading contacts and other kinds of relationships between Britain and Ireland to some degree.

These different kinds of contact between England and the rest of the British Isles would continue to develop and play a significant role as a single English kingdom emerged over the next 200 years. Arguably just as important in the making of that kingdom, however, if not more so in some ways, were the evolving links between England and mainland Europe. Britain was an island, but it was not isolated. Northumbria, specifically its great monastery on Lindisfarne, had been a centre of international learning and scholarship in the seventh century. And there were other regular contacts, not least commercial ones, between England and northern Europe – the modern Netherlands and northern Germany in particular – whilst Anglo-Saxon Christian missionaries contributed significantly to the conversion of the pagan peoples in those regions in the seventh and eighth centuries. But the most important international connections were probably those the English had with Italy and France. It had been Pope Gregory I's (590–604) idea to send a mission from Rome to convert the Anglo-Saxons at the end of the sixth century, and Anglo-Saxon pilgrims travelled regularly to Rome in the seventh and eighth. Closer to home, meanwhile, the dominant force in northern France and western Germany by the early sixth century were the Franks, and King Aethelberht of Kent married a Frankish princess, Bertha, in about 560. Frankish churchmen then played an important part in sustaining Christianity in southern England during the seventh century, and the number and range of Frankish objects found in the great Sutton Hoo ship burial in East Anglia confirm how extensive these links were at this time, at the elite level at least. In the second half of the eighth century, however, the situation in northern France and across continental Europe generally was transformed by the establishment of a new ruling dynasty, the Carolingians. When Charlemagne became king of the Franks in 771, he set about expanding his territories and imposing Christianity on the heathen peoples he conquered. He invaded Saxony in 772 and eventually achieved its total subjugation and conversion to Christianity. He also conquered the kingdom of the Lombards in northern Italy, and in 778, he invaded northern Spain, then controlled by the Moors. Between 780 and 800, Charlemagne added Bohemia to his empire and then secured its eastern border by crushing the Avars in the middle Danube basin. In 800, Charlemagne went to Rome to help suppress a rebellion against Pope Leo III (795–816), and as a token of thanks, Leo crowned him on Christmas Day that year, declaring the Frankish king emperor of the Romans. More than just a conqueror, however, Charlemagne introduced administrative reforms throughout the lands he controlled from his headquarters at Aachen; he issued laws, and he standardised weights, measures and customs dues. He also brought many eminent scholars to his court and sponsored a literary and artistic programme which historians call the Carolingian Renaissance. The most prominent amongst all these intellectuals was an Englishman, the Northumbrian monk Alcuin of York (c.735–804). The immense territories which Charlemagne controlled by the time he died in 814 became known as the Carolingian Empire, but during his lifetime and in subsequent generations, he was esteemed and revered as the greatest of all Christian rulers. His awesome military achievements could not be outdone, but they were something to emulate, and his court provided a model which lesser kings might seek to imitate in their own way. Over the next 200 years or so, Frankish influence of one kind or another on the development of English government, law and ecclesiastical structures would be profound.

The English in 796

So what was 'English' about England at the end of the eighth century? Certainly not its politics, which were fragmented and divided along regional and local lines. When King Offa of Mercia died in 796, the starting-point for this book, England was a long way from being a single kingdom ruled by a single king, and there was little indication that it would ever become one. Indeed, as the large number of small, insecure Anglo-Saxon kingdoms had been reduced to four large, stable ones over the previous 200 years, the chances of the latter or something like them becoming permanent features of the political landscape had arguably increased.

However, whilst allegiances and loyalties at an elite level might sometimes be expressed in provincial terms, as Mercians fought against Northumbrians or East Anglians against West Saxons, usually, and especially for the families who lived off the land they occupied, more intimate relationships and commitments mattered most, those with kin, neighbours and landlords. At this level, there would have been variations in customs and traditions between the different parts of England, and it is hard to know how much someone from south of the Thames and someone else from north of the Humber would even have understood what each other said. Nevertheless, wherever they lived, the people of England would have recognised much about their neighbours' ways of doing things. For one thing, they were all, nominally at least, Christians. The church calendar, based around religious festivals and saints' days, gave a common structure to the year; church buildings gave a physical focus to communities; and church services took more or less the same form wherever they were held, and obligations to the church (paying tithes, for example) would have been familiar to all. For another, the great majority of English people were involved in agriculture and worked the land to feed themselves and their families. Some of the larger Roman settlements, such as Canterbury, London or York, had survived as trading centres or *wics*, and others, such as *Hamwic* on the south coast and Ipswich in the east, had flourished during the eighth century. However, it is impossible to know how densely populated these places were, and towns in any recognisably modern sense did not really exist. Even villages were unusual, and most English people lived in small hamlets or scattered farmsteads on the estates of a powerful lord, perhaps the king himself, one of his followers, or a rich monastery. Typically, at the end of the eighth century, these landholdings were very large indeed (perhaps thousands of acres of fields, moors and woodland), and those who lived on them were organised to provide their lord, his family and his retinue with food, livestock and labour. For his part, the lord would usually be based at some central site, but he would also move around his estates from one hall or compound to another, consuming the tribute which the local people had produced.

Inevitably, evidence is extremely hard to find, but it seems clear that rural society in Anglo-Saxon England was based to a significant degree on the labour of slaves. Figures are notoriously elusive here, and estimating the size of England's population in the eighth century is really no more than guesswork (2 million, perhaps). However, slaves may have made up something between 10 and 20 per cent of that population. They were mostly captured in war, although those in extreme poverty might sell themselves into slavery, and slavery could also be a legal punishment in certain cases. They performed a range of physically demanding tasks in the fields (ploughing, sowing, harvesting and much else besides), they could be bought and sold, they were entirely subject to the authority of their master, and they had no legal rights. If a slave was abused, injured or killed, moreover, compensation was payable to the slave's owner, not to the slave's family. This made slaves 'unfree', a term which denotes not just a state of affairs for the individual slave, but a legal position: they could not swear oaths in legal disputes, pay tax or perform other public obligations. There were other peasants, too, who, in return for a small plot of land, would probably owe rent (paid in their own produce or livestock) and perform labour services on their lord's own lands at various fixed times in the year. Most of these lords were independent farmers. However, unlike their own tenants and labourers, these *ceorls* (as they were known) were regarded by the law as 'free': typically, a *ceorl* 'was oath-worthy and weapon worthy, a person of repute, possessed of a free kindred and capable of playing a full role in the army and the courts'.[13]

It was their possession of land and their ability to administer it themselves which set *ceorls* apart from those below them in the social scale. And higher up that same scale, land continued to denote status and rank. By the middle of the ninth century, it seems that the enormous estates which had hitherto dominated the rural landscape were beginning to fragment as the major lords divided up their lands and granted them in smaller parcels to their own followers. As a result, a larger landholding class made up of 'thegns' started to emerge across England. Thegns had more land than an ordinary *ceorl*, whilst their lifestyle, their local influence and, above all, their links to the royal government marked them out. The word 'thegn' means 'one who serves', and they were expected to carry out military and administrative duties in their areas. Some thegns ('king's thegns') would even find roles at the royal court performing services for the king himself or in the localities carrying out a range of duties on the king's behalf. The most successful of all might eventually be promoted by the ruler to the position of ealdorman ('chief man'), the king's deputy in a particular shire.

On a local level, however, the thegns began to reorganise the lands they controlled so that they could be farmed more efficiently and intensively. Many peasants moved from their isolated hamlets to be nearer the thegn's hall, and as these nucleated settlements multiplied and grew, open field-systems were often laid out around them to make farming even more viable and productive. Doubtless some peasants were forced to resettle, but others probably saw this new kind of more communal life as attractive, even if its main purpose was to enrich a relatively small number of increasingly powerful men. Larger populations meant a bigger labour supply; tools and materials could be pooled and shared; water-mills might be built to process grain. By the eleventh century, these developments were in full swing, although they were happening in some parts of England (eastern England and the midlands down to the south coast) more than in others (East Anglia and the south-east). Nevertheless, in them lay the origins of many English villages and the beginnings of England's landed gentry.

These rather crude social distinctions (free/unfree; slave/*ceorl*/thegn) must be used with care when discussing a situation which was inevitably more complex and nuanced in practice. The evidence is very thin, and more is known about some parts of England than others. There was almost certainly much variety within these classifications, too, and the dividing lines between them were probably quite blurred in practice. Nevertheless, they were clearly important to contemporaries. One way of defining a person's standing in Anglo-Saxon society was through their *wergild*. This was the amount of money payable to the relatives of someone who had been unlawfully killed, and all classes of society except slaves had one. In seventh-century Kent, the *wergild* of a thegn was fixed at 300 shillings and that of an ordinary *ceorl* at 100, whilst in Wessex at roughly the same time, the equivalent figures were 1,200 and 200 shillings.[14] Amounts may have varied from place to place, but these provisions in the laws of different kingdoms demonstrate that society across eighth-century England was hierarchical and highly stratified and that class distinctions such as these were keenly appreciated.

So it is probably fair to say that, by 796, despite the political, social, cultural and linguistic differences between them, the peoples of the different English kingdoms lived their lives in similar ways and had much in common. And on a more theoretical level, too, the idea that there was a distinct and separate English race or people (the Latin phrase is *gens Anglorum*, whilst the Old English word *Angelcynn* was later used to express the same notion), made up of people with things in common which transcended political frontiers and provincial rivalries, was established by this time and continuing to develop. This is important because notions of a uniquely English identity would be taken up and elaborated eagerly and repeatedly by the kings of the ninth and tenth centuries as they attempted to defend their kingdoms against foreign enemies and consolidate their control within their own realms. A growing sense of 'Englishness' underlay the creation of a single English kingdom.

It is impossible to know where or when the idea of a specifically English people originated, but one of the earliest expressions of the concept, and the one that turned out to be the most influential, came from eighth-century Northumbria. There, a monk named Bede (673/4–735), who lived virtually his whole life at the monastery of Jarrow, wrote a book called *Historia ecclesiastica gentis Anglorum*, which is usually translated as *The Ecclesiastical History of the English People*. For Bede, the English people were all descendants of those Germanic tribesmen (principally the Angles, Saxons and Jutes) who had come to England in the fifth and sixth centuries, then steadily established their dominance over the indigenous inhabitants, the Britons. When these tribesmen arrived in England, they were pagans, and Bede's primary purpose in the *Ecclesiastical History* was to describe how they were converted to Christianity from the late sixth century onwards. Bede's English people thus had several things in common: wherever they eventually settled and ruled in England, they all shared a history of migration; they spoke a common language, albeit one with differences in dialect, vocabulary and accent from area to area; and, crucial to any sense of a collective identity, they were bound together by their shared Christian faith.

There was more to Bede's conception of Englishness than any of this, though. First, Bede argued that the Anglo-Saxons had been visited upon the native Britons as a punishment for the latter's sins and their abandonment of proper Christian lives. These pagan invaders, having acquired a beautiful land with God's help, had then been further rewarded when they were converted and placed on the right Christian path, and in their story, Bede implicitly drew out parallels with the people of Israel in the Old Testament. He would not be the last author of this period to claim that the English were in some sense another 'chosen people'. Second, in Bede's view the responsibility for the conversion of the Anglo-Saxons to Christianity lay ultimately with the pope in Rome. Pope Gregory I had sent missionaries to England to begin the process at the end of the 590s, and although Bede was happy to acknowledge that other missionaries from Ireland had also played an important part in the conversion story, it was distinctively Roman forms of Christian doctrine and organisation that the Anglo-Saxons eventually adopted. Third, and on a more explicitly political level, Bede popularised the idea that there was potentially more to ruling the English than just regional kingdoms. He claimed that no fewer than seven kings before 671 had exercised *imperium* (empire) over all the English people south of the Humber, whilst three of them, as kings of Northumbria, had extended that *imperium* even further north.[15] These men were first and foremost kings in their own kingdoms. But Bede saw them as also exercising some kind of loose supremacy over the other Anglo-Saxon kingdoms of their day. And such a concept, however vague and ill-defined, lasted. Late in the ninth century, the *Anglo-Saxon Chronicle* repeated Bede's list, added an eighth king to it (King Ecgberht of Wessex) and gave these select rulers a title, *Bretwalda* or *Brytenwalda* ('Britain-ruler').[16] At a time when Alfred the Great was rebuilding and extending his kingdom in response to viking attacks, the West Saxon chronicler was using Bede's list to justify his kingdom's claims to authority beyond Wessex. Of course, it was extravagant and unrealistic at that stage to conceive of a kingship of Britain or even of a single realm below the Humber. Nevertheless, the theoretical underpinnings of a unified English kingdom were being constructed. Later kings would build more concretely on these foundations with common administrative structures, economic structures and laws; literature in English, poetry and prose, would play its part, too. But Bede's themes, that the English had common origins and language, that they were God's chosen people and that there existed the possibility for one king to exercise *imperium* over them all, would prove remarkably durable.

Notes

1 *BEH*, pp. 558–9.
2 Nicholas J. Higham, 'From Tribal Chieftains to Christian Kings', in idem and Martin J. Ryan (eds.), *The Anglo-Saxon World* (New Haven, 2013), pp. 126–65, at p. 140.
3 *EHD*, i no.32.
4 David Pratt, *The Political Thought of King Alfred the Great* (Cambridge, 2007), p. 36.
5 *BEH*, pp. 192–3.
6 *ASC* 855–8.
7 Pierre Chaplais, 'Who Introduced Charters into England? The Case for St Augustine', in F. Ranger (ed.), *Prisca Munimenta* (London, 1973), pp. 88–107.
8 *EHD*, i nos.56, 66.
9 Texts of the Tribal Hidage can be found in David Dumville, 'The Tribal Hidage: An Introduction to Its Texts and Their History', in Steven Bassett (ed.), *The Origins of Anglo-Saxon Kingdoms* (Leicester, 1989), pp. 225–30.
10 Peter Sawyer, *The Wealth of Anglo-Saxon England* (Oxford, 2013), p. 73.
11 *EHD*, i no.32 (Ine, 51).
12 *BEH*, pp. 220–1.
13 H.R. Loyn, *The Governance of Anglo-Saxon England, 500–1087* (Stanford, 1984), p. 51.
14 *EHD*, i nos.30 (H&E, 1, 3), 32 (Ine, 19, 70).
15 *BEH*, pp. 148–51.
16 *ASC* 829.

PART I
The origins of a kingdom, 796–899

1

THE EVENTS, 796–899

796–839

These years saw a dramatic and decisive change in the balance of political power in England. Mercia's supremacy was ended, and another kingdom, Wessex, became preeminent. Moreover, a royal dynasty was established in Wessex which, over the course of the ninth and tenth centuries, would come to rule the whole of England as a single kingdom.

King Offa's achievements were threatened as soon as died in 796. His son Ecgfrith succeeded him but was dead by the end of the year, and the task of preserving Mercia's dominance fell to a remote cousin, Cenwulf (796–821). Cenwulf immediately had to deal with an uprising in Kent, and he did so in 798 by capturing the leader of the insurgents, Eadberht Praen, and taking him to Mercia where his hands were cut off and his eyes put out.[1] He then installed his brother, Cuthred, as sub-king in Kent, and after Cuthred died in 807 Cenwulf ruled there himself. But if Cenwulf eventually managed to hang on to some kind of authority in Kent and in other parts of southern England, he did so with difficulty, and when he died in 821, 'much discord and innumerable disagreements' followed, 'between various kings, nobles, bishops and ministers of the Church of God, on very many matters of secular business'.[2] Cenwulf's brother Ceolwulf I, who succeeded him, was deposed in 823 and succeeded by Beornwulf.

Cenwulf's power across the rest of England also waned as his reign went on. There is no evidence that he exercised any kind of meaningful influence in Wessex or Northumbria, for example, and those kingdoms were left to develop during the first quarter of the ninth century, largely free of Mercian interference. In northern England, King Aethelred of Northumbria, Offa's son-in-law, was murdered in 796, and once his immediate successor had been deposed after only twenty days, the kingdom came into the hands of one of Aethelred's former rivals, returned from exile, Eardwulf. Eardwulf faced plenty of internal opposition and on one occasion, in 801, he led an army against the Mercians because King Cenwulf had given shelter to his enemies. In 806, Eardwulf was overthrown, only to be reinstated two years later with the backing of the pope and (by then, having been given an imperial coronation at Rome in 800) the emperor Charlemagne. After that, the chronology of Eardwulf's reign is confused and unclear. He probably lived until about 830, although he could have survived longer than this, and the numismatic evidence might actually support the theory that the rest of Eardwulf's reign was relatively stable. At the very least, he seems to have been able to pass the throne on to his son Eanred, who may have ruled until the mid-850s.[3]

The situation in Wessex during this period is more clear, because the *Anglo-Saxon Chronicle* records some of the things that happened. Some notes of caution need to be sounded about this, however. Having been produced in Wessex at the end of the ninth century, its emphasis on West Saxon affairs might sometimes endow them with a significance they did not in reality have. Second, and more specifically here, even the *Chronicle* does not provide much meaningful detail about events before the 820s, so it is difficult to get any clear sense of what was happening south of the Thames in the first two decades of the ninth century. The *Chronicle* does record how, in 802, King Beorhtric of Wessex, who had married Offa's daughter Eadburh in 789, died and was succeeded as king by Ecgberht. But even this simple statement probably conceals a much more complex story. On Ecgberht's death in 839, the chronicler described how, before he became king, Ecgberht had been forced by Beorhtric and Offa to take refuge in Francia for three years, and it may be that the exile returned in 802 with Frankish help. The *Chronicle's* entry for 802 also describes how, on the same day as Beorhtric himself died, so did one of the king's leading men, Ealdorman Worr. And not only that, still on the same day, a Mercian army entered Wessex and was defeated at Kempsford in Gloucestershire by a force from Wiltshire. It is hard to know what to make of all this, but it is at least clear that Ecgberht's reign began violently, and that he is unlikely to have been Beorhtric's chosen heir. It has also been argued that Ecgberht's origins were Kentish rather than West Saxon (his father, Ealhmund, may have been one of the last independent kings of Kent) and that therefore his exile at the hands of Beorhtric and Offa was intended to nip some kind of Kentish resurgence in the bud. So there is every chance that, in 802, Beorhtric was killed in a takeover led by his successor.[4]

Having described, albeit not very helpfully, the events of 802, the *Chronicle* proceeds largely to overlook the first twenty years or so of Ecgberht's reign. He is not mentioned again until the entry for 815 when he launched a campaign in Cornwall and ravaged 'from east to west', and later sources suggest that this might not have been Ecgberht's only expedition to the far south-west.[5] Much more important, however, and the *Chronicle* emphasises this by recording these events in some detail, was the battle Ecgberht won in 825 at *Ellendun* (Wroughton) in modern Wiltshire against King Beornwulf of Mercia.[6] The consequences of this defeat were catastrophic for the Mercians and momentous for Wessex. It was decisive enough to encourage the East Anglians to throw off Mercian control once and for all and look to Ecgberht of Wessex for protection instead. As proof of their good faith, they killed King Beornwulf in battle. At the same time, Ecgberht himself, buoyed by his success, sent a West Saxon army under his son Aethelwulf into Kent. The Mercian puppet-king there, Baldred, was driven out, the kingdom was occupied by the West Saxons and this in turn persuaded the people of Kent and Surrey, along with the South Saxons and the East Saxons, all of whom had been subject to Mercian authority of some kind since Offa's reign, to submit to Ecgberht and accept West Saxon overlordship.

The *Chronicle's* entry for 825 reads as if all these events happened quickly one after the other. In reality, the process it describes may have been more drawn out than it first appears, and it was certainly not over by the end of that crucial year. King Beornwulf was probably not killed until 826, and Ecgberht's overlordship may not have extended to the kingdom of the South Saxons until 828. The Mercians were not completely overcome by the defeat at Wroughton, either. Beornwulf's immediate successor as king, Ludeca, was quickly killed, probably in battle, in 827, but the truly pivotal moment did not come until 829 when Wiglaf, who had replaced Ludeca as king, was driven out of Mercia by Ecgberht. At this point the *Chronicle* pauses to assess Ecgberht's achievement. He had 'conquered the kingdom of the Mercians and everything south of the Humber; and he was the eighth king who was *Bretwalda*'.[7] Bede had compiled a list of seven English kings who, in his view, had exercised authority (*imperium* was the Latin word for it) over the English kingdoms south of the Humber. Ecgberht, in the *Chronicle's* view, was the latest in that line of masterful rulers and, from the chronicler's West Saxon perspective, the greatest yet. The special designation *Bretwalda*, meaning roughly 'Ruler of Britain', was coined to reflect his importance. His uniqueness was confirmed when, after taking control of Mercia, he travelled to Dore in Derbyshire and received the submission of the Northumbrians and when, in 830, he did the same in Wales. There is no suggestion that Ecgberht planned to rule these lands directly, but the symbolism of these events was obvious. Between 825 and 830 Ecgberht had overseen the disintegration of Mercian political power and successfully asserted West Saxon supremacy within Britain.

In 830, the *Chronicle* records how 'Wiglaf again obtained the kingdom of the Mercians'.[8] How he did this is unclear, and it may be that his recovery of power was sanctioned by Ecgberht. Ecgberht was certainly content to delegate royal authority elsewhere, and from 825 his son Aethelwulf ruled as sub-king of Kent. Arrangements like this, and perhaps the one in Mercia, may have amounted to an acknowledgement by the West Saxon king that he needed help to rule the extended territories which he had brought under his control. And, to be sure, as his reign drew to a close, he was confronted by new threats which would have challenged any ruler.

According to the *Anglo-Saxon Chronicle*, the first 'Northmen' came to England in 789, but the Vikings' first recorded and most notorious raid was on the great monastery of Lindisfarne off the Northumbrian coast in 793, an event which shocked western Europe. There may then have been further intermittent attacks and raids over the next forty years, particularly in and around Kent. The writers of the *Anglo-Saxon Chronicle* may not have been very interested in, or indeed aware of, these events; hence their failure to record them. So the evidence for them is patchy and inconclusive, and the prevailing impression continues to be that the viking threat did not become serious and sustained before the 830s. In 835, the *Chronicle* records, 'heathen men' ravaged the Isle of Sheppey off the Kent coast, and in the following year, King Ecgberht of Wessex himself fought and lost against the crews of thirty-five viking ships at Carhampton on the coast of north Somerset. Bruised but not fatally weakened, Ecgberht had to fight the Vikings once again in 838 when they joined forces with an army of locals at Hingston Down in Cornwall. This time Ecgberht was victorious, but it may be no coincidence that he died in the following year, from exhaustion perhaps if not injuries, after over thirty-seven years as king.[9] It is impossible to know what Ecgberht and his followers made of this formidable new enemy. They certainly would not have appreciated that 'the Viking Age' had begun or that, over the course of the next 250 years or so, these raiders and their successors would shape the course of English history and play a central role in the making of the kingdom of England.

DEBATE 1

The *Anglo-Saxon Chronicle*: facts or fake news?

'The fundamental authority for Old English history is the series of annalistic compilations known collectively as the *Anglo-Saxon Chronicle*'.[1] There is no dispute about this. Nevertheless, there are problems with the *Chronicle* which nobody studying this period can ignore. It is generally agreed that the first version of the *Chronicle* (the so-called common stock) was compiled in Wessex in the latter stages of Alfred the Great's reign. It is also conventional to claim that the compilation took place at Alfred's court itself. This view is not unreasonable: the contents of the *Chronicle* until the end of the ninth century are overwhelmingly oriented towards the affairs of Wessex and its kings, and especially towards Alfred and his struggle with the Danes; the creation of the *Chronicle*, which was written in English, would seem to fit in with the aims of Alfred's translation programme; an early version of the *Chronicle* was in circulation at Alfred's court in the early 890s, as Asser used a text of it in composing his *Life* of Alfred; and the various manuscripts of the *Chronicle* largely share the same material up to that point. It is important to remember, however, that there is no direct evidence (of the kind to be found in other works translated at Alfred's court, for example) linking the common stock to either the king or his circle. Additionally, once the common stock had been circulated and made available for copying after 892, different versions of the *Chronicle* began to be created by those who had access to it. What they chose to add, remove or change was down to them. As a result, multiple texts of the *Chronicle* were created, all of which had their own local and personal preoccupations and concerns. So the *Chronicle* is not now one source, but several: often they coincide, but frequently they differ. There are eight surviving manuscripts in all, labelled from A to H by historians. They were all compiled at different places and different times, and none of the surviving texts is contemporary before the mid-tenth century. The main purpose of the *Chronicle* was to provide a year-by-year ('annalistic') account of English history from its beginnings. Whether the account it gives is complete or reliable, though, is another question. The emphasis on the rise of Wessex in the ninth century is arguably self-serving, the description of the reign of Edward the Elder fails to give meaningful credit to his sister Aethelflaed, and the treatments of individual episodes such as *Brunanburh* and Edgar's coronation in 973 are decidedly grandiose. Issues such as these have led to the *Chronicle* frequently being seen as the 'official version' of West Saxon history. But this idea is too simplistic, and 'We should resist the temptation to regard it as a form of West Saxon dynastic propaganda'.[2] It is hard to fit the gloom-laden description of Aethelred the Unready's reign into this model, for example, and other parts of the *Chronicle*, on the mid-tenth century for example, when there were plenty of reasons why the spin doctors of southern England might have wanted to massage and manipulate evidence, are disappointingly thin and uninformative. But whatever the *Chronicle's* shortcomings, its influence has been profound. It was used in the twelfth century by John of Worcester, William of Malmesbury and Henry of Huntingdon, all of whom adapted and modified it in their own way and set historical writing in England on a new course through the middle ages. Bede's *Ecclesiastical History* is arguably the most important book ever written about English history, but it is the *Anglo-Saxon Chronicle*, warts and all, which underpins everything we think we know about the making of the kingdom of England.

1 F. M. Stenton, *Anglo-Saxon England* 3rd edn (Oxford, 1971), p. 688.
2 K&L, p. 40.

839–858

Ecgberht was buried at Winchester and succeeded as king of the West Saxons by his eldest son, Aethelwulf (839–58). The date of Aethelwulf's birth is unknown, but by 839 he was an experienced warrior and politician. He had been ruling the kingdom of Kent (actually modern Kent with Essex, Surrey and Sussex) since 825, and in 838, at an assembly held at Kingston upon Thames, he had been acknowledged as Ecgberht's heir in Wessex. As soon as Ecgberht died, Aethelwulf gave his own eldest son, Aethelstan, 'the kingdom of the people of Kent and the kingdom of the East Saxons and of the people of Surrey and of the South Saxons'.[10] This was clearly designed to be Aethelstan's training ground, although he was not given a completely free hand there by his father, who always kept a watchful eye on what Aethelstan was doing. Presumably, however, in due course Aethelstan was supposed to follow his father as king of Wessex, just as Aethelwulf had followed Ecgberht. But until then, it has been said, 'Aethelwulf ran a Carolingian-style family firm of plural realms, held together by his own authority as father-king, and by the consent of the distinct elites'.[11]

Within Wessex, Aethelwulf's main concern was the increasingly serious viking threat. Raids became more frequent – the *Anglo-Saxon Chronicle* records encounters between viking and local West Saxon armies in 840, 841 and 845. But the most serious battle of the 840s was in 843, when Aethelwulf himself was defeated, as his father had been in 836, at Carhampton. Viking activity intensified even more in the 850s. In 851, a fleet of 350 viking ships sailed up the Thames, stormed Canterbury and London and put the Mercian king, Berhtwulf (d.852?), to flight. It was left to King Aethelwulf and his son Aethelbald to confront the raiders at a place called *Aclea*, where the West Saxon army 'inflicted the greatest slaughter on a heathen army that we ever heard of until this present day'. Meanwhile, King Aethelstan of Kent won a significant victory of his own over the Vikings at Sandwich. The *Chronicle* also records the ominously important occasions in 850–1 when 'for the first time, heathen men stayed through the winter on Thanet', and in 854–5 when they stayed over winter, again 'for the first time', on Sheppey.[12]

As the Vikings continued to make their presence felt across southern England during the 840s and 850s, Aethelwulf's relationship with Mercia became ever more important. The Mercian king Berhtwulf, like his predecessor Wiglaf, probably ruled Mercia with Aethelwulf's permission and on the understanding that the king of Wessex had authority of some kind over his Mercian counterpart. It may have been around this time, too, that the disputed territory of Berkshire finally became part of the West Saxon kingdom. At the very least the two kingdoms cooperated, most notably in 853 when Berhtwulf's successor as king of Mercia, Burgred (852–74), asked Aethelwulf 'to help him to bring the Welsh under subjection to him'. As a result, Aethelwulf 'went with his army across Mercia against the Welsh, and made them all submissive to him'. This alliance was sealed in the same year when Burgred married Aethelwulf's daughter, Aethelswith.[13]

King Aethelwulf was not completely preoccupied with the viking raids and internal diplomacy. His relationships with some of his most prominent continental contemporaries were clearly important to him as well. In 853 he sent his son Alfred to Rome, where the young boy (he was only four at the time) met the pope. And three years later, in 856, Aethelwulf himself (accompanied by Alfred, who thus visited Rome twice before he was eight) made the same journey. According to the *Anglo-Saxon Chronicle*, the king travelled to Rome 'with great state, and remained there a twelvemonth'. Other evidence confirms how extravagant this pilgrimage was: Aethelwulf gave a gold crown, a gold sword, silver bowls and valuable textiles to St Peter and made lavish gifts to the Roman clergy and people.[14] Aethelwulf paused on his way to Rome and again on his return to England at the court of Charles the Bald (Charlemagne's grandson), king of the West Franks (843–77). On the outward leg of his trip, Aethelwulf was given supplies and an escort by Charles, whilst on his way home in 856 the West Saxon king stayed at the West Frankish court for no less than three months. Charles was having his own problems with viking raiders and presumably saw Aethelwulf as a useful ally. So useful, in fact, that he was prepared to formalise an alliance with him through marriage: in July 856 Aethelwulf married Charles's daughter, Judith, and in October she was consecrated and given the title of queen, 'something not customary before then to him or his people', in the view of one foreign chronicler.[15] If Aethelwulf was prepared to modify traditional practice here, and give Judith a status no previous West Saxon consort had enjoyed, he probably saw it as a small price to pay for the esteem he hoped to gain from an association with the most prestigious court in Europe.

This very association may have contributed to a developing crisis back in Wessex, however. Aethelwulf's marriage to Judith was doubtless intended to produce children. If it did, the position of the five sons he already had with his first wife, Osburh, would be brought into question by the arrival of half-brothers with a more exalted lineage than theirs. So news of Aethelwulf's plan to remarry may have prompted his eldest surviving son, Aethelbald, to pre-empt any attempt to alter the dynastic plan. King Aethelstan of Kent died in the early 850s, but shortly before he left for Rome in 855, Aethelwulf had divided his kingdom between his two eldest surviving sons, granting Wessex to Aethelbald and Kent (along with the other eastern territories Aethelstan had ruled) to Aethelberht. It is not clear what was supposed to happen when Aethelwulf came back to Wessex, but according to King Alfred's biographer, Asser, who was writing in the early 890s, 'a disgraceful episode' occurred as Aethelwulf was returning from Rome. Aethelbald, 'with all his councillors – or rather co-conspirators – attempted to perpetrate a terrible crime: expelling the king from his own kingdom'.[16] The *Anglo-Saxon Chronicle* does not mention this at all, and perhaps the chronicler chose to ignore it because it showed the West Saxon ruling dynasty in such a poor light. In any event, the *coup* was not completely successful, but on his return to England, it seems that King Aethelwulf was forced to accept a new arrangement: he received the kingdom's 'eastern districts' whilst Aethelbald kept control of the western ones. It is unclear what this actually meant. One view is that Aethelwulf was forced to accept the subordinate position as king of Kent (along with Surrey, Sussex and Essex) whilst his eldest son ruled in Wessex. Another is that Wessex itself was divided between Aethelwulf and Aethelbald whilst Aethelberht remained in control of Kent. Either way, Aethelwulf was compelled to accept a lesser position: Asser was clear that 'the western part of the Saxon land has always been more important than the eastern'.[17] Probably soon after these events, Aethelwulf had his will drawn up. It has not survived, but it is mentioned in other sources. Unfortunately, it does not clarify things significantly. Aethelwulf appointed Aethelbald his successor in Wessex whilst Aethelberht would be restored to (or keep?) his position in Kent once Aethelwulf was dead. It may even be the case that Aethelwulf intended the division between Wessex and Kent to be permanent and that he wanted Aethelberht to establish his own dynasty there. Within Wessex, moreover, there is a strong suggestion that Aethelwulf wanted his other sons, Aethelred and Alfred, to succeed Aethelbald as king if they survived him. There was little Aethelwulf could do to ensure that any of this actually happened, of course, and when he died early in 858, he left his four surviving sons to manage their own relationships. Buried first at Steyning in Sussex, Aethelwulf's body was later reburied at Winchester.

858–871

In the short term, Aethelwulf's scheme was implemented as Aethelbald (858–60) succeeded him as king of the West Saxons and Aethelberht became king of Kent. Soon, though, the plan began to unravel. One of the first things Aethelbald did was marry his father's widow, Judith. He may have done this (there were precedents) in order to identify himself with his father's rule, strengthen his own claim to succeed and give any children he had with Judith an illustrious Carolingian pedigree. But the *Anglo-Saxon Chronicle* does not mention the marriage at all (embarrassed again, perhaps, by Aethelbald's excessive behaviour), and Asser, when he reflected on it thirty years or so later, was clearly horrified by what had happened. The marriage, he said, was 'against God's prohibition and Christian dignity, and also contrary to the practice of all pagans'. It was widely regarded as a 'great disgrace', and when Aethelbald died in 860, Asser records, he had ruled Wessex for two and a half 'lawless' years. He was buried at Sherborne.[18]

At this point, if Aethelwulf's blueprint for the succession had been followed, Aethelbald would have been succeeded in Wessex by his younger brother Aethelred. But Aethelred, who may have been only twelve or thirteen, was probably thought too young to take on such an onerous responsibility, and it was actually King Aethelberht of Kent who followed Aethelbald as king of the West Saxons. In this way all of England south of the Thames was reunited under the authority of a single ruler, and this remained the situation as Aethelberht, unlike his predecessors, did not appoint anyone as sub-king of Kent. Asser and the *Anglo-Saxon Chronicle* described Aethelberht's five-year reign (860–5) as a success: he governed 'in peace, love and honour' and held the kingdom 'in good harmony and in great peace'.[19] Even so, the Vikings remained a threat. Winchester was attacked and plundered, whilst in the autumn of 864 in Kent, a viking army which had been paid off by the people there reneged on its promises of good behaviour and ravaged the eastern part of the kingdom. Viewed with hindsight, however, Aethelberht's reign must have looked tranquil by comparison with what preceded and followed it. When he died in the autumn of 865 and was buried at Sherborne alongside his brother Aethelbald, the real storm had not yet broken.

It was Aethelberht's younger brother, Aethelred I (865–71), who would eventually have to face an entirely new situation. Having succeeded his brother as sole king of the West Saxons in 865 when he cannot have been much older than sixteen, towards the end of the same year what the *Anglo-Saxon Chronicle* calls 'a great heathen army' arrived in England.[20] The size of this viking force, its origins and its leadership are all obscure. It might have sailed directly from Scandinavia, but equally elements of it could have come from Ireland, Northumbria or the European mainland. Later legend held that it was led by the great viking warrior Ivarr the Boneless and his brothers Halfdan and Ubba, the sons of Ragnar Lothbrok ('leather breeches'); but this is far from certain. Nevertheless, whatever the truth, those who wrote about these events later clearly recognised the arrival of this army in England as the moment when the scale and nature of the viking threat were drastically and permanently changed.

The Vikings spent the winter of 865–6 in East Anglia, where they had landed. They were given money, presumably in return for a promise not to plunder locally, and horses, presumably so that they could leave East Anglia quickly. And accordingly, they headed north in 866 to Northumbria. The northern kingdom may have been targeted by the army because, according to the *Anglo-Saxon Chronicle*, there was an ongoing civil war there between two rivals, Osberht and Aelle, and their supporters. Political leadership was therefore up for grabs, and it seems that the viking army was able to take advantage of the power vacuum and seize control of the city of York at the start of November 866. Osberht and Aelle then counterattacked, having put their differences aside for the time being in the face of a mutual enemy, and managed to retake the city. However, in March 867 they were both killed in a battle with the invaders at York, as a result of which the surviving Northumbrian leaders submitted to the victorious Vikings. The kingdom (or the southern part of it at least) had fallen to the great heathen army, although at this stage there is no evidence that the Vikings intended to rule Northumbria themselves. They installed a local man, Ecgberht (867–73), as king, presumably on the understanding that he ruled very much with their permission and as their agent.

At the end of 867, the Vikings left Northumbria. Turning their attention to Mercia they spent the winter at Nottingham. At that point Burgred, the king of Mercia, asked his brother-in-law Aethelred for help. As a result, the West Saxon king went with his younger brother Alfred and 'an immense army', Asser claimed, 'single-mindedly seeking battle'.[21] In the event, however, because the Vikings refused to fight, the brothers had to settle for a siege of Nottingham, but they were unable to break through the defences and in the end a truce was arranged. Having been paid off by the Mercians, the Vikings returned to York whilst Aethelred and Alfred returned to Wessex. Alfred, indeed, may have travelled home with his new bride, Ealhswith the daughter of a Mercian ealdorman. This marriage, which took place in the same year as the siege of Nottingham, was clearly designed further to reinforce the connection between Wessex and Mercia which had been developing since the 850s. During the late 860s, King Aethelred of Wessex adopted the same design for coins issued in his name as the King of Mercia, Burgred, used on his, and the coins for both kings were produced at either London and Canterbury. This established what has been described as 'a monetary union' between the two kingdoms which resulted in 'a common uniform currency circulating between Chester and Dover, Exeter and Lincoln'.[22] Such measures would have been intended to facilitate trade across southern England, but by establishing firm royal control over the system, the kings would also have hoped to maximise their income from the fees they charged for minting coins. At the very least, this numismatic evidence supports the idea that the two kingdoms were working very closely together to enforce internal controls and increase resources in a joint response to the viking menace.

In 869 the viking army left Northumbria once again and, having passed through Mercia, returned to East Anglia, where it settled down to spend the winter of 869–70 at Thetford. On 20 November 869, however, it was confronted by an army under the leadership of the East Anglian king, Edmund. During or very soon after a fierce fight which the Vikings won, Edmund was killed. He was later venerated as a martyr and saint and a successful cult developed around his relics at a place called *Beadricesworth*, now Bury St Edmunds. At the end of 869, however, all this lay in the distant future. The leaderless kingdom of East Anglia was now easy prey for the Vikings and, in Asser's words, after their victory, 'they subjected that entire province to their authority'.[23] The Great Army had conquered its second English kingdom, and it was soon looking for a third to invade.

Wessex was the Vikings' next target. Late in 870 they entered the kingdom of the West Saxons and made their base at Reading. Over the following year a series of battles was fought between the Great Army and the armies of King Aethelred and his followers. Initially the Vikings gained the upper hand. They defeated a force led by Ealdorman Aethelwulf of Berkshire at Englefield, and then, four days later, King Aethelred himself and his brother Alfred were beaten at Reading. The West Saxons were not fatally weakened, however, and only four days after the setback at Reading, Aethelred and Alfred won a major victory over the Vikings at Ashdown on the Berkshire downs. The *Anglo-Saxon Chronicle* attributes this triumph to the equally significant contributions of the two royal brothers, but Asser gave the lion's share of the credit to Alfred, who, he claimed, attacked the Vikings 'like a wild boar' while Aethelred was still praying in his tent. Both sources agree that 'many thousands' of Vikings were killed at Ashdown, but this may be an exaggeration given what happened next.[24] Two weeks after Ashdown, Aethelred and Alfred were defeated at Basing in Hampshire and two months after that they lost again at a place called *Meretun*. Their problems were compounded further when, probably late in March or early in April 871, what the *Chronicle* calls 'a great summer army' (in other words, a brand new viking host) entered Wessex under its leader Guthrum and came to Reading. Whether or not the arrival of these reinforcements was planned, the new army, Asser says, 'attached itself to the band' and only added to the pressure on the West Saxon leadership.[25] Then at this moment, as if the situation was not difficult enough, King Aethelred died. It is not clear why – perhaps he had been wounded in one or more of the recent battles. He was buried at Wimborne Minster in Dorset, and although he left two sons, he was succeeded as king of the West Saxons by his brother Alfred (871–99).

871–878

Alfred became king at a time of acute crisis for Wessex. As the Vikings seemed only to grow in strength, it must have looked very likely that he would suffer the same grisly fate as the kings of Northumbria and East Anglia. And his first encounter with the Vikings as king did not bode well: a month after his brother's death Alfred's outnumbered army was defeated by the Vikings at Wilton in Wiltshire. By then the fate of Wessex truly hung in the balance. According to Asser, the West Saxons had been 'virtually annihilated to a man' in no fewer than eight battles during 871.[26] Other writers differ about the precise number of battles which took place during this year (there may only have been six, or as many as nine), but that the position in general was dire seems clear. However, if the campaigns of 871 had exhausted the West Saxons, it seems that they had also taken their toll on the Vikings. Alfred's first significant achievement as king was to negotiate a ceasefire with them: Asser records how the West Saxons 'made peace with the Vikings, on condition that they would leave them; and this the Vikings did'.[27] This probably means that Alfred paid them money to leave his kingdom, just as the people of Kent, East Anglia and Mercia had done in 864, 866 and 868 respectively. He must have known that this was not a permanent solution to the viking problem and that they would almost certainly return to threaten Wessex again. But he was buying himself valuable time in which he could regroup and prepare for the battles to come.

The Vikings left Reading and spent the winter of 871–2 at London, forcing the Mercians to pay for their good behaviour. Then, having retired to Northumbria early in 872, the Vikings returned to Mercia again at the end of that year and wintered at Torksey in Lincolnshire. Once more, the Mercians had to pay for the privilege of having the Vikings as their guests over Christmas. The strain on Mercian resources must by then have been considerable and can only have been increased in the following winter (873–4) when the viking army made its winter base in the heart of the kingdom, at Repton in Derbyshire. The choice of Repton was no accident. It was the burial place of several Mercian kings and a site of great political and religious significance to the Mercian elite. Its seizure by the Vikings was a decisive demonstration of their power, and King Burgred was unable to respond. He was driven out of his kingdom and fled to Rome where he soon died and was buried.

Meanwhile, the Vikings in Mercia 'conquered all the land' and installed a certain Ceolwulf (Asser called him a 'foolish king's thegn', which at least suggests a man of some standing if not ability) as their puppet-king there. As in Northumbria in 867 and East Anglia in 869, there was no immediate sign that the Vikings wanted to rule Mercia or settle there. As far as the *Anglo-Saxon Chronicle* was concerned, Ceolwulf II was no more than a caretaker king, a viking stooge: he gave the Vikings hostages and swore subservient oaths about his new kingdom, 'that it should be ready for them on whatever day they wished to have it, and he would be ready, himself and all who would follow him, at the enemy's service'.[28] The reality appears to have been more complex than this, however, and contemporary evidence shows Ceolwulf acting with a significant degree of independence as king of the Mercians until he disappeared from the records in 879. Two charters from 875 survive, for example, both witnessed by members of the Mercian elite, in which Ceolwulf is called 'king of the Mercians'.[29] Three types of silver penny also survive in his name, two of which, the 'cross-and-lozenge' and the 'two emperors', and were also issued by Alfred in Wessex at the same time. This kind of monetary alliance between Wessex and Mercia was nothing new, as has been seen, but at this point it suggests a degree of contact and cooperation between the two kingdoms which later writers, keen to emphasise the loneliness of Alfred's struggle against the Vikings after 874, were perhaps reluctant to dwell on. Alfred's closeness to a neighbouring king who had been installed by the Vikings was probably not something they wanted future generations to know about, and their denigration of Ceolwulf makes more sense as a rewriting of recent history rather than an objective account of it. Because the combined evidence of Ceolwulf's charters and coins strongly suggests that, between 874 and 879, both Mercians and West Saxons regarded him as the legitimate and credible Mercian king.

Following Burgred's flight to Rome and Ceolwulf's assumption of power, the viking army in Mercia divided into two parts. One part under its leader Halfdan, perhaps what was left of the Great Army which had arrived in 865, returned to Northumbria, spending the winter of 874–5 somewhere by the river Tyne. In 867, the Vikings had left their puppet-king Ecgberht in charge in the north, but he had been overthrown in 873 and replaced by a certain Ricsige (873–6). The Vikings in 875–6 must have made short work of him as they are said to have 'conquered' the kingdom in that year. Then Halfdan 'shared out the land of the Northumbrians, and they proceeded to plough and to support themselves'.[30] This moment is usually regarded as signalling the start of viking settlement on a significant scale in northern England. These events are obscure, however, and it is hard to know what was actually going on. Halfdan may have 'conquered' Northumbria, but it seems that Ricsige was replaced by another King Ecgberht (876–8) as well. It is possible that the old division of Northumbria was reestablished at this point, with Halfdan ruling the ancient kingdom of Deira, centred on York, whilst the northern kingdom, Bernicia, remained in the hands of the English ruler, Ecgberht. He died in 878, and in the same year Halfdan himself was driven out of Northumbria by his own army – because he was too smelly, one source alleges![31] At this point, a Danish prince, Guthfrith (878–894/5), was elected 'king of Northumbria'. He is reputed to have converted to Christianity so may have been acceptable to the Northumbrian people as well as the viking army. It seems likely, however, that his power did not stretch beyond the Tees, where English lords based at Bamburgh held the line against complete surrender to the Vikings.

Meanwhile, as Halfdan's army had been setting out for the north in 874, the rest of the Vikings in Mercia, perhaps the survivors of the 'summer army' of 871, had moved from Repton to Cambridge under the leadership of 'the three kings, Guthrum, Oscetel, and Anwend'.[32] They stayed there for a year, presumably readying themselves for their next campaign, an attack on Wessex, which eventually began late in 875. Having 'slipped past the army of the West Saxons', the Vikings made their base at Wareham in Dorset.[33] But they were followed there by Alfred and agreed to a truce. Indeed, Alfred may have gained the initiative at this stage as the Vikings gave him hostages and swore to leave his kingdom straight away. In the event, however, they broke their promise, and under cover of darkness, part of the army escaped on horseback from Wareham and moved west to Exeter where it spent the winter barricaded inside a fortress. There it was soon joined by its ships, but not before 120 vessels had been lost in a storm on the way from Wareham. King Alfred pursued the Vikings to Exeter and, once again, he forced them to give oaths that they would leave Wessex. This time, perhaps seriously weakened by the damage to their fleet, they kept their word, and in August 877 the Vikings left Wessex and returned to Mercia. At this point some of the Vikings decided that they had campaigned enough. On arriving in Mercia, as their comrades in Northumbria had done in 875–6, they began to settle: the *Chronicle* says of Mercia that they 'shared out some of it, and gave some to Ceolwulf'.[34] He did retain some kind of authority over the south-western part of the kingdom, whilst the Vikings' territory further east in Mercia would have included London, Bedford and Northampton along with, in the north, the lands which came later to be known as the 'Five Boroughs' – Derby, Lincoln, Leicester, Nottingham and Stamford. Not all the Vikings had finished fighting, however, and enough of them remained determined to return to Wessex the next year.

878 was the pivotal year of King Alfred's reign, and a critical one in the making of the English kingdom. 'In this year in midwinter after twelfth night the enemy army came stealthily to Chippenham', the *Chronicle* records.[35] Both the date and the place were significant: Chippenham was a royal residence and the celebrations of Christmas and new year were probably still going on as the Vikings attempted to take the West Saxons by surprise. It is even possible that Alfred himself was at Chippenham for the Twelfth Night festivities (5 January) and the Feast of the Epiphany on the following day, and that the viking plan was to capture and kill him. If this was the case, they did not succeed, but the Vikings had done enough to imperil the survival of Wessex as an independent kingdom. They 'occupied the land of the West Saxons', the *Chronicle* says 'and settled there, and drove a great part of the people across the sea, and conquered most of the others, except King Alfred'.[36] What this actually meant in practice is far from clear (Asser's comment that, after the events at Chippenham, 'very nearly all the inhabitants of that region submitted' to the Vikings confuses rather than clarifies the situation), but it sounds at the very least like the start of a conquest.[37] And when a viking fleet arrived in Devon from south-west Wales, its purpose may have been to reinforce the achievements of the invading army, join forces with it and press further into the kingdom.

However, at this point, the viking takeover of Wessex began to falter. In Devon, they were defeated by a local army and, crucially, Alfred himself had survived to fight another day. He had escaped with a small number of followers and, in Asser's famous words 'was leading a restless life in great distress amid the woody and marshy places of Somerset'.[38] Asser depicts Alfred at the lowest point of his fortunes, forced to live from hand to mouth by ambushing viking patrols and raiding those locals who had submitted to the invaders. It is also during this phase of his reign that the most famous story about Alfred, when he burnt some bread (or 'cakes') that a local woman had asked him to mind, is set. This tale and others like it (none of which were written down until long after Alfred's death) are of course much more legend than fact. Another has Alfred being visited at Athelney by the great saint of seventh-century Northumbria, Cuthbert. Alfred gave Cuthbert food, not knowing who he was, and was rewarded by the saint for his generosity with advice on how to defeat the Vikings. A third story describes how Alfred, in disguise, visited the viking camp disguised as a minstrel and stayed there for several days gathering intelligence. But they were designed to show Alfred's suffering, his generosity and his ingenuity and, in the end, how great his recovery was. In reality, the Somerset marshes provided Alfred with an ideal hideout. He would have known them well from his youth, but to outsiders, they would have been impenetrable and dangerous, navigable only by boat and with specialised local knowledge. Once again, Alfred had gained time in which to assess his options and plan his response to the viking invasion.

His first move, around March 878, was to build a fortress at a place in the marshes called Athelney. Asser describes the site as 'surrounded by swampy, impassable and extensive marshland and groundwater on every side. It cannot be reached in any way except by punts or by a causeway'.[39] From here the king began a campaign of guerrilla warfare against the local viking forces, striking out against them 'relentlessly and tirelessly', Asser says.[40] But, if he was to defeat the invaders and regain his kingdom, Alfred needed a more decisive victory. So, in the second week of May, he rode to a place called 'Egbert's Stone'. It has never been established for sure where Egbert's Stone was, but it was presumably a place of local significance, a prominent landmark or regular meeting-place known to the people of the area. Perhaps it was near Penselwood on the boundary between Somerset and Wiltshire, because when he arrived at his destination Alfred was met by 'all the people' of those two counties, along with many from Hampshire, who 'rejoiced to see him'. Asser went further than the *Chronicle* at this point: 'When they saw the king, receiving him (not surprisingly) as if one restored to life after suffering such great tribulations, they were filled with immense joy'.[41] Asser clearly intended to liken Alfred's reception by his people with Christ's appearance before his disciples after the resurrection. More prosaically, the events at Egbert's Stone can only have resulted from the operation of an extensive and sophisticated underground communication system, a West Saxon resistance movement whose purpose was to fight back against the Vikings and restore Alfred to power.

The speed of these events and those that followed suggests that Alfred had determined on his strategy in advance. He was determined to stake everything on a battle with the Vikings in the hope that, unlike most of the previous clashes he had been involved in, he would win and win decisively. Two days' march after the rendezvous at Egbert's Stone, Alfred arrived with his followers, now transformed into an army, at Edington in Wiltshire. His spies may have told him that this was where the Vikings were encamped and perhaps he intended to take them by surprise.

Alternatively, the Vikings might have been waiting for him. Either way, 'fighting fiercely with a compact shield-wall against the entire viking army, he persevered resolutely for a long time; at length he gained the victory through God's will'.[42] This was not enough to guarantee lasting success, however, and it was what happened next that turned Edington into a conclusive triumph. As the Vikings turned and fled from the battlefield, Alfred and his men pursued them until they reached their stronghold at Chippenham. For the next two weeks, the king was encamped outside the walls of the fortress, intent on eliminating the viking threat once and for all; and eventually, 'thoroughly terrified by hunger, cold and fear, and in the end by despair', they agreed to surrender.[43] The terms were one-sided: the Vikings agreed to give Alfred as many hostages as he chose to take (he gave none in return, which was unprecedented in such a deal, Asser thought) and swore that they would leave Wessex immediately. Their leader, Guthrum, also agreed to convert to Christianity, and three weeks later, he along with thirty of his leading men came to Aller, near Athelney, where they were all baptised. Alfred acted as Guthrum's sponsor at the ceremony itself and the rituals were completed a week or so later at Wedmore, also in Somerset. In all Alfred and Guthrum were together for twelve days after the baptism, and surely during that time they discussed the future. Vikings had gone back on their promises before, of course, and Alfred cannot have been certain that his deal with Guthrum would last. Nevertheless, by the end of 878, he had at least proved that Wessex would not be conquered as easily as the other English kingdoms.

878–892

Guthrum (who after his baptism adopted the Christian name Aethelstan) took his time to lead his followers out of Wessex. They moved from Chippenham to Cirencester at the end of 878 and only after staying there for another year did they head for East Anglia. They 'settled there and shared out the land'.[44] As a result, by the start of the new decade, viking regimes and viking settlements had been established across much of eastern, midland and northern England: collectively these territories would later become known as the Danelaw. This process of settlement, which had been made possible by the conquests of the Great Army after 865, had only begun three years before in Northumbria, followed by eastern Mercia and East Anglia, and it was still in its earliest stages by the end of the 870s. Nevertheless, following the overthrow of three ancient kingdoms and the establishment of new ruling elites with different traditions, languages and aspirations, the political and social map of England had been transformed.

Wessex, however, had survived and showed how determined its resistance could be. So after another viking army had landed at Fulham and spent the winter of 879–80 there, its leaders decided not to waste any more time in England and set out for the continent. Perhaps the plan had been to join up with Guthrum's army and join in the conquest of Wessex, but Edington put paid to any such idea. Most of the entries in the *Anglo-Saxon Chronicle* for the next few years describe the fortunes of this army in the Frankish Empire, and there is notably little recorded about what was happening in England at the same time. As will be seen in Chapter 2,* however, this temporary respite from battles and campaigning gave Alfred the time he needed fundamentally to reorganise the way his kingdom's defences worked. He and his people had to be ready next time the Vikings returned to Wessex, as they surely would.

The first real test came in 885–6, when the viking army on the continent split in two and one part came back to England. The fleet sailed up the Thames estuary and laid siege to Rochester, but the locals were able to hold out until Alfred himself arrived with a relieving army and forced the Vikings to pull back. At this point some of the invaders left England once again, but others came to terms with Alfred, only to renege on them soon after. These diehards were now given help by some of those Vikings who had settled in East Anglia in the late 870s, and they were able to establish a new base at Benfleet on the north bank of the Thames estuary and prepare their next move. Unfortunately for them, their plans were frustrated when they quarrelled with their East Anglian allies, and most if not all of the invaders returned to the continent. Nevertheless, Alfred clearly took these developments very seriously. His response was to send a fleet to attack and punish the East Anglian Vikings who, as far as the *Anglo-Saxon Chronicle* was concerned had 'violated their peace' with Wessex.[45] Two battles at sea then took place, Alfred winning one and the Vikings the other.

It may have been these events which prompted what happened next. Some time between autumn 886 and autumn 887, 'King Alfred occupied London; and all the English people that were not under subjection to the Danes submitted to him'. Asser records the same event but presents it a little differently. According to him, Alfred

> restored the city of London splendidly – after so many towns had been burned and so many people slaughtered – and made it habitable again . . . All the Angles and Saxons – those who had formerly been scattered everywhere and were not in captivity with the Vikings – turned willingly to Alfred and submitted themselves to his lordship.[46]

It seems clear from Asser's account that Alfred's acquisition of London was violent and difficult, but the king presumably thought it was essential to have control there in order to establish a more intimidating presence on the Thames and deter further viking attempts to use the river as their gateway to England. But there was also much more to this event than matters of strategy. The assertions in the *Chronicle* and by Asser respectively that 'all the English people' or 'all the Angles and Saxons' who were not ruled by the Vikings submitted to Alfred at this point is obviously noteworthy. The implication is that Alfred was seen from this point on as more than

* Below, pp. 59–64

just a king of the West Saxons and that his authority now extended beyond the established borders of Wessex.

Other evidence confirms that something more profound was happening by the mid-880s. First, there were events in Mercia. After that kingdom had been divided in 877, King Ceolwulf had continued to rule the western part, including Worcester, Gloucester and Warwick, for another two years. Historians call this truncated territory English Mercia. After 879, however, Ceolwulf makes no further appearances in any record, and it is assumed that he died or was removed from power. Whatever happened to him, by the early 880s, English Mercia had come under the control of a certain Ealdorman Aethelred, and charter evidence suggests that he in turn had acknowledged the overlordship of King Alfred of Wessex by 883 at the latest. And to cement the alliance further, within two or three years, Aethelred had married Alfred's daughter, Aethelflaed. Second, it was during this phase of his reign that Alfred made a formal treaty with Guthrum, the man he had defeated at Edington in 878. There are different opinions about when this treaty was drawn up.[47] It was certainly made before Guthrum died in 890, and some historians would date it immediately after Edington. Others have contended that the treaty makes most sense in the context of Alfred's attack on East Anglia in 885 and his subsequent seizure of control in London in 886. A third argument gives the treaty a date between the other two, c.880, on the basis that this would coincide with the death (or disappearance at any rate) of King Ceolwulf of Mercia and an assertion of control over his lands (including London itself) by Alfred. Whenever it was made, the treaty touches on matters regarding trade and hostages, but in broader terms, and much more importantly, it purports to fix the boundary between Alfred's territory and the Viking-controlled parts of England. That line was set as running 'up the Thames, and then up the Lea, and along the Lea to its source, then in a straight line to Bedford, then up the Ouse to Watling Street'.[48] Put crudely, after winding through the Thames valley and then a little way north, a diagonal line was drawn between the south-east and north-west corners of the old kingdom of Mercia, putting English Mercia and London (which Alfred may already have controlled to some degree since the early 880s) once and for all out of viking reach. Significantly too, though, the treaty stipulates that its terms had been agreed, not just by Alfred and Guthrum and his followers, but also by 'the councillors of all the English race'. Again, the implication seems to be that Alfred was claiming to exercise authority on behalf of all those in southern England outside Danish control, whether West Saxon or not. If so, this would fit well with the evidence about the submissions he had received from that wider community following his capture of London in 886.

Whether such a claim could be translated into permanent political reality still remained to be seen, of course. And whilst Alfred's ambition seems clear there were still real problems to address. Not least among these was the return of the viking threat to England during the first half of the 890s. In August 891, the viking army on the continent was heavily defeated at Louvain on the river Dyle by an army under Arnulf, king of the East Franks. The survivors stayed where they were licking their wounds for nearly a year, but eventually a famine compelled them to move on, and they retreated to Boulogne. In the autumn of 892, having been given 250 ships by their Frankish hosts, they set out for England and, having crossed the Channel, sailed up the river Rother in Kent. On their way up the river, they destroyed a half-made fortress and then made their base at Appledore. Meanwhile, another viking army, eighty ships strong under its leader Hastein, had arrived in the Thames estuary and made its base at Milton Regis, near Sittingbourne, on the north coast of Kent.

893–899

Three hundred and thirty viking ships, probably carrying several thousand viking warriors between them, had arrived in south-eastern England by the autumn of 892. When news of this reached Alfred, he must have remembered the moment he first heard of the Great Army of 865, because these new arrivals potentially posed a similar threat. There were new complications, too: the viking settlers in East Anglia had not yet proved that they could be trusted (they had demonstrated this in 885–6), and Alfred could not be sure either that the Northumbrian settlers would ignore this chance to break their agreements with him.

The course of the next three years is described in the *Anglo-Saxon Chronicle*. These entries are very different from those for earlier years. They are long, densely packed with detail and significantly different in narrative style from earlier parts of the source. This is because, scholars largely agree, the entries for 893–6 were written up as a block by a different writer soon after the events had occurred and then added to the first version of the *Chronicle* which had been completed by 892–3. There are problems with the *Chronicle's* account of these years, however, beyond the fact that it was written with the benefit of hindsight. It is certainly very detailed, but also rather confusing and difficult to understand at times. It is also possible to argue that, despite its length, it downplays or even deliberately overlooks the role played by some important individuals in the campaigns it describes, not least Alfred's eldest son, Edward. Secondly, there is nothing from Asser to complement or confirm the contents of the *Chronicle* for this period, because Asser wrote his biography of Alfred during the early 890s and had certainly finished what survives by 893. This gap is plugged to some extent by the late tenth-century chronicle written by Ealdorman Aethelweard. He does deal with the events of 893–6, using a text of the *Anglo-Saxon Chronicle* which has now been lost, but his account is frequently obscure, even garbled, and so, once again, difficult to interpret or use conclusively.

Alfred's first step was to march with an army to a point somewhere between the two viking encampments at Appledore and Milton. Presumably he wanted to be well-placed to deal with any attempted breakout, but he also appears to have begun negotiations with Hastein, who was given money by Alfred in return for hostages and oaths. Alfred and his son-in-law Aethelred also became godfathers to two of Hastein's sons. Whilst Alfred was stationed in Kent, however, there was trouble elsewhere. At some point, probably early in 894, at least a part of the viking forces attempted to cross the Thames into Essex, but it was intercepted at Farnham in Surrey by an English army under (Aethelweard tells us) the king's eldest son Edward.

The Vikings were defeated and fled across the river where they took refuge on a small island and were besieged. However, and more ominously, viking fleets from Northumbria and East Anglia were now assembled: some besieged a fortress on the north Devon coast whilst others focused their efforts on Exeter, where Alfred now headed. As for Hastein, as soon as Alfred had moved off towards the Thames, he had broken his pledges and reoccupied a fort which the Vikings had used in 885 at Benfleet in Essex. Another English army confronted him there, however, and defeated him soundly. Hastein regrouped and gathered his forces at Shoebury in Essex. From there (joined by elements from Northumbria and East Anglia), they struck out across central England and into western Mercia. But they were pursued by armies led by Ealdorman Aethelred of Mercia and the ealdormen of Somerset and Wiltshire and finally forced to take refuge in a fortress called Buttington, per-haps near Welshpool in Montgomery. They were besieged there for many weeks, the *Chronicle* says, and eventually starving, they had no option but to try and break the siege by coming out of the fortress and fighting the besiegers. They were easily defeated, however, and many of the Vikings were slaughtered, although some were able to escape and find their way back to Essex. With winter approaching towards the end of 894, these survivors, having left their women and children in safety in East Anglia, then set out in yet another direction. This time, reinforced once again by East Anglian and Northumbrian allies, they headed north-west to Chester. They were pursued by an English army but reached their destination in enough time to set themselves up there for the winter.

All of these events took place, it seems, while Alfred himself was occupied at Exeter. His presence there eventually forced the Vikings to raise their siege of the city and leave. Having sailed along the south coast they tried to make their presence felt in Sussex by ravaging around Chichester, but they were seen off by a local army which killed 'many hundreds' of Vikings and captured some of their ships. Pickings were proving extremely thin wherever the Vikings attempted to find them, and their meagre gains were being bought at a high cost in terms of men and resources. Indeed, by the start of 895, the Vikings at Chester were also becoming desperate. Forced to move on once again by the threat of starvation ('they were deprived both of the cattle and the corn which had been ravaged', the *Chronicle* says), they went first into Wales and then back to Essex via Northumbria and Mercia 'so that the English army could not reach them'.[49] Eventually they made a temporary base on Mersea Island at the mouth of the Colne estuary on the south coast of Essex and, as the autumn of 895 drew in, they rowed their ships up the Thames and its tributary the river Lea where they made a fortress 'twenty miles above London', probably near Hertford.[50] But in the summer of 896, an army left London and saw the Vikings off. Alfred then arrived with his own forces to protect the city whilst the harvest was collected, and he then set about building two fortresses on the Lea which had the effect of cutting off the remaining Vikings from their ships. They retreated without them to Bridgnorth on the river Severn and were once again pursued by an English army. Having spent the winter at Bridgnorth, the Vikings then divided their forces. Some went to Northumbria, others to East Anglia 'and those that were moneyless got themselves ships and went across the sea to the Seine'. There were more raids on the south coast in the course of 896–7, but it seems clear that by this point the Vikings' attempts to repeat their predecessors' victories of the 860s and 870s had failed. At no point during the campaigns of 893–6 had they been able to pierce Alfred's defences, enter Wessex or English Mercia and remain there for any length of time. And although, to be sure, Alfred and his lieutenants had made considerable efforts to deal with the threat they presented, and many important men had been killed in the process, the *Chronicle* was clear that 'By the grace of God, the army had not on the whole afflicted the English people very greatly'.[51]

Little is known for certain about what happened over the following two or three years. Almost certainly Alfred continued with the work he had done in the 880s, repaired the defences which had been battered by the Vikings in the 890s and prepared for more attacks in the future. He cannot have known that he would never face another viking army. One source claims that Alfred made a formal peace treaty with the Vikings of Northumbria, apparently after the death of their King Guthfrith in 894 or 895.[52] There had certainly been Northumbrian involvement in the campaigns of 893–6, but whether this was supported by Guthfrith or not is unclear. In any event, his successor was Sigeferth, who may have been the 'pirate' of the same name whom Ealdorman Aethelweard records as raiding into Mercia or Wessex (it is unclear precisely where he attacked) in 893–4.[53] But if he was the same man, Sigeferth may have taken the end of the viking attacks on southern England in 896 as a sign that his reign should begin on a new footing with Alfred and his regime. As for Alfred himself, only just fifty but probably debilitated by years of illness and exhausted by years of hard work, he died on 26 October 899 and was buried in the cathedral church at Winchester. He had saved his kingdom from viking conquest not just once but several times, and in doing so, he had extended his authority more widely and embedded it more deeply than any of his predecessors. But his achievements were not necessarily permanent, and his successors would have to work just as strenuously as he had done to secure his legacy and build on it further.

DEBATE 2

Who were the Vikings?

The Vikings were an international phenomenon, and England was only one of the places they changed profoundly between about 800 and about 1100. They came from modern Denmark, Norway and Sweden, although not all early medieval Scandinavians were Vikings. Most carried on farming and hunting just as they had always done, and only those who left their homelands on ships to trade, raid and settle elsewhere qualify for this description. These adventurers were also given many other names by the people they encountered: Northmen, Danes, pagans, foreigners, robbers and more. As for the word 'Viking' itself, its meaning is obscure. First used in Old English, it may derive from the Old Icelandic *vik*, meaning bay or creek, or it may refer to people who came from the Viken, the area around the Oslo Fjord. Whatever its origins, the word was one of those used by the English to describe the hostile, heathen pirates (most of whom were Danish) who raided their coastline from the 790s onwards and then proceeded from the 860s to conquer and settle large parts of northern, central and eastern England, and it has been the pre- ferred term for historians describing these events ever since. Why these raids began remains up for debate, and there is still merit in the observation that 'No satisfactory explanation has yet been offered for the dramatic outburst of the Vikings from Scandinavia'.[1] Economic, political and technological explanations have all been given. The dominant view for a long time was that the Vikings were compelled to conquer new territories because of Scandinavia's growing population and resultant 'land hunger' at home. This theory is less popular today (arable land was scarce, but the early decades of viking activity were dominated by raiding not settling), and others have displaced it. For example, it has been argued that ambitious Scandinavians warlords or thwarted exiles who aspired to rule at home may have seen raiding as a way of recruiting fol- lowers, winning treasure and making a reputation, all of which might facilitate a bid for power on their return. But whilst there are some examples which fit this model, the evidence that this was a common phenomenon is hardly con- clusive. Others have suggested that when skilled Scandinavian boat builders added sails to their large rowing ships and improved their navigating meth- ods, they were able to travel long distances across open seas for the first time and encounter a new world of plundering opportunities. Against this, though, there is evidence that sails were adopted over a century before the viking raids began, so it is hard to see this development as their cause. Currently, perhaps the most popular explanation of the start of the viking raids is based on the increase in trade which took place between Scandinavia and north-western Europe from the late seventh century onwards. Scandinavians had long had contacts with Finland and Russia where furs as well as amber and walrus ivory could be acquired. These exotic commodities were sought after by merchants from England and Francia who could sail into the Baltic during the summer and pick them up at one of the growing number of trading centres along the coast. This may have been what first introduced the Scandinavians to sail technology; it certainly would have given them a favourable impression of how wealthy their trading partners were, and foreign ships in the Baltic may have been the first target for pirates who were soon emboldened to sail further afield in search of Christian riches.

1 R.H.C. Davis, *A History of Medieval Europe: From Constantine to Saint Louis*, ed. R.I. Moore, 3rd edn (Harlow, 2006), p. 174.

Notes

1 *ASC* F796.
2 S1435.
3 Alex Woolf, *From Pictland to Alba 789–1070* (Edinburgh, 2007), pp. 68–9.
4 *ASC* 802, 839.
5 *ASC* 815; for the later sources, see H. Edwards, 'Ecgberht, King of the West Saxons', in *ODNB*.
6 *ASC* 825.
7 *ASC* 829.
8 *ASC* 830.
9 *ASC* 789, 835.
10 *ASC* 839.
11 J.L. Nelson, 'Aethelwulf, King of the West Saxons', in *ODNB*.
12 *ASC* 851, 855–8.
13 *ASC* 853.
14 *ASC* 855–8; Nelson, 'Aethelwulf'.
15 J.L. Nelson (trans.), *The Annals of St Bertin* (Manchester, 1991), s.a.856 (p. 83).
16 K&L, p. 70.
17 K&L, p. 70.
18 K&L, p. 73.
19 K&L, p. 74; *ASC* 860.
20 *ASC* 866.
21 K&L, p. 77.
22 Mark Blackburn, 'Alfred's Coinage Reforms in Context', in T. Reuter (ed.), *Alfred the Great: Papers from the Eleventh-Centenary Conferences* (Aldershot, 2003), pp. 199–217 at pp. 204–5.
23 K&L, p. 78.
24 *ASC* 871; K&L, pp. 78–80.
25 *ASC* 871; K&L, p. 80.
26 K&L, p. 81.
27 K&L, p. 81.
28 *ASC* 874; K&L, p. 82.
29 S215, 216; *EHD*, i no.95.
30 *ASC* 875, 876.
31 Referred to in Woolf, *From Pictland to Alba*, p. 78.
32 *ASC* 875.
33 *ASC* 876.
34 *ASC* 877.
35 *ASC* 878.
36 *ASC* 878.
37 K&L, p. 83.
38 K&L, p. 83.
39 K&L, p. 103.
40 K&L, p. 84.
41 *ASC* 878; K&L, p. 84.
42 K&L, p. 84.
43 K&L, p. 85.
44 *ASC* 880.
45 *ASC* 885.
46 *ASC* 886; K&L, pp. 97–8.
47 For a date between 886 and 890 see, for example, R.H.C. Davis, 'Alfred and Guthrum's Frontier', *EHR* 97 (1982), pp. 803–10, and K&L, pp. 38–9, 311. For an earlier date, see D.N. Dumville, 'The Treaty of Alfred and Guthrum', in his *Wessex and England from Alfred to Edgar* (Woodbridge, 1992), pp. 1–27, and now S. Keynes, 'Alfred the Great and

the Kingdom of the Anglo-Saxons', in N.G. Discenza and P.E. Szarmach (eds.), *A Companion to Alfred the Great* (Leiden, 2015), pp. 13–46, at pp. 22–3.

48 K&L, p. 171.
49 *ASC* 894.
50 *ASC* 896.
51 *ASC* 896.
52 For the reference, see K&L, pp. 337–8, n.37.
53 K&L, p. 190.

2

RULING THE KINGDOMS, 796–899

By the start of the ninth century, kings across England were ruling their kingdoms in similar ways. There were differences of scale (the kings of Mercia faced larger challenges than their contemporaries elsewhere simply because they ruled more territory), but the strategies and methods used to establish and extend royal author-ity were essentially the same from Northumbria to Wessex. Kings travelled osten-tatiously around their kingdoms with their households; they held grand meetings with their *witan*; they provided lavish hospitality for and took it from their subjects; they gave magnificent gifts and rewards for loyal service, extracted tribute and raised money from trade. Rituals, genealogies, laws, charters and coins were already vital tools for expressing and enforcing royal control. And underpinning all of this, of course, was the kings' ability to maintain and where possible increase their power through war. That would not change after 800, but by the end of the ninth century, that ability would have been tested like never before.

Becoming king

How did a man become a king during the ninth century? There were no hard and fast rules about who should succeed a dead ruler, although there were developing conventions and a clear understanding that not just anyone was eligible. For a start, it seems to have been accepted by 800 that a new king should come from within the kindred (essentially the extended family) of the previous one. When he clearly did not, it prompted comment, as when the *Anglo-Saxon Chronicle* referred to Aelle, one of the Northumbrian kings killed by the Vikings in 867, as 'a king with no hereditary right'.[1] This did not necessarily mean that the eldest son of the late king would automatically succeed him (the establishment of primogeniture as a settled principle was still a long way off), or indeed that any of his sons would follow him on to the throne. However, some ninth-century kings were prepared to let their sons rule lesser kingdoms during their own lifetimes. The kings of Wessex were certainly keen on this kind of arrangement. Aethelwulf was sent to be sub-king of Kent by his father Ecgberht in 825, and Aethelwulf himself did something similar when he appointed his own second son, Aethelberht, as sub-king of Kent and the south-east in the mid-850s. In the first instance the intention seems to have been to give Aethelwulf experience of ruling before taking over in Wessex (which he did in 839), while in the second case Aethelwulf's plan may have been to establish a separate branch of the ruling dynasty in Kent. But at a higher level than that of the sub-kingdom, it was rare in this period for any son to take his late father's place as king. And even when special measures were taken to try and guarantee this, there were often problems. King Offa was determined to engineer the succession of his son Ecgfrith to the Mercian throne and went so far as to have him consecrated king in his own lifetime, the first reference to the consecration of a king in England.[2] Ecgfrith died less than a year after becoming king and was succeeded by a very distant relative, suggesting that he and Offa had worked hard to eliminate any closer claimants to the throne. It is arguable, albeit rather bluntly, that this troubled transition marked the beginning of the end of Mercia's supremacy within England. Half a century or so later, King Ecgberht of Wessex had his son Aethelwulf publicly acknowledged as his heir at a major gathering at Kingston in 838. Then, in the mid-850s, Aethelwulf himself attempted to ensure the succession of his two eldest sons, Aethelbald and Aethelberht, to Wessex and Kent respectively by setting out his intentions in his will. But events soon overtook this when Aethelbald seized power during his father's subsequent visit to Rome. Finally, in 899 when Alfred the Great was succeeded by his eldest son Edward, civil war ensued.

It was just as, if not more, common for a brother, a cousin or an even a more distant relative of the late king to take his place. There might be a range of such candidates (or athelings – roughly, princes of the royal blood) to choose from, but it was the man from within the royal kindred deemed fittest to rule (the one most 'throne-worthy' or 'king-worthy', as historians sometimes put it) who would succeed. The most obvious example of this comes from Wessex once again, where King Aethelbald (d.860) was succeeded by no fewer than three of his brothers, one after the other. This practice was pragmatic above all else. A king's first and most important duty was to lead his army in wartime and thereby protect his people, so it made no sense to allow a son to succeed his father as king if the former was very young or for some other reason incapable of campaigning and fighting battles.

There was clearly scope for controversy and argument here. Succession to the throne could be a vigorously competitive business and expectations about the kind of man who should succeed could easily be thwarted. To be sure, not every king succeeded as a member of his predecessor's kindred. Sometimes kings were simply imposed on a kingdom by a superior power: the Vikings did this in Northumbria and Mercia after they conquered those kingdoms in 867 and 874 respectively. At other times, the circumstances of a king's accession were suspiciously murky. For example, Ecgberht became king of Wessex in 802, but he probably did so by over-throwing King Beorhtric (who had driven Ecgberht into exile in the 790s), and not by any kind of hereditary right. Indeed, Ecgberht may have been from Kent rather than Wessex originally. Such a background and such a seizure of power could give rise to awkward questions about the legitimacy of Ecgberht's claim to rule the West Saxons, questions which might have hung over his successors' heads, too. So it is probably no coincidence that the *Anglo-Saxon Chronicle* took great pains to include a royal genealogy which gave Ecgberht and his son Aethelwulf impeccable West Saxon royal credentials. History was rewritten, showing that the possession of royal blood was seen as an important qualification for kingship; indeed 'so important that, if it did not exist, it had to be invented'.[3] There was also plenty of room for friction to develop between different members of a king's kindred about their respective rights to succeed him. When Alfred became king of Wessex in 871, the claims of his predecessor's two sons (Alfred's nephews) were overlooked. They may have been thought too young to succeed at such a difficult time, but one of them at least never forgot that he was an atheling. When Alfred died in 899, the new king Edward was challenged for the throne by his cousin Aethelwold, and it took more than three years of hard campaigning before the issue was settled in Edward's favour by Aethelwold's death.

But if, in the normal course of events, the next king was supposed to be the best kinsman for the job, who decided which person this was? It may be that the late king had designated a particular individual to succeed him. King Aethelwulf of Wessex made a will in about 856 in which he declared that his kingdom would be divided between his two eldest sons, Aethelbald and Aethelberht, after his death (the former would inherit Wessex, whilst the latter would get Kent, Surrey, Sussex and Essex, the dynasty's recent acquisitions). This plan was spoiled by events (rebellions and sudden deaths), but it is interesting to note Asser's claim that Aethelwulf made the will in the first place 'so that his sons should not quarrel unnecessarily amongst themselves after the death of their father'.[4] So a living ruler's wishes might have some impact on opinion, but they were no guarantee of promotion for his preferred nominee if others disagreed with the king's selection or if the unexpected happened. In the end 'succession was a matter of choice by the living', that is by those with the authority to identify a suitable candidate and the muscle to have him generally recognised as king: put another way, 'A man might be born king-worthy, but he had to be made a king'.[5] Those who made him would usually be the ones who had been most immediately and frequently connected with the old king, his *witan*, the military and ecclesiastical elite whose members knew how important it was for the new king to command the support and consent of the kingdom's leading warriors and leading churchmen. The choice may have been obvious and uncontentious – if there was more than a single candidate, perhaps one had already secured enough support to put him in a commanding position. Alternatively, they may have had to listen to the arguments of rival claimants and their supporters. Promises could have been made in return for backing, bargains could be struck about who would get what once the new reign had begun, rivals could be bought off or discouraged in other ways.

There is no reason to doubt that whispered conversations and secret deals characterised this process as much as public declarations and formal ceremonial. Doubtless some people were left feeling disappointed and aggrieved, but in the end, the successful candidate would be the one able to command sufficient support from the people who mattered politically. Was he the man best able to lead and protect his people? Was he the one most likely to keep the cream of society happy with lands, treasure and other gifts? Did he have other kingly attributes? If the answer to these questions was 'yes', then any other doubts (about his pedigree, his past or his personal foibles) would probably be put to one side and quietly suppressed. It is no surprise, for example, that the 'official version' of West Saxon history contained in the *Anglo-Saxon Chronicle* makes King Aethelwulf's death and his son Aethelbald's accession in 858 sound uncontroversial and straightforwardly smooth. It is only by reading Asser's account of Aethelbald's attempted *coup* during his father's absence in Rome and the events following Aethelwulf's return to Wessex that a clearer sense of the tensions within the ruling dynasty emerges. But in the end, however negative Asser's opinion of Aethelbald was, he would not have been able to outmanoeuvre his father and then succeed him without powerful backing from the great men of the kingdom.[6] This must have been the case once again following King Alfred's death in October 899. His son Edward was not crowned king until the following Whitsunday (8 June), and this interval of over six months is perhaps best explained as the length of time it took Edward to recruit the support he needed to fend off the alternative claim to the throne being made by his cousin Aethelwold. There was thus nothing inevitable about the succession of one particular individual or another, and this kind of dynastic in-fighting, with the plotting, power-brokering and factional squabbling which went along with it, must have been much more prevalent across the ninth-century English kingdoms than the surviving sources allow us to know.

The requirements of kingship

The ideal early medieval king was successful in war and generous to his followers. In practice, of course, these two things were inseparable: a king needed followers so that he could fight his wars, and he could only reward them and retain their support by sharing with them the spoils of his victories. It has been rightly said that 'The loyalty which the *witan* might show to a king was rooted in hard economic realities'.[7] The ideal king had more than just martial skill and wealth, however. He should be pious, of course, or at least publicly so, but more than this, he should be special, even unique and stand out from other men by virtue of his character, his charisma and perhaps even his physical appearance. By the start of the ninth century it was becoming more common for a king's superhuman status to be acknowledged by special ceremonies at the start of his reign. We know that Ecgfrith, son of King Offa of Mercia, was consecrated in 786 and Eardwulf, king of Northumbria, was also consecrated in York in 796. A charter of Ceolwulf I of Mercia dated 822 granted land to the archbishop of Canterbury in return for 'my consecration which . . . I have received from him the same day.'[8] And it is likely that Aethelwulf of Wessex was consecrated when he was publicly acknowledged as King Ecgberht's heir in 838, or when he succeeded as king a year later. The earliest surviving text of a royal coronation rite, the so-called First English Coronation *Ordo*, may have been written for this occasion. Equally, it has been argued that the *ordo* might reflect an already-established West Saxon tradition, one which Aethelwulf developed further when his Frankish wife, Judith, was consecrated shortly after their marriage in 856.[9] Precisely what 'consecrated' meant at this stage is unclear. From the tenth century, new kings were anointed with holy oils by leading churchmen, and this may have happened from the start. However, there is nothing before then to suggest that kings were yet being *crowned* at the start of their reigns. It is more likely that, on grand, formal occasions, the king wore a ceremonial helmet to denote his status as the leading warrior, and it is like this, helmeted, that kings of the ninth century are most frequently shown on their coins.

But if kings were denoted as exceptional men at the start of their reigns, they had to maintain that impression regularly and often after that. They could do so whilst travelling around their estates or visiting the lands of others, perhaps with banners held aloft at the front of the procession and large numbers of attendants around them. They could do so at major religious festivals, where they might attend services in their finest clothing and jewellery, again surrounded by an impressive entourage. There were other times, too, when a king might habitually display himself to his people. When the *witan* gathered, for example, the occasion might begin with some kind of ritual in which the king's authority was restated – perhaps he wore his helmet and took oaths of loyalty. When gifts were given, perhaps this happened publicly and ostentatiously to show the king's generosity. And when feasting took place, perhaps there were pre-arranged intervals where the king's prowess was proclaimed and his achievements praised.

It is unfortunately very hard to find specific examples of such ritualised activity in England before the end of the ninth century – Bede's description of King Edwin of Northumbria travelling around his kingdom in state is one rare survival.* But there is no reason to doubt that it was becoming increasingly common. Here the church, with its own experience of mystical, almost magical, ceremonies undoubtedly had an influence on kings eager to add an extra spiritual dimension to their power and status. But continental practices also permeated into England, not least those in use at the court of the great Frankish ruler Charlemagne. Offa of Mercia may have been inspired to consecrate his own son by Charlemagne's decision to have his two sons consecrated by the pope in 781. The division of Charlemagne's empire between his sons after his death in 814 may have been in King Aethelwulf's mind when he made his will dividing his territories in the mid-850s. Very soon after that, of course, Aethelwulf married a Frankish princess, Charlemagne's

* Above, p. 4

granddaughter Judith. She would certainly have brought companions with her from her own land; and her stepson, Alfred the Great, did the same thing to aid him in his educational and literary programmes. Regardless of their ultimate origins, however, such signs and symbols of power were particularly important in a largely pre-literate age. They had one principal aim, namely to exalt the king above ordinary men, but they were also designed to strengthen the connection between the king and his leading subjects and to identify the latter with the royal regime.

Nowhere was this aim more clearly evident than at the great assemblies periodically held by kings. The great men of the kingdom, secular and ecclesiastical, would expect and be expected to attend these. This gave the king the opportunity to socialise with them, either as individuals or as part of a group; to hunt, carouse and gossip with them; and to strengthen his networks of influence and exercise patronage. They in their turn would hope to catch the king's attention and make their plea for preferment or profit of some kind. But it was also at such assemblies that more formal public business could take place: laws could be issued, charters granted and policy discussed. Disputes could be resolved and cases judged. They were thus exercises in collective decision-making, designed to create consensus and a sense of common endeavour across the political elite.

The evidence for assemblies, for their frequency, their location, the business they conducted and the people who attended, is thin before the end of the ninth century. It has been argued that such occasions were as yet far from institutionalised, that they lacked defined procedures and functions and that 'they were more *ad hoc* and more inchoate than what came later'.[10] This is almost certainly true, but it does not mean that assemblies were not established features of the political landscape by the 800s. When King Aethelred of Wessex and his brother Alfred took an army to Nottingham to fight the Vikings in 868, they did so at the request of King Burgred of Mercia 'and his councillors'. When Ealdorman Wulfhere of Wiltshire lost his lands because he and his wife 'deserted without permission both his lord King Alfred and his country', he did so 'by the judgement of all the councillors of the West Saxons and of the Mercians'. And Alfred's own will was constructed expressly 'on consultation with Archbishop Aethelred [of Canterbury] and with the witness of all the councillors of the West Saxons'.[11] Moreover, the same document makes it clear that these 'councillors' were heavily involved in other important discussions about the royal family's inheritances on at least four other occasions. One was on King Aethelred's death in 871 when Alfred brought his father Aethelwulf's will to an assembly, had it read out 'before all the councillors of the West Saxons' and argued successfully that his interpretation of its provisions was correct. Alfred's will and those parts of Aethelwulf's which it mentions were only concerned with the family's private property, not with succession to the kingdom as such. But we know from Asser that Aethelwulf's will did make his intentions for the succession clear, and Alfred's negotiations with the *witan* about his father's bequests may have been an important part of his bid for the throne in 871. At the very least, that Alfred and his brothers had thought it prudent to include the *witan* in their family affairs speaks volumes for its power and influence.[12] Examples like this show very well that a king could not simply demand or expect his nobles passively to follow him. He needed their support at the start of his reign and throughout it, and he had to work hard to retain it by rewarding them with lands and including them in the processes of decision-making. King and *witan* ruled the kingdom together, and every reign (every successful one, that is) took the form of 'a working partnership' between them.[13]

'Tools and resources'

So a king might be brave and charismatic, and rituals could burnish his image. But he could accomplish little without the help of others. His *witan* were certainly crucial here, but in the first instance, the assistance a king received came from the members of his household. This would have included members of his immediate family, not least his wife. It is of course true that the exercise of military power in this period was an exclusively male preserve, and when it came to politics, the situation was not usually very different. Women could play important, albeit passive, roles in the diplomatic sphere when one of them was married in order to confirm an alliance: this happened in 789 when Eadburh, daughter of Offa of Mercia married King Beorhtric of Wessex to seal a pact between the two kingdoms, and when Ealhswith (a Mercian noblewoman) married Alfred (a West Saxon prince) in 868. Alfred's own sister, Aethelswith, had married King Burgred of Mercia in 853, the same year Mercian and West Saxon armies fought together against the Welsh. But when it came to influencing events more directly and actively, the conventions varied across kingdoms. There are enough examples from ninth-century Mercia of royal wives witnessing their husband's charters to suggest that this practice was common there. Aethelswith of Mercia regularly appears as a witness in her husband's charters with the title *regina* and made grants jointly with Burgred in her own name. She was referred to as queen when the *Anglo-Saxon Chronicle* recorded her death in 888.[14] And, of course, Aethelflaed of Mercia ruled English Mercia alongside her husband Ealdorman Aethelred. But even though these West Saxon women could feature prominently in royal business once they had moved to Mercia, the situation is Wessex itself was very different. Of all the West Saxon royal wives of the ninth century, only one, King Aethelwulf's second wife, Judith, left any significant impression on the historical record. And even then, her appearance as a witness in some of her husband's charters is probably attributable to her unique standing: she had been consecrated queen before leaving Francia as a way of safeguarding her prestige. Indeed, Asser implicitly confirms this: a West Saxon king did not customarily allow his wife to sit next to him on the throne, and 'nor indeed did they allow her to be called 'queen', but rather 'king's wife''. He attributes this reduced status to the wicked behaviour of Eadburh, Offa's daughter, who had accidentally poisoned her husband King Beorhtric after living scandalously as his queen. And revealingly, Asser does not even refer to Alfred's wife, Ealhswith, by name.[15] None of this means that royal women could not exercise influence behind the scenes, of course. They would talk to the king, almost certainly discuss affairs with him and give their opinions, and others might ask them to intercede in some matter on their behalf with the king. And through their relationships with their children, stepchildren and wider family they could attempt to build networks of support at court. Nevertheless, the impression remains that, in Wessex at least by the end of the ninth century, it was deliberate policy to give royal women a low profile.

Royal wives would probably have had households of their own, whilst other servants would have been responsible for meeting the king's basic needs – food, drink, clothes. When he moved around his kingdom, their job was to manage the convoy of horses, carts and equipment. Some of these servants would have become intimate friends of the king, trusted and respected by him. We know the names of some of the men who served King Alfred: Aelfric, keeper of the royal treasure, Sigewulf his cup-bearer, Deormod his steward, Ecgwulf his marshal. Asser also singles out Alfred's huntsmen for special mention, his 'falconers, hawk-trainers and dog-keepers'.[16] Precisely what duties many of these men carried out is unclear, but although their roles might sound menial, these positions would have been highly valued and sought after because they gave access to the king. We also know from Asser's biography of Alfred that the king's household servants were supposed to be divided into three separate groups, each group serving the king every third month and going home for the other two.[17] Things were probably not quite as well-organised as this in reality, however. People would come into the household and leave it as the king moved from one area to another, while others would cer-tainly have served him on a full-time basis. Nevertheless, the royal household would always have been a busy hub of activity. It was from this itinerant centre that the king's power radiated outwards around his kingdom.

But the household only provided the king with a basis for the exercise of power. Alfred the Great knew this very well, and when he translated Boethius's *Consolation of Philosophy*, this part must have struck a chord:

> You know of course that no one can make known any skill, nor direct and guide any authority, without tools and resources; a man cannot work on any enterprise without resources. In the case of the king, the resources and tools with which to rule are that he have his land fully manned: he must have pray-ing men, fighting men and working men. You know also that without these tools no king may make his ability known. Another aspect of his resources is that he must have the means of support for his tools, the three classes of men. These, then, are their means of support: land to live on, gifts, weapons, food, ale, clothing, and whatever else is necessary for each of the three classes of men. Without these things he cannot maintain the tools, nor without the tools can he accomplish any of the things he was commanded to do.[18]

So a king's principal 'resources and tools' were his subjects, and Alfred divided them into groups in a typically medieval way: those who prayed (monks and priests), those who fought (the warrior elite) and those (the bulk of the population) who farmed the land. This division is a crude one, of course, but the point here is that

Alfred appreciated his responsibility to provide in some way for all of his people of whatever background or class. If he failed to do this, he would be unable to rule. On a basic level this meant protecting them from external invaders and internal conflict. But it also meant that he needed to provide them with other 'means of support': land, food, gifts, weapons and the rest. But where did these things come from? Originally, they came from success in war. The defeated enemy would have its weapons taken away, and these would be redistributed among his men by the victorious king. Other things taken from the battlefield (belts, buckles, rings, brace-lets, clothing) would be collected and given away, too. Something like this must have happened after Ecgberht of Wessex defeated Beornwulf of Mercia at the bat-tle of Wroughton in 825. In the longer-term, however, it was the territory a king conquered that mattered most as far as resources were concerned. As he asserted his dominance over new lands, the king kept some for himself and gave others away as a reward, some to the church and some to his warriors. Once they had become landholders, these institutions or individuals would have the duty to run their lands so that they remained peaceful. If the land in question was bookland, it would have been immune from liabilities such as the payment of food-rents to the king. But if it had not been granted ('booked', historians say) in this way, it remained what is called folkland and therefore subject to all the traditional financial and other bur-dens. The king was also entitled to receive any profit made from the administration of justice over folkland, as well as fines imposed anywhere on those guilty of par-ticularly serious crimes. The administration of justice would develop into a useful source of royal income over the next century or so.

But there was much more to the exploitation of resources than this. The king would expect payments of tribute (probably in the form of cattle and other live-stock) from any people he had conquered. When the king of Kent was driven out by a West Saxon army in the mid-820s and the peoples of the south-east submit-ted to their new king Aethelwulf of Wessex, this was almost certainly part of the new arrangement. And something along the same lines might have happened in 886 after King Alfred's 'occupation' of London, 'when all the English people who were not under subjection to the Danes submitted to him'.[19] But a more regular and therefore more important element in his sustenance and wealth were the king's own lands. Rather than being vast expanses of defined territory, in the eighth and ninth centuries, these royal 'vills' tended to be specific places centred on a hall or large compound where the king would stay when he was in residence, whilst the inhabitants of the surrounding area had an obligation to pay a rent in kind (the Old English word is *feorm*), perhaps annually, to feed the king's travelling household. They, and other royal dependents from further afield who were perhaps not visited as regularly by the king himself, would bring their *feorm* to the vill for collection and distribution, and the whole process would have been overseen by the king's managers, his reeves. The *feorm* itself would be made up of specified amounts of livestock, grain, ale, cheese and the like, although over time it is likely that pay-ments in kind began to be replaced with payments in cash. This must have been particularly important during the second half of the ninth century when numerous

English kings were forced to 'make peace' with viking invaders. Invariably this meant paying them off, and the raising of such sums must have placed considerable strain on the kings' available resources and on his subjects' ability to keep supplying him with funds. More than one charter from this period reveals how even an institution as rich as the bishopric of Winchester struggled to meet the king's financial demands.[20]*

This rather cumbersome system of renders and food-rents, indeed, might have prompted further attempts to develop silver coinages in England during the ninth century. This proved difficult, however, as there appears to have been a serious silver shortage across western Europe at this time. There were five recoinages in Wessex and Mercia between 850 and 880, for example, and it seems likely that these were prompted in part by the need to remove large numbers of poor-quality coins from the system and replace them with fewer coins containing more silver. This must have had a considerable impact on prices in the short term at least. And more generally, the ninth century proved to be a difficult time for traders and the British economy. Some *emporia*, like *Eoforwic*, *Hamwic* and *Lundenwic* already seem to have been in decline during the first half of the 800s, perhaps because they were too reliant on overseas contacts and lacked sufficient connections with their own agricultural surroundings. But when the viking raids began in earnest in the middle third of the ninth century, trading centres and monasteries (the latter were also very important hubs of commerce and exchange) were easy and obvious targets, largely undefended and full of loot to plunder. *Hamwic* was attacked in 840, for example, and seems to have been largely abandoned soon afterwards, whilst the Thames and Humber estuaries (both vital trading routes) were regularly at the centre of viking activity for the rest of the century. Internal trade must have been severely disrupted, but overseas trade, already suffering as a result of the wider European silver shortage, was even harder hit. It reduced significantly between the 840s and the end of Alfred's reign, dramatically affecting the king's ability to profit from the control of business.

Perhaps the best glimpse we can get about the resources immediately available to a ninth-century English king is caught in the will of Alfred the Great. It is the first will of an Anglo-Saxon king to survive, and part of it outlines Alfred's wishes for the disposal of his private property after his death.[21] His wife, sons, daughters, nephews and other kin would receive approximately sixty different estates between them, spread across Wessex. Other lands were set aside for the monks of Winchester. Alfred's son-in-law, Ealdorman Aethelred of Mercia was to receive a valuable sword. Large sums of money were bequeathed to Alfred's children and three more of his ealdormen, whilst he stipulated that £200 was to be divided between 'the men who serve me' and that other sums would be given to various churchmen and in charity for the poor. In all the monetary gifts Alfred made amounted to £2,000. This was a large sum by any measure, and on a practical level, it would be interesting to know how it was eventually paid out, given that the only unit of currency was

---

* Below, pp. 103–4

the silver penny and that there were 240 of these in one pound. But the will does not give a full picture of all of Alfred's available resources. For one thing, he remarks himself in the will that 'I do not know for sure whether there is so much money, nor do I know whether there is more, though I suspect so'. And secondly, and more importantly, the will only deals with the disposal of the king's private property, not with those lands which were regarded as permanent and inalienable parts of the royal estate and which would have passed automatically to Alfred's successor as king. So it is certainly right to say that Alfred's exploitable resources must have exceeded those recorded in his will.

There also survives some idea of how Alfred distributed his wealth during his lifetime. Asser describes how the king ordered his servants 'to divide the revenue from all taxation in any one year into two equal parts'.[22] One of these parts was reserved for the church, and it in turn was divided into four smaller, equal amounts, one for the poor, one for the two religious houses Alfred had founded (a monastery at Athelney and a nunnery at Shaftesbury), one for the school he had established at court and the last for the other monasteries throughout his kingdom and Mercia. Sometimes his generosity extended further, Asser says, when the king made other grants to monasteries elsewhere in Britain, France or Ireland. The other half of Alfred's annual income was reserved, Asser says, 'for secular affairs' and divided into three portions for that purpose. One part went to 'his fighting men and likewise to his noble thegns who lived at the royal court in turns, serving him in various capacities'. The second part was given to the king's craftsmen (perhaps his gold-smiths and jewellers), while the third was reserved for those 'foreigners of all races who came to him from places near and far and asked for money from him (or even if they did not ask)'. Now it is hard to know how literally to take Asser's account of these matters. But two things are clear: Alfred was rich and he was generous. These qualities were crucial to the success of any king.

Ruling at a distance

Royal rule in the ninth century was an intensively personal business, and the king was no mere figurehead. As he toured his kingdom with his household, he ruled directly and by force of personality, making choices, issuing orders and resolving problems, the ultimate authority in matters of policy and law. Even so, he could not make every decision himself. The kingdoms of Wessex, Mercia, Northumbria and East Anglia were large, moving across them took time and means of communication were limited. So it was inevitable that forms of delegated regional authority developed to keep the kingdoms stable and productive as the king travelled from place to place. The most important individuals in this context were the ealdormen. The origins of this office are obscure, but by the ninth century, the ealdormen were the king's deputies, exercising power in his name in the areas assigned to them. It is probably the case that there were ealdormen, or at least men with equivalent roles and responsibilities, in all the ninth-century English kingdoms. They certainly existed in Mercia: the *Anglo-Saxon Chronicle* says that five Mercian ealdormen were killed in 827, and later in the century, King Alfred of Wessex became the son-in-law of one Mercian ealdorman and the father-in-law of another. But we know most about the ealdormen of Wessex at this time. By the 870s, the kingdom of Wessex seems to have been subdivided, mainly for administrative purposes, into about a dozen smaller areas or 'shires'. Some of these (Kent, Surrey, Sussex and Essex) were old kingdoms now under West Saxon rule; others further west (Wiltshire and Somerset, for example) had more ancient and indistinct origins. One ealdorman (perhaps two in the case of Kent) had overall responsibility for each shire, so there were probably about a dozen in post at any one time. In all (although the actual number was probably larger than this), sixty-six men have been identified who served as ealdormen in Wessex during the 800s, thirty-six of whom served between 858 and 899.[23] The ealdormen were appointed by the king (the office was not hereditary) and could be dismissed by him. Many came from established, distinguished families, long prominent in their shires, whilst others began their careers in the royal household, served the king well and became ealdormen as a result of this. But whatever their origins, they formed the top level of the West Saxon aristocracy.

Ealdormen had a range of duties. They might act as emissaries or ambassadors for the king. Ealdorman Aethelnoth of Somerset went to York in 894 on some kind of diplomatic or military mission, and it seems to have been customary for an ealdorman to take the annual tribute to Rome which, according to Asser, King Aethelwulf instituted in the 850s.[24] One such man was Ealdorman Aethelhelm of Wiltshire, who went to Rome in 887. He also took part in the siege of Buttington in 893 and almost certainly did much more for the king which went unrecorded in the sources. When King Alfred rewarded him with a grant of bookland in Wiltshire, it was probably no mere politeness which prompted the grateful king to describe him as 'my faithful ealdorman'.[25] But Aethelhelm was certainly not a unique case, and there were plenty of other ealdormen who worked just as hard for the king and thereby earned his respect and friendship. The bulk of the business they dealt with in their shires was unglamorous but essential. They oversaw the collection of tribute and rents payable to the king from his own estates and those of others; they had a general responsibility for maintaining law and order within their shires and for making sure that justice was administered and punishments enforced. If there were trading centres in their shires, they would supervise the merchants and the markets they attended. But perhaps their most important role was a military one: in wartime, it was the ealdormen who had the task of raising troops and leading them on campaign.

But even an ealdorman could not deal with all the details of routine business across his shire. He in turn was reliant on others, just as the king was reliant on him, and it was the king's reeves who managed the humdrum nitty-gritty of everyday life on the king's estates. They would collect the rents and renders due and extract the services owed, but they also had military duties and developing judicial ones, too. The reeves feature prominently and with a variety of functions in King Alfred's law code, and when Alfred embarked on his programme to improve literacy within his kingdom, the reeves were one group which he targeted (the ealdormen were another), much to the dismay of some, Asser says, who found learning to read a very difficult task indeed.[26]

A valuable insight into the king's relationship with his servants is provided by the entry for 896 in the *Anglo-Saxon Chronicle*. When in that year the Vikings abandoned their attempts to invade Wessex after three years of fruitless campaigning, the *Chronicle* recorded the event with a note of relief: 'By the grace of God, the army had not on the whole afflicted the English people very greatly', it said. Far worse over the same period in fact had been 'the mortality of cattle and men', and in particular the deaths of 'many of the best king's thegns who were in the land'. The bishops of Rochester and Dorchester were two of these men; there were three ealdormen (of Kent, Essex and Hampshire) 'and many besides', including 'Eadwulf, a king's thegn in Sussex, and Beornwulf, the town-reeve of Winchester, and Ecgwulf, the king's marshal'. Later in the same entry, the death of Wulfric, another royal horse-thegn as well as 'the Welsh reeve', was also recorded.[27] These men were all 'king's thegns', that is (strictly speaking) men who served the king in some kind of personal capacity, but they were much more than this, too, and together they constitute a good sample of those the king relied on and trusted to lead his armies, administer his estates, dispense his justice and give him advice. Their loss must have been a matter of sincere regret for Alfred – some of them had been his companions, even friends, for years. But he also knew very well that, without them and many others like them, ruling would be impossible.

Military organisation

There were no standing armies in the English kingdoms before the viking attacks of the ninth century prompted radical changes in methods of organisation and recruitment. Even then, ninth-century armies (the Old English word for an army which historians use more than any other is *fyrd*) were not large and probably consisted usually of hundreds of men and only occasionally thousands. The *Laws* of King Ine of Wessex stipulated that an 'army' consisted of any troop larger than thirty-five men, but they were written at the end of the seventh century or the start of the eighth and expectations may have been somewhat different 200 years later.[28] Some things had probably not changed all that much, however. When a king led a *fyrd* in pre-viking England, it consisted at its heart of those warriors whom the king kept around him permanently in his household – historians like to use the phrase 'hearth troop' to denote this group. They were the men who habitually hunted with the king (hunting was an important source of food, but also essential as a means of keeping these dedicated fighting men campaign-ready) and feasted with him. There was a bond between the members of this company, a camaraderie which was fostered by their common experiences in battle, their loyalty to each other and their lord and the gifts and rewards which they expected to receive from the king if they served him bravely. Land was what they ultimately hoped to acquire, of course, but they would also expect to be given their horses, weapons and other war gear by their leader. Many of these elite soldiers would have been granted magnificent double-edged, pattern-welded swords, daggers with jewelled handles and splendid sheaths and a spear, perhaps two metres long, topped with an iron head. A wooden shield covered with leather and reinforced by an iron band around the rim and an iron boss in the centre would be their main defence in a fight. But they would dress for battle, too, not just arm themselves. Some may have worn chain-mail armour and an iron helmet with a nose guard, but they would also have wanted to look magnificent so as to awe their enemy and communicate their status as adversaries who had always triumphed in the past. The bridles, saddles and harnesses of the horses on which they rode to the battlefield would be finely crafted, whilst their own buckles, clasps, brooches and rings would have been intended to glint and glimmer in the morning sun as it rose to signal the start of another fight to the death.

Such a fighting force must have been impressive, but it was not large enough on its own to conduct long campaigns or fight major battles. It probably consisted of no more than fifty to a hundred men, so in times of urgency it would need to be supplemented by forces (smaller *fyrds*) provided by local landholders, the thegns. Some of these men would have been eager to serve out of a sense of personal loyalty to the king, and in the hope of impressing him. Many would have been important enough to have military entourages of their own, and they would have brought these personal followings on campaign with them. But if a man had been granted bookland by the king, he would also be formally required to provide a number of troops for the royal *fyrd* at his own expense. This obligation to serve in and supply troops for the royal army was one of the three 'common burdens' that holders of bookland were obliged to shoulder. The number of men they were required to supply would depend on the size of their estates (perhaps one warrior from every five or six hides of land), the scattered levies would be managed and organised by the king's local officials, his reeves, and, once they were gathered together from a particular region, they would be led by the local ealdorman and brought to a pre-arranged meeting point. This seems to be what happened when King Alfred mustered his troops before the Battle of Edington in 878. Asser's account of the episode suggests that the king summoned the *fyrds* of Somerset, Wiltshire and Hampshire to gather at Egbert's Stone. We can imagine the king's reeves and ealdormen making their arrangements in response to the royal summons and gathering the troops within their own areas before leading them off to meet up with the king.[29]

This system had obvious shortcomings. More often than not, there was little if any time to recruit troops on a kingdom-wide scale. A viking raiding party could strike quickly and be gone long before the king and his officers were able to respond. So, frequently, the responsibility for raising forces lay first with the ealdormen in the localities, who perforce had to act promptly and without reference to the king. This gave the ealdormen a great deal of autonomy in terms of how and when they engaged the enemy. The *Anglo-Saxon Chronicle* records several occasions during the 840s and the 850s when individual ealdormen led their troops against the Vikings, and in 860, for example, two ealdormen, Aethelwulf of Berkshire and Osric of Hampshire, joined forces to confront a viking army. Eleven years later, the same Ealdorman Aethelwulf led the Berkshire *fyrd* to victory over the Vikings at Englefield. But such room for independent action cut more than one way: an individual ealdormen might prefer to make a deal with the enemy rather than fight, and sometimes even submit to them, choosing to prioritise his own or his region's interests over the king's or the kingdom's. Secondly, those who took part in the local levies, the rank and file troops, would be less well-trained, less well-armed and perhaps less motivated than their privileged leaders. For many, returning unscathed and as quickly as possible to their families and their crops would have been the overriding priority. Fighting for a king they had probably never seen, or for one who was unproven and quite likely to be killed very soon (like Alfred at the start of his reign), might have seemed an unwelcome and unnecessary risk. Loyalty unto death was probably much rarer in reality than some literary sources from the period would have us believe. Indeed, such pragmatic considerations may lie behind what happened in 878, when large parts of Wessex submitted to the viking invaders, forcing King Alfred into his marshy exile.

There was more to the military systems of the English kingdoms in the ninth century than just *fyrds* of one kind or another. Ships were important, and there are several references to ninth-century sea-battles with the Vikings in the *Anglo-Saxon Chronicle*. In 851, King Aethelstan of Kent and Ealdorman Ealhhere 'fought in ships and slew a great army at Sandwich in Kent'. Later, in 882, Aethelstan's younger brother, by then King Alfred of Wessex, 'went out with ships to sea', captured two viking vessels and forced the surrender of two others. Then, three years later in 885, Alfred sent a fleet from Kent to East Anglia which fought twice against viking naval forces, winning one encounter and losing the other.[30] How such vessels were manned and how such fleets were constructed and organised at this point is very obscure. It is possible that the service in the royal army expected of holders of bookland encompassed service at sea as well as on land in some areas. However, it is not until the tenth century that this starts to become a little clearer. Back on land, fortresses were clearly important, too; contributing to the maintenance of these was another of the three common burdens. Such places were not like the castles of later-medieval England, but larger sites containing a range of buildings surrounded by a man-made ditch, embankment and rampart. The Mercian royal vills at Hereford and Tamworth appear to have been fortified, and a joint West-Saxon/Mercian *fyrd* besieged the Vikings in the 'fortress' at Nottingham in 868. Asser describes how the Vikings 'went to a fortified site called Wareham' in 876 and how Alfred himself constructed a fortification of some kind at Athelney.[31] But despite such examples, it is likely that there were relatively few such places across England by the 870s. Major centres like Repton in Mercia and *Hamwic* in Wessex seem to have been undefended, and there is certainly no indication of any concerted or systematic attempt by any king before Alfred to change this.

The reign of Alfred the Great

The story of King Alfred is an exciting and stirring one, full of battles, adventures and colourful characters. But at the root of its appeal is the tale of an underdog who, in the face of the most overwhelming odds and almost certain defeat, fought back to rescue his people and set them on the road to greatness. Subsequent generations have seen Alfred's bravery, his resolute determination and his refusal to give up as characteristically 'English' qualities, and they have taken Alfred to their hearts as the archetypal 'Englishman'. However, Alfred's reign is a difficult one to approach objectively. Discussions of him and his achievements draw inevitably on centuries of propaganda, myth-making and wishful thinking. The process of constructing his reputation as one of the most successful English rulers began during his own life-time, and after a slow start when Alfred seems to have been regarded as simply one able king amongst many, by the later middle ages he had become the most famous of all the Anglo-Saxon kings. He was first referred to as 'the Great' in the sixteenth century, and after that, he was celebrated more and more.

How justified Alfred's reputation for greatness actually is remains to be seen. Nevertheless, there are clear, good reasons for seeing his reign as a turning-point in the story of how a single English kingdom was created. When he became king in 871, large parts of the kingdoms of Northumbria and East Anglia had already fallen to viking invaders. Wessex and Mercia had both been attacked by then, too; the latter would fall in 874, and there was every chance that Wessex would soon follow suit. A viking takeover of the whole of England seemed almost certain by the mid-870s. By the time he died in 899, however, Wessex had survived, Alfred had defeated the Vikings and his power extended across much of western-central England and as far north as Cheshire. He may not have realised it at the time or seen it in such terms, but Alfred had begun a process which ended with the political unification of England.

Such an overview is very general, of course, and there was much more to the pattern and detail of events than this. Alfred's ultimate victory was anything but inevitable, and we need to get beyond the conventional image of him as the pious, wise, benevolent ruler with only the interest of his people at heart if we are to understand how it happened. Alfred was a ruthless, hard-headed and pragmatic ruler who had to struggle against his own people as much as he did against the Vikings. Alfred becoming king at all seems to have been controversial and a matter of dispute. For the next few years, it can be argued, internal opposition to his rule grew and eventually boiled over as Wessex faltered in its response to the viking menace. And even after his great victory at Edington in 878, it is possible to see Alfred's reforms (military and educational) not just as gallant and radical attempts to deal with future viking attacks (which they certainly were) but as vital parts of Alfred's ongoing campaign to assert his own authority, and that of his dynasty, over his kingdom.

Alfred becomes king

It is almost a cliché to say that Alfred was an unlikely king. Nevertheless, he was. He was the fifth son of King Aethelwulf of Wessex, and three of his brothers became king before he did. For four brothers to rule the same kingdom one after the other was highly unusual, perhaps unique, and although the *Anglo-Saxon Chronicle* is at pains to make the succession from one to another appear smooth and untroubled, it almost certainly was not. King Aethelwulf himself had wanted permanently to divide his territories between his two eldest surviving sons, and in his will, made after his return from Rome in 857 or 858, he stipulated that his first son Aethelbald would succeed him as king of Wessex whilst his second son, Aethelberht, would become king of Kent (including Surrey, Sussex and Essex). It is important to remember, of course, that, when he made his will, Aethelwulf may himself have been ruling only as king of Kent, Aethelbald having usurped his place as king of Wessex during his absence abroad, so Aethelwulf's actual power to influence events in this way is questionable. Nevertheless, it seems that Aethelberht did indeed succeed as king of Kent in 858, whilst Aethelbald continued to rule in Wessex. Only two years later, however, Aethelbald died and Aethelberht succeeded him, thus reuniting the kingdoms of Wessex and Kent, and he was followed in turn as sole ruler of all these territories by his brothers Aethelred (in 865) and Alfred (in 871).

Each of these transfers of power, from one brother to another, can only have happened with the consent of the kingdom's great men, the *witan*. We can imagine discussions and negotiations going on in 860 and 865, promises being made and deals being struck. But practical considerations certainly mattered, too. Aethelred became king in the same year as the Great Heathen Army arrived in England, and the need for stability at the top of the political system may have been the best reason for preserving the *status quo*. By the time Alfred became king six years later, however, the circumstances had changed significantly. The Great Army had conquered much of Northumbria and East Anglia in 867 and 869–70 respectively, and in 871, Wessex itself had been heavily attacked. So when King Aethelred died in that year, the *witan* probably felt obliged to think carefully about who should succeed him. And the signs are that Alfred needed to try hard to convince them that he was the right candidate. He had already laid the basis for his succession whilst his brother was alive, when the pair of them had met the *witan* in an assembly at somewhere called *Swinbeorg*. Alfred recalled this meeting in his own will.[32] It probably took place towards the end of 870 or at the start of 871, and the purpose of it, as has been seen,* was ostensibly to get the consent of the *witan* to amend the arrangements King Aethelwulf had made in his will for the distribution of his private property after his death. Succession to the kingdom as such was not actually discussed (at least it is not referred to in Alfred's account of the meeting), but it is possible to see the agreement struck at *Swinbeorg* as a successful bid by Aethelred and Alfred to have the latter acknowledged as the former's heir.

Even so, Alfred was by no means certain to succeed his brother. After Aethelred's death, Alfred once again had to summon the *witan* to discuss Aethelwulf's will, and they met in a second assembly at another unidentified place called *Langandene*. Alfred's description of events is rather elusive, but he seems to imply that there were arguments at a high level about what should happen next, and that it was only at this meeting that his claims to succeed his brother were finally accepted, perhaps at the

* Above, p. 45

expense of his two nephews, Aethelred's sons.[33] In the end, these boys were probably too young to make a realistic bid for power at such a time of crisis, but there may have been men who, for whatever reason, wanted to see a son, rather than a brother, succeed the late king. For one thing, Alfred's ability to lead an army (the basic requirement of kingship) was as yet unproven. He had military experience (at the siege of Nottingham in 868 and in numerous battles and skirmishes during 871), and Asser tries his best to extol Alfred's martial talents when he describes how his hero, almost single-handedly and fighting 'like a wild boar', saw off the Vikings at Ashdown. Indeed, Asser says, Alfred could have succeeded Aethelred whilst the latter was still alive 'for he surpassed all his brothers in wisdom and in all good habits; and in particular because he was a great warrior and victorious in virtually all battles'.[34] In reality, however, Alfred was not the invincible warrior Asser depicted: West Saxon armies had lost more battles against the Vikings then they had won by the end of 871, and the future looked grim. What is more, Alfred seems already by this stage to have been suffering from a debilitating illness which would affect him for the rest of his life. Alfred had contracted piles as a youth, but by the time he was older, this seems to have developed into chronic internal problems, perhaps some version of irritable bowel syndrome or, it has been suggested, Crohn's Disease.[35] Alfred mentions his health troubles in his own writings, but Asser dwells on them in some detail.[36] In doing so, he intends to emphasise Alfred's torment and to portray him as an almost Christ-like figure who endured constant pain and suffering for the sake of his people, whom he eventually saved. A modern reader might prefer to interpret Asser's Alfred as highly strung, neurotic and permanently anxious, and his ailments as a physical manifestation of this. Either way, it seems that Alfred's condition was no secret, and his leading men would certainly have known about it. The king needed to be a man his warriors could esteem, and any kind of bodily frailty might bring their respect into question.

So, for a variety of reasons, the *witan* may have looked at Alfred in 871 and wondered whether he was made of the right kingly stuff. However, whatever their misgivings might have been, he was probably the only realistic candidate at that point. Publicly at least, solidarity was maintained across the ruling elite and Alfred's charters from the early years of his reign (871–7) suggest a good deal of continuity in personnel between Aethelred's reign and his. However, on the battlefield things were not going so well. Alfred had dealt temporarily with the Vikings in 871 by paying them off, but after conquering Mercia in 874, Guthrum and his army returned once again to Wessex. From late 875 they were stationed at Wareham then Exeter and Alfred once again could only negotiate their departure (probably with the payment of more tribute) in August 877. Then suddenly, within a few months, the Vikings were back, launching their third invasion of Wessex early in 878 with their surprise raid on Chippenham. This confirmed that Alfred had not been able to solve the viking problem, and both the *Anglo-Saxon Chronicle* and Asser describe how, following this event, parts of Wessex were occupied by the Vikings and large numbers of people submitted to them.[37]

It is worth wondering, however, whether important elements within the West Saxon elite had already lost faith in Alfred's leadership before the Vikings arrived at Chippenham and, indeed, whether some of them might actually have been involved in the viking attack. To deal with the Vikings in 871 and then again in 875–7, Alfred must have placed considerable strains on his kingdom. The duty of raising troops and raising money would have fallen most heavily on the great secular and ecclesiastical landholders, and some of them may have been asking by 878 whether the effort was worthwhile. After all, the Vikings had not been defeated and would surely be back for more soon enough. In around 877, Archbishop Aethelred of Canterbury complained to the pope about the level of royal pressure on the resources of his archdiocese, and as has been seen already,* a charter Alfred issued after 879 suggests how hard it was for as rich a landholder as the bishop of Winchester to raise funds for the king.[38] There is no reason to doubt that other lords had similar grievances. Ealdorman Wulfhere of Wiltshire may have been one such individual. He witnessed Alfred's charters regularly until 878, but not thereafter. We also know from a charter of 901 that, at some point, Wulfhere 'deserted without permission both his lord King Alfred and his country', and it is tempting to think that this is a reference to the events of early 878.[39]

By then, and however negatively the *Chronicle* and Asser might depict what happened in these other kingdoms, Northumbria, East Anglia and even Mercia might have looked to the great men of Wessex like havens of political stability and potential prosperity. This may have led some of them to conspire with Guthrum against Alfred and to plot his overthrow. If Alfred himself was in residence at Chippenham in January 878 (Chippenham is in Wiltshire, incidentally, where the treacherous Wulfhere was ealdorman), he was probably there for the festive season with many of his *witan*, and it has even been argued that elements within this group took this opportunity formally to depose Alfred and give him the chance, as Burgred of Mercia had done in 874, to leave his kingdom voluntarily.[40] This would have allowed the conspirators to conclude the agreement they had already made in secret with Guthrum by installing a viking nominee as king. Better this than what must have seemed like otherwise inevitable viking conquest. Unfortunately for them, however, Alfred rejected their ultimatum, escaped from Chippenham and fled to the Somerset marshes.

Talk of a coup, a deposition or a deal with Guthrum is all speculative, of course, and cannot be proved. And even if there was an attempt to remove Alfred designed to coincide with Guthrum's attack on Chippenham, support for it cannot have been universal. For one thing, Guthrum gained direct control only over parts of western Wessex in 878, and when a viking fleet appeared off the north coast of Devon later in the year and landed there, it was seen off by Ealdorman Odda and the shire *fyrd*. What is more, Asser says that Alfred spent his time in hiding 'with his small band of nobles and also with certain soldiers and thegns'.[41] The loyalty of his hearth troop can surely be taken for granted, but he also had the backing of Ealdorman Aethelnoth of Somerset. And when Alfred eventually felt able to launch his counter-offensive against Guthrum later in 878, he must have relied on a network

---

* Above, pp. 49, 103–4.

of support to convey his messages and instructions, raise the *fyrds* of Somerset, Wiltshire and Hampshire, and generally keep enthusiasm for his cause alive. But whatever happened in Wessex in 878 (and it will never be clear what really went on), there can be no doubt about the long-term significance of these events. Alfred's victory at Edington established once and for all that he was fit to rule. It was this event, reinforced by Guthrum's subsequent submission, baptism and removal to East Anglia, which made Alfred king in fact as well as in name.

Military reforms

Having finally proved himself in 878, Alfred set about the task of consolidating his power in Wessex. The main priority here was to protect his kingdom against future viking invasion, but if he was to achieve this, major reforms to the existing military systems of Wessex would be necessary. The kingdom had failed to deal with the scale and weight of the viking attacks. Three invasions between 871 and 878 had all but broken it, and it is perfectly fair to argue that Alfred's victory at Edington, whilst decisive, was lucky. He could just as easily have been killed as victorious, and then the viking conquest of Wessex would surely have been completed. So Alfred needed an army that was more mobile, more flexible and better able to respond quickly to problems as they arose. And so accordingly, rather than relying on ealdormen to raise troops as and when they were needed, and on landholders to recruit men from their lands in a hurry, historians have credited Alfred with the decision to establish a standing force, permanently on duty. The best evidence for this is in the *Anglo-Saxon Chronicle*'s entry for 893, which records that 'The king had divided his army in two, so that always half of its men were at home, half on service'.[42] In other words, those eligible for service in the *fyrd* would take it in turns to serve in rotating contingents, half of these men being on active duty at any one time whilst the other half remained at home to defend their lands and neighbourhoods.

Unfortunately, there are several problems with this analysis of the entry for 893. First, it should not be taken out of context. The Vikings had returned to England in 892, and the reference to the reorganisation of the *fyrd* makes up only a single sentence in a very long entry describing the campaigns of the following year. It is quite possible that, if Alfred did at that point make modifications to the *fyrd*, he did so only to meet the immediate needs of 893. There is no evidence that changes were made any earlier than this, and there is no evidence that they were permanent. Second, even if this entry does describe a major transformation in the way the *fyrd* was organised, there is no indication of how it worked in practice. The number of *fyrd*-worthy men in Wessex must have been considerable. It is hard to see how half of them could all have been on manoeuvres at the same time, especially when there was no enemy to fight. And beyond this, other questions arise. Did they serve all together in a single force or were they on duty in local divisions? If the latter, who was in charge? How were they selected? How long did they serve for before the other half took over? All these issues mean that, whilst something novel certainly appears to have happened to the *fyrd* in 893, it is too much to argue that this reform was 'revolutionary'.[43]

Similar reservations apply to the reforms Alfred is sometimes said to have made to his maritime military resources. The Vikings, of course, had shown conclusively how useful their fast, maneouverable ships could be as a means of transporting troops, horses and other supplies; and they were the main reason for the success of their hit and run raiding tactics. When the Vikings returned to England in 892, they came in 330 ships, according to the *Chronicle*, each of which might have carried between thirty and fifty men, perhaps over 10,000 troops in all. And Alfred certainly had experience of naval warfare himself (he fought at sea against viking ships in 875 and 882), and there is evidence that he experimented with ways of improving the design and capability of his own vessels. The *Chronicle's* entry for 896 records how

> King Alfred had 'long ships' built to oppose the viking warships. They were almost twice as long as the others. Some had sixty oars, some more. They were both swifter and steadier and also higher than the others. They were built neither on the Frisian nor the Danish pattern, but as it seemed to himself that they could be most useful.[44]

This was a demonstration of Alfred's ingenuity, and in the past, the lavish praise of Alfred's creativity in this entry has even been seen as proving that he was the founder of the Royal Navy. To be fair, few if any modern historians would subscribe to this view, not least because Alfred's new ships were a failure. They ran aground on their first outing, and although this may have been the fault of the crews who were unfamiliar with the design rather than the design itself, the expedition was a fiasco. In any event, there is nothing to show that Alfred's innovations were adopted more widely or that they influenced later ship design.

But if the evidence of Alfred's attempts to reform the army and navy of Wessex is thin and unpersuasive, this is not the case when it comes to the network of so-called *burhs* which were constructed across the kingdom from the 880s onwards. Fortresses of one kind or another already existed in Wessex before this, as has been seen, and Alfred may have known something about the fortified bridges erected over the rivers Loire and Seine by Charles the Bald in the 860s. But it is not in the end clear where he got his inspiration from, and anyway Alfred seems to have envisaged something much more extensive, systematic and coordinated than any earlier scheme. Individual fortresses are mentioned in the *Chronicle* and by Asser. The latter also writes admiringly of 'the cities and towns to be rebuilt [by Alfred] and of others to be constructed where previously there were none'.[45] But the best evidence for Alfred's achievement is a document known to historians as the Burghal Hidage. It survives only in a sixteenth-century transcript of an eleventh-century manuscript, and in several copies written after 1066.[46] So there is no original text of the Burghal Hidage, and there are differences between the versions which do survive. Nevertheless, most historians have been content to accept that these are based ultimately on an original document written at the start of the tenth century, during the reign of Alfred's son, Edward the Elder. The Burghal Hidage is usually dated in this way because it includes places like Oxford and Buckingham, which only came under West Saxon control in the early 900s. Despite this, it has been confidently stated (and most historians agree) that, 'there is little doubt that the burghal system was Alfred's creation'.[47]

The Burghal Hidage lists thirty-three fortified places spread across Wessex. None of them was more than twenty miles from another, a reasonable day's march for an army in need of supplies or a group of villagers in need of shelter. And in order to connect the *burhs* together even more closely, many were sited on the rivers, estuaries and overland paths and trackways which criss-crossed the kingdom. But they were also positioned in such places to prevent invading armies entering and roaming freely around Wessex as they had been accustomed to do in the 870s. Some of the *burhs* listed, like Wallingford, were new and specially constructed to meet the needs of the new system. Others were on old, established sites. Hastings and Chichester had been towns in Roman times, whilst Chisbury and Bredy were originally Iron Age forts. And after Alfred took control of London in 886 (London is not listed in the Burghal Hidage; it is not clear why), what was left of the existing settlement around modern Aldwych (*Lundenwic*) appears to have been abandoned and the old Roman city further east along the river repopulated. This must have been partly at least for defensive reasons as the ancient walls were still strong.

But none of the *burhs* would be much use without garrisons to defend them. The entry in the *Chronicle* for 893 which mentioned Alfred's division of the *fyrd* into two halves goes on to stress that they did not include 'those men who were to garrison the *burhs*'. So clearly, even by this date, the burghal system was up and running to some extent. The Burghal Hidage, however, gives much more detail about how the *burhs* were organised. As well as listing them, it specifies the number of hides said to 'belong' to each one. So, for example, 'to Winchester belong 2,400 hides . . . to Wareham belong 1,600 hides . . . to Wallingford belong 2,400 hides' and so on. By this time, it should be remembered, the hide no longer denoted an actual amount of land, but rather it was used as a unit to assess liability to pay tax or give other services to the king. The document then explains, albeit rather obscurely, how the number of hides for which a particular place was assessed translated into an obligation to man the *burhs*:

> For the maintenance and defence of an acre's breadth of wall [a length of about 20 metres], sixteen hides are required: if each hide is represented by one man, then every pole [an old unit of measurement equating to roughly five metres of wall] can be manned by four men.[48]

In other words, and for example, 2,400 men would be required to garrison each of the *burhs* of Winchester and Wareham, and from within these totals, sixteen men at a time would be required to man every twenty metres or so of wall. This means that the walls of late ninth-century Wareham and Winchester must have been 3,017 metres long. This sounds very precise, perhaps unrealistically so. But excavations at Winchester have shown that the walls of the town were in fact 3,034 metres long. The officials behind the Burghal Hidage had carried out their measurements meticulously.

If all the *burhs* listed in the Burghal Hidage had been fully manned at the same time, 27,071 men would have been required. It seems highly unlikely that this ever happened (this figure represents a significant proportion of the male population of Wessex at the time – perhaps as much as 10 per cent); but even so the *burhs* were certainly in use by the 890s and proving highly effective. In 893, the *Anglo-Saxon Chronicle* describes how the viking army in Kent was pursued and harassed by troops 'both from the English army and from the *burhs*'. And later in the same year, the ealdormen of Mercia, Wiltshire and Somerset 'and the king's thegns who then were at home at the fortresses assembled from every *burh* east of the Parret, and both east and west of Selwood, and also north of the Thames and west of the Severn' in order to confront and defeat a viking army at Buttington on the Welsh border. Ealdorman Aethelweard later commented in his *Chronicle* that 'These things done at Buttington are still proclaimed by old men'.[49] But the true value of the *burhs* during the campaigns of the 890s only become clear when all the movements of the different viking forces are plotted on a map of southern England.[50] Between 892 and 896, the invaders hardly managed to enter Wessex at all and spent most of their time circling around the kingdom trying vainly to find a way in. This contrasts very starkly with the way their predecessors had moved largely unhindered and unopposed around Wessex during the 870s, and the difference is best explained by the presence of the *burhs* and the efforts of their garrisons to track the Vikings, shadow their movements and intercept them where necessary. The burghal system was probably not complete by the early 890s, and not every fortress proved impregnable (a half-built and poorly manned one in Kent was captured by the Vikings in 892).[51] Nevertheless, there can be little doubt that, overall, they were a great success in military terms.

The *burhs* were more than just fortresses designed to keep invaders at bay, however. They were also instrumental in facilitating the growth of royal power within Wessex. Getting them built in such numbers and across such a wide area was first a test but ultimately a proof of royal authority. There can be little doubt that the labour of thousands of people must have been needed to construct the *burhs* and then maintain them. Significant numbers of officials must have been needed to compile recruitment lists, allocate tasks and monitor levels of individual service. On one level, of course, Alfred was only asking for his subjects to comply with their duty to shoulder the common burdens: building and keeping up a *burh*, or serving in a garrison, could be construed simply as extensions of the existing system. However, this extension was major and must have drawn significantly on the economic and human resources of Wessex. It was certainly not popular with everyone, and Asser makes it clear that there was resistance to Alfred's schemes from people 'who would undertake of their own accord little or no work for the common needs of the kingdom'. Indeed, he goes further, describing how Alfred had to use all his charm to persuade those who were dragging their feet to do their bit and, when this approach failed and his patience ran out, he had to resort to 'sharply chastising those who were disobedient'. Even then, when targets were not met or tasks were not completed 'those who had opposed the royal commands were humiliated in meaningless repentance by being reduced to virtual extinction'. Quite what Asser meant by this is unclear, but whatever Alfred did, it seems to have been enough to bring the shirkers round. Asser goes on:

> Those who were severely afflicted are contrite in untimely repentance, and are sorry that they had negligently scorned the royal commands; now they loudly applaud the king's foresight and promise to make every effort to do what they had previously refused – that is, with respect to constructing fortresses and to the other things of general advantage to the whole kingdom.[52]

This account gives us a rarely seen glimpse of Alfred the authoritarian ruler. We can only speculate what it was that finally persuaded those opponents of his plans to sign up to them, but it would be no great surprise to find that they were threatened with the loss of their lands, their positions or their status if they did not comply with Alfred's orders. How legal Alfred's threats might have been is another matter, but he was clearly not averse to the exercise of arbitrary power if it helped him achieve his objectives. This in turn suggests that whilst Alfred of course used the *burhs* to defend his kingdom against the Vikings, he also took advantage of their construction and maintenance to extend his control over his own people. And not just those at the top of the political system. It is reasonable to infer from the scale of the burghal system that significant pressure must have been placed on the countryside of Wessex, too, so that the *burhs* could be supplied with enough food to make them viable. This may have entailed wholesale changes to the way the rural economy functioned, although there is frustratingly little evidence about this. Nevertheless, the main point is clear enough. Alfred had nearly lost his kingdom and his life in 878 when many of his people had abandoned him: one way or another he was determined to keep them loyal now, even if that meant terrifying them into submission.

Alfred still used the carrot as well as the stick to get what he wanted. Many *burhs* developed into centres of trade with settled populations (not just military garrisons), and it is quite possible that this was part of Alfred's plan from the start. The streets of *burhs* such as Winchester, Wareham and Wallingford were laid out in similar ways, suggesting a common plan for them all which involved permanent habitation and commerce. The kings of the tenth century (and perhaps Alfred, too) were able to establish mints in some of these *burhs* and take their financial share from the business conducted there. They were also able to use the *burhs* as a source of patronage. In 898 a meeting was held at Chelsea to discuss the laying out of some streets along the river in what is now the City of

London.[53] It was attended by Archbishop Plegmund of Canterbury and Bishop Werferth of Worcester, as well as Alfred's son Edward, his daughter Aethelflaed and her husband Aethelred, who had been put in charge of English Mercia (of which London was a part) by the king. The two churchmen were granted lands on the site later known then as *Aetheredeshid* and later as Queenhithe. A few years earlier when the *burh* of Worcester was being fortified, three of the same people (Bishop Werferth, Aethelflaed and Aethelred) made an agreement, witnessed by King Alfred, in which Aethelflaed and her husband granted the bishop half of the rights they held through their lordship of the city, including all the fines for theft, fighting, dishonest trading, failure to maintain the *burh* walls and other offences.[54] It is not unreasonable to think that there were plenty of other deals like this made about other *burhs* and that they were intended to give the beneficiaries a valuable stake in the burghal system and a good reason for making it work. They have also been described as 'compensatory inducement to landlords for the supply of rural labour'.[55] In other words, these were not situations where the regime simply told people to do their duty or else; they were attempts to persuade and convince local landholders that it was in their own best interests actively to cooperate in the running of the *burhs*. And more broadly still, they provided Alfred with another way of developing a culture across the ruling elite of loyalty to, and dependence upon, him and his family.

Literacy and language

Alfred is virtually unique amongst medieval English kings in the extent to which he personally involved himself in a scheme designed to revive learning and standards of literacy within his kingdom. He may have been heavily influenced here by the explosion of cultural activity which had taken place in the Frankish Empire under Charlemagne and his successors (what historians call 'The Carolingian Renaissance'), but Alfred's approach remained distinctive and highly personal. Not only did he sponsor and support an educational programme; he conceived it and probably designed it to a large extent. He was even responsible for some of its products. For many historians, this is his greatest and most singular achievement. But the king's own enthusiasm for learning only accounts in part for what he attempted. There were religious and spiritual dimensions to what Alfred did (these are discussed more fully in Chapter 4),* but his plans were also made with purely practical and pragmatic goals in mind. Alfred's efforts in this context are as significant in their own way as his defeat of the Vikings. For him, both things contributed towards the same ends, the salvation of his people, to be sure, but also the consolidation of his own power. In the preface to one of his own translations from Latin into English, Alfred remarked how he wanted to be like earlier kings

---

* Below, pp. 101–2

who, because they had 'obeyed God and his messengers . . . not only maintained their peace, morality and authority at home but also extended their territory outside'.[56]

Asser stresses repeatedly how much Alfred himself craved the benefits of education.

> From the cradle onwards, in spite of all the demands of the present life, it has been the desire for wisdom, more than anything else, together with the nobility of his birth, which have characterised the nature of his noble mind.

Unfortunately, however, Alfred did not receive the teaching he wanted when he was young. His parents were neglectful in providing it and the tutors he did have were not up to the job. The king later told Asser

> that among all the difficulties and burdens of his present life this had become the greatest: namely, that at the time when he was of the right age and had the leisure and the capacity for learning, he did not have the teachers.[57]

Asser tells one story (presumably he had been told it by Alfred himself) to demonstrate the king's innate interest in the written word. His mother Osburh owned a book of English poems, and one day she told Alfred and his brothers that she would give it to the one of them who learned its contents by heart first. Alfred took up the challenge (he was 'attracted by the beauty of the initial letter in the book', Asser says), memorised the poems, recited them to his mother and was given the book. This experience may have been the origin of Alfred's preference as a grown man to have poems and other works recited to him, which he then discussed, dissected and remembered. How much Alfred could read himself is, in fact, a matter of some contention. He could probably read English, but he was never taught Latin as a boy, and he struggled to learn it later. He kept a little book with him, in which were copied certain psalms, prayers and other texts which Alfred liked. But it may be that he remained reliant on others to write these down and read them to him. Asser claims that Alfred did eventually learn to read and write Latin, but he depicts this as an almost miraculous event, and it is hard to know how proficient a Latinist Alfred actually became.[58]

Alfred was not interested in learning just for its own sake or as a pastime. He was convinced that it was only through the right kind of education that a person could acquire 'wisdom'. This was an important word for Alfred and it occurs regularly in his own writings and Asser's. It meant more than just 'knowledge' or 'good sense'. For Alfred, 'Wisdom is the highest virtue . . . Wisdom renders those who love it wise and honourable and temperate and patient and just, and it fills him who loves it with every good quality'.[59] The central text here is the Preface Alfred himself wrote to his translation of Pope Gregory the Great's *Pastoral Care*.[60] He begins by recalling a time in the past (he may have had the seventh century in mind, which he would have known about from Bede's *Ecclesiastical History*) when there were learned men throughout England, the people were happy and kings 'succeeded both in warfare and in wisdom'. However, learning then fell into decline, and standards of English scholarship collapsed. Suddenly there were no more good teachers, and by the time Alfred became king, there was hardly anyone in England 'who could understand their divine services in English, or even translate a single letter from Latin into English'. Now Alfred may have had a rose-tinted and overly nostalgic view of the past, but he probably did not exaggerate the extent to which scholarship had decayed over the previous half-century. The grammar and syntax of the surviving relevant documents (and there are only a few of them, which may itself be suggestive of decline) strongly indicate that the standard of Latin learning within the English ecclesiastical elite fell dramatically and quickly from the late 830s onwards. This has been described as 'a major breach, in a learned tradition which extended back to the school of Theodore and Hadrian in the late seventh century, and indeed beyond'.[61] And Alfred's point about this was clear: 'Remember what punishments befell us in this world when we ourselves did not cherish learning nor transmit it to other men'. In other words, the viking attacks of the ninth century had been God's judgement on an ignorant and uneducated people.

There are modern arguments about the impact of the ninth-century viking raids on the English Church,[*] but Alfred certainly thought they had been disastrous, and he set about the critical situation he faced with typical energy and commitment. First, he began his own process of instruction. He got 'helpers in this good intention of his, who would be able to help him attain to the desired wisdom and enable him to fulfil his wishes whenever possible'. In other words, he recruited a team of scholars from within Britain and from abroad to assist him at his court. These foreign imports were supposed to make up for the lack of scholars in Wessex itself. Amongst the most important of them were two Mercians – Werferth, bishop of Worcester, and Plegmund, later appointed archbishop of Canterbury – along with Grimbald, a monk from Flanders, and the German monk John the Old Saxon. Asser, of course, a Welsh monk, was one of them, too, and he devotes a long section in his biography of Alfred to the story of his recruitment by the king.[62] Alfred wanted these men to act as his own tutors and intellectual companions. It was part of their duties to read aloud to him and to discuss with him the meaning of the texts they were reading. Asser describes one such occasion in detail.[63]

Second, Alfred wanted to provide an education for others. To do this, the king established a school within his own court. His sons, Aethelweard and Edward, and his daughter, Aelfthryth, were trained to read and write there 'in company with all the nobly born children of virtually the entire area, and a good many of lesser birth as well'. They were exposed to books in English and Latin, learned the Psalms and English poems. Asser states with some pride that the king's children, now grown

[*] Below, pp. 98–9

adults, 'very frequently make use of books'. And back in the school, Alfred himself regularly gave lessons 'by day and night' in 'all virtuous behaviour and tutelage in literacy' to the sons of his 'his ealdormen, his officials as well as all his associates'.[64]

Third, Alfred gave his officials the task of learning to read English. In broad terms, this would have been a way of improving administrative efficiency. Alfred would be able to communicate with them in writing and convey his instructions clearly. But there were specific reasons, too, according to Asser. The king had grown concerned that his officials were not administering justice fairly because they had 'neglected the study and application of wisdom'. So they needed to learn to read the written laws and interpret them more prudently. Asser is clear about the success of this approach:

> nearly all the ealdormen and reeves and thegns (who were illiterate from childhood) applied themselves in an amazing way to learning how to read, preferring rather to learn this unfamiliar discipline (no matter how laboriously) than to relinquish their offices of power.

And even if they found learning to read difficult, Alfred insisted that they kept trying, with the help of a son, another relative or a servant who could read aloud to them in English.[65] This method had been good enough for the king, so it was good enough for his officials.

Clearly there were already established ways of teaching people how to read English when Alfred embarked upon his campaign to revive literacy. Memorising texts read aloud by a teacher seems to have been a usual starting-point for most pupils. But Alfred had favourite works of his own which he wanted people to use as they studied, so he arranged for the translation from Latin into English of these texts, which he described as 'certain books which are the most necessary for all men to know'.[66] This plan was announced by Alfred in the Preface he himself wrote to the first of these translations, of the *Liber Regulae Pastoralis* (or *Pastoral Care*, as it is usually called) written by Pope Gregory the Great in around 600.[67] *Pastoral Care* is essentially a handbook for bishops, and Alfred sent a copy of the translation to every diocese in his kingdom. But it is also a work relevant to anyone in a position of authority over others, and it addresses the qualities such individuals must have and the responsibilities they must carry out. Alfred himself was probably primarily responsible for the translation of *Pastoral Care*, as he probably was for several other translations: Boethius's *Consolation of Philosophy*, St Augustine's *Soliloquies* and the first fifty psalms of the Psalter. How the process of 'translation' actually happened, however, is not clear, and it seems quite likely that Alfred had help from one or more of his scholarly advisers. Even Alfred himself admitted that his translations could be quite loose: 'Sometimes he translated word for word, sometimes sense for sense', it says in the Prose Preface to Boethius's *Consolation of Philosophy*.[68] We also know that there were other translations completed at Alfred's court which were not by him: Bede's *Ecclesiastical History*, Orosius's *History against the Pagans* and Gregory the Great's *Dialogues* and perhaps others, too. Nevertheless, it seems clear that Alfred was deeply involved in this translation programme one way or another (Asser tells us that it was the king who ordered Bishop Werferth of Worcester to translate Gregory's *Dialogues*, for example), and such recollections may explain the otherwise rather random-looking list of works that were turned into English at Alfred's court.[69] They were ones which appealed to Alfred personally, which resonated and struck chords with him. Their selection tells us as much about his personality as they do about his plans.

But Alfred's ambitions extended far beyond training a few select people to read some poems, a random selection of books and the occasional law code. His stated intention was that eventually 'all the free-born young men now in England who have the means to apply themselves to it' should learn to read English. This would provide a foundation for a smaller number who wanted to learn Latin and go into the church, and this new cohort of learned scholars would take on the job of passing divine wisdom on to the next generation. In this way, Alfred's people would become observant, right-thinking Christians once again, able to understand God's Word and do His work. But, and just as importantly, Alfred's plans were aimed squarely at re-educating his serving and future bishops, ealdormen and reeves; at improving the effectiveness of his government; and at solidifying the loyalty of his leading men and their families. Collectively, those exposed to his learning programme formed 'the West Saxon political order in its entirety', and there can be little doubt that hard-headed political motives, as well as sincerely pious ones, prompted much of what Alfred did.[70]

We get most of our information about Alfred's learning programme from the king himself and from Asser. Naturally, they both emphasise the altruism of Alfred's scheme and stress how it was designed to improve the lives of his people and help them along the path to salvation. There is no reason to doubt the sincerity of their ambition or the depth of their Christian faith (the subject of Alfred's personal piety will be discussed in more detail in Chapter 4),* but at the same time, it is worth pondering whether the king and his bishop reveal anything else about why Alfred was so keen to pursue his reforms. It is interesting that, when Asser describes the education Alfred's children received at his court school, he emphasises how this bred in them certain kinds of virtuous behaviour: 'to the present day they continue to behave with humility, friendliness and gentleness to all compatriots and foreigners, and with great obedience to their father'.[71] And it is worth wondering whether it was this latter quality, obedience to the king, which Alfred was most interested in fostering across the ruling class. Asser portrays the school as an inclusive, nurturing environment and Alfred as the benevolent headmaster who took the children of his nobles under his wing. But it is not clear how happy the nobles were about this. Did they send their children to the school voluntarily, or were they required to do so? And what were the children taught when they arrived? Reading and writing, certainly. But Alfred would never have

---

* Below, pp. 99–101

forgotten the events of 878 and how his kingdom had nearly been lost through treachery. So it would be no great surprise if the children of the nobility were kept at the royal court in part at least as a means of guaranteeing their parents' good behaviour, nor if the need for loyalty to the king was inculcated from an early age at the court school so that the next generation would grow up instinctively dutiful and devoted to Alfred and his family. It is standard practice for authoritarian regimes to threaten the families of potential opponents and to manipulate the education system to influence young minds and instil the importance of compliance. Was Alfred doing anything different?

There are other indirect hints to suggest that Alfred used his learning programme to strengthen his own authority. If his officials did not learn to read as Alfred had instructed, for example, they ran the risk of losing their positions: 'I command you either to relinquish immediately the offices of worldly power that you possess, or else to apply yourselves much more attentively to the pursuit of wisdom', Alfred barked. It is not hard to interpret this threat a bit more generally ('do as I say or else!'), and even Asser is clear about how the ealdormen and reeves were 'terrified and chastened' into following Alfred's orders, 'preferring rather to learn this unfamiliar discipline (no matter how laboriously) than to relinquish their offices of power'.[72] It is perhaps going too far to argue that Alfred's nobles lived their lives in permanent fear of losing their positions if they were not considered to be loyal enough, or that their children were forcibly subjected to exercises in mind control at Alfred's court. Nevertheless, if Alfred wanted his leading men and their families to think and behave in certain ways, and if he had both selfless and selfish reasons for this, that is only to be expected.

It is inevitably impossible to know how successful Alfred's attempt to revive literacy was. We cannot discover how many people learned to read or how much more efficient administration became, although the frequent publication of written laws in English by Alfred's successors in the tenth century implies that there were officials by then who were able to read and expected to implement them. And of course, we will never find out how many souls were saved. What is more, when Alfred's achievements are compared with what had happened across the Channel during the Carolingian Renaissance, they can appear relatively low-key and small-scale, even rather crude. Nevertheless, no other English king had ever tried to do what Alfred did, and nothing quite like it happened again for centuries. And to be sure, Alfred's descendants knew that he had tried to do something novel. When in the late tenth-century Ealdorman Aethelweard wrote about Alfred, he described him as

> king of the Saxons, unshakeable pillar of the western people, a man replete with justice, vigorous in warfare, learned in speech, above all instructed in divine learning. For he had translated unknown numbers of books from rhetorical Latin speech into his own language – so variously and so richly, that [his] book of Boethius would arouse tearful emotions not only in those familiar with it but even in those hearing it [for the first time].[73]

Rhetoric and reality

It is common in autocratic regimes for a cult of personality to develop around the leader. Something like this certainly happened in Wessex under Alfred, and it is most obvious in the texts produced at his court. The propagandist-in-chief, of course, was Asser. For him, Alfred was brave, generous, just and wise, but above all he was saintly, even Christ-like, in his patient tolerance of trials and distress for the sake of his people, and in the way he eventually led them to salvation. His *Life of Alfred* is full of more or less direct allusions along these lines. When the king met the *fyrds* of Somerset, Wiltshire and Hampshire at Egbert's Stone in 878, he was received by them 'as if one restored to life after suffering such great tribulations'. Alfred's illnesses, too, far from being a divine punishment for sin of some kind (which is how most contemporaries would normally have seen them), were actually a divine gift, Asser claimed, bestowed on Alfred at his own request.[74] How many people were exposed to Asser's Alfred is another matter, of course. There is a theory that it was designed for a Welsh audience, to convince them of the benefits of submitting to Alfred's lordship. But the *Life* seems to have been left unfinished: there is no evidence that it ever reached Wales, and the signs are that it only ever became known to a small number of medieval writers.

Much bolder in its aims and more pervasive in its influence, it seems, was the *Anglo-Saxon Chronicle*. The consensus amongst historians is that the first version of the *Chronicle* had been completed in Wessex by the early 890s; Asser used it as the basis for his *Life* of Alfred, and he was writing in 893. It is generally agreed that the *Chronicle* was produced at Alfred's court as part of his literacy programme and that it recounts events from a decidedly West Saxon perspective. Beyond that, however, opinions differ about its wider purpose. On the one hand, it has been argued that

> We should also resist the temptation to regard it as a form of West Saxon dynastic propaganda, written for the consumption of the West Saxons in particular and intended to arouse their support for Alfred at a time when the very survival of his dynasty was at stake.[75]

Another argument, however, is that the *Chronicle* was consciously designed with an ideological objective at its heart. It described the origins of the different peoples of England, but its intention was to show that they had come together to share the same future under the rule of the kings of Wessex. Like Bede, and probably relying on him to a large extent, Alfred knew that the West Saxons, the Mercians and the people of Kent had different cultures and traditions, but the things they had in common, principally their Christianity and their language, were far more potent and made them a single English people, the *Angelcynn*. Alfred used this word himself several times at carefully chosen moments, in the prefaces to his *Laws* and *Pastoral Care* and in his treaty with Guthrum, and it was the *Anglo-Saxon's Chronicle's* job to describe the *Angelcynn's* shared history and create their collective memory. As a result, it has been said, 'King Alfred might be credited with the invention of the English as a political community'.[76]

The *Chronicle* is written in English, of course, the shared language of the *Angel-cynn*, and it is tantalising to wonder whether the pupils at Alfred's court school used it as their history textbook and how much they were exposed to the ideological subtext it contains. In any event, the *Chronicle* was not the only text which attempted to justify Alfred's rule beyond Wessex. His law-book, for example, which will be discussed more fully in Chapter 3,* was drafted in such a way as to present Alfred as the latest in a long line of distinguished lawgivers and as the heir to a divinely inspired tradition of law-making. Charter evidence also supports the idea that Alfred attempted to recast himself as a different kind of king once his position was secure. During the 880s, he began to be described in some of his documents as 'king of the Anglo-Saxons' or 'king of the Angles and Saxons'. No longer simply 'king of the West Saxons', Alfred was claiming authority over others beyond the traditional frontiers of his kingdom. And by the time Asser wrote his *Life* in 893, he referred to Alfred as 'king of the Angles and Saxons' every time he used his royal style. The coins issued in Alfred's name can also be interpreted, just like other kinds of text, to tell a similar story.[77] From the late 860s, the kings of Wessex and Mercia had jointly issued coins of the same weight and design, and Alfred continued this collaboration with Ceolwulf II of Mercia between 874 and 879. They went further, however, and at some point around 875, the poor-quality, debased currency circulating in both kingdoms was recalled, and a new type of silver penny, the 'Cross-and-Lozenge', which contained five times more silver than the old currency, was issued by both kings. This has been described as 'an astonishing demonstration of royal authority at a time of very great difficulty'.[78] During the same period, another coin type, the 'Two Emperors' was also struck in both their names. Less than a handful of these particular coins has ever been found, so they may originally have been issued in small numbers to mark a special event. Clearly, however, the image they carry on one side of two rulers seated side by side suggests a degree of cooperation and parity between the rulers of Wessex and Mercia which later chroniclers (Asser dismissed Ceolwulf as 'a foolish king's thegn') wanted to erase from the record.[79] From about 879–80, however, after his victory against the Vikings, Ceolwulf's disappearance from the records and the West Saxon assertion of control over English Mercia, Alfred moved to claim sole and exclusive control over the coinage system. Alfred issued another coinage (the 'Two-Line' or 'Horizontal' type) which was heavier still than the Cross-and-Lozenge, he introduced a new denomination of coin, the halfpenny (these had the same design as the pennies but were smaller and half the weight), and he increased the number of mints operating across his territories. More interesting still, at three mints, there were also special issues of coins some time during the 880s which combined Alfred's name on one side of the coin with the name of the mint on the other. These mints were

---

* Below, pp. 83–7

the ones at London, Oxford and Gloucester, formerly Mercian towns now under Alfred's control. It seems probable that the coins were designed and issued specifically to record and celebrate this new political situation.

The kingdom of the Anglo-Saxons

Perhaps the clearest depiction of this new political landscape is contained in the treaty which Alfred made with Guthrum some time after his victory at Edington in 878. As was seen earlier,* there is an argument about precisely when during the following few years the treaty was drawn up, but it is very tempting to link it with Alfred's acquisition of power in English Mercia from the early 880s and, ultimately, his occupation of London in 886 and the submission to him of 'all the English people that were not under subjection to the Danes'.[80] In any case, the important point here is that the treaty describes, with a good deal of precision, where the line was to be fixed between Alfred's area of authority and the rest of (still viking-controlled) England. That line, which had been agreed by 'the councillors of all the English race', was set as running 'up the Thames, and then up the Lea, and along the Lea to its source, then in a straight line to Bedford, then up the Ouse to Watling Street'.[81] The treaty (although it doesn't do so explicitly) thus gave practical expression to a wholly new political entity which historians have called 'the kingdom of the Anglo-Saxons', inhabited by a wholly new group of English, not just West Saxon, subjects. Bounded by Offa's Dyke in the west and by the line drawn diagonally across the midlands from north-west to south-east by the treaty, it also included London, which now began the next phase of its history as the centre of English political and commercial life.

The treaty, along with Alfred's seizure of London, put English Mercia firmly under Alfred's control, and although he allowed his future son-in-law Aethelred to continue governing there, the latter did so as Alfred's representative, not as an independent ruler. As will be seen, this connection between Wessex and Mercia would come under stress and be brought into question repeatedly during the tenth century; it was not bound to be permanent or develop further. Nevertheless, the treaty and the events of 886 demonstrate that the new titles which Alfred had given himself in his charters and coins were far more than empty expressions or straws in the wind. Their use from the 880s onwards, and the political developments they reflect, 'represented the union of two peoples for purposes or political organisation' and thus a crucial stage in the development of a single kingdom of England. When he died, it was no accident when the *Chronicle* described him as 'king over the whole English people [*Angelcynn*] except for that part which was under Danish rule'.[82]

---

* Above, p. 33

DEBATE 3

How 'great' was King Alfred?

Alfred is the only English monarch to have earned the title 'the Great'. The reasons seem obvious. He was a successful warrior who saved his kingdom from disaster and set it on a path towards future glory. Additionally, and uniquely, he was an intellectual who devoted himself to improving the spiritual welfare of his people. The problem for historians is that most of the evidence for Alfred's 'Greatness' is contained in sources produced near the king if not by the king himself. The biography of Alfred written by his friend and teacher Bishop Asser frequently and often implausibly extols his virtues; the *Anglo-Saxon Chronicle*, the main narrative source for the reign, was produced at or close to Alfred's court and gives a highly selective account of what happened; the king's own translations of works he regarded as 'most necessary for all men to know' can be seen as an idiosyncratic assortment of texts whose impact on a wider audience is impossible to gauge. So it remains fair to say that 'We hold that Alfred was a great and glorious king in part because he tells us he was'.[1] Nevertheless, it is not correct to say that Alfred's achievements went unappreciated by more detached observers. The late tenth-century chronicler Ealdorman Aethelweard referred to him as 'the magnanimous Alfred . . ., unshakeable pillar of the western people, a man replete with justice, vigorous in warfare, learned in speech, above all instructed in divine learning'.[2] English writers of the twelfth century developed Alfred's reputation further, and it was around this time that many of the most famous stories involving him (cakes and all) began to circulate. It was in Tudor England that Alfred was described as 'the Great' for the first time, and from that point, his reputation blossomed. In the 1730s, the designer William Kent included Alfred's bust alongside fifteen others in his Temple of British Worthies at Stowe. The inscription described him as 'The mildest, justest, most beneficent of Kings; who drove out the Danes, secur'd the Seas, protected Learning, establish'd Juries, crush'd Corruption, guarded Liberty, and was the Founder of the English Constitution'. He was also credited by then with founding Oxford University and the Royal Navy. But it was the idea that the origins of English representative government, crushed by the Normans and later revived during the Reformation, the Civil War and the Glorious Revolution, were to be found in Alfred's reign, which remained particularly persistent. The Victorians adopted it enthusiastically and saw Alfred as the embodiment of the solid British virtues they espoused. Modern scholarship has reined in this kind of unfounded fantasising, but in the process, attention has focused once again on what Alfred actually achieved during his reign. The unadorned facts are enough to show how extraordinary he was. He salvaged spectacular victory from the ruins of disastrous defeat. He then extended his power and entrenched his dynasty whilst, at the same time, writing profoundly about his duties as king. To be sure, the problems associated with the sources have not gone away, but those very sources are arguably the ultimate proof of Alfred's Greatness: 'The historical record plainly establishes that he was among the most remarkable rulers in the annals of human government'.[3]

1 K&L, p. 126; J.M. Wallace-Hadrill, 'The Franks and the English in the Ninth Century: Some Common Historical Interests', *History* 35 (1950), pp. 202–18 at pp. 216–17.
2 K&L, p. 191.
3 Patrick Wormald, 'Alfred', in *ODNB*.

Notes

1 *ASC* 867.
2 *ASC* 787.
3 *ASC* 855–8; P. Wormald, in J. Campbell (ed.), *The Anglo-Saxons* (Oxford, 1982), p. 116.
4 K&L, p. 72.
5 H.R. Loyn, *The Governance of Anglo-Saxon England 500–1087* (Stanford, 1984), p. 17; J.L. Nelson, 'Inauguration Rituals', in P.H. Sawyer and I.N. Wood (eds.), *Early Medieval Kingship* (Leeds, 1977), pp. 50–71; reprinted in her *Politics and Ritual in Early Medieval Europe* (London, 1986), pp. 283–307, at p. 284.
6 K&L, p. 73.
7 A.P. Smyth, *King Alfred the Great* (Oxford, 1995), p. 445.
8 *EHD*, i no.83; S186.
9 J.L. Nelson 'The Earliest Surviving Royal *Ordo*: Some Liturgical and Historical Aspects', in B. Tierney and P. Linehan (eds.), *Authority and Power: Studies in Medieval Law and Government Presented to Walter Ullmann* (Cambridge, 1980), pp. 29–48, reprinted in her *Politics and Ritual*, pp. 341–60.
10 J.R. Maddicott, *The Origins of the English Parliament 924–1327* (Oxford, 2010), p. 2.
11 *ASC* 868; *EHD*, i no.100; K&L, p. 174.
12 K&L, pp. 72–3, 174–5.
13 Smyth, *Alfred the Great*, p. 451.
14 S210, 214, 1201; *ASC* 888.
15 K&L, pp. 71–2.
16 K&L, p. 91.
17 K&L, p. 106.
18 K&L, pp. 132–3.
19 *ASC* 886.
20 S354, 1287.
21 K&L, pp. 173–8.
22 K&L, pp. 106–7.
23 S. Keynes, *An Atlas of Attestations in Anglo-Saxon Charters, c.670–1066* (Cambridge, 2002), Table XXII.
24 K&L, pp. 73, 190; *ASC* 883, 887, 888.
25 K&L, p. 179.
26 K&L, pp. 165, 167 (1.3, 34), 110.
27 *ASC* 896.
28 *EHD*, i no.32 (Ine, 13.1).
29 K&L, p. 84.

30 *ASC* 851, 882, 885.
31 *ASC* 868; K&L, pp. 82, 84.
32 K&L, pp. 173–8 at p. 174.
33 K&L, p. 175.
34 K&L, pp. 80–1.
35 Abels, *Alfred the Great*, pp. 98–100, and references.
36 K&L, pp. 76, 88–90, 91, 101, 131.
37 *ASC* 878; K&L, p. 83.
38 *EHD*, i no.222; S354.
39 *EHD*, i no.100.
40 J. Pollard, *Alfred the Great: The Man Who Made England* (London, 2005), ch.9.
41 K&L, p. 83.
42 *ASC* 893.
43 Abels, *Alfred the Great*, p. 197.
44 *ASC* 892, 896.
45 K&L, p. 101.
46 For a text of the Burghal Hidage, see K&L, pp. 193–4.
47 P. Wormald in Campbell (ed.), *The Anglo-Saxons*, p. 152.
48 K&L, pp. 193–4.
49 *ASC* 893; K&L, p. 90; *Chron. Aethelweard*, p. 50 ('vaunted by aged men').
50 See Abels, *Alfred the Great*, p. 357 for a good one.
51 *ASC* 892.
52 K&L, pp. 101–2.
53 S1648.
54 *EHD*, i no.99.
55 Pratt, *Political Thought*, p. 99.
56 K&L, p. 124.
57 K&L, pp. 74–5, 75–6.
58 K&L, pp. 99–100.
59 K&L, p. 133.
60 K&L, pp. 124–6.
61 Pratt, *Political Thought*, p. 50.
62 K&L, pp. 92–6.
63 K&L, pp. 99–100.
64 K&L, pp. 90–1.
65 K&L, p. 110.
66 K&L, p. 126.
67 K&L, pp. 124–30.
68 K&L, p. 131.
69 K&L, p. 92.
70 Pratt, *Political Thought*, p. 122.
71 K&L, p. 90.
72 K&L, p. 110.
73 K&L, p. 191.
74 K&L, pp. 84, 98–100.
75 K&L, p. 40.
76 Sarah Foot, 'The Making of *Angelcynn*: English Identity before the Norman Conquest', *TRHS* 6th ser. 6 (1996), pp. 25–49, at p. 25.
77 P. Grierson and M. Blackburn, *Medieval European Coinage I. The Early Middle Ages* (Cambridge, 1986), pp. 307–16, 602–9.
78 Sawyer, *The Wealth of Anglo-Saxon England*, pp. 82–3.
79 *ASC* 874.
80 *ASC* 886.
81 K&L, p. 171.
82 S. Keynes, 'Edward, King of the Anglo-Saxons', in N.J. Higham and D.H. Hill (eds.), *Edward the Elder 899–924* (London, 2001), pp. 40–66, at p. 45; *ASC* 900.

3

THE KINGS AND THE LAW, 796–899

It is very difficult to describe with clarity or discuss with certainty the ways in which justice was administered in Anglo-Saxon England. There are enormous gaps in knowledge and understanding because so little information survives about this topic, while the sources which do exist are often obscure and highly technical, decipherable only by specialists in the field who then cannot agree about their meaning and significance. The answers to very basic questions remain elusive and provisional. Where did laws come from? Where, how and by whom were they enforced? How were disputes heard and resolved? What happened to criminals and to others caught on the wrong side of the law? Nevertheless, despite the challenges, it is important to grapple with these issues. Laws and the ways they are applied reveal much about the priorities and standards of the society which produces them. Of more immediate relevance here, however, English kings of this period used the law (what it said and how it worked) to proclaim, define and extend their own power. To a significant degree, the making of English law went hand in hand with the making of the English kingdom.

Principles and practice

By the eighth century, it was firmly accepted that kings were more than just war-lords and that their duties extended beyond simply conquering territory so that they could reward their followers. Kings had also assumed a responsibility for the safety and security of the people they ruled. This meant defending them from invaders and external enemies, but it also meant protecting them against murderers, thieves and other evildoers within their own kingdom. This was very difficult in practice, however. There was no permanently employed police force or prosecuting authority in any of the English kingdoms. When crimes were committed, the means to investigate them were badly lacking. Unless the perpetrator was caught red-handed or their identity was somehow known for sure, they would probably get away with it. And disputes over land or inheritances were almost certainly settled as much by bribes and bullying as by impartial legal procedures.

Kinship and lordship

Kings simply did not have the kind of resources, infrastructure or coercive apparatus at their disposal which would allow them to control and regulate a universally applicable legal system. So they had to rely on other mechanisms and bonds to keep the peace and maintain stability, ones that were routinely out of their direct control. Members of the same kinship group or extended family would be expected to monitor each other's behaviour and look out for each other's safety, whilst lords were required to supervise the conduct of their followers and keep them under control. Similarly, kindreds and lords were duty-bound to make sure that accused members or followers appeared to answer charges made against them by others and to take action and seek justice on their behalf if they were injured, killed or needed to be compensated for some loss or other. One way they typically did this was by pursuing a feud or vendetta against the individual who had committed the wrong, or against their kin. This kind of private justice, if uncontrolled, had the potential to wreak havoc and create anarchy. However, the very fear of chaos may have led to the peaceful settlement of many disputes. These forms of collective responsibility and action were so fundamental to the functioning of Anglo-Saxon society that legal safeguards had to be put in place for those who lacked a kindred or a lord, including foreigners, illegitimate or abandoned children, freed slaves and so on. In practice, of course, ties of kinship and lordship might conflict, and then the law had to decide which took precedence, but broadly speaking, the duties and obligations imposed on all those connected in these ways were more important in ordering and stabilising society during this period than any kind of notional obedience owed to the king and his usually remote authority.

Codes and cases

Such limits on their effective powers of law enforcement did not stop some kings telling their subjects what, in their view, the laws actually were. The earliest surviving English royal laws are those of King Aethelberht of Kent (d.616). His successors in Kent, Hlothere, Eadric and Wihtred, also issued law codes during the seventh century, as did King Ine of Wessex (688–726). However, there are problems with all of these pronouncements and with the state of the evidence generally. The Kentish laws only survive in later, twelfth-century copies, and it is hard to know how accurate or comprehensive these are. Ine's Laws were only written down as part of the code which Alfred the Great issued during his reign; so, once again, it is far from certain that the extant evidence of their contents is reliable or complete.

What is more, no law codes from the eighth century survive (King Offa may have issued one but this is not clear), nor do any from the ninth before Alfred's, making it almost impossible to get a sense of royal aims and ambitions during this period.

Major questions also surround the purpose of the surviving codes. It is reasonable to presume that kings issued such documents intending them to be used in their courts and by their judges. However, most historians think that this was not their primary purpose and that the early law codes had an ideological objective more than a practical one. It has been argued that Aethelberht's code is not just the earliest to survive; it was probably the first to be made. He was the first Anglo-Saxon king to convert to Christianity, and he did so under the influence of St Augustine and his fellow missionaries from Rome. The idea of writing down laws was probably theirs, and Bede described Aethelberht's as 'a code of laws after the Roman manner'.[1] By this he meant not so much the content of the code as its form: Roman emperors (most notably the Emperor Justinian, whose compendium of Roman law, the *Corpus Iuris Civilis*, was completed in 534) wrote down and published their laws. And there were biblical precedents for written laws, too, most obviously those given to Moses and the Israelites by God in the Old Testament. Viewed in this way, the publication of laws (any laws) by an Anglo-Saxon king was an assertive statement of royal power and an attempt to associate himself with the great lawgivers of the past. This would explain why the contents of the surviving codes are sometimes rather chaotically, selectively and illogically arranged (Ine's laws in particular are hard to follow) and why they are not comprehensive catalogues of current principle and procedure: it mattered little what they actually contained, as long as they contained something and emphasised the king's law-giving capacity.

Having said all this, the early codes almost certainly do outline many existing customs and conventions. For example, they make it clear that oaths were of central importance in Anglo-Saxon society. Much more than just promises to do or not do something, they were solemn undertakings which bonded one individual to another in a whole range of social, economic and political relationships. But they were also of fundamental importance in the functioning of the justice system. In a wide variety of legal disputes, parties would be required to swear oaths as to the existence of a set of facts or the truth of what they said. But oaths were particularly significant as a way of establishing guilt or innocence in criminal cases. Most accusations of criminality were made publicly by one individual or his kin against another individual or group. Such accusations would have to be reinforced with oaths sworn by the accusers. In later periods, there were severe punishments for those who brought frivolous or malicious claims, and this was probably the case in earlier ones, too. The accused would then swear oaths as to their innocence. Obviously enough, this only got things so far, and other evidence would be needed to take the case further. Individuals might be called on whose testimony would support one or other of the parties, an eye-witness to the alleged offence or someone who witnessed an original land transaction which was now at issue. Their evidence would almost certainly be supported by oaths, too. But such third-party evidence might be either unavailable or inconclusive. So the oaths of the parties themselves would usually have to be supplemented by the oaths of others (historians call them 'oath-helpers') who would swear to the good character of the individual they were supporting. The greater the number of oath-helpers a party could recruit, and the higher their status, the more convincing their case became, and the more likely they were to win it. By contrast, if parties could not find enough or any oath-helpers to back them up, this suggested that they were regarded as suspect by their community, and they would struggle to prove their innocence or win their case.

Two references in Ine's code also show that, by the time it was published, another way of establishing guilt or innocence in criminal cases was recognised in Wessex: the ordeal.[2] These are the only mentions of ordeal in Anglo-Saxon England before the tenth century, so they should not be pushed too far. Also, they do not specify which kind of ordeal those behind the laws had in mind, but it has been argued that it was probably the ordeal by cauldron or hot water.[3] Other forms of ordeal (trial by cold water or hot iron in particular) were certainly being used in Francia by the early ninth century as well, and so it is possible that they were employed in England at the same time. But trial by hot water is the only type of ordeal known to have been in use anywhere in western Europe when Ine's code was published a hundred years or so before. It required the accused to put their hand into a cauldron of boiling water and take out an object, usually a stone or a ring. The burns were then bandaged, and if they had not healed after three days, guilt was established. The use of the ordeal amounted to a recognition that there was a limit to what human ingenuity could do to uncover the facts of a crime: sometimes a higher, divine authority had to be recruited to settle such questions. After all, if God was prepared to intervene and perform a miracle for an accused's sake (a scalded hand which healed after only three days would be seen in these terms), they must certainly be innocent. But presumably, the very possibility of having to undergo such an unpleasant procedure was supposed to act as both a deterrent to crime in the first place and, once an individual had been accused, as an incentive for them to confess and take a lesser punishment.

The early codes are also all concerned with the amounts of monetary compensation payable once guilt was proven in a bewildering range of more or less violent offences. For example, 'If anyone draws a weapon where men are drinking, and yet no injury is done there, [he is to pay] a shilling to him who owns the house and twelve shillings to the king', and 'If anyone fights in the house of an ealdorman or other important councillor, he is to pay sixty shillings compensation and is to give another sixty shillings as a fine'.[4] It is clear that the kings accepted the inevitability of violence and that, rather than trying to eliminate it, they sought to control it and minimise its negative consequences. But this was also an area where concern about law and order overlapped with concerns about status. So in Ine's code, for example, the free men of Wessex (those who were not slaves, that is) were divided into three ranks, each with a different *wergild* (1,200, 600 and 200 shillings). Earlier Kentish laws had done something similar.[5] A man's *wergild* (literally 'man-price') was the monetary value set on his life by law and a badge of social standing: the higher his position in society, the higher his *wergild*, with the king's *wergild* the highest of all.

If someone committed a crime, they might be able to clear themselves or avoid further punishment by payment of their own *wergild*: thus, Ine's code ordered that 'If a thief is caught [red-handed], he is to die the death, or his life is to be redeemed by his *wergild*'.[6] More broadly, if a man was killed unlawfully, the kin or lord of the convicted killer would have to pay the victim's *wergild* to his kindred. *Wergild* was important in other situations, too. For example, one of Aethelberht's laws states that *wergild* (whose is not clear) can be paid as compensation in cases of adultery.[7] So the codes are far from worthless as evidence of what the laws actually were, and they reveal a good deal about the kind of issues that preoccupied seventh-century kings and their subjects. Nevertheless, it is certainly right to say that 'the extant texts can never be more than a partial guide to the law as experienced'.[8]

The challenge, however, is to find any evidence of 'the law as experienced' before the end of the ninth century. Information about roughly twenty individual lawsuits survives from the period up to 899. This is not very many, the detail is usually very thin and almost all of them concern disputes over land in which a monastery or other church was one of the parties. It is worth stressing at the outset, too, that nowhere in any of these recorded decisions is there a reference to a piece of enacted royal legislation. The law codes, in other words, are conspicuous by their absence from accounts of actual legal proceedings, and this further supports the idea that they were not designed for practical use. This does not mean that the laws contained in the royal codes were not used at all, of course, but most of them were probably already laws before the kings decided to start codifying them. In other words, whilst a king like Ine may have introduced some novel elements into his laws here and there and expressed in the Prologue to the code his wish that 'none of the ealdormen or any of our subjects might afterwards pervert these our decrees', the laws used in real disputes were almost certainly ones based on long-held local tradition and oral custom, not ones written and handed down from on high by the king.[9] This means that the substance of the law would have varied between and within kingdoms. Kentish law was almost certainly different in many respects to West Saxon law; West Saxons and Mercians would have dealt with similar events using different principles and procedures; people in Yorkshire may have treated cases differently from their fellow Northumbrians north of the Tees and Tyne. There would have been much overlap and much in common, of course: shared linguistic, cultural and social patterns would have ensured that. Nevertheless, provincial variety and regional particularity must have characterised the legal systems of pre-viking England.

Courts: local and royal

Wherever there was a serious dispute over property or a grave accusation against an individual, there needed to be a place where the issues could be publicly and formally dealt with – a court. The law codes of the seventh century already take the existence of such bodies for granted. The laws of Hlothhere and Eadric stipulate, for example, that if one man makes an accusation against another 'and he meets the man at an assembly or a meeting', he is to do him 'such right as the judges of the people of Kent shall prescribe'. And Ine's code sets out what someone should do if left unsatisfied after asking 'for justice in the presence of any official (*scirman*) or other judge'.[10] These references are rather oblique, though, and there is little sign that the occasions they refer to took place regularly or in any kind of systematic, institutionalised way. Indeed, it is perfectly possible that most of the time these courts met as and when the local communities involved needed them, and not in response to instructions from above. It is also particularly unclear whether any royal officials were routinely involved and, if they were, what role they played. These meetings were decidedly local, it seems, both in terms of the laws they used and in terms of the experts who presided over them and gave judgements. They provided a forum of some shape and size in which the people of an area could settle their disputes, respond to charges, impose punishments and exact compensation.

Apart from this kind of local tribunal, however, there is no evidence of any other kind of court in early Anglo-Saxon England – except, that is, the king's own court. The best evidence of this dates from Alfred's reign onwards, as will be seen,* but there is no reason to doubt that earlier kings behaved in significantly different ways to their successors. After all, the king was the ultimate judge in his kingdom. Inevitably he would be more concerned to hear cases which touched upon his own rights and property, or those which concerned his leading subjects, but he could hear any dispute between his subjects and listen to accusations made by one of them against another at any time. He might do this quickly and informally as he moved around his kingdom from estate to estate and as petitioners managed to make their way into his presence. In practice, though, he would probably tend to deal with such matters when he was in company with his leading men, especially if the case in question concerned members of the landowning or military elite. The doing of justice was one of the fundamental requirements of good kingship. The development of such ideas was encouraged by the church, which emphasised the importance of Old Testament figures like David and Solomon as models. Christianity also brought with it the prestige of the late Roman Empire and the example of (once again) the Roman emperors. And increasingly by the end of the eighth century, the English kings' continental contemporaries were also having an influence on how they saw and presented themselves as judges and lawgivers. The Frankish kings (especially Charlemagne) had placed enormous emphasis on the production of written law, but also on the person of the king as the main component in the judicial machine. Without him in his proper place at its heart, the ideological theory went, that machine would not function. When King Aethelwulf of Wessex returned from Rome via Francia in the 850s, it is hard not to think that he brought some of these ideas with him. His son Alfred, who visited Rome twice as a child and had a Frankish stepmother, would act on them in furtherance of his own political and military objectives.

---

* Below, pp. 82, 87–8

Alfred the Great and the law

Courts and judges

King Alfred of Wessex was deeply involved in the administration of justice within his kingdom. At least, this is what Asser his biographer tells us. The relevant description is long, detailed and worth dwelling on.[11] According to Asser, Alfred used to hold judicial hearings for those nobles and 'common people' who were dissatisfied with the results of hearings they had already been involved in before ealdormen and reeves. Alfred would even compel parties who were unwilling to appear before him in such cases to do so, 'since the king was an extremely astute investigator in judicial matters as in everything else'. The king was also in the habit of looking into 'nearly all the judgements which were passed in his absence anywhere in his realm, to see if they were just or unjust'. And if he uncovered a problem, especially if he detected any hint of corruption or incompetence on the part of the judges in question, he would contact them and ask them to explain the reasons for their decisions. If it transpired that the judges had acted as they had through ignorance, they were forcefully commanded by Alfred 'either to relinquish immediately the offices of worldly power that you possess, or else to apply yourselves much more attentively to the pursuit of wisdom'. In practice, this meant learning to read English, although, as was seen earlier,* 'wisdom' for Alfred was a highly charged word which meant much more than just 'knowledge'. But, more pertinently here, if Asser's account is accurate, then Alfred allowed his subjects to make appeals to him from lower courts, and he aggressively ordered them to participate if they were reluctant. He also collected judgements made in other cases which had not been directly referred to him, studied them closely and intervened when he was unhappy for some reason with their outcome. He was prepared to confront his judges robustly and demand improved performances under threat of dismissal if they failed to respond.

All of this raises significant questions (and suggests some answers) about the way the legal system worked in Alfred's Wessex. First of all, the king could only have heard appeals from the decisions of his ealdormen and reeves if there were courts ('assemblies', Asser calls them) where these officials presided. Unfortunately, Asser gives no more information about this, although Alfred's own law code clearly does. It refers to charges being brought 'in a public meeting of the king's reeve' and to the need for traders and their men to appear before the king's reeve 'at a public meeting' before they began their work; 'and they are to take with them such men as they are able thereafter to bring to justice at a public meeting'. There are also references to meetings before the king's ealdorman, and the latter also had a role to play in the prosecution of feuds. Presumably these were the officials whom, Asser tells us, Alfred habitually harassed and harangued.[12] Two clauses from the law codes of Alfred's successor, Edward the Elder, may cast a little more light on this. In the first

---

* Above, pp. 65–6

of his two codes, Edward 'commands all the reeves that you give such just judge-ment as you know most right and as it stands in the law-book'. At the very least, this hints strongly at some kind of active participation by the king's officers in courts of some kind, perhaps the local courts described above, if not courts of their own. And in the second, Edward may have recorded an already current practice when he decreed that 'every reeve shall hold a meeting every four weeks'.[13] Furthermore, the 'law-book' (*Domboc*) which Edward required his officials to use in the first of these clauses was almost certainly his father's law code, so by this time, there was already an organised body of law which the king expected them to refer to when making their judgements. But Alfred's code may have been completed by the time Asser wrote in the 890s, and if it was, it is not unreasonable to suppose that the king expected his own judges to use it. And even if it was not in use by then, Ine's code probably was. Alfred's emphasis on the importance of his judges learning to read supports this argument further: it would be helpful if they could read a range of things, but perhaps a collection of laws most of all.

So already under Alfred, there is clearer (albeit far from conclusive) evidence for royal involvement in the legal process below the level of the king's own court and for royally produced laws being used in those proceedings. Asser did not write this account to provide future generations with information about the administration of justice in late ninth-century Wessex, however. He wrote it to reveal yet more about Alfred, and it should be read with this deeper purpose in mind. There are plenty of parallels, for example, between the way Asser portrays Alfred in this section of his biography and the ways in which the Frankish kings are known to have involved themselves in the exercise of justice. They heard appeals, settled disputes, enquired into abuses of power and investigated miscarriages of justice. So Alfred was a great modern ruler in the same mould as his continental contemporaries, and Asser is always keen to imply this. But even more, and explicitly, he was seeking to reinforce his recurring depiction of the king as a man constantly striving for wisdom as a means of getting closer to God. For Asser, Alfred was a new Solomon, and he says or implies as much more than once.[14] Alfred craved the ability to distinguish good from evil and right from wrong, and he wanted his officials to have that too.

The Domboc

Alfred's *Domboc* was probably devised and drawn up by the king and his advisers in the late 880s or early 890s. Alfred is the first English king since Ine who is known to have produced a law code, and it is interesting to speculate why he revived this seemingly lapsed practice. It makes sense to see the *Domboc* as another element in Alfred's wider plan for the revival of learning and literacy in Wessex, which was discussed earlier,* and there is no reason to doubt that Alfred's wish to improve the administration of justice in his kingdom was sincere. But he would also have

* Above, pp. 64–9

known that the issuing of laws was a divinely sanctioned prerogative of kingship. His advisers would certainly have stressed this idea, and in particular, those with a Frankish background would have been keen to remind Alfred of the importance placed by Charlemagne and his successors on the making of written laws. Publishing the *Domboc*, in other words, gave Alfred another way of proclaiming and enhancing his own authority as king.

It is clear from the way the *Domboc* is organised that it had political and ideological functions as well as strictly legal ones. Most obviously, it is very long; indeed, it is by far the longest of all the surviving Anglo-Saxon codes, and that in itself suggests that it was designed to make an impression simply by existing at all. It begins with translated extracts from the Old Testament, in particular those parts of the Book of Exodus which deal with the Law (the Ten Commandments) which Moses received from God on Mount Sinai. It then goes on to describe how these laws were adapted and applied by Christian nations with the help of the church. Alfred then acknowledges his debt to earlier English royal legislators, Aethelberht, Offa and Ine, before he finally begins to set out what he claims is a selective compendium of these earlier laws, with a few additions of his own. At the end of this list, the Laws of Ine are copied into the text in their entirety.

Various significant points emerge from this. Alfred's intention was not to supersede Ine's legislation but to incorporate it into his *Domboc* and thereby construct a composite set of West Saxon laws. However, by openly asserting that he was also drawing on laws issued by Kentish and Mercian kings in his own code, Alfred was firmly positioning himself as the inheritor of their traditions as well as Ine's and affirming his right to legislate for English people more generally. It was during this part of his reign that Alfred was staking his claim to rule the Kingdom of the Anglo-Saxons, not just the kingdom of Wessex, and it has been argued that that these parts of the *Domboc* 'would have represented a dramatic assertion of his role as the shepherd and guardian of an amalgamated English people'.[15] But the *Domboc* was clearly even more ambitious than this. By dwelling at the start on the importance of law in the Old Testament, Alfred was extending his pedigree as a law-giver even further back, as far back, indeed, as the history of legislation went. That this legislation was given by God only added to its lustre, but that it was given to Moses and the people of Israel was even more important. It is almost certainly no coincidence that there are 120 provisions in Alfred's *Domboc* (if Ine's provisions are included in the number). According to tradition, Moses was 120 years old when he died. Alfred saw himself as another Moses, and he wanted his subjects to see themselves as 'a new holy people' specially favoured by God under his own divinely inspired (wisdom-based) leadership. The *Domboc*, therefore, 'proclaimed the destiny of a kingdom that had survived God-given punishment, and might now enter its inheritance'.[16]

How deeply such extravagant ideas permeated below the level of an intellectual elite around the king is impossible to say. Some historians have argued, indeed, that the *Domboc's* purpose was almost entirely symbolic and that it was not a document intended for practical use. The important thing may have been 'simply to get something into writing that *looked like* a written law code, more or less regardless of its actual value to judges sitting in court'.[17] However, the explicit references to the *Domboc* in Edward the Elder's first law code, and in several law codes later in the tenth century, strongly imply that the ealdormen, reeves and thegns who had been assigned legal duties were expected to know its provisions and apply them. But more broadly still, it has also been argued that the best evidence for the impact of the *Domboc* 'lies not in dispute settlement but the character of later legislation, extensively dependant on Alfredian legal principle'.[18] So the *Domboc's* ideological and political concerns do not preclude either its use as a working document or its value as a source of information about how Alfred and his successors expected justice to be administered in their kingdom.

The *Domboc* was principally concerned with the criminal law and with the duty incumbent on the king and on elements within wider society to maintain order and stability. Collective responsibility (of a kindred or of a lord's following) had always been crucial here, as has been seen, but the mutual obligations owed to each other by members of these groups had to be underpinned by something other than vague assumptions and expectations. So Alfred declared, 'First we enjoin, what is most necessary, that each man keep carefully his oath and his pledge'. If the oath was broken or left unfulfilled, the accused must hand over his weapons and belongings and remain in prison for forty days. If he refuses to cooperate and go willingly his weapons and possessions will be forfeited, and if he runs away, he will be outlawed and excommunicated.[19] Clearly, when he legislated about oaths in this way, Alfred had something more in mind than just polite promises to behave in a certain way or keep one's word. And it has been argued that he was referring here to a specific oath of loyalty sworn to him by his subjects, and that anyone who broke such an oath was committing treason. When Ealdorman Wulfhere of Wiltshire deserted Alfred, he may have broken an oath like this.* If so, Alfred was probably the first Anglo-Saxon king to require such an oath from his subjects, and it would sit well with the emphasis which is placed throughout the *Domboc* on the need to respect the person and status of the king: 'If anyone plots against the king's life ... he is to be liable for his life and all that he possesses'; 'If anyone fights or draws his weapons in the king's hall, and he is captured, it is to be at the king's judgement – either death or life, as he wishes to grant him'. And there were punishments listed for those found guilty of fighting at a meeting in the presence of the king's ealdorman or his deputy, and for forcibly entering the king's residence.[20]

It has also been argued that the oath mentioned in the first chapter of the *Domboc* was not just a promise of loyalty to the king, but that it might have included undertakings not to commit crime or aid those who did.[21] In other words, crime was coming to be seen not just as something which affected its victims and required the payment of compensation or the physical punishment of the perpetrator. All crimes were reprehensible, but theft and homicide in particular threatened the

---

* Above, p. 58

social order and disturbed the peace which it was the king's duty to preserve. This made their commission breaches of loyalty to the king and therefore a form of treason. This is certainly the way criminality had come to be regarded by the early tenth century. The second law code of Edward the Elder, for example, regarded the failure to pursue thieves as a breach of 'oath and pledge, which the whole nation has given', and it possible that the history of that development began with Alfred's innovatory approach in the *Domboc*.[22]

The virtues of loyalty and the potency of the bond between a lord and his followers were stressed in other parts of the *Domboc*, too. So other lords, not just the king, could look to it for confirmation of their privileged position: 'he who plots against his lord's life is in return to be liable for his life and all that he possesses'. Elsewhere it was stipulated that if a man fought for his lord, no feud could be initiated against him by the lord's enemy, whilst a man was allowed to pursue a feud on behalf of his kinsman 'unless it is against his lord'.[23] In this case, the lordship bond prevailed over ties of kinship. But both were overridden by the loyalty and obedience which all subjects owed to their king. And by 899, this loyalty may well have been formally embodied and expressed in a public oath taken by all men of appropriate age and status.

Although a man could not pursue a feud against his lord, rules about the feud more generally feature prominently in the *Domboc*.[24] Importantly, Alfred did not attempt to abolish or prevent the practice; rather he planned to manage the system and limit the disorder and bloodshed it might produce. He accepted feuding as an inevitable fact of life in a self-regulating society and largely confined his involvement and that of his officials to matters of procedure and payment. Actual violence should only be used by those involved in a feud as a last resort, so a man should surround and besiege his enemy's home for seven days rather than attack it, in the hope of forcing the enemy to submit. This compelled the parties to cool off in situations where impulsive reactions could prove fatal. If he did submit, the enemy's kinsmen would be informed, and he should be kept prisoner safely for thirty days whilst waiting for their response. Again, this was supposed to give the parties more time and space which they could use calmly and rationally and, ideally, to reach a settlement. If one of the parties did not have the resources to besiege his enemy, however, he could ask for help from the local ealdorman; if no help was given, he was then allowed to seek out the king and request his intervention. How far and how often such procedures were observed, of course, is quite unknown and self-help in such cases probably remained as common as self-restraint.

The *Domboc* also contains long lists of punishments to be imposed for various offences. Some of them are predictable: penalties for assaulting women, for raping young girls or for theft of livestock.[25] Others are less so: penalties for assaulting nuns, for betrothed women who commit fornication or for offences committed by an owner's dog.[26] Either way, these were the kind of issues which preoccupied the members of this society. Status was another such issue, of course: the fine payable by a man who slept with another man's wife depended on the rank of the wronged husband. A 'twelve-hundred man' (a wealthy landowner with a *wergild* of

1,200 shillings) received most compensation in this situation (120 shillings); a 'six-hundred man' (a less substantial landowner whose *wergild* was 600 shillings) received 100 shillings, and a *ceorl* (an ordinary freeman with a small amount of land and a *wergild* of 200 shillings) least of all, forty shillings.[27] *Wergild* in fact features regularly throughout the *Domboc* in a range of situations. If a man accused of plotting to kill the king wished to clear himself of the charge, for example, 'he is to do it by the king's *wergild*'. Similarly, a man charged with plotting to kill his lord could clear himself 'by his lord's *wergild*'. In other words, the accused in these cases would need to arrange for oaths to be sworn as to their innocence by men whose combined *wergild* equalled that of the king or their lord. And in another case, if a man came unexpectedly across his feuding enemy and the latter agreed to submit and give up his weapons, anyone who subsequently fought against him 'is to pay *wergild* or wound in accordance with what he has done'.[28] So in this case, a full *wergild* payment would be required if the man was killed and a smaller amount, depending on the nature of the injury, if he was just injured. Feuds and *wergild* may seem like brutal and crude ways of settling disputes and inflicting punishments, but they were regarded by Alfred as disincentives to crime and the best available way of preventing even more violence.

Helmstan's case

But for all their interest and value, the sources discussed so far do not reveal anything about how real legal disputes were conducted in Alfred's Wessex. Very occasionally, however, it is possible to strip away the layers of propaganda and get beyond the official language of government to catch a glimpse of the king himself at work as a judge. A letter written to Edward the Elder describes in detail a dispute which had begun at the end of Alfred's reign over an estate at Fonthill in Wiltshire.[29] The letter was written by, or at least in the words of, someone prominently involved in the case, Ealdorman Ordlaf. But the central character in the story is Helmstan, a king's thegn and the owner of the land at the start of the quarrel. The arguments began when Helmstan fell foul of the law: he stole a valuable belt and was found guilty of the crime. The letter does not record how he was punished, but Ine's Laws specified death or the payment by the convicted thief of his own *wergild*.[30] In addition, however, such public disgrace would have dealt Helmstan's reputation and standing a severe blow, and this in turn would have made him vulnerable to others who coveted his land. The most forceful of these opportunists was called Aethelhelm Higa, who tried to take advantage of Helmstan's predicament by making a claim to his five hides at Fonthill. Helmstan, desperate for help, looked to his godfather, the man who had sponsored him at his confirmation, Ealdorman Orldaf of Wiltshire, and asked him to intervene in the case on his behalf. Ordlaf did so by approaching King Alfred who happened to be staying nearby at Wardour. Alfred was persuaded by Ordlaf that Helmstan should be given the chance to defend himself, and he appointed a group of important figures to arbitrate. These men listened to Helmstan and Aethelhelm Higa and concluded that Helmstan should be allowed to formally prove his right to the Fonthill estate. Helmstan then explained how the land had come into his possession, produced a charter to back this up and convinced the arbitrators that he should be permitted to swear an oath as to his rightful possession of the estate and reinforce this with the oaths of other reputable supporters. But Aethelhelm Higa refused to go along with this 'until we went in to the king and told him in every respect how we had decided it and why we had decided it; and Aethelhelm himself stood in there with us'. So Alfred was asked to intervene once again:

> And the king stood in his chamber at Wardour – he was washing his hands. When he had finished, he asked Aethelhelm why what we had decided for him did not seem just to him; he [Alfred] said that he could think of nothing more just than that he [Helmstan] should be allowed to give the oath if he could. I [Ordlaf] then said that I wished to attempt it, and asked the king to appoint a day for it, and he then did so.

What is striking here is the informality of the scene – as he dried his hands, the king listened to what the arbitrators had decided, approved it and then gave his decision. No rules or fixed procedures are used; there is no reference to Alfred's *Domboc* here or to any kind of court other than the one the king ordered to be constituted on the spot. Of course, the parties to this dispute were important men known to Alfred, so it is hard to know how typical this kind of occasion was. But it seems fair to assume that the king dealt with this kind of disagreement regularly and that he was accustomed to doing so in this kind of way. The case serves as a valuable reminder that, whether at this elevated level or lower down the social scale, most disputes were probably settled with pragmatism and common sense, not with laws and technical procedures.

Clearly, though, if this was a case in which connections and networks of influence were of central importance, so were oaths. After Alfred made his order, Helmstan feared he would be unable to find other men willing to support his own oath with theirs, and so he asked Ordlaf to provide some for him. The price of this, it seems, was Helmstan's agreement to surrender the estate at Fonthill to Ordlaf, who would then permit Helmstan to occupy it for the rest of his life. Accordingly, on the appointed day, Helmstan swore his oath and was backed up by Ordlaf's men. He therefore won his case against Aethelhelm but then immediately handed over his charter for Fonthill to Ordlaf. Ordlaf gave Helmstan the right to stay on the estate for life 'if he would keep out of disgrace'. So it becomes clear by the end of the letter that Ordlaf was writing it to explain how he had come into possession of the estate at Fonthill and to quash any suspicion that he had done so in an underhand way. He was at pains to emphasise that he had agreed to help Helmstan as a dutiful godfather should, and that Helmstan had offered him the estate freely and willingly, not as a bribe. 'And, Sire', he asked of King Edward, 'when will any suit be ended if one can end it neither with money nor with an oath? And if one wishes to change every judgement which King Alfred gave, when shall we have finished disputing?'

But, despite what Ordlaf hoped at the time, this was not the end of the matter. Two years or so after the case had apparently been resolved, Helmstan was caught stealing cattle, deprived of his estates by the king (not Fonthill, which belonged to Ordlaf by this point) and declared an outlaw. Interestingly, what happened at this point may cast a little more light on those developing ideas about crime as treason which were mentioned earlier.* A convicted cattle rustler might normally expect to be executed or pay his *wergild* (this is what Ine's Laws required), but neither of these things appears to have happened to Helmstan.[31] He lost his lands instead, and when Ordlaf asked the reeve who confiscated Helmstan's estates why he had done so, 'he said that he [Helmstan] was a thief, and the property was adjudged to the king, because he was the king's man'. This implies that Helmstan had pledged himself to the king in some way, presumably by an oath, and that this theft constituted a breach of that oath. So stealing a third party's cattle was equated with disloyalty to the king, and from this flowed the king's right to take away Helmstan's lands. That Ordlaf was puzzled by this and wanted the reeve to explain what he had done might also hint that this idea was a new one.[32] In any event, Helmstan responded to this latest setback by fleeing to King Alfred's tomb at Winchester. He swore another oath there (presumably about his innocence) and obtained a sealed document to this effect which he then took to Ordlaf. Ordlaf once again intervened with the king (by this time Edward the Elder) who revoked Helmstan's outlawry and gave him back one of his estates. A few years later, Ordlaf gave Fonthill to the bishop of Winchester in exchange for other lands in Wiltshire. This prompted Aethelhelm Higa to make another bid for the estate, which in turn led to Ordlaf writing his letter to the king to explain its history. He concluded:

> Now, Sire, it is very necessary for me that it may remain as it is now arranged and was before. If it shall be otherwise, then I must and will be satisfied with what seems right to you as a charitable gift.

In other words, Edward's decision would always be the final one; so when Aethelhelm Higa finally withdrew his claim to Fonthill, he must have done so knowing that the king was against him.

The limits of the law

Evidence about the operation of the law during this period is patchy, obscure and hard to interpret. Almost all of it, moreover, comes from Wessex, and it is impossible to get any meaningful sense of the extent to which the mechanisms and laws in place there were replicated in Mercia, East Anglia or Northumbria. And even where there is material available to get a sense of what was happening, whole sections of the population are still largely overlooked. Women, for example, when they feature in the early law codes at all, tend to do so as victims of violent sexual crime or adulteresses, not as active litigants. Nevertheless, it is possible to make some tentative observations at this point. There is no reason to doubt that the laws applied across England during the ninth century remained overwhelmingly local

* Above, pp. 85–6

and customary. Royal law codes were assertions of authority more than practical working documents, and they had no detectable influence on the law as it was applied and enforced in real situations. Having said that, it can be argued that, by 899, ideas about crime were developing so as to give the king a greater stake in its prosecution and punishment, and notions of loyalty to the ruler were being hardened and clarified. There are also signs that the central government was using its own officials more often to supervise and run courts of some kind. In other words, kings were starting to define the law in their own interest and royal involvement in ordinary judicial processes was beginning to intensify. Alfred's reign was an important one in this area as in so many others. But it would be his successors who developed the substance of the law and the structure of the legal system even more in order to express and fulfil their imperial ambitions within England.

Notes

1   *BEH*, pp. 150–1.
2   *EHD*, i no.32 (Ine, 37, 62).
3   Robert Bartlett, *Trial by Fire and Water. The Medieval Judicial Ordeal* (Oxford, 1986), pp. 7–8.
4   *EHD*, i no.30 (Hlothhere and Eadric, 13), no.32 (Ine, 6.2).
5   *EHD*, i nos.32 (Ine, 70), 30 (Hlothhere and Eadric, 1, 3).
6   *EHD*, i no.32 (Ine, 12).
7   *EHD*, i no.29 (Aethelberht, 31).
8   Wormald, *MEL*, ii p. 12.
9   *EHD*, i no.32 (Ine, Prologue).
10 *EHD*, i nos.30 (Hlothhere and Eadric, 8), 32 (Ine, 8).
11 K&L, pp. 109–10.
12 K&L, pp. 163–70 (Alfred, 22, 34, 38, 42.3).
13 Attenborough, *Laws*, pp. 114–15 (I Edward, Prologue), 120–1 (II Edward, 8).
14 K&L, pp. 92, 106.
15 K&L, p. 39.
16 Patrick Wormald, 'Lex Scripta and Verbum Regis: Legislation and Germanic Kingship from Euric to Cnut', in Sawyer and Wood (eds.), *Early Medieval Kingship*, pp. 105–38, at p. 132; reprinted in his *Law and Culture in the Early Medieval West: Law as Text, Image and Experience* (London, 1999); idem, *MEL*, i p. 427.
17 Wormald, 'Lex Scripta', p. 115.
18 Attenborough, *Laws*, pp. 114–15, 120–1, 130–1 (I Edward, Prologue; II Edward, 5, 5.2; II Aethelstan, 5); Robertson, *Laws*, pp. 20–3 (II Edgar, 3, 5); Pratt, *Political Thought*, p. 241.
19 K&L, p. 164 (Alfred, 1–1.2).
20 Wormald, 'Lex Scripta', p. 114; K&L, pp. 165, 166, 167, 168 (Alfred, 4, 7, 38, 40)
21 See, for example, Wormald, *MEL*, ii pp. 112–29.
22 Attenborough, *Laws*, pp. 120–1 (II Edward, 5). Pratt, *Political Thought*, pp. 232–8.
23 K&L, pp. 165, 169 (Alfred, 4.2, 42.5, 42.6).
24 K&L, pp. 168–70 (Alfred, 42).
25 *EHD*, i no.33 (Alfred, 11, 16, 29).
26 *EHD*, i no.33 (Alfred, 18, 23).
27 K&L, p. 166 (Alfred, 10).
28 K&L, pp. 165, 169 (Alfred, 4.1–2, 42.4).
29 *EHD*, i no.102.
30 *EHD*, i no.32 (Ine, 12).
31 *EHD*, i no.32 (Ine, 12).
32 Wormald, *MEL*, i pp. 147–8.

4

THE KINGS AND THE CHURCH, 796–899

The institutions and practices of the Anglo-Saxon Church had been developing for 200 years by the time King Offa of Mercia died in 796. Through its services, its teachings and its wider pastoral efforts, it played a crucial role in the spiritual lives of the English people as it guided them along the difficult and dangerous path to salvation. But the church also had an essential contribution to make in politics and government. It controlled large amounts of land along with the people on it. This gave the church and its leading personnel wealth, power and influence, all of which the kings of England were wise to cultivate and, if they could, control. But the church was also main source of learning and scholarship in England, and as such, it was co-opted by secular rulers to create and articulate ideas about the nature of their royal power. The church was expected to dignify the office of king-ship, legitimate individual rulers and their dynasties and justify their wars. In return, kings would protect the church and keep it safe from covetous abusers. That was the theory, at least. But in the ninth century, this collaborative and mutually supportive relationship between the kings and their clergy came under unprecedented strain as viking attacks on England overwhelmed many in positions of secular power, devas-tated vulnerable religious communities and arguably jeopardised the very survival of English Christianity itself. In the end, of course, the faith survived, the pagan plunderers were converted to the one true religion, and the productive partnership between royal and ecclesiastical power was reestablished. Alongside King Alfred and his successors, the English church would make its own distinctive contribution to the creation of a single English kingdom.

The structure of the English Church

By the end of the eighth century, the inhabitants of what would eventually become the kingdom of England were all Christians, and the land was divided into areas called dioceses, each under the control of a bishop. But this seeming uniformity was very recent and its roots, whilst strong, were still developing. There had been Christians in Roman *Britannia*, and by the time the Romans abandoned their province in the fifth century, Christianity had become the official religion of the Empire. However, the extent to which Christianity survived in England in the immediate post-Roman period is very unclear, and when the Anglo-Saxons began to arrive from northern Europe shortly after the Romans left, they brought their paganism with them. It was Bede who described their conversion to Christianity in his *Ecclesiastical History of the English People*, written in the first quarter of the eighth century. Missionaries from Rome (led initially by St Augustine of Canterbury (d.604)) in southern England and from Ireland in northern Britain (led by St Aidan (d.651)) spearheaded the process in the first half of the seventh century by targeting the rulers of the different Anglo-Saxon kingdoms. But their task was difficult and far from straightforward: for every king who was keen to accept Christianity, there was another who resisted, and progress was slow and inconsistent. Even when a king did convert, moreover, there was no guarantee that his subjects would do the same quickly or at all, and every chance that his successor would revert to paganism. The Roman and Irish missionaries also had different beliefs about the kind of Christianity they wanted their converts to practise. Most famously, they disagreed about the correct way to calculate the date of Easter, and this argument was only settled in 664 at the Synod of Whitby when King Oswy of Northumbria chose the Roman method of dating.

Pope Gregory the Great (d.604), who sent Augustine and his fellow Roman missionaries to England, had originally envisaged two ecclesiastical provinces in England, one based at London and the other at York, with each province made up of twelve dioceses. In practice, however, these plans were frustrated by the political problems the missionaries faced. Canterbury rather than London became the centre of the southern province, because the king of Kent was more powerful than the king of the East Saxons and more prepared to give the new religion a chance to establish itself. And although Paulinus (d.633) became the first bishop of York in 625, an archbishopric was not yet established there. Indeed, ecclesiastical organisation was only rudimentary at best by 668 when Theodore of Tarsus (d.690) became archbishop of Canterbury. Bishops had a crucial role to play in the church's efforts to hold on to the converts they had made and create yet more. They were the leaders of their local Christian communities and were expected to set an example. So they should preach and teach themselves, and live an exemplary Christian life, but they were also needed to ordain new priests so that new congregations were properly provided with pastoral care and spiritual help. However, south of the Humber in the late 660s, there was only one bishop in office, whilst in the north there were bishops only at York and Ripon. The danger of Christianity simply fizzling out in England must have been a real one, and Theodore was determined to prevent this happening. He quickly appointed new bishops at Rochester, Winchester and Dunwich, and he held a great church council at Hertford in 672 which declared that the number of dioceses should continue to increase along with the number of converts and that church councils should be held twice a year so that standardised approaches to church practice and doctrine could be adopted and taken around the country. By the time Theodore died in 690, further dioceses had been established in East Anglia (at Elmham), in western Mercia (at Hereford and Worcester) and in Lincolnshire (at Lindsey), whilst in the north the situation had clarified somewhat and there were bishops at Hexham and Lindisfarne as well as York. This work was carried on by Theodore's successors, and by the middle of the eighth century, the church in England was divided into manageable territorial areas. South of the Thames, there were five dioceses: Canterbury, Rochester, Selsey, Winchester and Sherborne. There were two in East Anglia (Dunwich and Elmham); five in Mercia (Lichfield, Lindsey, Hereford, Worcester and Leicester); and one more (originally the diocese for the kingdom of the East Saxons) at London. In Northumbria, the bishops at Hexham and Lindisfarne were joined by one at Whithorn (from the 730s), whilst the bishopric of York was made into an archbishopric in 735.

There was more to the English Church in 796 than dioceses and bishops, however. As it increased its institutional strength, so it became richer. Rules on the payments due to the church (principally tithes) had been tightened up by the end of the century, but most of the church's wealth by then came from the lands which it had been given by kings and other wealthy families. And often, the main feature of that land was the church, dedicated to a local saint, built on it. Historians call these churches 'minsters', but this is a rather confusing term and needs a little explanation. In early medieval England, the Latin word used to describe any group of people living together in a religious community was *monasterium*, and the Old English version of this was *mynster*. But these words covered a wide range of different establishments. Minsters could be big, complex places (wide, enclosed areas with some stone buildings and many residents) or small, simple ones (a single wooden structure on a little plot with a handful of occupants). They also differed in purpose and function. At one end of the spectrum were monasteries in the more conventional sense: groups of ascetic, contemplative men or women who lived an enclosed, communal life according to a clear set of rules. Their lives were spent praying, studying and working. At the other end were communities staffed by clergy (not monks, but priests and lesser clerical ranks – so-called secular clergy) who met the pastoral needs of the surrounding population. And somewhere in the middle were the minsters run by monks who did some pastoral work, those run by secular clergy who lived more like monks and those where monks and secular clergy lived side by side performing different duties.

By the late eighth century, there were probably hundreds of minsters in England, and clearly there was a great deal of diversity within this system. Individual minsters were organised according to the preferences and principles of their own abbots and abbesses. The important points to note at this stage, however, are, first, that all who lived a religious life during this period, whatever their rank and status (monks, nuns, bishops, priests or even lower orders such as deacons and acolytes), lived communally, and second, it was these communities, under the overall but inevitably sometimes rather distant supervision of the local bishop, which were responsible for meeting the pastoral and spiritual needs of the areas they were in. It has been said that 'by 800 most people who lived in England, outside the highland zone, were within what they would have considered a reasonable walking distance from a minster'.[1] Doubtless people could come to many of the minsters for a range of reasons: to visit the shrine of the saint who was buried there and sometimes perhaps even to worship in the minster church or make confession. The larger minsters were also likely to be centres of education and knowledge as well as artisanal skill and craftsmanship; they might therefore develop into centres of trade and commerce. But it was probably more common for priests and even some monks regularly to leave their minsters and travel through the villages and settlements which surrounded their churches, in order to carry out baptisms and marriages, to visit the sick and bury the dead. Bede describes what must have been a typical scene:

> If by chance a priest came to a village, the villagers crowded together, eager to hear from him the word of life; for the priests and the clerics visited the villages for no other reason than to preach, to baptise and to visit the sick, in brief to care for their souls.

His description of the kind of ministry overseen by Cedd, bishop of the East Saxons (d.664), is also probably a fair representation of how some early minsters were founded and of how their communities worked after that: 'He established churches in various places and ordained priests and deacons to assist him in preaching the word of faith and in the administration of baptism'.[2] Elsewhere great minsters like Whitby in North Yorkshire and *Medeshamstede* (later Peterborough) in Cambridgeshire had the resources and influence to allow them to establish a number of minsters within their surrounding areas, linked to the head-minster and dependant on it to a significant degree for personnel and direction. But these smaller establishments were still centres of communal living which served the local community, and by 800, when there were still as yet no parish churches and no parish priests in England in any recognisable sense, services (Mass in particular) would often be held in the open air by a wooden or stone cross erected to mark the meeting-place.

Not surprisingly most early minsters were mission stations, designed to provide a platform for further conversion in their surrounding area. Most were placed in or at least near established centres of population or royal administration. Zealous and enthusiastic though they were, however, the early missionaries and their successors could not simply travel around England setting up minsters wherever they pleased. If they were to succeed, they needed lay assistance, and this came in the first instance from the kings and their leading subjects. Seventh-century kings might do this to show their adoption of the new faith, whilst later endowments could be made for a variety of reasons: to display the power and wealth of the donor, to provide somewhere for the donor to retire to or somewhere his family members (younger sons and daughters in particular) might live and work. What this meant, of course, was that many of these secular benefactors came to regard the minsters they had endowed as their own property which might be inherited by their heirs.

Minsters were also vulnerable to unscrupulous rulers and lords who might simply take a fancy to some of their lands and seize control of them. The West Saxon ruling dynasty, for example, assumed direct control over the minsters in Kent as they asserted their political power over that region in the 820s.[3]

So from the very start, the Anglo-Saxon Church had an ambivalent relationship with its lay supporters. On the one hand, it needed their help if it was to survive and prosper, whilst on the other it could fall prey to their greed and opportunism if circumstances changed. At the same time, what bears emphasis here is the way in which these diocesan structures and monastic networks covered more or less the whole of England by the end of the eighth century. This gave the English Church a chance to develop an integrity, a coherence, even a unity, of its own, although in order to do so it would need strong lay allies to protect it against predators. The wealth and resources of the church would always tempt greedy speculators, but at the same time, this pre-existing national framework of power and wealth would be a crucial asset for those kings from Alfred onwards who aspired to rule more than just one part of England.

English kings and the pre-viking church

An early medieval king would never have been far from a clergyman. The church, of course, gave a ruler divine legitimacy at his coronation, and this would almost certainly have been reaffirmed on ceremonial occasions throughout a reign. More than this, however, the practice of consecrating a king at the start of his reign became standard procedure during this period. In what soon became a quasi-religious ceremony, spiritual lustre and mystical power were added to the king's newly acquired earthly authority.[*] On an everyday level, however, the king would have had priests in his household, whose job it was to say Mass, hear confession and give instruction. Only the clergy were routinely literate, and they would have had an important role in writing a proportion of the documents issued in the king's name (although, where these recorded royal grants of land, many would also have been written by the beneficiaries), but also in reading a variety of texts to him – letters and legal documents, certainly, but also scripture and other religious writings. But at the top end of the ecclesiastical hierarchy, the bishops and other leading churchmen (the heads of the more important minsters, for example) would have served the king as members of his *witan*. They would have met him when he attended or presided over a church council: King Beornwulf of Mercia did this at the unidentified site of *Clofesho* in 825, and the witness list to one of the charters he issued there contains the names of the archbishop of Canterbury, twelve other bishops, four abbots, one prior, three deacons and nine priests.[4] But the king and his ecclesiastical advisers probably came together more often when he summoned them to attend one of his own assemblies. The growing importance of these gatherings during this period

* Above, pp. 43–4

was discussed earlier,* but it is worth repeating here that they dealt with a range of ceremonial, political, diplomatic and legal business, and there is no doubt that the bishops and abbots were involved with all of that. The charters issued on these occasions show how substantial the ecclesiastical contribution could be.[5]

The story of the relationship between the archbishops of Canterbury and the kings of Mercia and Wessex in first half of ninth century reveals much about the need both royal and ecclesiastical leaders had for each other's support. For the last decade of his reign at least, and probably for longer than that, King Offa ruled Kent and treated it as part of his kingdom of Mercia. This was not a straightforward situation, however, and there are plenty of signs that Mercian rule was resented and disputed in Kent at various points during the 770s and 780s. The archbishop of Canterbury played a central role in either supporting or frustrating Offa's ambitions there, and it is not surprising that, when the archbishopric became vacant in 793, Offa appointed his own nominee, Aethelheard, to the position. However, when Offa died in 796, the Kentish opposition was quick to reassert itself, and for the next two years, Kent was ruled as an independent kingdom once again by one if its own leading men, Eadberht Praen. Archbishop Aethelheard, the representative of the unpopular Mercian regime, was forced into exile and only restored to power in 798 when the forces of King Cenwulf of Mercia overran Kent, captured Eadberht and later killed him. One of Aethelheard's main roles after this was to support Cenwulf's younger brother Cuthred, who was installed as sub-king of Kent, and in return for his loyalty, the archbishop was able to recover estates which had been lost by Canterbury to the Mercian kings during the latter part of the eighth century. He was also able to hold numerous reforming councils (or synods), at one of which, held at *Clofesho* in 803, Aethelheard was finally able to put an end to Offa's plan for a separate Mercian archbishopric at Lichfield. This scheme had been short-lived, but the division of the southern English province into two had been potentially very damaging indeed to the interests of Canterbury. A single archbishopric for southern England suited Cenwulf, who needed ecclesiastical support at a time when his regime was still struggling to establish itself, and it certainly suited Aethelheard who, by the time he died in 805, had reasserted the authority of the archbishopric of Canterbury over the whole of the English Church.

However, this coincidence of interest between king and archbishop did not last long. Aethelheard's successor, Wulfred (805–32), must have been acceptable as a candidate to Cenwulf and Cuthred, but he soon quarrelled with the Mercian king. And although this particular dispute (its causes are unknown) seems to have been resolved reasonably quickly, the two were at loggerheads again between 815 and 821. For more than a century the English Church had tried to insist that ministers should not fall under the hereditary control of royal or local noble families. In 803, indeed, the synod held at *Clofesho* had forbidden minster communities to choose laymen as lords and had required them to observe monastic discipline.[6] The

---

* Above, pp. 45–6

concern here was about the decline in standards that secular control of minsters might provoke, and the habit lay lords had of taking a minster's lands for themselves or their families. And in 816 at another synod, this time at Chelsea, similar principles were set out. Lay lordship of minsters was again prohibited, and it was declared to be the responsibility of the local bishop to appoint the heads of minsters in his diocese.[7] Such ideas challenged powerful royal and noble vested interests and they brought Wulfred into direct conflict with Cenwulf over the Kentish minsters of Reculver and Minster in Thanet, which the Mercian kings had claimed as their own after taking control of Kent. First the king managed to persuade the pope to suspend Wulfred from office, and he acquired papal privileges confirming his rights over the monasteries he had inherited or acquired. The archbishop used some forged charters to support his claims, and he may also have responded to his own suspension by deposing the king. Shortly before his death in 821, Cenwulf imposed a settlement whereby the archbishop kept the lordship of Reculver and Minster in Thanet, but only after agreeing to surrender to the king an estate of 300 hides and a large fine. Wulfred tried hard to work more fruitfully with Cenwulf's successors, but all his efforts were frustrated in 825 when King Beornwulf of Mercia was defeated in battle by King Ecgberht of Wessex at Wroughton. Over the next two years, Kent was taken over by Ecgberht and his son, Aethelwulf, who was installed as sub-king there. They did not recognize the archbishop's claims to authority over the Kentish minsters and claimed it for themselves.

By the time Wulfred died in 832, the political situation in England had been radically transformed: the supremacy of Mercia was over, and the rise to dominance within England of the rulers of Wessex had begun. This may not have been completely clear to contemporaries, of course, but the signs were ominous at the very least, and Wulfred's successor as archbishop of Canterbury, Ceolnoth (833–70), had to adjust to this altered landscape. In 836 he convened a church council at Croft in Leicestershire, which was attended by King Wiglaf of Mercia, but this was the last time the archbishop appears to have worked at such a level with a Mercian king. Thereafter his focus seems to have shifted towards the rulers of Wessex, and in 838, he pledged his loyalty to King Ecgberht, Aethelwulf his son and their heirs in return for a promise by the two kings to respect the liberties of the church. At the same time, Aethelwulf granted several estates to Canterbury, in return for which Ceolnoth formally surrendered authority over the Kentish minsters to the king, who became their lord and secular patron. Ceolnoth also gave up his claim to control the lands and incomes from the minsters and to influence the election of abbots and abbesses. This accord was made at Kingston upon Thames in Surrey, a royal estate which would become the preferred coronation site for the rulers of Wessex in the tenth century. Even at this early date, however, the choice of location for this meeting was almost certainly politically significant. Ecgberht and Aethelwulf were attempting to secure the support of the leading English churchman for their dynasty, whilst for Ceolnoth, the events at Kingston amounted to a recognition of West Saxon control over Kent, but also of West Saxon supremacy within England. He may even have consecrated Aethelwulf in recognition of his status as Ecgberht's heir. 'It would seem that Archbishop Ceolnoth and the church of Canterbury had come decisively off the fence and had tied themselves to the fortunes of Ecgberht's lineage'.[8] For their part, Ecgberht and Aethelwulf now had the high-level ecclesiastical backing they needed to legitimise their political and military successes.

The English Church and the Vikings

After 838, the kings of Wessex were directly responsible for the defence of the Kentish minsters, not just against the covetous local aristocracy, but against a quite new danger. The greatest challenge the English Church faced during this period came from Scandinavia. In 835, the *Anglo-Saxon Chronicle* records, 'heathen men' ravaged the Isle of Sheppey off the Kent coast, and King Ecgberht himself fought against the Vikings in Somerset in 836 and in Cornwall in 838.[9] After that, and until the arrival of the Great Heathen Army in 865, viking raids on England were sporadic and uncoordinated. However, that does not mean that they were insignificant. There were viking forces in Kent in 835, 841, 851, 853, 855 and 865, and on at least one of these occasions (851), the city of Canterbury was sacked, and almost certainly, the cathedral church (Christ Church) was attacked and plundered. And as the Great Army made its way through Yorkshire and East Anglia in the second half of the 860s and early 870s, it is very likely that the churches of those regions suffered at its hands, with buildings burnt, books destroyed, precious treasures looted and members of the communities killed and maimed. By the 870s, there were no bishops at Leicester and Lindsey in Mercia, nor at Elmham and Dunwich in East Anglia. All of this, along with the poor scholarly quality of surviving bishops' manuscripts and the absence of recorded synods after 845, has led one historian to argue for 'a fundamental collapse of episcopal cohesion' south of the Humber in the middle decades of the ninth century.[10] Meanwhile in the north, the diocese of Hexham ceased to function, and the monks of Lindisfarne had to evacuate their church and flee to Chester-le-Street. The situation in other dioceses in the midlands and the north is less clear; but it cannot have been good, and the diocesan structure of these areas seems to have been severely damaged.

Minsters suffered along with the episcopal centres. The plundering of the monastery at Peterborough in 870 was described in graphic terms in the *Anglo-Saxon Chronicle*; after killing King Edmund of East Anglia and seizing control of the kingdom, the Vikings came to Peterborough, 'burnt and destroyed it, killed the abbot and the monks and all they found there, and brought it to pass that it became nought that had been very mighty'.[11] Other churches, including Abingdon, Evesham, Ely, Thorney and Whitby, were also devastated and some, such as Dover and Minster in Thanet, disappeared from the records entirely. When King Alfred later wrote regretfully of the prosperous time 'before everything was ransacked and burned', he had the havoc wreaked by the Vikings in mind, and there is other evidence to suggest that he was not exaggerating the problem to suit his own purposes. When Fulco, archbishop of Rheims, wrote to Alfred in the mid-880s, he agreed that the church 'has fallen into ruin, whether by the frequent invasion and onslaught of

Vikings, or through decrepitude, or through the carelessness of its bishops or the ignorance of those subject to them'.[12]

But having said all this, the viking raids did not affect the whole of England, or its churches, in the same way or to the same extent. Indeed, it has been argued very strongly that there was 'fundamental regional diversity' as far as the impact of the attacks was concerned.[13] In the south-west or (particularly) the west midlands, raiding was much more intermittent and there was no permanent viking settlement. In these areas, many minsters survived the raids and there was a good deal of continuity in ecclesiastical organisation. And even where there was eventually more viking settlement, in Staffordshire, Cheshire, Lancashire and Cumbria, for example, and even in Yorkshire and the east midlands, it has been argued that the disruption, whilst intense during the second half of the ninth century, was not so catastrophic as to wipe out all traces of religious life. Not surprisingly, perhaps, the most serious damage was probably done in East Anglia: no East Anglian bishops are recorded between the 860s and the 940s, and it is likely that church lands, buildings and personnel all suffered badly at the hands of their new viking lords. And how much this changed after Guthrum's conversion to Christianity in 878 is far from clear. Nevertheless, even in this part of England, there is no compelling evidence to suggest that religious life was completely wiped out after 865. Indeed, overall across England, 'a high proportion of the pre-viking minsters remained in some sense in existence' during this traumatic period, and the remarkable resilience displayed by the English Church testified to its institutional strength and gave it a base on which it could later rebuild.[14] That is not to deny that the survivors emerged poorer and smaller from the experience, but, as will be seen, during these chaotic years, their lost estates are just as likely to have fallen into opportunistic Christian hands as into marauding pagan ones.

Alfred the Great and the church

Alfred's attempts to revive Christian life within his kingdom were discussed in Chapter 2.* However, the emphasis there was on how his reforms were designed to help Alfred defend Wessex more effectively and administer it more professionally. More still needs to be said about Alfred's personal approach to religion and about how he sought to utilise the structures of the West Saxon Church and use its human and material resources to increase his own power. Not surprisingly, his faith and his realism are hard to disentangle.

The pious king

In his biography of Alfred, Asser portrays the king in saintly, almost Christ-like, terms. Alfred's piety was profound from an early age, we are told, when he learnt

---

* Above, pp. 64–9

psalms and prayers and collected them in the book which he always kept with him. Alfred heard Mass every day, took part in other services and distributed alms to the poor. He secretly visited churches at night to pray, and he was particularly concerned to suppress his own carnal desires which were leading him towards temptation and sin. The illnesses he suffered throughout his adult life were depicted by Asser as gifts given to Alfred by God at the king's own request. They revealed Alfred to be a kind of living martyr, even Christ-like, a saviour who suffered for the sake of his people. Alfred also enjoyed listening to scripture being read out, and this was one of the reasons why he recruited scholars such as Asser to attend his court. He wanted to take advantage of their knowledge and expertise to increase his own spiritual awareness, and above all he wanted them to help him acquire more 'wisdom', which meant getting closer to an understanding of God's plan for the world. Still according to Asser, Alfred showed his devotion to the church in other ways as well. He founded two monasteries, one at Athelney (the site of his greatest victory) for monks and another at Shaftesbury for nuns, and he divided both his time and his income into secular and religious halves:

> this man of holy resolve promised devoutly and faithfully with all his heart to give to God one half of his service, both by day and by night, and one half of all the riches which, acquired by right, steadily accrued to him throughout the year.[15]

He even devised his own candle clock which burnt for twenty-four hours a day to help him measure the time he was giving to his devotions.

To be sure, Asser may have overstated the depths of Alfred's faith and the lengths to which he went in his attempts to develop it. Nevertheless, there is no obvious reason to doubt that Alfred was an intensely devout Christian king. His own writings reinforce this and take it further. In his will, Alfred left several estates to the Old Minster at Winchester, and he bequeathed significant sums of money to several bishops and for charitable distribution. In the prose preface the king wrote to Bishop Werferth of Worcester's translation of the *Dialogues* of Pope Gregory the Great, he reflected on what he had

> frequently heard from statements in holy books that for us, to whom God has granted such a lofty station of worldly office, there is the most urgent necessity occasionally to calm our minds amidst these earthly anxieties and direct them to divine and spiritual law.[16]

So for Alfred, religious commitment was clearly a private obsession and priority, but it also had wider significance beyond his own salvation. As king, Alfred considered himself to be responsible for his people's security, but also for their spiritual well-being, even their chances of eternal life. In the words of Fulco, archbishop of Rheims, who wrote to Alfred about the king's plans in the mid-880s, 'you attend to the good of the kingdom divinely entrusted to you, seeking or safeguarding its peace with warlike weapons and divine support'.[17] As has been seen,* Alfred's view was that standards of learning had declined so much in recent years that people had quite simply lost the ability to worship God properly. In the most literal and basic sense, they could not understand His word (in the Bible and in the works of those who had interpreted it), and there was nobody with the expertise to explain it to them. If this situation was not addressed, all hope of doing what God wanted in the way He wanted it done would be lost, along with all chance of going to Heaven. The viking invasions were one obvious cause and consequence of this decline in standards of divine learning; they were God's punishment (or warning) inflicted on those whose attention had drifted from what was required for redemption, and the invasions themselves had of course compounded the problem by causing such chaos and disruption to monasteries and other centres of learning. 'We were Christians in name alone, and very few of us possessed Christian virtues', Alfred said, and his characteristically ambitious response was to seek 'the renewal of religion through the revival of literacy'.[18]

The reform of the clergy

Central to Alfred's plans were his bishops. In time, his literacy programme would produce a new generation of learned, loyal church leaders, but meanwhile, the king appointed bishops in whom he had confidence. Asser, of course, became bishop of Sherborne some time between 892 and 899. He was also given control of two Somerset monasteries by Alfred, at Congresbury and Banwell, and another at Exeter, and he was referred to by Alfred as 'my bishop' in the preface to the *Pastoral Care*.[19] Plegmund, another of Alfred's scholarly recruits from Mercia, became archbishop of Canterbury in 890, a sure sign that West Saxon control over Kent remained strong. And more broadly, by the 890s, Alfred was able to thank God for the 'learned bishops' who were 'now nearly everywhere'.[20] Meanwhile, Alfred's translations, particularly the *Pastoral Care* which was distributed to all the West Saxon dioceses, were designed to provide insight and instruction. The *Pastoral Care* had much to teach anyone in a position of authority, but it was first and foremost a handbook for bishops. It dealt with important questions such as what kind of men should become bishops; how they should live; how they should instruct their subordinates and give them correction; and how they should continually reflect, contemplate and examine their own consciences. It warned of the dangers of pride and arrogance in leaders who should be humble, and of the need to learn from adversity.

One of the surviving copies of the *Pastoral Care* was sent to Bishop Werferth of Worcester (d.907x915). He was already in post when Alfred became king in 871, and he was clearly someone the king came to trust deeply. Werferth was one of the Mercian scholars recruited by Alfred to help with his plan to revive learning and literacy, and one of the named beneficiaries in his will. In Asser's opinion, he was

* Above, pp. 65–6

'a man thoroughly learned in holy writings', and he translated Gregory the Great's *Dialogues* 'at the king's command'.[21] Part of this work contained an account of the life and miracles of St Benedict (d.*c.*547), one of the founders of western monasticism, so it would have been of particular relevance to those in charge of a religious community. The ultimate aim of the translation programme, however, as was explained earlier,* was to improve standards of literacy and learning across the West Saxon clerical and secular elites. The books 'which are the most necessary for all men to know' were translated from Latin into English at Alfred's court and then circulated around the kingdom.[22] Those who received them could then teach others how to read and write in the vernacular. If any of these pupils later wanted to join the church as a monk or a priest, they could then be taught Latin, and eventually, a new generation of knowledgeable, scholarly clergymen would be created, men who could preach God's word properly to the people of Wessex and help them regain God's favour. If they preached loyalty and obedience to the king and his dynasty at the same time, so much the better.

Power and politics (again)

So Alfred was personally and actively devout, and he developed an ambitious plan to improve the quality of religious life in his kingdom. He did not attempt any sweeping reorganisation of the church in Wessex, however, and its institutional structure remained largely unchanged throughout his reign. Nevertheless, there can be no doubt that Alfred regarded the church as a vital asset when it came to ruling his kingdom. The bishops controlled extensive lands and exercised authority over the people who lived on them: they were important political figures as much as religious ones and the king expected them to do more than just care for their congregations' souls. They had legal duties to perform, for example: a dispute about whether a holder of bookland was entitled to give it away to someone other than a kinsman would be heard in the presence of a bishop; and a man who contravened Alfred's first law and broke his 'oath and pledge' would be imprisoned and then sentenced by a bishop.[23] Alfred's bishops were also encouraged to play their part in the king's burghal policies, as was seen earlier.† Of course, the bishops had much to gain from these transactions, financially in particular and also in terms of security. But they entailed administrative responsibilities, too, and there was almost certainly an expectation that the bishops would do their best to run their new acquisitions in the king's interests as well as their own: 'If their churches were to be secure from viking assaults in the future, the bishops had every reason to assist Alfred as best they could in creating effective burghal defences'.[24]

But if Alfred was keen to cooperate with the church in order to achieve mutually beneficial ends, he was also prepared to exploit what the church had to offer

* Above, pp. 66–8
† Above, pp. 63–4

more ruthlessly and selfishly. As the English minsters suffered at the hands of the Vikings, many of their estates were left untended and unprotected. Much of this land seems sooner or later to have ended up under new lay ownership, and it has been argued strongly (although not all historians share these opinions) 'that Alfred and his heirs profited from ill-gotten monastic lands'.[25] Estates which were linked to minsters in the seventh and eighth centuries were given away by Alfred to his followers or officials in the ninth, and by the early tenth century, the religious houses of England might justifiably have felt that they had as much to fear from their own rulers as they did from the Vikings. In the twelfth century, Alfred was remembered by the monks of Abingdon in Oxfordshire as a Judas who stole their lands, and the king's relationship with his first archbishop of Canterbury, Aethelred (870–88), appears to have been far from smooth, probably for similar reasons.[26] Pope John VIII (872–82) wrote to the archbishop after Aethelred had made a complaint to him. Aethelred's own letter is lost so it is hard to know exactly what his concerns were, but in his reply the pope referred to 'certain adversities' and 'certain hardships' facing the archbishop and encouraged him 'to resist not only the king, but all who wish to do any wrong'. The pope went on to explain that he had also sent a letter to Alfred (this has not survived either), in which 'we have been at pains to admonish and exhort your king . . . not to neglect to be obedient to you and a devoted helper for the love of Jesus Christ our Lord in all things'.[27]

It is quite possible that the dispute between king and archbishop on this occasion, as on previous ones, concerned control of the Kentish monasteries and that Alfred was asserting his control over them too forcefully for Aethelred's liking. However, the pope's letter was written late in 877 or early in 878, and it cannot have been sent very long after he received the archbishop's complaint. This was a time of crisis for Wessex. A viking army was encamped in Dorset and then Devon from late 875 until the summer of 877, and when it returned early in 878, it nearly conquered the kingdom. Every resource Alfred could get his hands on must have been used to deal with this existential threat, and the king would have expected the church to do its share. So it may be that Archbishop Aethelred had become unhappy with Alfred's financial demands, or with other kinds of royal pressure for services or material sacrifices. One bishop of Winchester, Ealhferth (d. by 877), certainly felt squeezed by Alfred's need for tribute to pay the Vikings. Alfred's father, King Aethelwulf, had left two estates in his will to the church at Winchester, but some time before 877, Ealhferth was forced to hand them back to Alfred because he could not afford to pay his share.[28] And his successor, Bishop Denewulf (d. 908), also struggled to keep his church's lands beyond royal reach. Before he became bishop, an estate belonging to the Old Minster at Alresford in Hampshire had been leased to the family of a man called Alfred. Bishop Denewulf later renewed the lease, but Alfred was subsequently found guilty of adultery, and his possessions were forfeit to the crown. In spite of his church's prior claim, Denewulf was only able to recover Alresford from the king after paying him 120 mancuses of gold (a mancus was a gold coin worth thirty silver pennies, minted rarely and usually just for ceremonial purposes). Denewulf was also unable to obtain lands left to the Old Minster in the will of King Aethelwulf, despite surrendering another large estate to Alfred to secure them.[29]

It is right to say of John VIII's letter to Archbishop Aethelred of Canterbury that 'It comes as a shock, in view of his work later in his reign, to find Alfred mentioned in the company of the enemies of the Church'.[30] However, that shock is only so great partly because the campaign undertaken by Asser and by Alfred himself to portray the king as virtuous and unselfish, the ideal Christian ruler, has been so successful over the centuries. And anyway, Alfred would not have seen anything wrong about what he was doing. He was only following his predecessors' example when he bore down heavily on the church, and if he pushed things further than they did, that should come as no surprise given the particularly sizeable challenges he faced. What is more, the evidence suggests that Alfred was not seizing monastic lands wherever he could simply to enrich himself and that there was a strategic dimension to his approach. Some of the estates which eventually found their way into lay hands were along the border fixed by Alfred's treaty with Guthrum, for example, and the acquisition of lands in this region may have begun under Alfred in order to shore up defences and install loyal officials at important points. After all, the church in Alfred's Wessex was not an autonomous, independent entity: it was an integral part of the political, financial and military fabric of the kingdom, and it had to play its part in protecting it. Nevertheless, it has certainly been argued that the king and his nobles stood to gain financially and politically from the secularisation of former ecclesiastical estates and that the sheer amount of land lost to the English minsters during Alfred's reign and the following decades 'had an important impact on the development of royal power in England. The house of Wessex emerges as the greatest and most immediate beneficiary of what can only be described as a revolution in landholding'.[31]

Between a viking rock and a royal hard place

There is no reason to doubt that the English Church was put under great strain during the ninth century. The temptation to put all the blame for this on the Vikings, however, should be resisted; predators from closer to home were also guilty of appropriating ecclesiastical lands and abusing ecclesiastical vulnerability. What is more, the truth about how much physical damage was caused by the Vikings and others is hard to assess objectively. It was in Alfred's interest to emphasise how disordered things had become by the time he came to write about them in the 880s; however, the material impact of the mid-century traumas on the southern English Church appears to have varied from region to region. Nevertheless, as argued already,* the decline in standards of Latin literacy and learning which Alfred set out to reverse does appear to have been real, and although this set in before the viking attacks began in earnest, it can only have been accelerated by them. So Alfred did

---

* Above, pp. 65–6

have a meaningful job to do on behalf of his spiritually deprived subjects when he started his programme to revive Christian belief and practice in his kingdom. Having said this, the church possessed assets (personnel and property) which were open to exploitation by an ambitious and determined king. It was the church's job to provide pastoral care to Alfred's people, but it was also expected to support him ideologically and practically. Many of its leaders cooperated with the king in his schemes to extend and consolidate royal power, because it was in their own interest to do so. Others meanwhile, and at considerable cost, were given little choice but to service the king's needs. One way or another, by indoctrinating his subjects or by filling his coffers, the church helped to strengthen Alfred's regime and further his plans for the assertion of West Saxon supremacy across southern England.

Notes

1   J. Blair, *The Church in Anglo-Saxon Society* (Oxford, 2005), p. 152.
2   *BEH*, pp. 310–11, 282–3.
3   N. Brooks, *The Early History of the Church of Canterbury* (Leicester, 1984), pp. 197–203.
4   Robertson, *Anglo-Saxon Charters*, no.V.
5   See, for example, *EHD*, i nos.80, 85, 86, 90–2.
6   Brooks, *Early History*, pp. 179–80.
7   Brooks, *Early History*, pp. 175–7.
8   Brooks, *Early History*, p. 147.
9   *ASC* 835, 836, 838.
10 Pratt, *Political Thought*, p. 50.
11 *ASC* 870.
12 K&L, pp. 125, 182–3.
13 Blair, *The Church in Anglo-Saxon Society*, p. 295, map on p. 296.
14 Blair, *The Church in Anglo-Saxon Society*, p. 320.
15 K&L, pp. 105–6.
16 K&L, p. 123.
17 K&L, p. 182.
18 K&L, p. 125; Abels, *Alfred the Great*, pp. 230–1.
19 K&L, p. 126.
20 K&L, p. 126.
21 K&L, p. 92.
22 K&L, p. 126.
23 K&L, pp. 164, 168 (Alfred, 1.2, 41).
24 Brooks, *Early History*, p. 154.
25 R. Fleming, 'Monastic Lands and England's Defence in the Viking Age', *EHR* 100 (1985), pp. 247–65, at p. 250. Compare D.N. Dumville, 'Ecclesiastical Lands and the Defence of Wessex in the First Viking-Age', in idem., *Wessex and England from Alfred to Edgar* (Woodbridge, 1992), pp. 29–54, for a more restrained view of the issue.
26 J. Stevenson (ed.), *Chronicon Monasterii de Abingdon*, 2 vols (London, 1858), i p. 50.
27 *EHD*, i no.222.
28 S354.
29 S1287 (Robertson, *Anglo-Saxon Charters*, no.XV), 814 (A.R. Rumble, *Property and Piety in Early Medieval Winchester: Documents Relating to the Topography of the Anglo-Saxon and Norman City and its Minsters* (Oxford, 2002), no.V(v), pp. 116–18), 354.
30 Brooks, *Early History*, p. 150.
31 Fleming, 'Monastic Lands and England's Defence', p. 264.

The birth of a kingdom, 899–975

PART II

The birth of a kingdom

995–975

5

THE EVENTS, 899–975

899–902

Alfred the Great died on 26 October 899 and was succeeded as king of the Anglo-Saxons by his eldest son Edward, later called 'the Elder'. He 'was crowned with the royal crown' on 8 June 900 at Kingston upon Thames in Surrey, 'having been elected by the chief men'.[1] Edward was probably born in the 870s, but the *Anglo-Saxon Chronicle* did not mention him before Alfred's death, and Asser only referred to him briefly, as an obedient and well-educated son. It only becomes clear from the late tenth-century account of the 890s written by Ealdorman Aethelweard that Edward had been heavily involved in the campaigns against the Vikings during that decade. And other evidence also testifies to Edward's increasing importance before 899. He was granted extensive estates by Alfred in his will, particularly in Kent where he inherited all of his father's bookland, and in a charter of 898, Edward is referred to as *rex*. The charter in question concerns land in Kent, and it is possible that by this point Alfred had appointed Edward sub-king there, just as his predecessors Aethelwulf and Ecgberht had promoted their eldest sons during their reigns.[2] This is not certain, but whatever Edward's formal status was by the time of his father's death, he was a mature and experienced warrior steeped in the ethos of Alfred's court, and the obvious person to follow him as king.

This does not mean he was unchallenged, however. The *Anglo-Saxon Chronicle* describes in some detail how, as soon as Edward became king, his cousin, the atheling Aethelwold, rebelled against him. Aethelwold was the eldest son of Edward's uncle (and King Alfred's older brother), Aethelred I (865–71), and probably thought that his claim to the throne was just as good, if not better, than Edward's. He began his revolt by seizing Wimborne in Dorset (where his father was buried) and Christchurch, about fifteen miles to the east. But Edward moved quickly with an army to confine Aethelwold at Wimborne. The rebel prince sounded his defiance ('he would either live there or die there', the *Chronicle* reported him saying), but soon enough he escaped during the night and fled.[3]

Having escaped from Wessex, Aethelwold and his supporters regrouped in the north. In the words of the *Chronicle*, he 'went to the Danish army in Northumbria, and they accepted him as king and gave allegiance to him'.[4] Then, in autumn 901, he sailed with a fleet down the east coast of England and took control of Essex. In the following year, the Danes of East Anglia gave him their support, and they raided into Mercia, getting as far as Cricklade in Wiltshire. But when Aethelwold and his troops crossed the Thames into Wessex in 902, this was a step too far for King Edward. A royal army now entered Essex and East Anglia determined to bring the uprising to an end. This expedition was punitive and its effects were widespread (the king's forces harried all the land between the Devil's Dyke in Cambridgeshire and the Great Ouse river, 'all as far north as the fens', the *Chronicle* reported), although subsequent events would show that it had not ended the rebellion.[5] For when the time came to withdraw his forces, Edward was determined to keep his troops together. But despite repeated orders to keep up, the contingent from Kent became separated from the rest of the army. Cut off and exposed, on 13 December 902, they were overtaken by Aethelwold and his allies and defeated at the so-called battle of the Holme (perhaps close to the modern village of Holme in Cambridgeshire, although the precise location of the battle is unknown). However, if the battle was lost, the struggle for the succession was now over, as amongst the many high-ranking casualties of this bloody encounter was the atheling Aethelwold himself.

903–918

Aethelwold's revolt had been prolonged and serious. It is impossible to know what would have happened had he survived the battle of the Holme and continued to challenge his cousin. But certainly, the pressure on King Edward would have been sustained, and he might have found it difficult to withstand. The evidence is thin and inconclusive, but one text of the *Anglo-Saxon Chronicle* hinted at the enduring strain on Edward when it referred to the peace deal which 'from necessity' he struck with the Danes of Northumbria and East Anglia in 906.[6] This may be the chronicler's way of saying that Edward had to pay the Vikings off (just as his father Alfred had in the 870s), but other than this brief reference, there is nothing to cast any further light on Edward's situation before serious fighting resumed in 909.

In that year, a joint West Saxon and Mercian army entered Northumbria, where it ravaged for five weeks. However, this only seems to have provoked a brutal Danish response, and Aethelweard described it at length in his chronicle later in the century.[7] Large areas of English Mercia, as far south as the river Avon in Gloucestershire, were plundered and wasted by the invaders, but as they returned north with their spoils, they were intercepted by the West Saxons and their Mercian allies at Wednesfield, near Tettenhall (now part of Wolverhampton) on 5 August 910. The date was probably carefully chosen. It was the feast day of St Oswald, the great seventh-century Northumbrian saint, whose relics had been seized in Lincolnshire during the raids of 909 and brought to Gloucester where a new priory in his name was subsequently constructed. Inspired by the saint (this is how contemporaries would have seen it), the Danish defeat at Tettenhall appears to have been crushing and decisive. Aethelweard claimed that the English secured their victory 'without delay . . . and the army of the Danes was put to flight, overcome by weapons'. The *Anglo-Saxon Chronicle* described how the West Saxon and Mercian troops 'put the [Danish] army to flight and killed many thousands of its men'. The damage inflicted on the Danish leadership seems to have been particularly severe – two or three of their 'kings' were killed as well as numerous other leading warriors.[8]

In 911, the most important political event was the death of Ealdorman Aethelred of Mercia. The resulting redistribution of power saw Aethelred's wife (King Edward's elder sister), Aethelflaed, become the sole ruler of English Mercia, whilst Edward himself took direct control of London, Oxford and the lands surrounding these two centres. Over the next few years, Edward and Aethelflaed worked together to enforce their control over the kingdom of the Anglo-Saxons, and also to extend it outwards into Danish territory. Late in 911, Edward ordered the construction of a *burh* at Hertford, whilst in summer 912 another was started at Witham in Essex. Together these two forts would block any viking attempt to put pressure on London from the north or the east. Meanwhile, in Shropshire, Aethelflaed built a *burh* on the river Severn at Bridgnorth in an attempt to prevent the Vikings using the river as they had in earlier campaigns. She followed this up in 913–14 with a series of *burhs* (at Tamworth and Stafford in 913 and at Warwick and Eddisbury in 914). The first three of these were designed to strengthen her grip on the northern frontier of English Mercia and provide a springboard for attacks against the centres of viking power in the Five Boroughs, whilst Eddisbury was built to reinforce Aethleflaed's grip on the Wirral peninsula and the mouth of the river Mersey. This fort, along with the neighbouring *burh* at Runcorn which was constructed in 915 and the one at Chester which had been in use since 907, would serve as barriers in the way of any viking attempt to enter north-western England from Ireland.

Before he could take the initiative against the northern Danes, however, Edward had to deal with a viking attack from Brittany in 914. Having ravaged first in Wales, the invaders came inland, only to be defeated by English armies raised from Herefordshire and Gloucestershire. Then, having given hostages and undertakings to leave, the rump of the viking army evaded the troops Edward had stationed on the south side of the Severn estuary and began their raids once again. The English defenders finally put them to flight, however, and the few Vikings left were compelled to take what refuge they could get on the island of Steepholme in the Bristol Channel. By the autumn, starving according to the *Chronicle*, they had managed to find their way back to south Wales and from there to Ireland.[9] These attacks were not particularly serious, but they were a distraction which took up time and consumed resources. As a result, it was not until the end of 914 that Edward could return his attention to the physical consolidation of his power. In November, he stayed with his army at Buckingham for a month and built a *burh* on each side of the river there, whilst in the following year he did something similar at Bedford. Buckingham and Bedford are about twenty miles apart, the former roughly ten miles west of Watling Street (the Alfred-Guthrum frontier) and the latter about ten miles east. Edward's intention was clearly, once again, to strengthen his control over this stretch of territory, but there were other consequences, too, as Edward's demonstrations of power at Buckingham and Bedford persuaded many of the principal viking leaders and their supporters in those areas to submit to him. Something similar almost certainly happened when in 916 Edward supervised the building of another *burh* at Maldon in Essex, a few miles from the one at Witham he had ordered in 912.

917 and 918 were pivotal years in the making of the kingdom of England. The Mercian Register recorded Aethelflaed's seizure of Derby 'with all that belongs to it' some time before the start of August 917.[10] This was one of the Five Boroughs and a major centre of viking power south of the Humber. Its capture was a significant statement of intent and demonstration of force by Aethelflaed. Meanwhile, further south, Edward had to fight to survive. Just a few miles to the north and west of Buckingham and Bedford respectively, some time in the spring of 917, the king ordered two more *burhs* to be built, one at Towcester and the other at an unidentified place called *Wigingamere* in the *Chronicle*.[11] By the summer Towcester was under attack from the Danes of Northampton and Leicester. The assault was ultimately a failure, and the attackers were turned away, but this was only the first of several challenges Edward had to face. Another viking army now gathered from Huntingdon and East Anglia and built its own fortress at Tempsford, a few miles east of Bedford. From there it attacked Bedford, but the *burh's* new defences again held fast and the Vikings were defeated. Meanwhile, a third viking army which had besieged *Wigingamere* was also repelled by the defenders. Edward's line of new forts had held in the face of concerted efforts to break through, and it was now the turn of the English armies to counter-attack. One took Tempsford, and then another from Kent, Surrey and Essex successfully laid siege to the Danish power-base at Colchester. A viking attempt to seize the new fortress at Maldon was also thwarted with 'many hundreds' of casualties on the enemy side, according to the *Chronicle*. By the autumn Edward was back at Towcester, where he ordered stone walls to be built. The viking leaders and their armies based a few miles north at Northampton, perhaps awed by this show of strength, then 'sought to have [Edward] as their lord and protector', whilst soon afterwards, having captured the viking fort at Huntingdon, the people of that district submitted to Edward as well 'and asked for his peace and protection'. 917 ended with Edward returning to Colchester. He repaired the damage caused by his followers earlier in the year and took submissions from the viking armies in East Anglia and Cambridgeshire, as well as from 'many people who had been under the rule of the Danes'.

By the start of 918, therefore, Edward and Aethelflaed had successfully consolidated their frontier with the Danelaw. Crucially, however, they had also begun to break out of the kingdom of the Anglo-Saxons and take control of viking territory and viking subjects. This process continued in the new year. Edward took his army to Stamford, ordered the building of a *burh* and took the submission of the inhabitants. As for Aethelflaed, she took control of Leicester early in the year, whilst, according to the Mercian Register, the people of York promised to submit to her, too. Before this happened, however, on 12 June Aethelflaed died at Tamworth, the *burh* she had built in 913.[12] On hearing this, Edward went straight to Tamworth and, in the *Chronicle's* words, 'occupied the borough'.[13] Following this, he received the submission of all the Mercians who had been subject to Aethelflaed, as well as that of the Welsh princes and their people. Then he travelled with his army north to Nottingham and captured it. Four of the Five Boroughs (after Derby, Stamford and Leicester) were now under his control. The *Anglo-Saxon Chronicle's* final entry for 918 bluntly recorded that 'all the people who had settled in Mercia, both Danish and English, submitted to him'.[14] This implies that the last of the Five Boroughs, Lincoln, also surrendered to Edward and that, by the end of 918, the kingdom of the Anglo-Saxons had been extended to the river Humber.

919–924

Edward's ambitions extended beyond England and even Britain. Some time between 917 and 919 his daughter Eadgifu married the king of the West Franks, Charles the Simple (898–922). In this way Edward was carrying on a recent West Saxon tradition of finding marriages at foreign courts for members of the ruling dynasty. His grandfather Aethelwulf and his uncle Aethelbald had both married Judith, the daughter of Charles the Bald, and his sister Aelfthryth had become the wife of count Baldwin II of Flanders. Eadgifu's marriage was prestigious and added lustre to Edward's kingship. But it was also supposed to be helpful in a more practical sense, too: information, resources and mutual support were supposed to flow between the allies in good times and in bad.

The last few years of Edward's reign are described only patchily in the *Anglo-Saxon Chronicle*. There was more *burh*-building in 919, at Thelwall and Manchester, to further strengthen the English grip on the north-west and the river Mersey. In 920 another *burh* and a bridge over the river Trent were constructed at Nottingham, whilst yet another, at Bakewell, plugged a gap on the river Derwent between the other new forts at Manchester and Nottingham. As Edward went north into the Peak District in 920, he was met by the king of Scots and by Ragnall, the viking ruler of York; with them were other leading men of the north, and according to the *Chronicle* 'all who live in Northumbria, both English and Danish, Norsemen and others, and also the king of the Strathclyde Welsh and all the Strathclyde Welsh, chose him as father and lord'.[15]

There is little sign in the *Chronicle* that Edward's progress north during these years was particularly difficult. But there is other evidence to hint at the problems he was dealing with in the last phase of his reign. Events in the north of his extended kingdom probably preoccupied Edward more than anything else. With its emphasis on the affairs of southern England, the *Anglo-Saxon Chronicle* contains little if any information about what was happening in the north during the second decade of the tenth century. There are no surviving royal charters from the period 910–924 either, so it is impossible to get any kind of insight into the dynamics of

Edward's court or the allegiances he was able to cultivate. There are other written sources, however, English, Irish and Scottish, which, together with surviving coins, provide at least some detail about what was clearly a significant period in the history of this region. Perhaps the two most important individuals in this context were Ragnall and Sihtric. They were probably brothers, but they were certainly grandsons of Ivarr the Boneless, one of the viking leaders against whom Alfred the Great had fought in the 870s. The careers of Ragnall and Sihtric are hard to piece together, but it seems that they, along with other grandsons of Ivarr, were expelled from Norse-controlled Dublin in 902. For the next dozen years or so, they had various adventures in Scotland, northern England and back in Ireland, but it was from 914 that their campaigns began to have a significant political and military impact. In that year Ragnall sailed north to the river Tyne and seized the lands of Ealdred, the ruler of Bamburgh. Having been forced to flee, Ealdred joined forces with Constantine, the king of Scots, and returned to confront Ragnall, only to be defeated by him in battle at Corbridge. After dividing his conquered territories between his followers, Ragnall returned to raiding in Scotland and Ireland, but in 918, he was back in the north where he won a second victory at Corbridge over the Scots and the English of Bamburgh. Ragnall now felt strong enough to take power in York early in 919, the same year his brother Sihtric recaptured Dublin. Sihtric then followed this up with an attack on north-western Mercia in 920, getting as far as Davenport in Cheshire. It is in the context of the rise to power of Ragnall and Sihtric in York and Dublin that the submissions made to Edward in 920 and described in the *Chronicle* should be put. Not so much acknowledgements of subjection to Edward by the northern leaders, they perhaps amounted more to a declaration of a general truce between all those who took part – an attempt to stop events getting out of control and to prevent Sihtric's raid of 920 becoming the first of many. To be sure, Edward seems to have been perfectly content to allow Ragnall to wield power over much of Northumbria from his base at York until his death in late 920 or early 921. He was succeeded as ruler there by Sihtric.

Edward's relationship with the Mercians who had been ruled by his sister and her husband might not have been straightforward either. The Mercian Register records how, in 919 after Aethelflaed's death in the previous year, her daughter Aelfwyn 'was deprived of all authority in Mercia and taken into Wessex'.[16] This may imply that the Mercians had expected Aelfwyn to carry on acting as their ruler in the same ways Aethelred and Aethelflaed had, but that Edward removed her in what amounted to a *coup d'état* because he wanted to exercise personal control over English Mercia himself. This is speculation, however, and there is nothing else from the tenth century to cast light on Edward's relationship with the Mercians after this. However, the twelfth-century historian William of Malmesbury mentions a Mercian revolt at Chester in 924. Perhaps this was a result of enduring Mercian bitterness at the way Aelfwyn had been treated and at the imposition of direct West Saxon rule over her inheritance, but in the end, the causes of this obscure event remain unclear. It was important, though, William of Malmesbury claims, because it was only a matter of days after suppressing the revolt, on 17 July 924 at Farndon, about ten miles south of Chester, that Edward died.[17] His body was taken and buried at the New Minster, Winchester, the monastery he had founded in 901.

924–939

The events immediately following Edward's death are confused in the evidence and hard to piece together. The late king was married three times and had at least fourteen children. His first wife, Ecgwynn (whose background is obscure), was the mother of the future King Aethelstan, who was probably born about 893/4. By 901, however, Edward had married Aelfflaed, daughter of the ealdorman of Wessex, and their eldest son, Aelfweard, was presumably born soon after that. Finally, Eadgifu, daughter of the ealdorman of Kent, had become Edward's third wife by about 920. Two of their sons, Edmund and Eadred, were later kings. Before this, however, Aethelstan's position as Edward's eldest surviving son clearly gave him a strong claim to succeed his father as king in 924. However, by the time of his death, it seems that Edward had made plans to involve Aelfweard, the eldest son of his second marriage, in his succession plans as well. Indeed, it is likely that Aelfweard had become Edward's principal heir by then and that he was supposed to become king. But if this was the intention, it was frustrated almost immediately. Aelfweard himself died very soon (only sixteen days, the *Chronicle* reported) after his father. And what is more, Aethelstan was chosen as their king by the Mercians.[18] Whether the second of these events preceded or followed the first is unclear, but they gave Aethelstan the chance to succeed to the whole of his late father's kingdom. He was consecrated and crowned king by Archbishop Aelfhelm of Canterbury at Kingston upon Thames on 4 September 925.

It is perfectly possible that King Edward had wanted his kingdom of the Anglo-Saxons to be divided between his two sons after his death – Wessex to Aelfweard and Mercia to Aethelstan. It is just as possible, though, that he wanted Aelfweard to be his sole successor and that the Mercians elected Aethelstan as their king in a show of defiance. Edward was near Chester when he died, and William of Malmesbury later alleged that he was there to put down a revolt, presumably by elements in that region who had remained unreconciled to Edward's kingship since Aethelflaed's death in 918.[19] Having been brought up at his aunt's court, as will be seen, Aethelstan was perhaps seen more as Aethelflaed's heir than Edward's.

Aelfweard did have a younger brother, Edwin, who may have harboured ambitions to take Aelfweard's place in Wessex, but in the end, Aethelstan was able to assert himself over the entire kingdom. This was not inevitable, however. Over a year passed between the death of Edward the Elder and the consecration of King Aethelstan. This alone hints at the difficulties which surrounded the latter's succession to the throne, but there is other evidence, too, of tensions within royal circles during the mid-920s. Aethelstan's personal connections with Wessex were not strong. In the twelfth century, William of Malmesbury described how in the 890s Aethelstan was sent by his grandfather King Alfred to be educated and trained at the court of Aethelflaed and Aethelred in Mercia. It is reasonable to assume that he subsequently took part in his aunt's campaigns against the Vikings, and he may even have exercised some sort of political and military leadership in Mercia after her death in 918. So his upbringing and experiences in Mercia probably explain why he was chosen as king there in 924. But if he was respected in Mercia, Aethelstan cannot have been well known to the leading men of Wessex, and William of Malmesbury later claimed that Winchester (where Edward the Elder and Aelfweard were buried) was a particular centre of opposition to him.[20] Aethelstan's decision to be crowned at Kingston upon Thames, on the border between Wessex and Mercia, suggests that he was keen to start afresh and rule a united kingdom, but soon after his consecration, rumours about Aethelstan's legitimacy began to circulate, and there are suggestions of a Winchester-based plot to blind and depose the new king. Aethelstan's half-brother, Edwin, may have been implicated in this plot and his death in 933 (he was 'drowned at sea', the *Chronicle* said) was mysterious enough to justify suspicions that his relationship with Aethelstan never improved. A source from Flanders alleged that Edwin was driven out of England 'by some disturbance in his [*sic*] kingdom', and Symeon of Durham (writing in the twelfth century) went so far as to include an explicit allegation in his chronicle that, in 933, 'King Aethelstan ordered his brother Edwin to be drowned at sea'.[21]

Once established as king, Aethelstan set about continuing the work of Edward and Aethelflaed on his northern frontier. His first impulse was to consolidate what he had inherited and so in January 926, he met Sihtric, the viking ruler of York, at Tamworth. It is likely that each agreed not to invade the other's lands or support the other's enemies, and the arrangement was sealed by the marriage of Sihtric to Aethelstan's sister. But any hope the two rulers might have had of establishing a stable working relationship were dashed when Sihtric died in 927. Aethelstan promptly invaded Northumbria on the pretext of coming to his sister's aid. But whilst this was opportunistic to an extent, it may also have been a necessary pre-emptive strike against others looking to secure Sihtric's kingdom for themselves. Aethelstan's principal rivals in Northumbria after Sihtric's death appear to have been Olaf, Sihtric's son, and Guthfrith, another grandson of Ivarr the Boneless. Guthfrith came with a fleet from Ireland, perhaps to support his young kinsman Olaf or to make his own bid for power. Aethelstan may have had to drive Guthfrith out of York, and Olaf may have fled to Ireland. Guthfrith may even have returned and made another unsuccessful bid to capture York. In any event, precisely what happened is unclear. The *Anglo-Saxon Chronicle*, and later William of Malmesbury, were both at pains to claim that Aethelstan added Northumbria to his kingdom lawfully and smoothly; other sources, most notably a Latin poem written soon after the events, have been seen as supporting the idea that Aethelstan's acquisition of Northumbria was more akin to a military takeover.[22] Either way, by the summer of 927, the other rulers of Britain felt compelled to recognise Aethelstan's supremacy. On 12 July, at Eamont near Penrith, the king of Scots, the ruler of Strathclyde, two Welsh princes and the lord of Bamburgh made peace with Aethelstan and accepted his overlordship. According to William of Malmesbury, Aethelstan followed this with a trip to Hereford, where he compelled the Welsh princes to submit to him once again, imposed a huge annual tribute and fixed his frontier with Wales at the river Wye. He then travelled further south-west, William claimed, drove 'the Western Britons who are called Cornish' out of Exeter, which he refortified, and fixed the limit of their territory at the river Tamar.[23]

Submissions like those at Eamont and Hereford had taken place before, most notably in 920 when Edward the Elder had been king. But the events of 927 were more profoundly significant. In 920, there was no suggestion that Edward would exercise any practical authority over territory north of the Humber. After 927, by contrast, it is clear that Aethelstan regarded Northumbria as part of his kingdom, and a southern king was intending to rule the north directly for the first time. At the same time, using force or at least the threat of it, he had taken active and assertive steps to define his frontiers with the Welsh and the Cornish.

The meetings and events of summer 927 took place almost exactly three years after the death of Edward the Elder. In that short time Aethelstan had averted the division of his father's kingdom, reconstructed it, reinforced its western frontiers and extended it to the Scottish border. And as Aethelstan's power increased, so his reputation spread abroad. One of his half-sisters, Eadhild, had already married Hugh, duke of the Franks, in 926, and William of Malmesbury describes at length the magnificence of the embassy sent to Aethelstan's court by Hugh to make his proposal.[24] But an alliance with the English king became even more attractive to foreign rulers as Aethelstan's reign went on. So, in 929 or 930, another of his half-sisters, Eadgyth, married Otto (later emperor Otto I the Great), the son of Henry the Fowler, king of the East Franks (d.936). This marriage was followed soon by that of yet another of Aethelstan's half-sisters, probably called Aelfgifu, to Louis, the brother of Rudolf II of Burgundy. Such alliances were designed to bring cultural and intellectual benefits to both sides as English and Frankish scholars and experts crossed the Channel to share knowledge and intellectual resources. But they were primarily political and military arrangements which aimed to provide increased security for the rulers and limit their opponents' opportunities for resistance. Even so, Aethelstan's successes did not go unchallenged. Political events in the years immediately after 927 are poorly recorded and it is impossible to know what was happening in northern Britain. But by 934, for reasons which are unclear, the peace with the Scots had broken down. Aethelstan took an army and a fleet to Scotland 'and ravaged much of it', the *Chronicle* said.[25] In the twelfth century, Symeon of Durham went into further detail about this expedition. On his way north, Symeon records, Aethelstan stopped at Chester-le-Street to pay his respects to Saint Cuthbert and ask for his support, and from there, he took his army as far north as Dunnottar (south of modern Aberdeen) and his fleet even farther north, to Caithness.[26] No English king had campaigned on such a scale or over such distances before, and Aethelstan's awe-inspiring show of force quickly persuaded King Constantine to submit to him once more and hand over his son as a hostage. Constantine's defeat seems evident, too, from a charter issued by Aethelstan in September 934 when the two kings were together at Buckingham. Not only did the king of Scots find himself deep in Aethelstan's territory (surely not something he would have wanted), but in the witness list to the charter he is described as 'subregulus'. A king, yes, but unequivocally an inferior one.[27]

But even these intimidating demonstrations of force and authority did not keep Aethelstan's enemies subdued for long. Having concluded that they would stand a better chance of defeating him if they acted together rather than separately, by 937 a coalition had been formed, and armies led by King Constantine, his son-in-law Olaf Guthfrithson, the Norse ruler of Dublin, and Owain, the ruler of Strathclyde, confronted Aethelstan and his forces at a place called *Brunanburh*. It has never been established with certainty where this battle took place, and good cases have been made for sites in Cheshire, Yorkshire and Dumfriesshire. Nevertheless, commemorated and described in a poem in the *Anglo-Saxon Chronicle*, Aethelstan's victory at *Brunanburh* is the most famous event of his reign. According to the poem, the battle was long (it lasted a whole day) and brutal. But an English victory, inspired by the king himself ('lord of nobles, dispenser of treasure to men') and by his half-brother Edmund, was never in doubt, and ultimately it was total and decisive. As the battle ended, the *Chronicle* recorded, 'five young kings lay on that field of battle, slain by the swords, and also seven of Olaf's earls, and a countless host of seamen and Scots'. Olaf and Constantine had been forced to flee for their lives, with the latter leaving his dead son behind him. In the concluding words of the *Chronicle*,

> Never yet in this island before this, by what books tell us and our ancient sages, was a greater slaughter of a host made by the edge of the sword, since the Angles and the Saxons came here from the east, invading Britain over the wide seas, and the proud assailants, warriors eager for glory, overcame the Britons and won a country.[28]

In other words, nothing as important had happened in Britain for over 500 years, and other sources only reinforce the view that, in contemporary minds, this was an event of deep significance. The *Annals of Ulster* described *Brunanburh* as 'a great, lamentable and horrible battle' in which thousands of Norsemen were killed. And at the end of the tenth century, Ealdorman Aethelweard explained how it was referred to simply as the 'great battle' by the common people.[29]

Little is known about the last two years of Aethelstan's reign. Continental sources record that he sent a fleet to Flanders in 939 to help his nephew Louis IV, king of the West Franks, suppress a revolt.[30] Louis was the son of King Charles the Simple (d.929) and his wife (Aethelstan's half-sister) Eadgifu. Charles and Eadgifu were married some time between 917 and 919, but Louis (born in 920 or 921) had been sent for his own protection to Aethelstan's court following his father's deposition and imprisonment in 922–3. Later, in 936, when envoys arrived in England from France intending to take Louis back and install him as king, it was Aethelstan who insisted that an English escort should accompany his nephew. The bond between uncle and nephew was clearly still strong three years later. But other than that, nothing survives to cast light on Aethelstan's activities between his victory at *Brunanburh* and his death at Gloucester on 27 October 939. He was buried at

Malmesbury Abbey, a monastery to which the king was particularly devoted. This may be enough to explain Aethelstan's wish to rest there, but it is interesting that he did not choose to be interred with his predecessors at Winchester. Perhaps this was his final snub to the forces which had struggled to prevent his succession in 924, but if there were still those in England who resented his success, others could only marvel at it. According to the *Annals of Ulster*, Aethelstan was 'the pillar of the dignity of the western world', whilst, half a century or so after his death, Ealdorman Aethelweard described Aethelstan as 'a very mighty king and worthy of honour'. During his reign, 'The fields of Britain were consolidated into one, there was peace everywhere, and abundance of all things'.[31]

DEBATE 4

Where was *Brunanburh*?

It is not unusual for early medieval battles to be poorly described in the surviving sources. Hardly anything is known about what happened at *Ellendun* in 825, Edington in 878 or even Ashingdon in 1016. But at least we are fairly certain where these battles took place. Frustratingly, this is not the case with arguably the greatest battle in Anglo-Saxon history, *Brunanburh*. The *Annals of Ulster* described *Brunanburh* as 'a great, lamentable and horrible battle', whilst Ealdorman Aethelweard said it was remembered simply as 'the great battle' by the time he was writing at the end of the tenth century. But almost all our detailed information about this event comes from seventy-three lines of verse in the *Anglo-Saxon Chronicle's* entry for 937. These contain valuable evidence about the participants, the course of the battle and its outcome; nevertheless, the poem fails to specify where it actually took place, saying only that Aethelstan and his brother Edmund that day 'won by the sword's edge undying glory in battle around *Brunanburh*'.[1] Meaning something like 'The stronghold of someone called Bruna', naturally many attempts have been made over the years to identify the site. Claims have been made for places with similar-sounding names across all parts of the British mainland. Brinsworth near Sheffield, Bromswold near Huntingdon and Burnswark in Dumfriesshire have all been suggested. But ultimately more than spelling is required in a case like this. It is not clear how the allied armies from Ireland, Scotland and Strathclyde (led respectively by Olaf Guthfrithson, King Constantine and Owain) reached the battlefield, but it is likely that the Dublin Norse crossed the Irish Sea by the route which usually took them as quickly and directly as possible to York, and it is perfectly possible that the Scots and the Strathclyde Welsh sailed down the west coast as well. It is also reasonable to argue that the allied armies came together somewhere in northern England. If so, a rendezvous somewhere around the Wirral peninsula in Cheshire would make sense. Here, on the Mersey estuary at a strategically vital point on the frontier between Norse and Mercian areas of influence, is the modern village of Bromborough, and place-name evidence suggests that an Old English form of Bromborough was indeed *Brunanburh*. There may have been another stronghold belonging to someone called Bruna, of course, but linguistic and logistical considerations strongly support the case for Bromborough as the likely site of this most legendary and mysterious of battles. Meanwhile, 'Exaggerating the importance of this victory is difficult, for had Aethelstan's opponents won, the West Saxon hegemony over the whole mainland of Britain would have disintegrated'.[2] True enough, if *Brunaburh* is seen as an essentially defensive exercise on Aethelstan's part. But the fragility of his hold on northern England was exposed as soon as he died. Olaf Guthfrithson regained control of York, and it was not until the death of Erik Bloodaxe in 954 that Aethelstan's successors could confidently begin to see northern England as permanently theirs.

1 *Annals of Ulster*, pp. 384–5; *Chron. Aethelweard*, pp. 54–5; ASC 937.
2 Foot, *Aethelstan*, p. 171.

939–946

Aethelweard was writing during the reign of Aethelred II, when Aethelstan's achievements were under serious threat, so perhaps there were elements of nostalgia or wishful thinking in the chronicler's assessment. And to be sure, Aethelstan's successors had to struggle to keep his kingdom together, and there was no guarantee it would survive intact. The first challenges came almost as soon as Aethelstan was dead. Childless (perhaps deliberately so), Aethelstan was succeeded by his half-brother, Edmund, the eldest son of Edward the Elder and his third wife, Eadgifu. Edmund was eighteen in 939, and the events of his short reign (he died in 946) are poorly recorded in the *Anglo-Saxon Chronicle*. It is clear enough, however, that much of Edmund's reign was taken up with his struggle to hold on to Aethelstan's acquisitions. In particular, the resurgent Vikings of Dublin challenged him for control of the north-east midlands and the kingdom of York.

By the end of 939, the ruler of Norse Dublin, Olaf Guthfrithson, who had been amongst those defeated by Aethelstan at *Brunanburh*, was back in England. The Vikings of York had acclaimed him as their king and invited him to return. In 940, Olaf advanced as far south as Northampton, but after being seen off there, he turned on the Mercian royal centre at Tamworth and took it 'by storm', with heavy losses on both sides.[32] King Edmund then confronted Olaf at Leicester, but the viking leader escaped and soon a truce was made. It is likely that Edmund was compelled to make significant territorial concessions to Olaf, perhaps ceding control of the north-east midlands to him. But if this is what happened, it proved to be only a short-term setback for Edmund. When Olaf died in 941, the king was able to recover his losses. The *Anglo-Saxon Chronicle*, again shifting into verse in recognition of the importance of these events, recorded how Edmund 'overran' Mercia and the Five Boroughs. This was portrayed almost evangelically by the chronicler as a liberation of the (presumably Christian) Vikings who had lived in these areas since the late ninth century from the tyranny of the (presumably pagan) Norsemen.[33]

But York was still under viking control, after Olaf had been succeeded as ruler there by his cousin, Olaf Sihtricson. In 943, however, this Olaf was baptised with King Edmund as his sponsor, and soon after that, Olaf Guthfrithson's brother Ragnall, who was at York by 943, was also baptised. So clearly there were contacts between the two sides, and perhaps some kind of negotiated settlement was being prepared. However, if this was the plan, it did not work. The *Anglo-Saxon Chronicle* recorded how, in 944, 'King Edmund reduced all Northumbria under his rule, and drove out two kings, Olaf, Sihtric's son, and Ragnall, Guthfrith's son'. Later in the century Ealdorman Aethelweard gave the credit for this success to Archbishop Wulfstan of York and Ealdorman Aethelmund of Mercia.[34] Either way, the initiative was with the English king once again. In 945, Edmund ravaged the kingdom of Strathclyde, blinded the two sons of the ruler there and then gave the territory to Malcolm I (d.954), who had become king of Scots some time between 940 and 945 when his cousin, the aged King Constantine, had retired to a monastery. In return, probably with the threat from the Vikings of Dublin still in mind, Malcolm agreed to be Edmund's ally 'both on sea and on land'.[35] Strathclyde had not been one of Aethelstan's conquests, and Edmund did not intend to incorporate it into his restored kingdom in 945. But, having taken back control of Mercia and Northumbria, by attacking Strathclyde and then recognising it as within Malcolm's sphere of influence, he would have stirred memories of Aethelstan's campaigns in northern Scotland and in the process reasserted his predecessor's claim to be the dominant ruler in Britain.

After having been forced to stomach Olaf Guthfrithson's victory in 940, Edmund's successes over the next five years were remarkable. If anything, he had managed to build on Aethelstan's achievements and consolidate them, and all of this when he was only in his mid-twenties. Unfortunately, however, he did not live to enjoy his victories, because on 26 May 946 he was murdered. 'It was widely known how he ended his life', the *Chronicle* recorded, 'that Leofa stabbed him at Pucklechurch' in Gloucestershire. Later, in the twelfth century, John of Worcester added some more detail which suggests that the killing was not politically motivated: Edmund was slain as he tried to rescue his steward, who was being robbed by Leofa, 'a most wicked thief'.[36]

946–955

King Edmund was buried at Glastonbury by abbot Dunstan. He left two sons, Eadwig and Edgar, but the former was only five or six and the latter only about three, so Edmund was succeeded as king by his brother, Eadred, who was consecrated at

Kingston upon Thames on 16 August 946. The chronology of Eadred's reign is confused, and the surviving sources contradict each other about what happened. Most importantly, whilst the *Anglo-Saxon Chronicle* gives the fullest account of the main events, its dating of them is often questionable. Having said this, it is possible to put forward a reasonably coherent description of Eadred's reign, even if much of the detail remains uncertain. One thing is quite evident, however: for Eadred, as it had been for Edmund and Aethelstan, northern England was the king's main priority.

In 947 at Tanshelf, near the river Aire at Pontefract in the West Riding of Yorkshire, Eadred received pledges of loyalty from Archbishop Wulfstan of York 'and all the councillors of the Northumbrians'. Shortly after this, however, these same men 'were false to it all, both pledge and oaths as well', and they accepted another viking leader, Erik 'Bloodaxe', as their king.[37] He was the son of Harald 'Fairhair', king of Norway (d.*c*.930) and was destined to become a celebrated character in the Icelandic sagas of the twelfth and thirteenth centuries. His epithet 'Bloodaxe', for example, was first used in one of these works, but much of what was written in them is hard to credit as historically accurate. Nevertheless, back in the 940s, Erik's short-lived contribution to the politics of northern England was certainly dramatic. King Eadred responded to what amounted to a declaration of northern independence (in 948, according to the *Chronicle*) by ravaging the rebellious land. Amongst the casualties was St Wilfrid's 'glorious minster' at Ripon, which was burnt to the ground. Thinking, presumably, that he had made his point, Eadred began his march south, only to be intercepted by a northern army at Castleford where 'a great slaughter' took place and the rearguard of Eadred's army was wiped out. The furious king then decided to return to the north and 'destroy it utterly', but before he did, Erik's erstwhile supporters abandoned him and paid compensation to Eadred.[38] Linked with these events (although dated to 952 in the *Chronicle*) may have been an order by Eadred to arrest Archbishop Wulfstan and remove him from his position. He was reinstated a few years later, but presumably only after Eadred felt sure of the loyalty of the northern elite.[39] An entry in the *Chronicle* for 949 then records the return to Northumbria of Olaf Sihtricson. He may even have returned with Eadred's approval but, if he did, royal support did not prevent him from being driven out of Northumbria in 952 and replaced as king there by Erik (this may also have been the reason for Wulfstan's arrest, if the *Chronicle's* date of 952 for this event is correct). Two years later, though, Erik was expelled from York for the second time, and this time the consequences were decisive. According to the *Chronicle* entry for 954, after Erik's departure 'Eadred succeeded to the kingdom of the Northumbrians'. Later, in the twelfth century, Symeon of Durham referred to the same event (although he wrongly dated it to 952): 'Here the kingdom of the Northumbrians came to an end, and henceforward the province was administered by earls'.[40]

As for Erik Bloodaxe, later evidence purports to describe what happened to him after his expulsion. In the thirteenth century, the chronicler-monk of St Albans, Roger of Wendover, described how Erik, his son and his brother were killed 'treacherously' by a man called Maccus at Stainmore, 'a certain lonely place', where the Roman road between York and Carlisle crosses the Pennines. He added that Erik had been betrayed to Maccus, an old enemy of Erik's, by Oswulf, lord of Bamburgh, whose English family had been ruling much of the territory between the rivers Tees and Tweed (the old kingdom of Bernicia) for nearly a century by this time.[41] And it is certainly correct that, following Erik's death, it was this same Oswulf who was appointed by Eadred as the first ealdorman of all Northumbria (north and south) and who ruled it under, or at least with the consent of, the king. Concerned, perhaps, that Erik or his relatives might make another bid for power in Northumbria, Oswulf had good reason to plot their assassination. King Eadred himself, however, like his brother before him, did not live to enjoy the fruits of his success. He appears to have suffered from some kind of chronic illness for most of his life, and this was probably the cause of his death at Frome in Somerset on 23 November 955. He was buried at the Old Minster, Winchester, and having had no sons of his own, he was succeeded as king by his nephew, the elder son of King Edmund, Eadwig.

956–959

Eadwig was probably no more than fifteen when he became king, and his short reign was not viewed positively by many of those who survived him and wrote about it. He was immoral, impious and incompetent, it was alleged. The most scandalous story about him records how, the day after his coronation, no less a figure than abbot Dunstan of Glastonbury discovered the new king in bed with his future wife, but also with his future mother-in-law. Such reports are not necessarily to be taken at face value, however. They are found first in the earliest biography of Dunstan, written about 1000, and one thing that is known for certain about Eadwig is that he and Dunstan quarrelled seriously, as a result of which the latter went into exile. Dunstan and his biographer cannot be considered impartial observers of Eadwig's reign.

Eadwig was certainly not an inactive king. About ninety charters survive from his reign – a remarkably large number for a period of only four years. Most of those (about sixty) were issued in 956–7, when perhaps Eadwig was trying to bolster his support with lavish gifts of land or attempting to raise money through the sale of privileges. It may be significant, however, that many of those estates granted by the king in 956–7 had recently been granted, also by royal charter, in the previous twenty years. So there is a possibility that the king was taking lands from individuals or institutions he did not favour and re-granting them to those he did. If this was the case, such conduct was dangerously provocative and would almost inevitably have resulted in the development of rivalries and factions within the ruling elite. It may therefore provide the background to the exile of abbot Dunstan in 956 and the events of 957. In that year, Archbishop Oda of Canterbury, in the words of one text of the *Chronicle*, 'separated King Eadwig and Aelfgifu, because they were too closely related', whilst another version recorded that 'In this year the atheling Edgar succeeded to the kingdom of the Mercians'.[42] Dunstan's biographer characterised Edgar's taking of power as a legitimate *coup*: Eadwig 'was wholly deserted by the northern people, being despised because he acted foolishly in the government committed to him, ruining with vain hatred the shrewd and the wise, and admitting with loving zeal the ignorant and those like himself'.[43] It is worth repeating that this interpretation is hardly neutral, and it is possible that the division of 957 was more amicable and peaceful than it appears at first sight. When Edgar issued charters after that he was usually referred to as 'king of the Mercians' and occasionally as 'king of the Northumbrians', too, although there are a small number of charters which gave him a grander title, two in particular referring to him as 'king of the English'. Meanwhile, Eadwig's charters styled him 'king of the English' for the rest of his reign. In addition, Eadwig's coins were the only currency in England between 957 and 959; Edgar issued no coins until his brother was dead.[44] In other words, it is reasonable to conclude that Eadwig retained supreme authority in England until he died and that the division of 957 was a negotiated settlement designed to delegate power north of the Thames to Edgar – perhaps it was even Eadwig's way of acknowledging Edgar as his heir. However, the possibility remains that the division of the kingdom between north and south had been in place since 955. One text of the *Anglo-Saxon Chronicle* records how, on King Eadred's death in that year, Eadwig became king of Wessex and Edgar king of Mercia. The chronicler is usually blamed here for misdating the division and placing it two years too early. But it may just be that Eadwig and Edgar aimed to partition the kingdom and act as joint kings from the start. Perhaps the events of 957 were simply a confirmation of this.[45]

So the evidence about Eadwig's reign remains obscure and ambiguous. It is hard to know what to make of Bishop Aethelwold's of Winchester's view that Eadwig 'had through the ignorance of childhood dispersed his kingdom and divided its unity, and also distributed the lands of the holy churches to rapacious strangers'.[46] This might mean that Eadwig's actions had alienated so many influential people that Mercia seceded from his realm in 957. Alternatively, it might simply indicate that Eadwig's own decision to divide his kingdom was simply, in Aethelwold's view, a mistake. Ealdorman Aethelweard's judgement was clearer and more positive: Eadwig was very beautiful, the chronicler claimed, and was called 'All-fair' by the common people. And more importantly in this context, Eadwig 'held the kingdom for four years, and deserved to be loved'. But by the twelfth century, the negative view of Eadwig had largely prevailed. To William of Malmesbury, Eadwig was 'a wanton youth, and one who misused his personal beauty in lascivious behaviour'. John of Worcester, referring to the events of 957, claims that Eadwig 'was abandoned by the Mercians and the Northumbrians with contempt'.[47] Unfortunately for the historian, the frantic, arguably reckless, charter activity of 956–7 was not maintained, and little is known about what really happened in England between summer 957 and Eadwig's death on 1 October 959. He was buried at the New Minster in Winchester, and his sixteen-year old brother, Edgar, succeeded to the whole kingdom.

959–975

Many of those who wrote so critically of Eadwig did so, at least in part, to provide a contrast with the king they esteemed and revered, Edgar. These contemporary observers successfully ensured that their portrayal of Edgar as a wise, pious and successful ruler was the one which stuck. And the epithet given to him in the twelfth century, *pacificus* ('the Peacemaker' or 'the Peaceable'), is evidence of the way in which, even by then, his reign had come to represent a golden age of stability and prosperity.[48] The *Anglo-Saxon Chronicle* entry for 959, written later, set the tone when it described how 'things improved greatly' whilst Edgar was king,

> and God granted him that he lived in peace as long as he lived; and, as was necessary for him, he laboured zealously for this; he exalted God's praise far and wide, and loved God's law; and he improved the peace of the people more than the kings who were before him in the memory of man.

And there is more along the same lines before the entry ends.[49]

Edgar was lauded by those who subsequently described his reign (most of whom were monks) because he was reputedly such an enthusiastic and active supporter of efforts to reform and refound monasteries across southern England. Indeed, this movement was at its height during the 960s and 970s, and many of the most significant recorded events of Edgar's reign relate to it. Thus, the leading reformers were promoted by him: Dunstan became archbishop of Canterbury almost as soon as Edgar became king in 959, whilst Oswald held the bishopric of Worcester (from 962) and the archbishopric of York (from 971) together. Meanwhile, Edgar's old tutor, Aethelwold, became bishop of Winchester in 963. Within a few months, Aethelwold had expelled the secular clergy from the Old Minster at Winchester and replaced them with monks. Perhaps in the same year, Edgar ordered that all secular priests should be expelled from monastic sites and replaced with monks and nuns, an order that seems to have been implemented at several monasteries in 964. The high-point of the reign in this context came some time between 966 and 973, at Winchester again, when a church council was held to standardise monastic practice in England. A document, the *Regularis Concordia*, was drawn up to set out in detail what had been agreed. This desire for uniformity on the king's part was evident in other areas in the early 970s, too, when Edgar reformed the English coinage: henceforth (from about 973), all silver pennies issued throughout England would be of the same type, whilst new measures were introduced to control coin production.

More will be said about these developments in later chapters,* but they all only serve to compound the difficulty of assessing more objectively whether Edgar's reputation as a great king is deserved. The fundamental problem remains that very little information is recorded about the basic political outline of his reign. The

* Below, pp. 145–7, 178–88

Chronicle, after the long hymn of praise in the 959 entry, hardly mentions Edgar again until 973, and after that, the only entry relevant entries record his death in 975 and lavish yet more undiluted tribute on him. It does seem right to say, however, that England between 959 and 975 was relatively free of either external attack or internal upheaval. No viking activity is recorded in the kingdom, for example, between the death of Erik Bloodaxe in 954 and the resumption of attacks in 980, although Edgar did order Thanet to be ravaged in 969, and it is conceivable that this might have had something to do with viking raiders trying to use one of their traditional bases. And there was certainly other military activity in Britain whilst Edgar was king. Twelfth-century chroniclers described, without a hint of doubt as to the practicalities of such an undertaking, how Edgar's fleet would circumnavigate the whole of Britain every summer.[50] And indeed, such events as are recorded for his reign suggest that regular shows of force like this, albeit on a more manageable scale, might have been regarded as necessary by the king. The *Chronicle* reported, for example, how a certain Thored, Gunnar's son, ravaged Westmoreland, on the frontier with the kingdom of Strathclyde, in 966. Then, Welsh sources record an English expedition to north Wales in 967, led by Ealdorman Aelfhere of Mercia, and attacks on Anglesey in 971 and 972 by two brothers, Maccus and Gothfrith. Meanwhile, the new king of Scots, Kenneth II, raided into English territory, probably in 971, reaching Stainmore and the Lake District.[51] Clearly, the situation on the northern and western frontiers of the English kingdom was still unsettled by the 970s, and, whilst not perhaps too threatening individually, collectively these events may have lain behind the most famous events of Edgar's reign in 973. On 11 May of that year, the feast of Pentecost, Edgar was consecrated king at Bath. This may have been his second consecration (following an unrecorded one at the start of the reign) and the first stage of a symbolic declaration by Edgar of authority over the whole of Britain. The second stage followed immediately after the rituals at Bath when the king sailed with a large fleet around Wales to Chester. There he was met by six or eight other British rulers (the surviving accounts differ in detail) who acknowledged the English king's overlordship by rowing him along the river Dee with Edgar himself taking the helm.[52]

The events at Bath and Chester, some have suggested, took place in the same year (973) as the standardisation of the coinage and the publication of the *Regularis Concordia*. But even if they did not happen simultaneously, together these measures can still be considered as different elements of the same scheme on Edgar's part – to underpin England's dominance within Britain by strengthening some of his kingdom's most important internal systems and structures. But if this was the plan, it was still being implemented when Edgar died on 8 July 975 at the age of only thirty-one or thirty-two. He was buried, like his father Edmund before him, at Glastonbury Abbey.

Notes

1 *Chron. Aethelweard*, p. 51.
2 K&L, p. 175; S350.

3 *ASC* 900.

4 *ASC* 900.

5 *ASC* 903.

6 *ASC* 906.

7 *Chron. Aethelweard*, pp. 52–3.

8 *ASC* 910.

9 *ASC* 914.

10 *ASC* 917 (Mercian Register).

11 The rest of this paragraph is based on *ASC* 917.

12 *ASC* 918 (Mercian Register).

13 *ASC* 918.

14 *ASC* 918.

15 *ASC* 920.

16 *ASC* 919 (Mercian Register).

17 *WMGRA*, i pp. 210–11.

18 *ASC* 924.

19 *WMGRA*, i pp. 210–11.

20 *WMGRA*, i pp. 222–3.

21 *ASC* 933; Flanders source quoted in Woolf, *From Pictland to Alba*, p. 163; *EHD*, i no.3 (p. 278).

22 *ASC* 927; *WMGRA*, i pp. 206–9, 212–15; Sarah Foot, *Aethelstan: The First King of England* (New Haven, 2011), p. 19.

23 *WMGRA*, i pp. 214–17.

24 *WMGRA*, i pp. 218–21.

25 *ASC* 934.

26 *EHD*, i no.3 (p. 278).

27 S426.

28 *ASC* 937.

29 Seán Mac Airt and Gearóid Mac Niocaill (ed.), *The Annals of Ulster (To AD 1131)* (Dublin, 1983), pp. 384–5; *Chron. Aethelweard*, pp. 54–5.

30 Foot, *Aethelstan*, pp. 183–4.

31 *Annals of Ulster*, pp. 386–7; *Chron. Aethelweard*, p. 54.

32 *ASC* 940–3.

33 *ASC* 942.

34 *ASC* 944; *Chron. Aethelweard*, p. 54.

35 *ASC* 945.

36 *ASC* 946; *JW*, ii pp. 398–9.

37 *ASC* 947.

38 *ASC* 948.

39 *ASC* 952.

40 *ASC* 954; *EHD*, i no.3 (p. 280).

41 *EHD*, i no.4 (p. 284).

42 *ASC* 957.

43 *EHD*, i no.234 (p. 901).

44 S. Keynes, 'Edgar, *rex admirabilis*', in Donald Scragg (ed.), *Edgar, King of the English 959–975* (Woodbridge, 2008), pp. 3–59, at pp. 7–9; C.P. Lewis, 'Edgar, Chester and the Kingdom of the Mercians, 957–9', in ibid, pp. 104–23, at pp. 116–17.

45 *ASC* 955.

46 *EHD*, i no.238 (p. 920).

47 *WMGRA*, i pp. 236–7; *JW*, ii pp. 406–7.

48 *JW*, ii pp. 424–5 ('pacificus rex Eadgarus').

49 *ASC* 959.

50 *WMGRA*, i pp. 256–7.

51 *ASC* 966; Woolf, *From Pictland to Alba*, pp. 206, 208–9.

52 Six 'kings': *ASC* D 973; eight 'sub-kings': *JW*, ii pp. 422–3.

6

RULING THE KINGDOM, 899–975

Alfred the Great transformed the kingdom of Wessex into the kingdom of the Anglo-Saxons. In the three-quarters of a century following his death in 899, Alfred's successors transformed the kingdom of the Anglo-Saxons into the kingdom of the English. The size of this kingdom is a matter of some dispute, but it is safe to say that, by the last quarter of the tenth century, it extended in practical terms from the English Channel to the river Tees and, in theoretical ones at least, as far north as the Scottish frontier. Precisely when this kingdom came into existence is also a keenly debated topic. Edward the Elder and Aethelstan have traditionally been seen as its principal architects. However, it has been argued most recently that the reign of King Edgar was the pivotal one in this context.[1]

The bumpy road to a single English kingdom

Put simply, three main factors underpinned the creation of a single English kingdom by the southern kings during the tenth century: their military success, their administrative reforms and their wealth. These three elements worked together, of course, and there were others (not least the nature of the opposition they faced, a degree of dynastic stability and sheer good fortune) which contributed greatly to their achievements. Moreover, it would be a mistake to think that the emergence of a single English kingdom was an inevitable, let alone an irreversible, process. There is no evidence that Alfred set out to create any such entity or that his successors did anything but act assertively to defend their territories and then capitalise on their successes as and when they could. There was little if any predestination or long-term planning in what they achieved, there were numerous times after 899 when developments might have headed in different directions, and there were plenty of forces tending towards political fragmentation rather than unity. The relationship between Wessex and Mercia was often tense, and the bonds between them often proved fragile. Historians have argued, for example, about the nature of the connection between the two in the first quarter of the tenth century.[2] Were they separate, independent realms whose rulers cooperated in a common cause? Or, far from being autonomous rulers, were Aethelred and Aethelflaed simply Edward the Elder's agents, answerable to him and bound to follow his lead? There is certainly room for interpreting Edward's actions on the deaths of Aethelred in 911 and Aethelflaed in 918, and his treatment of their daughter Aelfwyn in 919, as a series of aggressive and illegitimate power grabs which left a disgruntled and aggrieved Mercian ruling class reluctant to cooperate with its new West Saxon masters. Alternatively, however, it has been persuasively argued that English Mercia was already by 899 an integrated part of 'the kingdom of the Anglo-Saxons' which King Alfred had created and which King Edward inherited, that Aethelred and Aethelflaed ruled there under Edward as his willing subordinates and that the latter took over direct rule from them smoothly and with an impeccable right to do so once they were dead. It has even been argued that a new consecration ritual or *ordo* may have been devised for Edward the Elder which took account of his undivided rule over Wessex and English Mercia. Equally, it may have been written for the coronation of Aethelstan in 925.[3] Either way, the relationship between Wessex and Mercia remained under stress for some time to come, as the events following the death of King Eadred in 955 show.

From 924 onwards, royal power was retained by members of Edward's immediate family and their close relatives. This dynastic stability was an important reason why the southern kings continued to be successful. Having said that, issues surrounding the succession arose regularly and always had the potential to destabilise or undermine the regime. That they were usually resolved quickly (within a year or two) and (as far as can be judged from the evidence) peacefully may have had as much to with good luck as good judgement. Edward himself would not have been king for long if his cousin Aethelwold's revolt had been successful. It also seems likely that Edward's eventual successor, Aethelstan, was not his preferred choice as principal heir. Aethelstan was Edward's eldest surviving son, but he had been brought up at the court of his uncle and aunt in Mercia. Meanwhile back in Wessex, it was the king's son by his second marriage, Aelfweard, who looked set to succeed Edward. However, the Mercian Register records that Aethelstan was chosen by the Mercians as their king when Edward died in 924, and it was only Aelfweard's sudden death (a fortnight or so after his father's) that prevented a division of the old king's realm which might have become permanent.[4] Aethelstan's coronation did not take place until the end of September 925, more than a year after Edward had died, and, as was suggested earlier,[*] this may reveal something about the amount of resistance Aethelstan had to overcome in Wessex before he was able to succeed to the whole kingdom.

---

[*] Above, pp. 115–16

After that, Aethelstan may have seen success in war not just as a means to acquire glory and new territory (most notably, Danish-controlled Northumbria), but as an essential way of maintaining a dominant position within his own realm. Concerns about the legitimacy of his kingship might also explain why Aethelstan never married and had no children. There could have been religious or physical reasons for this, but equally, he may have agreed to remain single and childless as part of the deal he struck with a sceptical and nervous West Saxon elite in 924–5. Aethelstan was succeeded easily enough by his half-brother Edmund in 939 (this transfer of power might have been planned and agreed far in advance), but when Edmund was murdered in 946, his two sons were too young to succeed him and his younger brother, Eadred, became king. During these two reigns the unpredictability and volatility of political and military events were very obvious, and although the kingdom of Northumbria had been incorporated into the English kingdom once more by 955, at the time it cannot have been at all clear that this development would last for long. And, of course, after Eadred's death, uncertainty reigned again as England was split between Eadwig south of the Thames and Edgar to the north. These events were discussed at greater length in Chapter 5,* but the division may have been the result of a revolt against Eadwig's incompetent and scandalous rule, or it may have been a negotiated partition of the kingdom. Whether or not the division was supposed to endure is also far from certain. It is clear, however, that even as late in the period as this, a unified kingdom under a single king was still not everybody's idea of the best, or even the most viable, political arrangement. King Edgar would put that kingdom back together once more after 959, but it is important to remember that its eventual permanence was anything but certain.

Military power

Victory in war lay at the root of these momentous developments. First of all, Edward the Elder came out on top in the struggle with his cousin Aethelwold over the right to succeed King Alfred. One of the most striking aspects of this conflict was Aethelwold's seeming inability to attract support for his claim to the throne from within Wessex or English Mercia. His backing came overwhelmingly from the Vikings of Northumbria and East Anglia, an indication perhaps that Alfred had been successful in his efforts to instil loyalty to him and his chosen heir amongst the ruling elites of his extended kingdom.

With Aethelwold's challenge disposed of, and after a few obscure years, King Edward began to flex his military muscles further afield. From 909 onwards, a series of effective campaigns and some decisive victories in battle (at Tettenhall in Staffordshire in 910, for example) enabled him to advance into the southern midlands and East Anglia and force the Danes based in York back beyond the Humber. Crucial to Edward's success throughout the years until her death in 918 was the work

* Above, pp. 123–4

of his sister Aethelflaed. She took over as ruler of the Mercians following the death of her husband, Aethelred, in 911, and although she conducted her own military campaigns apart from those of her brother, it seems almost certain that their joint efforts were coordinated to a significant degree. Central to both of their strategies was the construction of *burhs* on the Alfredian model in their newly acquired territories. They were used to defend strategically valuable sites and consolidate control of surrounding areas, but they were also launch pads for further advances into enemy territory. Edward built *burhs* at Witham in Essex and at Hertford in 912, at Buckingham in 914, Bedford in 915, at Maldon in Essex in 916 and at Towcester in 917. Whilst Aethelred was still alive, *burhs* had been constructed at Chester and in Worcestershire by the Mercian rulers, and Aethelflaed carried on the same policy when she was left in sole charge. Between 911 and 915 alone *burhs* were constructed at Bridgnorth, Tamworth, Stafford, Eddisbury, Warwick, Runcorn and Chirbury, and there were others recorded whose sites are hard to locate. She died in June 918 having recently taken control of Derby and Leicester. Thanks in no small part to her, the conquest of the southern Danelaw was almost complete.

Aethelflaed's death was an important moment in the further development of a single English kingdom. On hearing that his sister had died, King Edward occupied Tamworth and 'all the nation in the land of the Mercians which had been subject to Aethelflaed submitted to him'.[5] Some in Mercia may have hoped that the delegated rule exercised by her would continue in some form, but any prospect of this was ended in 919 when Aethelflaed's daughter, Aelfwyn, 'was deprived of all authority in Mercia and taken into Wessex'.[6] From this point on, Edward ruled Mercia directly and looked to increase his power even more along his new northern frontier. He built more fortresses in 919 at Thelwall and Manchester, and after constructing another at Nottingham in 920, he pushed on into the Peak District. A *burh* was established at Bakewell, and at the same time Edward was visited by Constantine II, king of Scots, Constantine's brother Donald, king of Strathclyde, Ealdred lord of Bamburgh and his brother Uhtred, and Ragnall, the ruler of York. According to the *Anglo-Saxon Chronicle*, having met with Edward, these great lords of northern Britain 'chose him as father and lord'.[7] Quite what this means is unclear. If the *Chronicle* was implying that Edward had now acquired some kind of practical, meaningful control beyond the Humber, it is almost certainly exaggerating. At best his authority there remained theoretical, and those at the meeting saw it as 'probably no more than a mutual definition of their spheres of interest'.[8] Nevertheless, it was the first time in generations that a king based in southern England had done anything of this kind, and the significance of the moment was not lost on Edward's successors.

Only seven years after this meeting, Edward's son, Aethelstan, took control of the kingdom of Northumbria. Whether he succeeded there peacefully following the death of his brother-in-law Sihtric, or violently by ousting Sihtric's heirs, is far from clear. Either way, his seizure of power in 927 was followed immediately by meetings with other British rulers at Eamont near Penrith and Hereford and by the submission of the Cornish at Exeter. The *Anglo-Saxon Chronicle* says that

Aethelstan 'brought under his rule all the kings who were in this island'. This might be another exaggeration, and the other British rulers probably saw things differently. Nevertheless, Aethelstan became the supreme ruler of all the English people in 927, and his claim to be the dominant leader in Britain was certainly justified. It was shortly after this that his coins started to show him crowned and to describe him (as do his charters from about 931) as 'king of the whole of Britain' (*Rex totius Britanniae*). The witness lists to his charters, too, which regularly include the names of Welsh and Scottish rulers, suggest that there was substance behind the imagery. Aethelstan was challenged more than once over the next dozen years, of course. In 934 he campaigned into the far north of Scotland, and in 937, he had to confront a coalition including Scottish, Irish and Norse armies at *Brunanburh*. He was successful on both occasions, however, and he died in 939 secure as the first ruler of a single English kingdom extending from Cornwall to the Scottish frontier.

It is worth asking at this point where Aethelstan and his fellow rulers got their armies from. This is a difficult question to answer given the lack of relevant evidence, but it is reasonable to assume that at the heart of his forces, as it had been in the previous century, were the king's hearth troop and the personal armed followings of the great men who accompanied him on campaign. They would serve out of a sense of honour, duty and loyalty, and in the hope of reward. It is also perfectly possible that the king employed mercenaries, perhaps from abroad, to increase the number of those under his command. However, it is harder to be sure how far the king could expect or successfully demand military service from his subjects beyond the select confines of the warrior elite. By 899, the principle was embedded that those who held bookland were required to take their turn serving in the *fyrd*, manning the *burhs* and maintaining bridges. However, there is little if any sign that Alfred's supposed reform of the *fyrd* in the 890s had any lasting effect or that there was any kind of standing army in place for the tenth-century kings to use. Alfred's successors must therefore have continued to rely on their own household retainers and those of their leading men to form the core of any royal army. But troops raised locally from within individual shires and hundreds by royal reeves and ealdormen were also indispensable. The obligation to serve in these regional armies would have fallen first and foremost on the holders of bookland. The extent of that obligation would have depended on the value of the estates an individual held, which in turn determined how many hides the lands were assessed at for tax purposes. The landholder probably then had the job of finding the appropriate number of men to serve in the shire *fyrd* from estates with his specified hidage assessment. When larger 'national' armies were raised, this would initially have been done along local lines, too. Levies from particular shires would then assemble together for battle behind the landholders who had summoned them to fight or other shire commanders, whilst the king, his great men and their personal military followings took the lead. Inevitably, arrangements in practice were almost certainly more hand to mouth and improvised than this neat description suggests. How the hidage assessment of particular estates related to the number of men recruited is quite unclear at this time. By 1066 in certain parts of England, it appears that the practice was for one soldier to be recruited from every five hides, but it is dangerous to regard this as typical of the whole kingdom and to project it back into the tenth century.[9] What is more, there is no clarity about the kind of men recruited: were they designated individuals with military training and experience, or was it just a case of local men taking turns to serve? Then, who provided them with food and equipment, and how long were they expected to serve for? Nevertheless, whatever the practical realities of raising a tenth-century army were, it was the bonds formed by lordship and land tenure which held it together.

For most of the 940s and 950s, Aethelstan's successors had to struggle to hold on to his conquests and keep the kingdom of the English intact. His half-brother Edmund first lost control of Danish Northumbria and north-eastern Mercia before recovering both in 942 and 944 respectively. He ravaged in Cumbria and made an alliance with the king of Scots in 945 before he was murdered in the following year. The situation in the north remained fluid and confused during the reign of Edmund's brother, Eadred (d.955). He had to see off challenges from Erik Bloodaxe and Olaf Sihtricson, but in 954, the northerners expelled Erik for the last time and accepted Eadred as king. With hindsight, it is possible to see this as the moment when Northumbria became a permanent part of the English kingdom. It was also at this point that the campaigning stopped.

The evidence is thin to say the least, but the reigns of Eadwig and Edgar appear to have been peaceful ones, free from serious external threat or internal armed conflict. Decades of almost continuous warfare may have exhausted the reserves or enthusiasm of potential opponents, and of course, as the grip of the English kings on their new (and, indeed, their traditional) territories tightened during the middle decades of the tenth century, so the resources at their disposal increased. Underpinning Edgar's considerable power, for example, may have been the largest fleet ever assembled by an English king. In the twelfth century, John of Worcester outlined the extent of Edgar's sea-power: a fleet of 3,600 ships was assembled every year after Easter – 1,200 on the east coast, 1,200 on the west and 1,200 in the north. The king would then circumnavigate the island of Britain in a clockwise direction every summer to patrol his coastline, practise manoeuvres and intimidate anyone thinking of challenging him.[10] These claims are extravagant, but they probably contain elements of truth. Edgar may have hired some of these ships and crewed them with foreign mercenaries. But other more formal mechanisms may have been used, too. Another twelfth-century source, the so-called *Laws of Henry I*, states that the shires of England were divided into hundreds (these are discussed later)* and 'shipsokes'. It has been suggested that the latter were groups of three hundreds, each group being required to produce a ship with a crew of sixty, and it has been argued that Edgar was the most likely inventor of this system.[11]

Whether he was or not, however, contemporaries were certainly struck by the fleet Edgar took to Chester in 973. He must have sailed it around the coast after his

---

* Below, p. 143

consecration at Bath in May and it can only have impressed the other British rulers he met at Chester. Accounts of what happened there differ in detail, but two texts of the *Anglo-Saxon Chronicle* described how 'six kings came to meet him, and all gave him pledges that they would be his allies on sea and on land'.[12] Amongst these 'kings' were Kenneth of Scots, Malcolm of Strathclyde, the ruler of Man and the Isles and two princes of north Wales. Then, according to John of Worcester, once they had made their pledges to Edgar, they all proceeded to get on board a boat and row it along the Dee, with Edgar at the helm.[13] To be sure, the English sources had a vested interest in portraying the events at Bath and Chester in grandiose terms. Nevertheless, something significant certainly happened in 973. At the very least, the meeting at Chester was a summit arranged to delineate the spheres of influence of the rulers involved. But it may be more realistic to see it as a ceremonial assertion of overlordship by the king of the English, the most powerful ruler in Britain, and the ceremony at Bath in particular as 'an imperial inauguration rite and Edgar in his later years as ruler of a British Empire, tenth-century style'.[14] Edgar's charters performed a similar function. The usual practice from the 960s onwards was for him to be styled 'king of the whole of Britain' (*Rex totius Britanniae*) in the opening address and 'king of the English' (*Rex Anglorum*) in the witness list.[15] This was not sloppy draftsmanship. Like Aethelstan before him, Edgar was concerned to project the grandeur and extent of his power. Unlike his illustrious predecessor, however, Edgar was able to leave a stable and durable English kingdom to his heirs.

Household government

For all rulers during this period, the beating heart of power was their household. Their immediate family (spouses, siblings, children) would have exercised significant influence over them. Royal women in particular seem to have carried more political clout in the tenth century than they had been allowed in the ninth. A queen would have spent much of her life apart from her husband and with her own household, but her role as representative of the ruling dynasty remained important even then. Following King Edgar's coronation in 973, for example, Queen Aelfthryth presided over a feast of her own for the abbots and abbesses. She was 'dressed in linen garments and robed splendidly, adorned with a variety of precious stones and pearls, [and] she loftily surpassed the other ladies present'.[16] Such splendour befitted Aelfthryth, who is the first tenth-century queen believed with any confidence to have been crowned and anointed.[17] But her predecessor Eadgifu, the third wife of Edward the Elder, had already shown how important a queen could be, not just as a channel for suitors and litigants seeking access to the king, but as the mother and even grandmother of her husband's successors. Eadgifu's sons Edmund and Eadred both became king (and she appears to have been a forceful presence at their courts), as did her grandsons Eadwig and Edgar. It is impossible to know in detail what went on behind the scenes when the succession was disputed, but it seems very likely that Eadgifu played a key role in securing the throne for her direct descendants.

Both Eadgifu and Aelfthryth owed their ability to affect events to their potent family connections. Eadgifu was the daughter of Ealdorman Sigehelm of Kent whilst Aelfthryth's father was Ordgar, ealdorman in south-west England. Edward and Edgar may have married them in part at least to shore up their positions in these regions, but Aelfthryth also had other links which made her an attractive match for the king. Her first husband had been Ealdorman Aethelwold of East Anglia, the son of Aethlestan 'Half-King'. At the peak of their power, the Half-King and his family had controlled most of England in the king's name. That peak had probably passed by the time Edgar married Aelfthryth in 964 or 965, but that may not have been obvious to the king, and it was still essential for him to maintain good relations with this clan. King Edmund's second wife, Aethelflaed, was the daughter of one ealdorman, the widow of a second, the sister-in-law of a third and probably the daughter-in-law of a fourth. Marrying her enabled Edmund to maintain his connections with all these families. Moreover, as daughters from rich backgrounds, these queens had access to lands of their own, and surviving wills suggest that women of their class were able to hold and grant estates. Aethelflaed (Edmund's widow) and Aelfgifu (the widow of King Eadwig) disposed of extensive properties in their wills, and it is only reasonable to assume that, during their lifetimes, they and other tenth-century queens were able to use at least some of their land to build up an income and attract support from those who aspired to get access of some kind to it.[18] They could also exercise patronage towards the church by granting endowments and encouraging reform, and in return, they might expect the support of those churchmen they had favoured when it came to questions of royal succession and inheritance. But of course, the most successful royal woman of this period was not a queen at all. Aethelflaed, 'Lady of the Mercians', was quite as effective a politician and military leader as her brother Edward, and she was instrumental in laying the foundations of a single English kingdom. She may even have planned for her daughter, Aelfwyn, to succeed her and continue her work.

Back in the king's household, domestic servants would have met his daily needs (food, drink, clothing, transport). Other officials would look after his treasure; priests would have preached mass daily, heard the king's confession, guarded his relics and perhaps written his documents. Warriors would have hunted and feasted with the king, and fought alongside him when necessary. The composition of the household was not fixed. Certainly, there would have been a permanent core of personnel in virtually continuous attendance, but beyond that, and depending on things like the season of the year, the area the household was in and the business it needed to conduct, its membership would vary and its size would fluctuate. The viking rulers of York, as well as Aethelred and Aethelflaed in Mercia would all have spent their days surrounded by a throng of such people. But the most valuable insight into the way a royal household was staffed in the tenth century is provided by the will of King Eadred, who died in 955.[19] It begins with various bequests to the church for the good of his soul, and then he grants extensive lands to his mother Eadgifu and sums of money to his bishops and ealdormen. His household officials then feature prominently: the seneschal (*discthegn*), chamberlain (*hraeglthegn*) and butler (*biriele*) each received eighty mancuses of gold (whether they were minted on this occasion is not clear). The chaplains in charge of the royal relics each received fifty gold mancuses and £5 of silver pennies (there were 240 pennies in a pound), the other priests received £5, and each steward (*stigweard*) and all the lesser officials received thirty gold mancuses. Clearly this is not a list of every member of the king's household, but it shows very well just how valuable his close servants were to him.

The household was itinerant, and the ruler would move from place to place, often from one royal estate to another. This remained a crucial means by which people beyond the immediate centre of power came into contact with, or at least caught a glimpse of, their leader, and it allowed the king himself to exercise authority personally and directly. In the twelfth century, the chronicler John of Worcester described how King Edgar had travelled around his kingdom and what he did along the way:

> in winter and spring, he was accustomed to enquire diligently within his kingdom, travelling right through all the English provinces, about the manner in which the legal rights and the statutes he had promulgated were observed by the magnates, lest the poor should be crushed by injustices they suffered from the powerful.[20]

More mundanely, the constant travelling also enabled the ruler to feed his entourage: if it stayed put in one place for too long, the household might strip the neighbourhood of its food and fodder. Like a predatory shark, it had to keep moving to survive. Having said all this, the kings of southern England rarely ventured beyond the Thames in this period. If military campaigning required them to travel north, that could not be avoided, but in the normal course of events, they preferred to stay in the south. Furthermore, as will be seen in more detail shortly,* the southern kings had their preferred regular residences, and where they were based at any particular time depended to a large extent on the season, the available hunting, the political and military situation and the religious calendar.

One issue which historians have continued to debate concerns the extent to which the royal household during this period was responsible for producing the documents issued in the king's name, his charters (or diplomas, as they are sometimes called). It is natural enough to assume that royal charters were produced by the king's scribes, and certainly, by the tenth century, it seems that they usually were. The centralised production of charters by priests of the royal household seems to have been the norm under Edward the Elder and during the middle decades of the 900s. And most notably, between 928 and 935, it was almost certainly one such priest, known to historians as 'Aethelstan A', who wrote a series of charters in the name of King Aethelstan. This does not mean, however, that the royal household exercised a monopoly over the making of royal documents. It was a long-established practice in England for charters to be drafted by the beneficiary receiving the land

---

* Below, pp. 139–40

or privilege, not by the scribes of the king who was granting them. This was often a monastery or a bishop, although a layman might use an ecclesiastical writing office to prepare his charters, too, and in the tenth century this continued to happen. So, historians have identified charters thought to have been produced by the monks of Glastonbury or Worcester around the middle of the 900s. And perhaps the most famous tenth-century charter of all, the so-called Foundation Charter of the New Minster at Winchester, was produced at the Old Minster there in 966. It has been argued most recently, however, that, far from showing a loss of royal control over charter production during Edgar's reign, the differences in the language and style of the charters produced in the 960s and 970s suggest 'that the Anglo-Saxon bureaucracy had expanded and evolved, and that it had become markedly more sophisticated in the process'.[21] Even if they were drafted locally and even if the idiosyncrasies of individual scribes are clear, they wrote with centrally dictated procedures and instructions in mind, especially where the formal, legalistic components of the texts were concerned. Consequently, these documents share an underlying consistency and provide evidence 'of the extent of Edgar's royal authority, but also of the sophistication of the Anglo-Saxon administration in the 960s and 970s'.[22] This argument is perhaps rather strained, but it is important to consider it because charters, especially when studied together in significant numbers, reveal so much about how royal power was exercised at this time. They show how the king rewarded his great men, how he handled his resources and (through the witness lists included in the charters) who was influential and regularly in attendance at court. They are also public declarations of status and prestige: the titles the king is given in his charters can provide important insights into developing ideas about the nature and extent of his authority and power. The symbolic importance of the charters issued by Aethelstan and Edgar has already been mentioned,* but it is worth emphasising once again. At the start of his reign, King Aethelstan was described in his charters as 'king of the Anglo-Saxons', but after 927, as his military conquests continued, he was styled 'king of the English' (*Rex Anglorum*) and even, on occasions, 'king of the whole of Britain' (*Rex totius Britanniae*). Later, from the 960s Edgar was regularly referred to as 'king of the whole of Britain' and 'king of the English' in the same document. Royal charters contained ideological statements as well as practical measures, so it is crucial to know as much as possible about who wrote them, where and when.

Government by assembly

One thing charter witness lists can reveal is the identity of those who attended the king's assemblies. Anglo-Saxon kings had always consulted their *witan* at important times and about important business. They would discuss matters of diplomacy and warfare, laws would be issued, charters granted, disputes settled. And beyond the formal activities, the assemblies provided a space in which the leading men of the kingdom could socialise, gossip, network and deal. They were designed to be

* Above, pp. 132, 134

collusive, collaborative occasions where the king and his leading subjects worked together to manage their own affairs and the affairs of the realm. In this way, they would all gain a stake in the outcome of the decisions they reached: 'achieving and presenting consensus' was their ultimate *raison d'etre*.[23]

So there was nothing new in the tenth century about a king holding such gatherings. But there is also no doubt that royal assemblies acquired an extra degree of importance during this period. As the territory ruled by the kings of southern England expanded east and north, the challenge of exercising effective royal power increased. The regular and systematic holding of large gatherings, attended by important men from all over England, became an essential way of managing this new political reality.

It is hard to know exactly when royal assemblies began to become larger and more frequent. The best evidence of when they were held, where and who attended is contained in the royal charters which were issued while the assemblies were taking place. But unfortunately (and the reasons for this are unclear), no royal charters survive from *c.*910 until 924, when Edward the Elder was king. Given that the granting of charters came to be one of the main functions of later assemblies, the absence of any charters during these years may imply an absence of assemblies over the same period. And indeed, whilst the *Anglo-Saxon Chronicle* does indicate that some assemblies were held by Edward during the second decade of his reign, they do all seem to have been concerned with a particular kind of business, namely submission by defeated peoples or individuals, and it is not at all clear what form they took. On the face of things, therefore, Edward the Elder does not seem to have been particularly interested in holding assemblies in any organised way or in order to deal with a range of business.

By contrast, Edward's successor, Aethelstan, saw things differently, and it was during his reign that the role of the assembly developed significantly. It is not known for sure why this was the case, but Aethelstan was a king with extensive foreign connections, and it has been suggested that at least some of the inspiration for certain aspects of his kingship may have been taken from Carolingian tradition. Aethelstan would certainly have been exposed to this one way or another, as Chapter 5 showed.* One of his half-sisters, Eadgifu, had married Charles the Simple, king of the West Franks, during Edward the Elder's reign. When Charles was deposed and imprisoned in 923, his wife sent their son Louis to be protected and brought up at the West Saxon court. Louis was restored to power in Francia as Louis IV with Aethelstan's help in 936. A second half-sister, Eadhild, married Hugh, duke of the Franks in 926, whilst a third, Eadgyth married Otto, the son and heir (he became Otto I) of Henry the Fowler, king of the East Franks.[24] These marriages brought prestige and status to all concerned, along with strategic and political benefits. But they may also have brought ideas about the nature of royal rule and theories of imperial ideology from Carolingian Europe into England.

Charters were issued in Aethelstan's name from 925. This in itself, it has been said, 'testifies to a reinvigorated monarchy'.[25] And thereafter, the charter evidence

---

* Above, p. 117

shows that assemblies were held much more frequently and regularly than ever before. It has been suggested, mainly on the basis of the charters produced by Aethelstan A, that between two and five assemblies were held each year from the mid-920s onwards and for the rest of this period.[26] Each one probably lasted a minimum of two or three days, but during Aethelstan's reign, the holding of assemblies annually at Christmas, Easter and Whitsun appears to have become more regularised, and these gatherings during the great festivals of the church year may have extended over two or three weeks.

But the increased frequency and regularity of assemblies during the tenth century were arguably not their most striking features: it was their membership which made them special. First the sheer number of those attending Aethelstan's assemblies set them apart from anything which had happened before. The charter witness lists suggest that over a hundred men might have attended some of these meetings, although the lists more usually contain between twenty-five and forty names.[27] Most of the names come as no surprise: men of the highest status such as the archbishop of Canterbury, other bishops, ealdormen and king's thegns, men who owed their lands and their status to the king and who played personal roles in government at the highest level. But, from this point onwards, it is also possible to see men of lesser status (landholders to be sure, but ones with local rather than national profiles) appearing regularly as witnesses. Others came from regions beyond the traditional frontiers of Wessex: Scandinavian names appear on charters issued by Aethelstan and Eadred, and Edgar's witness lists include the names of men from Mercia and Northumbria. Rulers from Wales and Scotland also feature as witnesses, particularly in Aethlestan's charters.

So these assemblies were more geographically and socially diverse, as well as larger and more frequent, than those which had been held before Aethelstan's reign. And the lists of those who attended them, when studied collectively, suggest that they were capable of dealing with local, national and even supranational business. All this activity was a direct result of having to rule more territory, and an attempt to assert lordship over peripheral areas within the expanding English kingdom and dominance over areas beyond its frontiers. It was still vital for the king to travel, but it was impractical for him to do so often or swiftly over the greater expanses of territory he now controlled. It made more sense, as a practical response to this new situation, for the king to summon his subjects to him. Consequently, the king tended to hold his assemblies in towns like Winchester (934), but more usually at royal vills in the countryside of Wessex, like Cheddar in Somerset (941, 956, 968) or Amesbury in Wiltshire (932). It has been calculated that, of the twenty-one meetings held during Aethelstan's reign at which royal charters were issued, only six or seven were held outside this royal heartland and only four north of the Thames.[28] Assemblies did take place at Colchester (931), Nottingham and Buckingham (934) and York (936), but these were unusual, and much the same southern-dominated pattern emerges from later reigns as well. The usual venues would be able to provide food and other facilities for large gatherings (there were few if any royal estates in the newly acquired lands), but there was another aspect to this geographical concentration as, by bringing people to him, the king was again demonstrating his

authority over them. Thus, it was the very increase in the size of the English kingdom during the tenth century that led to the kings spending the bulk of their time
where the hub of royal power firmly remained, in the south.

Once those attending the assembly had gathered, its business would begin. It
is reasonable to think that a good deal of ritual and theatricality characterised the
formal parts of the event and that these activities were carefully choreographed.
We can imagine seating plans and processional lists being made to correspond
with rank and status, prayers being said publicly at the start and end of sessions
and oaths being given and received. Most of the ceremonial detail would have
been designed to focus attention on the authority of the king, enhance the mystical and charismatic dimensions of his power and show him as exceptional, unique
amongst men, almost superhuman. A surviving account of King Edgar's coronation
in 973 gives some idea of what went on.[29] It took place at Easter 'in accordance
with custom', when the archbishops, bishops, abbots and abbesses of the kingdom
came together with all the ealdormen, reeves and judges. Once they had arrived at
Bath in response to the king's summons, the members of this 'splendid and glorious
army', followed by a long procession of other worthies, led Edgar, 'crowned and
chosen', to the church. The two archbishops, Dunstan of Canterbury and Oswald
of York, took him into the sacred space to the sound of everyone singing, and
having reached the altar and removed his crown, the king prostrated himself on
the floor. Dunstan sang the *Te Deum*, following which Edgar recited his coronation oath, a set of three promises probably formulated for this occasion. He would
protect the church, 'proscribe theft and all manner of wickedness for persons of
all stations' and be just and merciful. After more prayers, he was anointed by both
archbishops. They then gave him a ring, strapped a sword around his waist, put the
crown on his head and handed him a sceptre and a rod. Mass was said, and the day
ended with a feast, at which the king sat 'raised up . . . on his lofty throne', with
an archbishop on each side and surrounded by his great men who were 'gleaming
attractively'.

This was a coronation, of course, and not a typical occasion – the rites and formalities employed must have been particularly elaborate. Nevertheless, there is no
reason to doubt that ceremonial on a smaller scale than this formed a part of all the
major meetings the king had with his great men during this period. It might have
been in the tenth century, for example, that so-called crown-wearings became a
feature of royal assemblies. These were staged events during which the king sat on
his throne, fully robed, crowned and with the rest of his regalia, and when hymns
of praise were sung to his glory. They served as periodic reminders of his splendour
and regality in 'a society where visual culture counted for more than literacy'.[30]
A charter of King Eadred, issued on Easter Day 949, describes how the king 'was
exalted with royal crowns', and this may have been an evolving seasonal practice by
then.[31] This evidence is far from conclusive, but it seems clear at least that the crown
became an increasingly important symbol of royal authority during this period, and
it has been argued that Aethelstan was the first English king to be crowned as well

as anointed at the start of his reign, and he is depicted (on his coins and elsewhere) wearing a crown, unlike earlier kings who were conventionally shown wearing helmets.[32] Continental, principally German, influence may have been at work here, and it would be no great surprise if, like his Ottonian counterparts, Aethlestan wore his crown during assemblies, or if a formal crown-wearing ceremony took place during them. After all, an assembly only gave the king a limited amount of time to make an impression on those attending, and memories of his magnificence and majesty may in the end have been what the visitors from Wales, Scotland and elsewhere took away from these occasions and recounted in awe-struck terms when they returned home.

Beyond the stage-managed ritual, the practical work of the assemblies carried on. Questions of domestic policy, warfare, diplomatic relations, royal marriages and the succession would all have been examined. Important appointments (bishops, abbot, ealdormen) would also have been debated and disputes resolved. But assemblies were social occasions as well as political ones. Feasting, drinking and hunting would have broken down some personal barriers and allowed for some frank conversation, but the assemblies also provided the kings with the opportunity to give gifts and distribute patronage. During the mid-tenth century, the English kings made a remarkable number of grants of bookland. Indeed, between 940 and 975 there were more such grants than for any comparable period before 1066, and most of these were issued at assemblies. This may tell us plenty about the king's position during this period, about how he needed to forge bonds with his great men by buying their support and about the political manoeuvring behind the scenes. But it is clear at least that the issuing of royal charters and the distribution of royal patronage became an essential function of the royal assembly at this time. The same goes for the making of legislation. Assemblies expressed a real concern for law and order and the maintenance of stability, and there is no reason to doubt that the king looked to his *witan* for counsel and relied on their experience when dealing with such matters. So the law code known as II Aethelstan (or 'the Grately Code') ends by declaring that 'All this was established at the great assembly at Grately [in Hampshire], at which Archbishop Wulfhelm [of Canterbury] was present and all the nobles and councillors whom King Aethelstan could gather together'. A later code, II Edmund, which attempted to deal with issues surrounding the blood feud, begins with a statement by the king: 'I have been inquiring with the advice of my councillors, both ecclesiastical and lay, first of all how I could most advance Christianity'.[33] Plenty of other codes say something similar, and it may not be going too far to suggest that law codes were authoritative because they were issued by the king on the basis of such advice.

So assemblies had symbolic functions (to transmit the image of the king and heighten his dignity) and practical ones (to keep the king in touch with the fringes of his expanded kingdom and carry out a range of important work). But perhaps the most important purpose of the assemblies was to create ties of mutual trust and dependence between the king and his leading subjects by promoting consensus amongst them. These gatherings served to bring men from within the established areas of royal power into contact with others from the recently acquired, more distant regions and to include them all in the king's decision-making processes. And by opening up to all the members of this group the prospect of royal reward for loyal service, and by giving this new, broader political elite a say as well as an interest in what was decided at the assemblies, they could contribute to the dilution of provincial loyalties and to the creation of a new form of English unity based on a shared allegiance to the kings in the south.

There were other ways of building up an aristocratic *esprit de corps*, of course, through marriages, other kinship links and ties of personal loyalty which bound members of the ruling class to each other and to the king. Either way, the signs are that, by the second half of the tenth century the leading families of England formed an increasingly tight-knit group with shared interests and common expectations.[34] But it was at royal assemblies that these men met most often and in the greatest numbers. These meeting thus 'helped to stabilise and harmonise the relationship between the king and his great men on which peace ultimately depended', but they also furthered the development of a single English kingdom.[35]

Regional government

The tenth-century English kings exercised personal rule through their mobile households and the summoning of assemblies. However, routine, everyday government necessarily had to be conducted away from the royal centre, most of it without the direct involvement of the king himself. To allow for this at a time when the area under the kings' control was growing rapidly, a significant amount of delegation and institutional innovation had to take place. These developments were far from complete by 975, but by then, administrative structures and standardised mechanisms were evolving and a framework of power was taking shape, through which kings could implement their commands and enforce their authority over a vastly extended English kingdom.

Wessex had already been divided into shires by the end of the ninth century. At that stage, they were used first and foremost as units of military organisation (shire *fyrds* led by local ealdormen feature regularly in the *Anglo-Saxon Chronicle*'s account of the viking wars). But they could also be used for the assessment of other dues and the extraction of other services (tax collection and the performance of legal duties, for example), and this is the direction in which they later developed. As King Alfred's successors extended their rule beyond their West Saxon heartlands, they imposed this familiar system on their new territories. New shires in the midlands, most (like Warwickshire and Leicestershire) centred on the *burhs* built by Edward the Elder and Aethelflaed during the first quarter of the tenth century, gradually came into existence during this period, although it is hard to say precisely when. The process of dividing English Mercia into shires may have been begun by Edward the Elder. It is tempting, too, to argue that Aethlestan's reign was the turning-point here, and that the establishment of shires in the east midlands took place as part of a wider process of political consolidation. The text historians refer to as VI Aethelstan, for example, records the requirement 'that every reeve should receive the pledge in his own shire', and it has been inferred from the wording and its context that this was a reference to the midland as well as the southern shires of the kingdom.[36] Alternatively, the peaceful years of King Edgar's reign may have provided the breathing-space required to refine and embed these structural changes.[37] And because no new shire is named in the records until the start of the eleventh century, some historians have argued that they were not established until then. None of these theories about the establishment of the new shires can be proved, however, and the precise chronology of shire formation is impossible to establish.

Nevertheless, those shires which did exist at the end of King Edgar's reign were probably already subdivided by then into smaller administrative areas called hundreds (or wapentakes in the former viking-controlled parts of England), because they were originally made up of one hundred hides of land. Hundreds were used to facilitate tax assessment and collection and to organise other public obligations. This enabled the king, through his officers, to supervise and control the behaviour of his subjects in new and direct ways. A document known as the Hundred Ordinance makes it clear that, by the time it was produced, the hundred was an established unit of local administration and played an important role in the enforcement of local justice. Once again, however, it is not at all clear when that date was. Many historians think that the Hundred Ordinance was issued by King Edgar (it is sometimes known as I Edgar, his first law code), but it could also have been issued by King Edmund, who died in 946 or King Eadred, who died in 955. In the law code which King Edmund certainly did issue at Colyton in Devon, he ordered that a person who failed to pursue a thief should pay 120 shillings to the king and 30 to the hundred.[38] But it is unclear what kind of entity this provision had in mind when it used the term: it could receive payments and had some role in criminal justice, but whether it was a geographical area with a fixed size and shape is not clear. Fortunately, another document, Edgar's law code issued at *Wihtbordesstan* (IV Edgar), probably some time between 966 and 975, mentions hundreds and wapentakes far more definitively, so both were definitely in existence and in use by the time he died. Indeed, it seems very likely that these units of local administration only began to take on their final forms and functions during Edgar's reign.[39]

Both shires and hundreds had their own courts, as did the *burhs*. These will be discussed more in Chapter 7,* but it is worth emphasising here that the meetings of these courts were important, not just for the administration of justice, but for the exercise of royal power by the king's agents on his behalf. Meetings of the shire court were political occasions as well as legal ones, at which the great men of the shire would gather and come into contact with royal authority. Something similar, perhaps a little lower down the social scale, happened at meetings of the hundred

---

* Below, pp. 161–3

court. The courts were regulated by royal legislation and supervised by royal officials. The Hundred Ordinance stipulated that the hundred court should be held once a month, whilst King Edgar directed that the *burh* court should meet three times a year, presumably to enforce burghal obligations (King Aethelstan had ordered that repairs to the *burhs* should be carried out annually). Meanwhile the shire court was supposed to meet twice a year in the presence of the local bishop and ealdorman.[40] In the ninth century, each shire in Wessex had had its own ealdorman, but as the southern kingdom extended northwards in the tenth century, the size of the areas under the control of individual ealdormen also increased. It seems likely that, from about the 920s onwards and for the rest of this period, there were about a dozen ealdormen in office at any one time. Some of them became very powerful indeed. Aethelstan 'Half-King', for example, was ealdorman of East Anglia from 932 until 957, but the territory under his control also included eastern Mercia. His brothers were also ealdormen: Eadric in Wessex (942–9) and Aethelwold in the south-east (940–6). Between them, they controlled the greater part of the emerging English kingdom, and after the Half-King's death, much of his authority passed to his eldest son Aethelwold and then, after the latter's death, to a younger son, Aethelwine. By the 960s, the whole of western Mercia was under the authority of another mighty ealdorman, Aelfhere, and the chronicler Aethelweard began his long career as ealdorman 'of the western provinces' in around 973. There was an obvious risk to the kings in placing so much authority in the hands of men like this: they might try to establish ruling dynasties of their own or at least networks of influence in which they, not the king, were central. At least until the end of King Edgar's reign, however, the system seems to have worked reasonably well, and the ealdormen, for all their power, remained what they had always been, royal officers overseeing the king's rights in the areas they governed in his name.

But just as the king could not exercise personal rule over his whole kingdom and relied on his ealdormen, so the ealdormen necessarily had to delegate local power and use subordinates of their own. The regions under their control often encompassed several shires, so individuals were probably appointed to supervise each one of these, and they in turn would have depended on officials on the ground. The royal reeves were the most important of these men. Their daily routine would have been taken up in supervising the royal estates, collecting taxes, tolls and information, organising meetings and court sessions. It is hard to pinpoint individual examples of reeves at work, but the importance of their contribution to the smooth running of royal government in the localities is clear from the law codes of the tenth century. More will be said about this in due course,* but suffice it to say here that Edward the Elder's first law code was aimed directly at them:

> King Edward commands all his reeves: that you pronounce such legal decisions as you know to be most just and in accordance with the written laws

* Below, pp. 154–5

(*domboc*). You shall not for any cause fail to interpret the public law (*folcriht*); and at the same time it shall be your duty to provide that every case shall have a date fixed for its decision.

And towards the end of his reign, in his second code, Edward ordered his reeves to hold a meeting every four weeks to arrange days for the hearing of disputes (this was perhaps an early stage in the development of the hundred court). Similarly, the laws issued by Aethelstan and Edgar assigned their reeves various judicial duties and expected them to work hard to keep the peace locally and follow the king's orders.[41] These men were the everyday face of royal government: as the English kingdom expanded in the tenth century and the demands of government became more onerous, the kings were increasingly reliant on them, and it was through them that his authority was transmitted and enhanced.

Mints and coins

Royal reeves would have been hard at work in the *burhs* as well as the countryside. The burghal system, established by Alfred and extended by his successors for military reasons, was also a crucial component of the political machine which drove forward the development of a single English kingdom. As has been seen, *burhs* had courts of their own, and many of them were beginning to flourish as trading centres which the king could control and profit from ('all buying is to be within a town', Aethelstan ordered in the Grately Code).[42] Many, too, were established during the tenth century as mints where coins were produced. There were mints in all the different kingdoms and regions of England when King Alfred died in 899, not least in Danish-controlled York and East Anglia where the treasure acquired by the Vikings over the course of their English conquests had allowed them to produce large numbers of good-quality coins. Of course, Edward the Elder and then Aethelstan secured control of these resources and greatly increased their own wealth as Danish territory was incorporated into their expanding kingdom, and they used them to stamp their own royal authority on their newly acquired lands. By the end of his reign, it has been estimated that Edward had well over a hundred moneyers working in at least sixteen *burhs*, from Exeter in the far south-west to Chester in the north and Cambridge in the east. Aethelstan later had coins minted at Nottingham, York and Norwich.[43] Ultimately, by 975, there were perhaps sixty or seventy English mints in operation across England.

On an initial inspection of the surviving evidence, it seem that it was Aethelstan who first attempted to impose more centralised order on the coinage system: 'there is to be one coinage over all the king's dominion and no one is to mint money except in a town', he declared in the Grately Code, and the number of moneyers allowed in certain towns was also specified.[44] But it has been suggested that this part of the code was not new and that the provision about the coinage, along with others around it, may first have been introduced by Edward the Elder, only to be incorporated later in his son's laws. Those towns allowed to have moneyers were all deep in southern England, for example (none is further north than London), which suggests that royal influence over the coinage had not yet extended much beyond Wessex when the list was originally made. In addition, it seems that the Grately provision was not even an attempt to introduce a single type of coin across the kingdom; rather it was intended to ensure that only the coins of Aethelstan and his West Saxon predecessors were used in the areas they ruled.[45] This would have meant that the coins of Edward the Elder and even Alfred remained in use and that they continued to circulate along with the coins of later kings. Many of these coins must have been in poor condition, however, and worth very little by the 970s (this was still a time when the value of a coin depended to a large extent on how much precious metal it contained). This would have made trading frustratingly difficult if coins were expected as payment. And even more basically than this, the variety of different kinds of circulating coins must have been confusing. King Aethelstan's 'Circumscription Cross' coin, with its grand royal title (*Rex totius Britanniae*) around the edge, made a powerful statement about how the king wished to be seen by his subjects after 927. But these coins probably only circulated within a limited area and alongside other coins issued by Aethelstan and his predecessors. Depending on where they had been produced, these varied considerably in size, weight, design and fineness.

What is more, in the century or so before the 960s, very little new silver had been imported into England, mainly because the material was in seriously short supply across Europe. This meant that the quality of the coins in circulation in England gradually declined during this period, and that by the start of Edgar's reign they were in a poor state. It was in the 960s, however, that rich new sources of silver were discovered in Germany, first in the Harz mountains in Saxony and then elsewhere in the kingdom. New German mints were established, and much of the bright new currency they produced found its way to Scandinavia where it was used to pay for furs. Then, as Germany's economy quickly expanded, the demand on the continent for English goods, most notably wool, was revived and foreign silver again started to arrive in England in large quantities. This influx of new silver as coin or bullion stimulated what has been described as 'a remarkable revival of cross-Channel trade' towards the end of Edgar's reign and may have made possible one of the most lauded episodes of the period, Edgar's reform of the coinage, which was implemented some time around 973.[46] The outline of this plan seems reasonably clear. New coins of a prescribed uniform size, silver content and design were to be introduced across the kingdom, and no other coins (mainly those of previous kings) would any longer be legal tender. The design of the coins would be changed every few years, but each coin would still carry Edgar's name and title and also the names of the mint where it was struck and the moneyer who struck it. And to enforce centralised control even more, the dies used to make the coins were all manufactured together at a single location, probably Winchester, where the moneyers had to collect them (presumably after payment of a hefty fee).

It is worth wondering how successful Edgar was in securing the withdrawal from circulation of obsolete coins, and worth noting that standards of weight and fineness varied even in the reformed issues. Whether he envisaged frequent recoinages from the start or just a one-off replacement of old pennies is also open to question. Nevertheless, there is no reason to doubt that, as far as the late tenth-century English coinage was concerned, 'there was a dramatic switch from diversity to uniformity between the Channel and the Tees'.[47] Underlying these changes may have been a perfectly understandable desire to introduce some regularity into a still rather messy system and a straightforward determination to make trading (and payments to the king) easier. But there were political and ideological considerations at work here, too. Edgar's reforms brought a decisive end to a fragmented, and to some extent regionalised, system of multiple coinages and replaced it with a coherent, completely national one, embodied by a single coin type which would be the only valid currency from Cornwall to the river Tees. The scale and sophistication of this new system were in themselves potent expressions of English administrative unity and royal authority. During the 930s, after his victories in northern England and the submission to him of other British kings, King Aethelstan had developed the imagery and text on his coins 'to place his stamp on the newly exalted position in which he found himself'.[48] Forty years later, Edgar was surely attempting something even more profound when his bright new coins showed him in stately profile and described him as *rex Anglorum* ('king of the English'). This time, the use of the title was 'no more and no less than the recognition of political reality'.[49]

Royal wealth

Kings used coins to proclaim and spread ideas about the nature of their kingship. They also made money from the coinage system, not least when the moneyers had to pay royal officials for the dies they were required to use and, in time (although it is not clear whether this was already happening by 975), when old coins were brought in to mints to be replaced (for a fee) with new ones. But the bulk of the king's revenue in the tenth century, as it had in the ninth, came from his lands. The kings of Wessex had some estates which belonged to them personally and others which were regarded as belonging to the monarchy itself. They could dispose of the former as they wished (as Alfred had done in his will), but the latter were supposed to pass intact from one ruler to the next. All the kings of the tenth century would have inherited these West Saxon royal estates, but it is less clear whether any such resources were available to them in the rest of England. Edward the Elder presumably took control of whatever was left of the old royal estates in English Mercia after 918, and Aethelstan must have inherited these in 924 and then those in Wessex when he became king there. But in the areas of England which had been under Danish control since the 860s and 870s, it seems unlikely that there were many royal estates left to take over by the second quarter of the 900s. Most such lands had probably come into private ownership one way or another, so as the southern kings extended their political and military control into the north and east, it is difficult to see how they can have added much to their own property portfolios. Nevertheless, the estates they did control were crucial sources of wealth. The kings would be paid rents, increasingly in cash during this period but also in food, other produce and labour services, and the collection and distribution of this income would be organised by the king's reeves.

The king was also able to make money from other people's lands, not just his own. Anglo-Saxon kings had been using the lands they controlled to extract taxation and impose other public obligations perhaps since the sixth or seventh centuries. The standard unit for assessing liability was the hide, and individual estates were notionally divided into a number of these either by custom or by imposition from above. Originally the hide had been a measure of land (the amount of land farmed by, and supporting, a peasant family), but by the tenth century, it had become more 'an expression of productive capability'.[50] In other words, a physically smaller but more fertile estate might be given a larger hidage assessment than a larger, less fruitful one, and so have to pay more tax or provide more troops. This system was still evolving during the tenth century, but as more land was acquired by Edward the Elder and his successors, it seems reasonable to assume that they at least began the process of imposing these familiar mechanisms on it and that they expected their new subjects to pay taxes to them in the same way as their established ones. And here the gradual imposition of the system of shires and hundreds/wapentakes across the newly conquered territories must have encouraged standardised requirements and procedures. Indeed, the spread of these uniform administrative structures, administered by royal officials, can only have increased royal wealth. Although detailed records and figures do not start to become available before the eleventh century, it is reasonable to assume that King Edgar was significantly richer than Alfred the Great.

Royal power in the north

Edgar's coinage reforms may in fact have been part of a wider programme of royal image-making which culminated in the king's extraordinary coronation at Bath and the ensuing ceremonies at Chester in 973. Edgar had probably been consecrated king in 960 or 961, in other words, as soon as possible after he succeeded Eadwig in Wessex. In this respect, he was following the examples of his tenth-century predecessors. In 973, by contrast, as has been seen already,* he was arguably asserting a much wider authority over the whole of the British Isles. He had hinted at something similarly ambitious in his fourth law code, where one provision was expressly decreed to be 'common to all the nations, whether Englishmen, Danes or Britons, in every province of my dominion' and another applied to 'all who inhabit these islands'.[51] Despite the rhetoric, however, there were certainly limits to the king's authority within Britain and even within his new English realm. Most obviously, the process of incorporating the far north into the English kingdom had barely begun by 975. Northumbria north of the river Tees (the ancient kingdom of

* Above, p. 126

Bernicia) had been ruled by an English dynasty based at the great coastal fortress of Bamburgh since the second half of the ninth century, whilst a series of Scandinavian rulers based at York had controlled the southern part of the old kingdom. They had all submitted to both Edward the Elder and Aethelstan when compelled to do so (or, at least, they had reached some sort of understanding with their southern neighbour), but it was not until after the death of Erik Bloodaxe in 954 that the English kings could even begin to think of ruling directly north of the Humber. King Eadred appointed Oswulf of Bamburgh as the first ealdorman of all North-umbria after 954, but whilst this was a way of the king asserting his power to make such a choice in his newly annexed territory, it was also an acknowledgement of the entrenched power of the lords of Bamburgh and the political reality that Northum-bria could only be effectively governed by someone with local resources, connec-tions and experience. After Oswulf died in about 966, he was replaced as ealdorman by Oslac. His Scandinavian name suggests that he was probably based at York, and his regular witnessing of royal charters in the last five years of Edgar's reign indicates that he was close to the king and regarded by him as his representative in the north. It was Oslac who was given the task by Edgar of implementing the *Wihtbordesstan* decrees there, for example.[52]* Even so, it is likely that his meaningful authority extended as far as the river Tees and not much beyond; further north, power probably remained in the hands of the lords of Bamburgh. Oslac was exiled in 975 in mysterious circumstances, perhaps having fallen victim to the intrigues which followed the death of King Edgar in that year. Certainly, the *Anglo-Saxon Chronicle* lamented his loss: 'the valiant man Oslac was driven from the country, over the tossing waves, the gannet's bath, the tumult of waters, the homeland of the whale; a grey-haired man, wise and skilled in speech, he was bereft of his lands'.[53]

Edgar's English kingdom

It is evident enough that kings needed to be wealthy, but this basic fact is worth emphasising. As he moved around his own estates, the king had to feed himself and maintain his household. Any surplus produce could be sold for a profit, and any surplus funds could be given away as alms or used to purchase essentials (horses, carts, cooking pots) as well as royal finery (the king's jewels, books, drinking vessels, robes and weapons). In wartime, moreover, there is no reason to doubt that kings spent money on hiring paid troops to fight in their armies or crew their ships. But the king also needed wealth to reward his followers with: both his position and his prestige depended greatly on how much and how successfully he was able to do this. He could dole out the treasure and loot plundered from, or given as tribute by, his defeated enemies. But increasingly by the tenth century, it was gifts of land that his men wanted more than anything else, and the public distribution of estates became one of the main features of royal assemblies during this period. Of course,

* Below, pp. 159–60

the paradox here is that the king had to keep acquiring new lands in order to give them away, both to his established followers and to the powerful new subjects whose loyalty he needed to secure. So it is quite right to say that, in this period, 'war was a major economic activity' and that kings needed to keep fighting in order to gather resources, manage their great men and simply survive.[54]

Even so, the exception to this rule is obvious: King Edgar *pacificus* was famously successful because he fought no wars and faced no revolts. In the twelfth century, John of Worcester attributed Edgar's achievements and the stability of his reign to his personal qualities, but also to his ceaseless activity – his annual circumnavigations of Britain and his judicial tours of his kingdom.

> By the first action concentrating on strength, by the second on justice, he sought the advantages of the state and kingdom in both. Hence the fear of his enemies on every side and the love of all those subject to him grew.[55]

This view is perhaps a little rose-tinted, and there may have been wider factors at work here. Edgar's ruling style may have been harsher than the available evidence allows us to see, and the grateful monks who later wrote about him may have wished to disregard the king's more disciplinary tendencies. It is arguable, too, that the political situation across England, which had been volatile and unpredictable earlier in the century, had stabilised by the 960s, and that earlier military conquests were now being successfully reinforced by institutional and administrative change. Edgar was the sole and undisputed ruler of a single English kingdom which stretched from the Channel coast to the river Tees at the very least. That kingdom was well on the way to being divided up into a network of shires and hundreds/wapentakes which allowed royal tax assessors and other officials to influence and direct the lives of the population to an unprecedented degree. A new coinage system tended towards uniformity in trading and commercial practices and, at the same time, further developed the image as well as the reality of royal power. Regular royal assemblies were held to magnify the aura of kingship, encourage collective action and forge consensus across the ruling elite. The seeds of royal bureaucracy had been sown as charter production had become more centralised. Meanwhile, landholders may have welcomed an end to the almost constant demands of warfare as the respite gave them the chance to develop the estates they or their forebears had been given by the king and to cultivate new, peaceful ways to profit from their allegiance to him. If they wanted more land, then rather than fight for it, they could seek out royal patronage, plan the marriages of their children or get involved in the property market and start buying from or exchanging with their neighbours and their peers. It has been said that, in England during the century before the Norman Conquest, 'careful management of estates, rather than deft swordplay, was the best guarantee of the good life'.[56] If so, it may have been during the evidently tranquil reign of King Edgar when this first became clear to the English political and military elite. After seventy-five years of trauma, a single English kingdom had been born by the time King Aethelstan died in 939.

A short, troubled adolescence followed, but it came of age and got down to business under Edgar the Peaceable.

Notes

1 George Molyneaux, *The Formation of the English Kingdom in the Tenth Century* (Oxford, 2015).
2 The arguments are best considered in Keynes, 'Edward, King of the Anglo-Saxons', *passim*.
3 Keynes, 'Edward, King of the Anglo-Saxons', pp. 48–9; Nelson, 'The Second English Ordo', in her *Politics and Ritual*, pp. 361–74, especially at pp. 366–7.
4 *ASC* 924 (Mercian Register).
5 *ASC* 918.
6 *ASC* 919 (Mercian Register).
7 *ASC* 920.
8 Williams, *Kingship and Government*, p. 84.
9 The evidence comes from the Domesday Book record for Berkshire, *Domesday Book: A Complete Translation*, ed. Ann Williams, G.H. Martin (London, repr.2002), p. 136.
10 *JW*, ii pp. 425–7.
11 E. John in Campbell (ed.), *The Anglo-Saxons*, pp. 172–3; Williams, *Kingship and Government*, pp. 116–18.
12 *ASC* 973.
13 *JW*, ii pp. 424–5.
14 Nelson, 'Inauguration Rituals', in her *Politics and Ritual*, p. 303.
15 Keynes, '*Edgar, rex admirabilis*', p. 25.
16 *VSO*, pp. 110–11.
17 P. Stafford, 'The King's Wife in Wessex, 800–1066', *Past and Present* 91 (1981), p. 17 and nn.42, 44; idem, *Queen Emma and Queen Edith. Queenship and Women's Power in Eleventh-Century England* (Oxford, 1997), pp. 62–3, 162–4.
18 Stafford, King's Wife, p. 22 n.64.
19 *EHD*, i no.107.
20 *JW*, ii pp. 426–7.
21 Ben Snook, *The Anglo-Saxon Chancery. The History and Production of Anglo-Saxon Charters from Alfred to Edgar* (Woodbridge, 2015), p. 168.
22 Ibid., p. 169.
23 Levi Roach, *Kingship and Consent in Anglo-Saxon England, 871–978: Assemblies and the State in the Early Middle Ages* (Cambridge, 2013), p. 44.
24 Maddicott, *Origins of the English Parliament*, p. 31; Roach, *Kingship and Consent*, p. 203.
25 S. Foot, 'Aethelstan, King of England' in *ODNB*.
26 Roach, *Kingship and Consent*, p. 75.
27 Maddicott, *Origins of the English Parliament*, p. 5.
28 Roach, *Kingship and Consent*, p. 60.
29 *VSO*, pp. 104–11.
30 Maddicott, *Origins of the English Parliament*, p. 23.
31 S549.
32 Maddicott, *Origins of the English Parliament*, pp. 19–20; Foot, *Aethelstan*, pp. 216–23.
33 *EHD*, i nos.35, 38.
34 R. Fleming, *Kings and Lords in Conquest England* (Cambridge, 1991), pp. 22–39.
35 Maddicott, *Origins of the English Parliament*, p. 31.
36 *EHD*, i no.38 (pp. 426–7) (VI Aethelstan, 10); Pratt, 'Written Law', p. 345.
37 Molyneaux, *Formation*, pp. 157–64.
38 Robertson, *Laws*, pp. 12–13 (III Edmund, 2).
39 Molyneaux, *Formation*, pp. 141–55.

40 *EHD*, i nos.35 (ch.13), 39 (ch.1), 40 (chs.5.1–2).

41 Attenborough, *Laws* pp. 114–15, 120–1 (I Edw, Prologue, II Edw, 8).

42 *EHD*, i no.35 (II Aethelstan, 13.1).

43 Lyon, 'The Coinage of Edward the Elder', in Higham and Hill (eds.), *Edward the Elder*, pp. 67–78, at pp. 71–2, 77.

44 *EHD*, i no.35 (II Aethelstan, 14, 14.2).

45 Foot, *Aethelstan*, pp. 152–3.

46 P. Sawyer, *The Wealth of Anglo-Saxon England* (Oxford, 2013), p. 98.

47 Molyneaux, *Formation*, p. 141.

48 Foot, *Aethelstan*, pp. 154–5.

49 Keynes, 'Edgar, *rex admirabilis*', p. 24.

50 Molyneaux, *Formation*, p. 93.

51 *EHD*, i no.42 (pp. 435, 437) (IV Edgar, 2.2, 14.2).

52 *EHD*, i no.42 (p. 437) (IV Edgar, 15).

53 *ASC* 975.

54 J. Campbell, 'The Sale of Land and the Economics of Power in Early England', *Haskins Society Journal*, 1 (1989), pp. 23–37, at p. 37; reprinted in his *The Anglo-State* (London, 2000).

55 *JW*, ii pp. 426–7.

56 Robin Fleming, *Britain After Rome: The Fall and Rise, 400 to 1070* (London, 2010), p. 317.

7

THE KINGS AND THE LAW, 899–975

It is rather misleading to end one chapter on the development of English govern-ment in the tenth century and then start another on the development of English justice during the same period. Because far from being separate, the two things were intimately connected: there was no 'separation of powers' in Anglo-Saxon England and no meaningful sense in which executive, legislative and judicial authority were distinct from each other or kept each other in check. The king was the ultimate law-giver, judge and decision-maker in his kingdom, and so the law, what it said and how it worked, was an essential weapon in the royal armoury and another means of exercising control. There was more to the legal system than this, of course, and jus-tice at a local grassroots level remained very much a matter of custom, tradition and communal duties. Nevertheless, as Edward the Elder and his successors extended their political and military authority across a single English kingdom, the evolving apparatus of justice and the ideas about kingly power which an expanding body of royal law expressed, helped them dominate it and justify the entire process.

Law and government

The very act of law-making was a forceful and assertive exercise of political power. Earlier English kings had appreciated this, but the history of royal legislation before King Alfred's reign was patchy and intermittent. In the tenth century, however, his successors enthusiastically took up the practice which Alfred had revived: Edward the Elder issued two law codes, Aethelstan and Edmund issued three each and Edgar at least two more and perhaps as many as four, depending on how the texts are classified. More will be said shortly about the content of these codes,* but some important points about their form and purpose need to be emphasised here. First

---

* Below, pp. 155–61

of all, legislating was a collaborative affair and reveals much about decision-making at the highest level. The codes nearly all make it clear that, far from being unilateral royal pronouncements from on high, they were devised by the king acting in concert with his great men. Just two examples will serve for now. At the start of his third law code (issued at Exeter and conventionally if confusingly referred to as V Aethelstan by historians), the king announced that:

> I, King Aethelstan, make known that I have learnt that our peace is worse kept than I should like . . . And my councillors say that I have borne it too long.

Similarly, King Edgar began the code known as II Edgar by declaring:

> This is the ordinance which King Edgar determined with the advice of all his councillors, for the praise of God and for his own royal dignity and for the benefit of all his people.[1]

Second, the increased emphasis placed by the kings of this period on the publication of written law is good evidence of the expanding role of writing in government. All of the codes were written in English and designed to be read. They might be read quietly and silently by the recipients or out loud in public to a wider audience. Either way, the regular issuing of royal laws in English presupposes 'the existence of a functionally literate class able to comprehend their meaning and disseminate it yet further'.[2] King Edgar's final code, which was probably issued early in the 970s, exemplifies this when, at the end, it declares:

> And many documents are to be written concerning this, and sent both to Ealdorman Aelfhere [of Mercia] and Ealdorman Aethelwine [of East Anglia], and they are to send them in all directions, that this measure may be known to both the poor and the rich.[3]

It was almost certainly the local reeves who would eventually have received these 'documents'. They feature prominently as the enforcers of royal orders right from the start of Edward the Elder's reign. In his first code, Edward 'commands all the reeves that you give such just judgement as you know most right and as it stands in the law-book [Alfred's *domboc*]'. And in his second code, he decreed that 'every reeve shall hold a meeting every four weeks'. Aethelstan expected his reeves to work hard and professionally, too. He issued direct orders to them about the collection of tithes (I Aethelstan) and the distribution of royal alms (the so-called Ordinance on Charities), and there are echoes of the way Alfred had berated his under-performing officials throughout his decrees: 'If any of my reeves will not carry out this ordinance and is less zealous about it than we have pronounced, he is then to pay the fine for disobedience to me, and I shall find another who will'. And towards the end of the document known as VI Aethelstan:

> Aethelstan commands his bishops and his ealdormen and all his reeves over all my dominion, that you observe the peace just as I and my councillors

have enacted it. If any of you neglects and will not obey me . . . and will not so concern himself with keeping order as I have commanded and as it stands in our writings, then is the reeve to be without his office and without my friendship.[4]

The stern emphasis placed here on the need for reeves to act efficiently and effectively suggests how important they were to the implementation of royal justice. What is more, perhaps this is the best evidence available (indirect though it is) of the success of King Alfred's plans to create a new breed of officials who could read and act on written instructions. But the documents known as III and VI Aethelstan also suggest that the transmission of ideas about the law in writing was at least sometimes a two-way process and not just a royal preserve. The first of these texts was a report (it survives in Latin but may have been written originally in English) prepared by the bishops, thegns, nobles and free men of Kent, which thanked the king for his help in keeping the peace, referred to some of his legislation and made its own recommendations about what else might be done. The second was another report sent to the king, this time by 'the bishops and reeves who belong to London . . . both nobles and commoners' which also referred to Aethelstan's earlier laws and recorded the arrangements made to implement the king's decrees.[5]

Finally here, and as these texts make clear, the royal law codes of the tenth century were practical documents and their provisions were supposed to be implemented. There are doubts about whether the earlier codes of Alfred, Ine and the seventh-century Kentish kings were designed to have anything more than a symbolic value. But there are no such doubts about the tenth-century codes. They reflect the preoccupations of the king and his leading subjects, they address contemporary concerns about order and criminality and they try to provide specific solutions to the problems they addressed. They were not always successful, of course, but the law codes of this period were pragmatic attempts by the kings to achieve results and, in the process, bend all their subjects to their will.

Law codes and their concerns

Theft and public order

The royal law codes of this period were overwhelmingly concerned with the problem of theft and the preservation of order. Several of them set the tone right at the beginning by bemoaning the state of affairs they set out to improve. Edward the Elder's second code, for example, starts with an account of how the king 'exhorted all his councillors, when they were at Exeter, to consider how the public peace for which they were responsible could be kept better than it had been'. The opening in similar terms of V Aethelstan has already been mentioned,* whilst Edmund in his second code declared it 'most necessary that we should keep most firmly our

* Above, p. 154

peace and concord among ourselves throughout my dominion' and remarked how 'the illegal and manifold conflicts which take place among us distress me and all of us greatly'.[6] But it was Aethelstan who focused most frequently and intensively on thieving. His earliest code, issued at Grately in Hampshire, begins by stating 'First, that no thief is to be spared who is caught with stolen goods, if he is over twelve years old and if the value of the gods is over eight pence', and it continues with multiple provisions about prosecuting and severely punishing various forms of theft.[7] By the time V Aethelstan was issued at Exeter a few years later, however, not much seems to have improved and Aethelstan remarked with frustration on how the laws 'pronounced at Grately' had not been kept. He adopted a different approach as a result and offered a temporary amnesty to thieves who paid compensation to their victims by a specified date.[8] This idea was then developed further at another council meeting held at Faversham in Kent when a pardon was promised to criminals 'for any crime whatsoever . . . on the condition that henceforth and forever they abstain from all evil doing' and 'confess their crimes and make amends for everything of which they have been guilty'.[9] This change of strategy apparently did not work to the king's satisfaction either, however, and in the end, Aethelstan opted to revive a more conventionally ferocious approach to crime. Another assembly, this time at Thunderfield in Surrey, produced IV Aethelstan. All convicted thieves would now be executed, whether they had been caught red-handed or not. Any thief who ran away had to be pursued and killed, and if anyone came across a runaway, they were required to kill them on the spot. If the thief was a free woman, 'she shall be thrown from a cliff or drowned'; a male slave would be stoned to death and a female slave burned. The king did subsequently moderate his orders somewhat when he ordered that nobody under the age of fifteen should be executed, because 'it seemed too cruel to him that a man should be killed so young, or for so small an offence, as he had learnt was being done everywhere', and when he raised the lower limit on the value of goods whose theft would incur the death penalty to twelve pence. Nevertheless, it is provisions like this which have led one historian to detect 'an obsessional, even fanatical tone in Aethelstan's theft legislation'.[10]

But theft was not Aethelstan's only concern, and there were other threats to public order, too (we might call this 'anti-social behaviour'), which he tried to address in his legislation. 'Lordless' and 'landless' men stood out in this society because they lacked some of those crucial ties which bound individuals together and gave them responsibilities for each other's conduct. In both of these cases, crimes committed by such men would be answered for by their kindred. Similarly, lords who protected their followers so that justice was denied and the king had to intervene would be fined, and powerful kindreds who sheltered known disturbers of the peace would be removed from their neighbourhoods and, the king declared, 'go whither I wish'.[11] Others who gave such offenders any refuge would be punished, as would those who assisted in theft or were accessories to it. Aethelstan also issued laws against witchcraft and sorcery, and cattle-rustling appears to have been a particular problem which the king returned to several times.[12] Generally, however, the repeated (perhaps increasingly desperate) emphasis in Aethelstan's codes on the iniquities of crime and the obvious difficulties he had in combatting it might suggest that he was not very successful in the end. Of course, crime statistics are unavailable for the tenth century, but the sheer number of provisions Aethelstan issued might have made it difficult for his officials (however literate and conscientious they were) to keep up with what the law actually was. And, to be sure, later kings returned to the issue of criminality and treated it as if it was quite unresolved: the theft of livestock, in particular, seems to have been a serious concern for all of them.[13] It has been argued that 'the hallmark of Aethelstan's law-making is the gulf dividing its exalted aspirations from its spasmodic impact'.[14] But whilst there is obviously some justification for this observation, it might yet be too harsh a judgement on a king who, more than any of his predecessors, tried actively to maintain the peace within his kingdom at a time of rapid and enormous political change.

Loyalty

Another theme which recurs throughout the royal law codes of the tenth century is the importance of loyalty. As was argued earlier,* Alfred may have been the first English king to require an oath of loyalty from all his male subjects of a certain age and status. Edward the Elder's second code gets closer to making this obligation clear:

> If anyone neglects this and breaks his oath and his pledge, which the whole nation has given, he shall pay such compensation as the *domboc* declares.

And during Aethelstan's reign, it was agreed in a royal assembly at Thunderfield 'that every reeve should receive the pledge in his own shire, that they would all maintain that peace as King Aethelstan and his councillors had enacted it'.[15] But by the middle of the 900s, when King Edmund issued his third law code at Colyton in Devon, there is no doubt at all that the oath in question was not just a general one to behave well, but an undertaking given directly to the king:

> In the first place, all shall swear in the name of the Lord . . . that they will be faithful to King Edmund, even as it behoves a man to be faithful to his lord, without any dispute or dissension, openly or in secret, favouring what he favours and discountenancing what he discountenances.[16]

As for loyalty to one's lord, that was of central importance, too:

> And we have pronounced concerning treachery to a lord, that he who is accused is to forfeit his life if he cannot deny it or is afterwards convicted at the three-fold ordeal.

And in a similar vein:

> no one is to receive the man of another man, without the permission of him whom he served before.[17]

* Above, pp. 85–6

But there was more to loyalty than being dutiful, and here criminality and theft become relevant once again. It was seen in Chapter 3* how King Alfred may have attempted to develop the notion of theft as tantamount to treason, that is an offence not just against the victim but against the king. But whether Alfred was the first to have this idea or not, it took hold decisively in the tenth century. The royal legislation of this period contains regular references by the kings to 'the peace' being poorly kept or the need to maintain 'the peace'.[18] By 'the peace' in this context, the drafters of the laws did not just mean keeping things quiet, but they had in mind an almost tangible entity, a state of national security and stability which in some sense belonged to the king and which it was his duty, with the help of his people, to preserve. Thus, anyone who disturbed or broke the peace in any way (thieves, robbers, criminals in general) was also being disloyal to the king and in breach of the oath they had taken to him. There is no reason to doubt that Aethelstan and his fellow kings were sincere in their ambition to protect their people and enhance their safety through the implementation of strict laws and harsh punishments for wrongdoers. However, the system of courts would need to be reorganised and expanded in order to keep the peace across the new English kingdom, and a new force of literate, competent and obedient royal officials would be needed to administer it. The development of this new notion of a national peace would therefore help the king's subjects, but it would also give the king more opportunity to involve himself in their lives, and more power over them as a result.

Money and the economy

The kings of the tenth century repeatedly stressed how important it was for trading to take place in towns: 'all buying is to be within a town', Aethelstan said in his Gratley code, following a principle previously set out by Edward the Elder. But more than this, transactions should only be carried out under the supervision of appointed witnesses or officials. Goods should only be bought 'in the witness of the town-reeve or of another trustworthy man, or, again, in the witness of the reeves in a public meeting'.[19] And by Edgar's reign, the witnessing of commercial transactions had seemingly become a specialised affair. He declared that every borough should have thirty-six witnesses available to oversee deals (twelve if the borough was small). Each hundred should have twelve witnesses on standby, too: 'And every man is with their witness to buy and sell all goods that he buys and sells, in either a borough or a wapentake'. There should be two or three witnesses at every sale.[20] Certainly the kings were motivated here by their desire to keep traders honest and save their subjects from exploitation. It needed to be clear that the goods being bought and sold were not stolen, for example, and that the prices being demanded and paid were fair. But, of course, this kind of tight supervision gave the kings, through their officials who oversaw the system, even more control over the daily

* Above, pp. 85–6

lives of their people. This was obviously the case with the coinage, too. First Aethelstan and then Edgar declared that there should be a single coinage throughout their
kingdom. Again, this was a way of facilitating trade (Edgar attempted to standardise
prices for wool, too), but that trade was to be on the king's terms and with his
money made by his moneyers.[21]

Danish England

Edgar was the first tenth-century king who could meaningfully legislate for a single
English kingdom which extended beyond the river Humber. Edward the Elder's
realm had been much smaller than Edgar's, and, for all of Aethelstan's military and
political successes, it is hard to think that his laws had had much impact beyond
Mercia before he died. After Aethelstan's death, whatever authority he had managed to establish in northern England was seriously weakened anyway, and it was
not until the mid-950s that the English kings could begin realistically to regard all
the people from Cornwall to the Scottish frontier as subject to their laws.

Edgar's final law code, which was issued at an unknown place called *Wihtbordesstan*, probably in the early 970s, attempted to address aspects of this new situation.
On the one hand, he acknowledged the differences between southern England,
where his power was strongest, and those parts of northern England which had
been occupied and settled by the Vikings and their descendants since the late ninth
century:

> [I]t is my will that there should be in force among the Danes such good laws
> as they best decide on, and I have ever allowed them this and will allow it as
> long as my life lasts, because of your loyalty, which you have always shown me.

This was a pragmatic response to the fact that these areas had their own customary
laws and procedures which, even had he wanted to, Edgar would have found hard
to change. And what Edgar meant by 'the Danes' in this case seems to be clarified
more precisely later in the code when he refers to the support he expected 'Earl
Oslac and all the people who dwell in his ealdormanry' to give him in enforcing
it.[22] Oslac became ealdorman of Northumbria in about 966, but as was seen earlier,[*]
his practical authority probably extended no further north than the Tees. On the
other hand, however, whilst allowing for some Danish particularity when it came
to individual laws, Edgar was keen to use his legislative power to assert ultimate
authority over all his people. He does this several times in the *Wihtbordesstan* code.
Most resoundingly:

> this measure is to be common to all the nation, whether Englishmen, Danes
> or Britons, in every province of my dominion, to the end that poor man and

[*] Above, p. 149

rich may possess what they rightly acquire, and a thief may not know where to dispose of his stolen goods, although he steal anything, and against their will they be so guarded against, that few of them shall escape.[23]

Here was another way of articulating the idea referred to earlier,* that it was the king's duty to preserve the peace across his whole kingdom. But in explicitly referring to the different ethnic origins of his subjects at the same time, the king was recognising a new political reality and asserting his supremacy over it.

The church

At his coronation, the first promise the king gave was to protect the church. There were many ways to do this, but one was through royal legislation. Several law codes from this period deal almost exclusively with ecclesiastical matters. This has led some historians to argue that these codes were the result of separate meetings held by the English bishops and other leading clergy, perhaps at councils of their own or during a royal assembly where they discussed such matters among themselves, and that they were probably then explained to the king and the rest of the *witan* who gave their authority for the decrees to be issued.[24] So I Aethelstan attempted to tighten up the system whereby tithes and other payments were made to the church and warned priests who were not carrying out their duties properly that they risked losing their positions. II Edgar dealt with similar issues and set out sanctions for those who failed to pay what they owed. I Edmund laid heavy stress on the importance of clerical celibacy and ordered that churches should be kept in repair.

But ecclesiastical laws stamped with royal approval did not serve simply to support the church and enforce its rights. Much of the royal legislation issued during this period, whether secular or religious in its concerns, was influenced by the ideas of leading churchmen around the kings, men such as Archbishops Wulfhelm (926–41) and Oda (941–58) of Canterbury under Aethelstan and Edmund respectively, and by the teachings of the church more generally. The opening sections of Edgar's *Wihtbordesstan* suggest as much.[25] These laws, the king declared, were being issued in response to 'the sudden pestilence which greatly oppressed and reduced his people far and wide throughout his dominion', and he went on to observe that 'a calamity of this kind was merited by sins and by contempt of God's commands, and especially by the withholding of the tribute which Christian men ought to render to God in their tithes'. Just as Alfred had seen the viking attacks on his kingdom as divine punishment for sin, so Edgar saw 'the sudden pestilence' (perhaps the one referred to in the *Anglo-Saxon Chronicle* under the year 962) in the same way. The code then emphasised once again the importance of prompt and full tithe payments and urged the royal reeves to press for as much payment as they could. But the influence of the church was clear in other matters, too. The church encouraged

---

* Above, p. 158

reconciliation and settlement in disputes, as well as the importance of mercy and forgiveness. The ordeal, too, was essentially a religious ceremony conducted by priests, and when King Edmund issued his laws regulating the conduct of feuds he did so having first considered 'how I could most advance Christianity'.[26]

Courts

For all this legislative effort on the part of the kings, however, they would have been unable to achieve any of their objectives without effective legal machinery. As Chapter 3 showed,* there was little resembling a 'system' or 'network' of courts in England at the end of the ninth century. As far as the limited evidence allows any firm conclusions to be drawn at all, there was the king's court and there were local courts. None of these was convened consistently at fixed times, with set procedures, defined powers or permanent personnel. The king could hear cases whenever he wanted. Often he would have done so during meetings with his leading subjects, but Helmstan's case shows that royal involvement could be spontaneous and improvised, too. Local courts may have met more regularly, and there may have been some participation there by royal officials, but this is all very unclear. Seventy-five years later, however, the situation was quite different. A hierarchy of separate and distinct courts certainly did exist in England by the end of King Edgar's reign, making this period a pivotal one in the development of England's judicial system.

At the top of this hierarchy, of course, was the king's own court. The king was the ultimate judge in his kingdom, and there was no appeal to any higher authority from his decisions. He was expected to be an active promoter of justice, and the expectations were set out in the 'three precepts declared to the people by the newly ordained king' at his coronation: 'that the Church of God and all Christian people have true peace for all time . . . that robberies and every injustice be forbidden to all ranks, and . . . that he offer equity and mercy in all judgements'. By the time Edgar became king, these 'precepts' or instructions had been recast as three promises solemnly given by the new ruler to his subjects, to defend the church, to destroy wickedness and judge with justice and mercy. This new version of the king's oath was probably written for Edgar's coronation at Bath in 973.[27] John of Worcester's description of King Edgar was written some time later, in the twelfth century, and is perhaps a little rose-tinted. But it also gives a strong flavour of the kind of thing a king of this period was expected to do for the sake of his people:

> in winter and spring, he was accustomed to enquire diligently within his kingdom, travelling right through all the English provinces, about the manner in which the legal rights and the statutes he had promulgated were observed by the magnates, lest the poor should be crushed by injustices they suffered from the powerful.[28]

---

* Above, pp. 80–1

It is hard to imagine the kings travelling quite so far so often, but the emphasis on the doing of justice as a fundamental royal duty is valid, and Edgar himself summarised his aims at the start of one of his codes: 'it is my will that every man, whether poor or rich, is to be entitled to the benefit of the common law [*folcriht* in Old English], and just judgments are to be judged for him'.[29]

However, there are indications that the kings of this period were actually trying to reduce the number of cases they heard personally, so that their intervention in a dispute would become a matter of last resort when all other options had been exhausted. Aethelstan specified fines payable by someone 'who appeals to the king before he demands justice as often as he ought', and Edgar said something similar: 'no one is to apply to the king in any suit, unless he may not be entitled to right or cannot obtain justice at home'.[30] So in practice, it is likely that most of the disputes the king was personally involved in were special in some way (between two or more of his leading men, perhaps, or involving a great church), that they concerned land and that they were heard at one of the assemblies he regularly held. The developing importance of these meetings during this period was stressed in Chapter 6,* and it was emphasised above when the making of royal legislation was discussed. But it is important to remember here that the king's obligation to do justice between and for his subjects was also one of their main features. More than this, however, the making of a judgement on one of these occasions was another kind of collaborative decision on the part of the king and his councillors and part of that wider effort to cultivate consensus among the ruling class and broaden the base of the king's authority.

Below the level of the king's court, by 975 every hundred, shire and *burh* had its own court as well. The so-called Hundred Ordinance (also known as I Edgar), which may have been issued by Edgar at the start of his reign or by one of his immediate predecessors, stipulated that the hundred court should be held once a month, and Edgar's law code issued at Andover (III Edgar), probably during the 960s, restated this. Meanwhile the shire court was supposed to meet twice a year in the presence of the local bishop and ealdorman. Edgar also directed that the *burh* court should meet three times a year, presumably to enforce Aethelstan's earlier order (or something like it) that repairs to the *burhs* should be carried out annually.[31] But it is very unlikely that these provisions actually created these courts. To be sure, the expansion of the English kingdom during the first half of the tenth century presented the king and his government with enormous challenges of control and organisation. So, as territory was acquired in midland England and divided into shires on the West Saxon model (this process was well underway by 975 and perhaps complete, as Chapter 6 argued),† it made sense to have a regular meeting of that shire's elite community presided over by a high-status representative of the king, either the bishop, the ealdorman or both. Disputes could be aired and settled, accusations and announcements could be made and the important men of the shire could begin to appreciate that their best interests now lay in cooperating with the new regime. But, having said this, it is only sensible to

---

* Above, pp. 137–42
† Above, pp. 142–4

suggest that meetings like this must have happened reasonably often across the shires of Wessex during the ninth century. According to Asser, King Alfred held judicial hearings for those nobles and 'common people' who were dissatisfied with the results of hearings they had already been involved in before ealdormen and reeves.[32] Edgar's decree that the shire court should be held twice a year, therefore, may have been a way of acknowledging the importance of a time-honoured West Saxon institution, and of standardising its operations, as it was introduced across the newly acquired parts of his enlarged kingdom. And similar considerations may apply to the emergence of the hundred court. The first precisely dateable reference to the term 'hundred' is found in King Edmund's laws, and therefore coincides broadly speaking with the extension of the shiring system into the midlands. But Edward the Elder probably had a similar tribunal in mind in his second law code when he ordered his reeves to hold a meeting every four weeks to arrange days for the hearing of disputes. It is also conceivable in turn that Edward was simply referring in writing to a practice which was already current and, perhaps, long-established. It seems very likely that the hundred court of the later tenth century was 'essentially the old local court with a new name, and a more regulated system'.[33]

Hearing a case

So shire courts and hundred courts, it can be argued, were probably versions of already-existing tribunals, reorganised from above by the king's government. But if a more systematised court structure was evidently in place by 975, the number of reported cases which reveal any aspect of legal practice and procedure is so small that it is virtually impossible to get any coherent sense of how these courts actually worked, other than on an individual case-by-case basis. Legal disputes of one kind or another might be mentioned in several different types of evidence: chronicles, for example, or biographies of prominent individuals, usually churchmen. But most of the recorded cases are referred to in charters because the disputes in question concerned rich individuals or institutions with property, and this in turn means that most of the surviving case law was written by or on behalf of the successful party in the dispute. As for the criminal law, there are only about thirty surviving references before 975 to specific crimes which were actually committed, and more than half of these are from Edgar's reign. And even where an argument about property or the commission of a criminal offence is revealed in a source, the details provided are typically thin, elusive and hard to interpret with conviction.

One unusually detailed example of a recorded case will illustrate some of these problems.[34] Some time during the reign of King Eadred, at Yaxley in Cambridge-shire, 'a woman was stolen' from a man called Aelfsige. Aelfsige tracked down the woman (presumably she was one of Aelfsige's slaves; her name was Thurwif) and found her in the possession of a certain Wulfstan. Wulfstan claimed that he had acquired the woman from Aethelstan of Sunbury (Middlesex), who in turn claimed that he could prove how she had come to him. However, Aethelstan failed to do this and had to return the woman to Aelfsige and pay him two pounds compensation. At this point, the local ealdorman, Brihtferth, got involved. Since Aethelstan had failed to show how the woman had come into his possession, he was deemed to have stolen her, and Brihtferth demanded his *wergild*. Aethelstan said he did not have the money, but when his brother Edward offered to pay it if Aethelstan handed over his estate at Sunbury to him, Aethelstan refused and said that 'he would rather that it perished by fire or flood than suffer that'. Edward's argument that it would be better for one of them to have the estate than to lose it completely fell on deaf ears, and the lands were confiscated by the ealdorman in default of Aethelstan's *wergild* payment. After King Eadred's death, Aethelstan tried to repossess his lost estate, but his claim was thrown out. Later he appealed to King Edgar to intervene, but it was decided once again that he could only recover the lands if he paid his *wergild* as he had been ordered to do in the first place. Aethelstan still lacked the necessary funds, however, and still would not let his brother pay for him. Sunbury eventually ended up in the possession of a certain Ecgferth. When Ecgferth died, he left the estate to Archbishop Dunstan of Canterbury who had agreed to act as guardian for Ecgferth's widow and child, but when Dunstan tried to take up the bequest, the king refused to let him. 'My councillors have declared all Ecgferth's property forfeit, by the sword that hung on his hip when he was drowned', Edgar declared, before seizing the property himself and granting it to one of his ealdormen, Aelfheah. Dunstan offered to pay Ecgferth's *wergild* in order to recover the estate, but the king once again refused: 'That might be offered to obtain a consecrated grave for him, but I have left the whole case to Aelfheah'. The archbishop had to wait another six years before he finally acquired the land at Sunbury, having paid Aelfheah 200 mancuses (twenty-five pounds of silver) for it.

Here, with the archbishop seemingly in secure possession of the disputed estates, the record of the case ends. It obviously leaves some important questions unanswered. Why was Aethelstan so unwilling to accept his brother's help? What had Ecgferth done that led King Edgar to ignore the terms of his will, confiscate his property and, it seems, deny him a Christian burial? But beyond these narrow issues, several broader considerations emerge. First, the extent of royal involvement in this case is particularly striking. More than once after Aethelstan lost his estate at Sunbury, a king was personally involved in determining how the case would progress. Second, and even more significantly, when Aethelstan could not pay his *wergild*, he was not executed for theft as the laws suggest he should have been; rather his estate at Sunbury was confiscated by Ealdorman Brihtferth and it became in effect royal property which the kings subsequently, and on several occasions, disposed of as they pleased. It has already been explained how, by this time, theft was equated with treachery to the king.* The loss of one's property was an appropriate punishment in both cases. Third, there is no mention whatsoever in the case report of any official tribunal (a shire or hundred court, for example) being used during the course of this dispute, or of any specific royal laws being relied upon. Aethelstan was clearly regarded by the authorities as guilty of stealing Thurwif, but how and where that verdict was reached (if it ever formally was) is quite unclear. Of course,

* Above, pp. 85–6

that is far from saying that shire and hundred courts were not functioning or dealing with a whole range of legal matters just like the ones in this case, but a good deal of imaginative speculation, based on evidence from later periods, is required in order to reconstruct something of what they did.

The outcome of all legal disputes depended at least in theory on the quality of the evidence which the parties could produce. Testimony could be written or oral. In cases concerning land, the former might often be in the form of charters or other such documents which gave evidence of title. However, charters were probably only available in cases where high-status individuals or institutions were involved (most transfers of property lower down the social scale were still made verbally), and anyway, such written evidence as did exist may only have been regarded in this period as partial proof at best. It was the ceremonial, public act in which land was often conveyed, rather than the written record of that ritual, which transferred title, and so oral evidence of that event would have been preferable. Where oral evidence was given, oaths of course were vital. Parties would swear their own oaths as to the facts and issues in dispute (the higher an individual's rank and the better his reputation, the more 'oath-worthy' he was), but they might also bring in witnesses and oath-helpers to bolster their own oath and give their case more credibility. The more oath-helpers a party could recruit, and the higher their status, the better. Thus, the reputation of those making and defending the claims in question was of central importance in determining who would win. Edward the Elder's early legislation gives some idea of what would happen in a property dispute:

> in cases where a man wishes to substantiate his plea of ownership, he shall produce trustworthy witness to this effect, or he shall produce such an oath – an unselected oath if he can – as the plaintiff shall be bound to accept.[35]

By 'trustworthy witness' here is probably meant either documentary or sworn oral testimony, whilst 'such an oath' refers to the cumulative value of the oaths sworn by his oath-helpers. Ideally, these should be 'unselected', that is individuals nominated by the litigant and willing to help, rather than others appointed by the court whose oaths would inevitably be less compelling.

Sometimes, however, oaths could not be used at all. If one party was a known criminal or a stranger in the neighbourhood, for example, he would lose his 'oath-worthiness' and, almost certainly, his case. And Aethelstan's Grately code ordered that anyone who was found to have sworn a false oath would never be entitled to swear an oath again.[36] But in criminal cases more broadly, the use of oaths was less common anyway. This might be because of the value of the stolen goods in a case of theft, or because of the nature of the accusation (crimes of stealth such as robbery at night) could not be dealt with by the accused's oath. Often, too, it might be because there was just a general suspicion about a particular accused (someone who claimed to have acted in self-defence in a case of alleged murder, for example), and so no direct accuser or witnesses.

Most criminal cases would begin with a direct accusation (an 'appeal') by one person or their kin against another individual. If the accuser was of reasonably high status, the accusation might be supportable with an oath and perhaps a reputable accused would be able to swear as to his innocence, too. But in situations where oaths were inappropriate or inconclusive for whatever reason, another form of proof had to be used to establish guilt or innocence: the ordeal. Edward the Elder's first law code stipulated what happened to those convicted of perjury:

> if the charge has been proved or the oath on their behalf has collapsed, or has been overborne by more strongly supported testimony, never again shall they have the privilege of clearing themselves by oaths, but only by the ordeal.[37]

But the fullest explanation yet of how the ordeal actually operated is found in the laws of Aethelstan. The accused was required to attend mass on each of the three days before the ordeal, and during that time, he was to remain under the supervision of a priest, eat no food but bread and vegetables, and drink nothing but water. On the day of the ordeal itself, he would make a charitable offering, take communion and swear an oath as to his innocence before beginning.[38] What happened next depended on the kind of accusation which had been made. A moneyer accused of producing sub-standard coins could clear himself by undergoing the ordeal of hot iron. That is, he would have to carry a piece of red-hot iron in one hand over a fixed distance. The burnt hand would be bound, and if, after three days, it had healed enough to be deemed 'clean', he would be acquitted. If the hand was not clean, however, it would be cut off and displayed at the mint.[39] Those who plotted against their lords, broke into churches or practised witchcraft which resulted in death would undergo the triple ordeal, as would arsonists and 'those who avenge a thief'.[40] In other words, they would go through the same process as an accused moneyer, but carry a piece of red-hot iron three times the usual weight: the Hundred Ordinance stipulated that the iron used in the triple ordeal should weigh three pounds.[41] If they were found guilty, different punishments followed according to the nature of the offence. The Grately code also refers to the ordeal of water, in which the accused was 'to sink one and a half ells on the rope', and there are other mentions in a text now known as *Ordal*, which may originally have been part of one of Aethelstan's codes, of the ordeal by cauldron, in which (in the single ordeal) the accused plunged his hand into hot water up to his wrist to retrieve a stone and (in the triple ordeal), the arm had to be submerged up to the elbow.[42] It is by no means always clear which type of ordeal was used in which case or quite what they all entailed. But it seems to have been a procedure largely reserved for those accused of serious criminal acts: homicide and theft as well as those mentioned already. There is no evidence to suggest that ordeals were used in cases concerning land before 1066.

Policing and punishment

Not every dispute was settled by an appearance in court or the outcome of an ordeal, however; far from it. Private justice in the form of the feud still had an important role to play in the management of relationships between individuals and groups. King Alfred had tried to impose tight procedures on the way feuds operated so as to make violence very much a last resort. Half a century later, King Edmund attempted to go further. In order to minimise the consequences where a feud had resulted from a killing, he prohibited vengeance being taken against anyone but the killer himself. If one of the killer's kin was attacked by a kinsman or associate of the deceased, the latter 'is to incur the hostility of the king and all his friends, and to forfeit what he owns'. The code also outlines an elaborate system for negotiating a settlement in such cases. 'Leading men' should oversee such processes, and the ultimate aim was to extract the payment of the dead man's *wergild* from his killer and avoid violence completely.[43] How successful such attempts to keep the peace were is unknowable, and King Edmund's obvious concerns about this issue suggest that unregulated feuding remained a common problem.

By the mid-tenth century new mechanisms were emerging which would be essential to the maintenance of order for the rest of the middle ages. The most important of these was the tithing or frankpledge ('free-pledge') system. This was designed to impose policing responsibilities on local communities and give individuals responsibility for monitoring and responding to the illegal conduct of their neighbours. In its fully developed (post-1066) form, the sheriff would hold a special meeting of the hundred court twice a year and take the 'view of frankpledge'. This meant ensuring that every free male of twelve or over in the hundred had taken an oath of loyalty to the king and his heirs and promised not to steal, and that every such male was attached to a tithing (a group of ten free householders). The members of a tithing were obliged to ensure each other's performance of their legal duties. This might mean apprehending one of their number if he was accused of committing a crime. If they failed to do so, or if the accused escaped, the tithing would be fined for its failure to control him. In the event of an escape, too, the rest of the tithing was expected to launch the hunt for the fugitive. The only clear evidence of this system in operation dates from later periods, but it seems clear that its origins lie in the mid-tenth century, and perhaps even earlier in embryonic form. There are references to tithings, and to units very like them, carrying out policing duties during Aethelstan's reign, and the picture is even clearer by the time Edgar became king. The Hundred Ordinance (I Edgar) outlined what should happen when a thief had to be pursued and captured: 'If the need is urgent, one is to inform the man in charge of the hundred, and he then the men over the tithings; and all are to go forth, where God may guide them, that they may reach [the thief]'.[44] The frankpledge structure was supposed to give all free men a direct interest in the conduct of their fellow tithing members and, therefore, a stake in the maintenance of local order. But it is important to remember that, once again, it gave the king, through his officials and the workings of an increasingly coherent system, the power to organise and discipline his subjects. In keeping the peace, the king was increasing his power.

But local communities were not just passively put-upon by an ever more dominant central power. Sometimes, the evidence suggests that the kings' subjects took up their responsibilities eagerly and conscientiously. The documents known as III Aethelstan and VI Aethelstan were not royal products at all, but rather responses to the king's legislation issued by local communities. The first was 'The decree of the bishops and other councillors in Kent, concerning measures for the preservation of the public peace'. It thanked the king for his efforts to preserve the peace and referred to his laws issued at Grately and Faversham. It then set out the principle that 'every man shall stand surety for his own men against every charge of crime'. This was a reaffirmation of the importance of the lordship bond and of the duties of lords to control their followers' behaviour. The text concluded by asking the king to correct anything in it which needed amending, 'And we are zealously prepared to carry out everything you are willing to order us, in so far as it lies within our power to do so'.[45] The second of these documents was prepared by 'the bishops and reeves who belong to London' and expressed the views of what historians refer to as the London peace guild, an organisation responsible, it seems, for policing the London area. Once again, it referred to some of Aethelstan's earlier legislation, but this was added to by the Londoners to reflect their own particular concerns. The prosecution of theft (of livestock and slaves) featured heavily, as did the obstacles presented by an over-powerful kindred in the pursuit of criminals. But deference to royal authority was obvious once again, too: 'But let us keep our pledge and the peace, as it may please our lord; there is great need for us to carry out what he wishes, and if he commands and directs us further, we are humbly ready to obey'.[46]

These two texts may together hint at the existence of a whole apparatus of local law enforcement which is otherwise unrecorded: if local communities were responding to royal legislation in their own way in London and Kent, there is no reason why this could not have been happening in other areas at the same time. But this was far from a free-for-all. The emphasis on shared mutual responsibilities for keeping the peace is common to all the surviving evidence, whether royal or local, and the seriousness with which these duties were taken is clear. But what remains plain above all is the respect for the king as the ultimate authority in these matters. That might be expected in documents like III and VI Aethelstan, which may for one reason or another have been designed to curry favour with the king, but there is no reason to doubt their sincerity in attempting to deal with matters of crime and social order. Traditional ties of neighbourhood, family and lordship remained hugely powerful during this period and would have formed the basis of much dispute settlement in practice. But these ties were gradually being co-opted and developed by the government (in the form of the tithing system, for example) and falling under more centralised control. Explicit oaths of loyalty to the king and dutiful obedience to royal officials both supplemented these customary obligations and served to make royal power a more consistent and predictable presence in local affairs. All of this only helped to foster the idea of a single English people under a single English king.

The longer arm of the law

The burst of legislative activity presided over by the English kings during this period can be seen as a sign of their growing confidence and enormous ambition. When they issued laws, Edward the Elder, Aethelstan, Edmund and Edgar were all attempting to define their status and proclaim their achievements. Law-making expressed their imperial aims and confirmed their success in first acquiring and then retaining control over a vastly extended kingdom. Beyond this, however, it remains hard to get a clear view of how the law was routinely applied and enforced. In southern England, the degree of uniformity of practice and custom remains obscure, whilst in Northumbria the picture is perfectly dark. More generally, the extent of Scandinavian influence on the workings of the law is uncertain. Even so, between 899 and 975, some important developments did take place. A hierarchy of courts and a system of policing with some kind of national coverage are discernible in outline by the time of Edgar's death, whilst the idea (embryonic under Alfred) that the law might be used as a way of establishing and testing loyalty to the king had become firmly established. The notion that theft amounted to treason and the associated sense that there was a 'peace' which the kings were bound to preserve were enormously helpful in allowing the rulers to tighten the grip they and their officials held on the legal machine. And the early development of the tithing system gave the king's servants the chance to exercise direct control over the lives of individuals and their connections at ground level. By 975 Alfred's successors had asserted their dominance over much of England in a variety of political and military ways. Less obviously, the marked intensification of routine royal involvement in the operation and administration of the law was also a crucial part of this process. Increased royal activity of this kind, which gradually served to define how the law worked and what it said, could only in the end give the kings even more power over their subjects.

DEBATE 5

How Danish was the Danelaw?

By the start of the tenth century, people from Scandinavia ruled much of northern, eastern and midland England. Most of them were descendants of the viking warriors who had come to England in 865 as members of the Great Army which quickly conquered East Anglia, Mercia and much of Northumbria. These conquests, first recognised implicitly in the treaty between Alfred the Great and Guthrum which drew the line between their respective territories, formed what later became known as the Danelaw and this term is still used by historians to describe those parts of England most profoundly affected by the viking invasions of the later ninth century. *The Anglo-Saxon Chronicle* records the settlement (as opposed to the conquest) of Northumbria, Mercia and East Anglia by Scandinavians in 876, 877 and 880 respectively. However, what settlement actually amounted to is far from clear: 'According to who you believe, immigration was confined to a small group of elite land-takers or it was a secondary mass migration in the wake of the raiding parties'.[1] How many settlers were there? What was their social status? Did they integrate with the indigenous population or enslave them? Did they convert to Christianity or stick with their pagan ways? The hundreds of place names with Scandinavian elements surviving in Lincolnshire and Yorkshire (those ending in -by, for example, which means 'settlement' or 'village' in Old Norse) suggest that foreign settlers could have a significant impact on local spaces and language. However, such toponymic evidence is late (mostly from Domesday Book) and is not consistent across the Danelaw. It reveals little about the time-scale or the nature of settlement. Archaeological evidence is also frustratingly elusive. The relative scarcity of Scandinavian-style burials found in England might suggest that the settlers were happy to be buried like their new neighbours, the Anglo-Saxons. This could point towards a rapid adoption of the local customs and perhaps even the local religion. Scattered evidence from excavated farms and settlements shows that Scandinavian fashions and designs were being combined with Anglo-Saxon ones on brooches and buckles, all of which hints at the development of a hybrid culture in the generations after the first settlers arrived. Crucial here was the conquest of central England by Edward the Elder and his sister Aethelflaed in the first quarter of the tenth century and the gradual incorporation of the north into the English kingdom after that. In return for their lands and the acceptance of their customs, the viking leaders accepted the southern rulers as their kings. Thereafter, special provision was regularly made for the Danelaw in royal law codes, and political stability (with some interruptions) was gradually established there. This allowed the church to recover largely unmolested after its ninth-century traumas and spread its influence over its new mixed congregation. It also allowed the Danelaw to prosper economically. Urban markets boomed at Chester and York; in the midlands the Five Boroughs (Derby, Leicester, Lincoln, Nottingham, Stamford) grew into successful towns, as did Ipswich and Norwich in the east. The Danelaw, of course, was a not a single entity. Scandinavian settlement, along with political and military pressures, affected parts of it differently and at different times. Relations between the new and established populations and between the settlers themselves cannot always have been harmonious. Nevertheless, from the late 800s onwards, the people living in these areas of England, with their different languages, customs and religious beliefs, assimilated to a remarkable degree. And whilst it may be going too far today to describe the society they created as one 'abnormal in structure and unique in racial composition', it was undoubtedly rich, complex and distinctively Anglo-Scandinavian.[2]

1 Julian D. Richards, *The Vikings: A Very Short Introduction* (Oxford, 2005) p. 64.
2 Stenton, *Anglo-Saxon England*, p. 513.

Notes

1 *EHD*, i nos.36 (V Aethelstan, Prologue), 40 (II Edgar, Prologue).
2 Foot, *Aethelstan*, p. 137.
3 *EHD*, i no.41 (IV Edgar, 15.1).
4 Attenborough, *Laws*, pp. 114–15 (I Edward, Prologue), 120–1 (II Edward, 8), 122–7; *EHD*, i nos.36 (II Aethelstan, 25), 37 (VI Aethelstan, 11).

5 Attenborough, *Laws*, pp. 142–7 (III Aethelstan); *EHD*, i no.37 (VI Aethelstan).

6 Attenborough, *Laws*, pp. 118–19 (II Edward, Prologue); *EHD*, i nos.36 (V Aethelstan, Prologue), 38 (II Edmund, Prologue 1–2).

7 *EHD*, i no.35 (II Aethelstan, 1).

8 *EHD*, i no.36 (V Aethelstan, Prologue, 3.1).

9 Attenborough, *Laws*, pp. 144–5 (III Aethelstan, 3).

10 Attenborough, *Laws*, pp. 148–9 (IV Aethelstan, 6, 6.3–7); *EHD*, i no.37 (VI Aethelstan, 12.1, 12.3); Wormald, *MEL*, ii p. 128.

11 *EHD*, i nos.35 (II Aethelstan, 2–2.2, 8), 36 (V Aethelstan, Prologue 1), 37 (VI Aethelstan, 8.2); Attenborough, *Laws*, pp. 144–5 (III Aethelstan, 6).

12 *EHD*, i nos. 35 (II Aethelstan, 6, 9), 38 (VI Aethelstan, 8.7–8)

13 See, for example, Robertson, *Laws*, pp. 14–15 (III Edmund, 5–6); *EHD*, i no.41 (IV Edgar, 8–11).

14 Wormald, *MEL*, i p. 300.

15 Attenborough, *Laws*, pp. 120–1 (II Edward, 5); *EHD*, i no.37 (VI Aethelstan, 10).

16 Robertson, *Laws*, pp. 12–13 (III Edmund, 1).

17 *EHD*, i no.35 (II Aethelstan, 5, 22).

18 Attenborough, *Laws*, pp. 118–19, 142–5 (II Edward, Prologue, III Aethelstan, 2, 5); *EHD*, i nos.36 (V Aethelstan, Prologue), 37 (VI Aethelstan, 10).

19 *EHD*, i no.35 (II Aethelstan, 12, 13.1); Attenborough, *Laws*, pp. 114–15 (I Edward, 1).

20 *EHD*, i no.41 (IV Edgar, 3–6).

21 *EHD*, i nos.35 (II Aethelstan, 14, 14.2), 41 (III Edgar, 8, 8.2).

22 *EHD*, i no.41 (IV Edgar, 12, 15).

23 *EHD*, i no.41 (IV Edgar, 2.2).

24 M.K. Lawson, 'Archbishop Wulfstan and the Homiletic Element in the Laws of Aethelred II and Cnut', in Alexander R. Rumble (ed.), *The Reign of Cnut. King of England, Denmark and Norway* (Leicester, 1994), pp. 141–64, at pp. 144–6; idem, *Cnut. England's Viking King 1016–1035*, 2nd edn. (Stroud, 2011), p. 60.

25 *EHD*, i no.41 (IV Edgar, Prologue, 1–1.8).

26 *EHD*, i no.38 (II Edmund, Prologue).

27 Nelson, 'Second English *Ordo*', in her *Politics and Ritual*, pp. 369–70; Wormald, *MEL*, i pp. 446–8; Maddicott, *Origins of the English Parliament*, pp. 34–5.

28 *JW*, ii pp. 426–7.

29 *EHD*, i no.40 (III Edgar, 1.1); Robertson, *Laws*, p. 24.

30 *EHD*, i nos.35 (II Aethelstan, 3), 40 (III Edgar, 2).

31 *EHD*, i nos.39 (I Edgar, 1), 40 (III Edgar, 5–5.2), 35 (II Aethelstan, 13).

32 K&L, pp. 109–10.

33 Robertson, *Laws*, pp. 12–13 (III Edmund, 2); Attenborough, *Laws*, pp. 120–1 (II Edward, 8); Wormald, *MEL*, ii p. 196.

34 S1447; Robertson, *Anglo-Saxon Charters*, no.XLIV (pp. 90–3).

35 Attenborough, *Laws*, pp. 114–15 (I Edward, 1.3).

36 *EHD*, i no.35 (II Aethelstan, 26).

37 Attenborough, *Laws*, pp. 116–17 (II Edward, 3).

38 *EHD*, i no.35 (II Aethelstan, 23).

39 *EHD*, i no.35 (II Aethelstan, 14.1).

40 *EHD*, i no.35 (II Aethelstan, 4–6.3).

41 *EHD*, i no.39 (I Edgar, 9).

42 *EHD*, i no.35 (II Aethelstan, 23.1); Attenborough, *Laws*, pp. 170–3; Wormald, *MEL*, i pp. 373–4.

43 *EHD*, i no.38 (II Edmund, 1, 1.3, 7).

44 *EHD*, i nos. 37, 39 (VI Aethelstan, 3, 8.1; I Edgar, 2).

45 Attenborough, *Laws*, pp. 142–7 (III Aethelstan, Prologue, 7, 8).

46 *EHD*, i no.37 (VI Aethelstan, Prologue, 8.9).

8

THE KINGS AND THE CHURCH, 899–975

Alfred the Great tried hard to revitalise Christian practice and worship in his kingdom. He founded monasteries, he encouraged literacy in English and Latin and he instructed bishops. But when he died in 899, religious life in England was still varied and diverse, whilst ecclesiastical structures and routines were far from uniform. Alfred's successors appreciated just as he had done how much a strong, centrally organised church could offer them in terms of personnel, material resources and ideological support. Kings from Edward the Elder to Edgar exploited the church (particularly its lands, many of which they acquired), but they relied on it, too, to underpin royal power and shape the image of kingship. In this regard, the church was simply another branch of government.

Royal government and the church

The English clergy played a prominent role in the government of the expanding English kingdom during this period. They did so at the highest of levels around the king as well as in the localities, and they did so in a wide range of capacities. Their presence was most obviously felt at court. Constantly in attendance on the king would have been a group of literate churchmen whose job it was to say Mass, hear the royal confession and provide spiritual guidance. But they would also read and write many of the king's documents and perform other routine administrative tasks for him. At a higher level than this, however, the English archbishops and bishops, along with some of the leading abbots, were regularly in attendance at royal assemblies, as the witness lists to the kings' charters show. Collectively they, along with the ealdormen, thegns and *ministri* also included in the lists, were the king's *witan*, and they would advise him on all manner of political, diplomatic, military and legal matters. Ecclesiastical influence on both the tone and content of royal legislation of this period, for example, was obvious and profound, as Chapter 7 showed.* But behind the formality of the witness lists were more personal relation-ships between the king and his most powerful ecclesiastical advisers. Much here would have depended on how much the king liked or disliked one individual or another, but great figures like Archbishops Oda and Dunstan of Canterbury and Bishop Aethelwold of Winchester would certainly have exercised the kind of inti-mate influence over the king's routine decision-making and the direction of royal policy which is now impossible to recover in any detail.

When away from court, the bishops in particular had their own duties to per-form. They would have needed their own staff to run their estates and to ensure that tithes and other church dues were collected, church buildings were maintained and (most crucially) pastoral care was properly provided across their dioceses. But the clergy had public responsibilities, too. The ordeal, as King Aethelstan's Grately law code made clear, was essentially a religious ceremony conducted by priests. And bishops were more broadly involved in the organisation of local peacekeeping, too, as texts like III and VI Aethelstan make clear. Later, King Edgar required that, alongside the local ealdormen, the local bishop should preside over the twice-yearly meetings of the shire court.[1]

It is hardly surprising that the king prized his power to appoint bishops, as they contributed hugely to the projection and implementation of royal authority across the kingdom. In addition to controlling their dioceses and carrying out their offi-cial duties in the shire court, they were expected to preach loyalty and obedience to the king and to ensure that the priests appointed to meet the spiritual needs of their local congregations did the same. Above all, however, the church gave the king divine legitimacy, and it did this most visibly and splendidly at his coronation. The detailed content of the coronation ceremony (its rituals, procedures, prayers and hymns) developed significantly during the tenth century as it evolved to reflect and endorse the growing power of the kings of Wessex over the whole of England. Most relevantly here, by the end of this period, the first part of the royal coronation oath took the form of a promise by the king to protect the church. In return for this undertaking, he would be anointed and crowned. The high-point of these develop-ments came with Edgar's so-called imperial coronation at Bath in May 973 which, although its precise significance remains unclear, was probably designed at least in part to proclaim the king's lordship over the whole of Britain.† The involvement of individual clergymen in this event should not be overlooked, however. Behind the scenes they would have been responsible for the religious, ideological and symbolic character of the ceremony – not just what the king and others said, but the appear-ance and choreography of the event, too. The king was consecrated and crowned by Archbishop Dunstan of Canterbury whilst other bishops and leading abbots looked on close at hand. Byrhterth of Ramsey's account of what happened repeatedly stresses the number of clergymen present and the centrality of their role before, during and

---

* Above, pp. 160–1
† Above, pp. 133–4

after the ceremony. He refers to 'a multitude of priests' and 'a crowd of clerics' who took part in addition, whilst the *Anglo-Saxon Chronicle*'s entry for 973 also records how 'There was assembled a crowd of priests, a great throng of learned monks' at Bath.[2] Their job was to chant, sing and process as loudly and impressively as possible.

It was suggested in Chapter 6* that coronations began to be supplemented by periodic crown-wearings during this period. If this is what happened, then church-men would have been heavily involved in the management of these occasions as well, where the power of the king was restated and publicly proclaimed once more. All such ceremonial served to define the king's responsibilities in ways which suited the church, but also, in ways which very much suited him, these elaborate rituals expressed the king's unique status, elevated him above ordinary mortals and gave the stamp of heavenly approval to his more earthly achievements in politics and war.

Kings and dioceses

The original diocese of the West Saxons was split into two smaller ones (Winchester and Sherborne) in the early eighth century. This arrangement was still in place when King Alfred died in 899 – Asser was bishop of Sherborne and Denewulf was bishop of Winchester. Winchester, however, was more than just an episcopal centre. It was probably the most populous and largest urban settlement in Wessex (it was one of only two places assessed at 2,400 hides in the Burghal Hidage; the other was Wallingford), and this gave it a huge economic importance. But it was a royal centre, too, and the relationship between the town and the kings of Wessex was a long-established one. Alfred, his father Aethelwulf and his grandfather Ecgberht were all buried in the cathedral church (the Old Minster, as it is usually known), and as part of his burghal programme, Alfred had entirely remodelled the town's street plan to enhance its defensive capabilities. The first mint there was probably established at the same time. Alfred may well have been planning further developments in Winchester when he died, but, if he was, these were carried on by his relatives. By the end of 902 (when she died), his widow Ealhswith had founded a convent there, the abbey of St Mary, known as Nunnaminster, but the most important new foundation was the monastery, dedicated to St Peter, established by Edward the Elder and usually known as the New Minster. Edward almost certainly had grand plans for his new church. It was probably intended from the start to serve as the mausoleum of the ruling dynasty: Edward had his father reburied there, and Alfred was joined by Ealhswith when she died. Eventually, Edward himself was interred there, as were two of his sons and (probably) one of his wives and his brother. Cults were manufactured there, too: the relics of the Breton saint, Judoc, were enshrined in the monastery, as were the remains of Grimbald, who had been one of Alfred's closest advisers. Miracles were soon said to have taken place at his tomb, and this

* Above, pp. 140–1

could only have added to the impression Edward was trying to cultivate of the New Minster as 'the shrine church and pantheon of the West Saxon monarchy'.[3]

On the face of things, new religious houses such as these, with their obvious royal connections, would serve to enhance Winchester's prestige further and consolidate its position as the chief town of Wessex. However, Edward's project can also be seen as part of an attempt by him (which his father may have begun) to assert more direct royal control over the town at the expense of its bishop. It is hard to believe that Bishop Denewulf watched happily as the construction of the New Minster went ahead. It was built immediately to the north of, and directly alongside, the Old Minster, and it was significantly bigger than its venerable neighbour. This aggressive expression of royal patronage, moreover, was built on land given to the king by the bishop for the purpose, and it is quite possible that Denewulf was put under pressure by the king to give up this land and other estates to him as well. Surviving charters show that the bishop and the king entered into a series of transactions in the early 900s. In each the bishop either leased lands to the king or exchanged lands with him, but it is at least worth wondering whether Denewulf did this willingly. In a letter to King Edward, the bishop referred to an estate at Beddington in Surrey 'which you were desirous I should lease to you'. Denewulf then set out the details of the estate and the stock it had, only to finish with a rather piteous plea: 'Furthermore, the bishop and the community at Winchester beg that . . . you desire no more land of that foundation, for it seems to them an unwelcome demand'.[4] Not for the first time, and perhaps even more intensively than before, the king of Wessex appears to have exploited his power over the church to cherry-pick its resources and increase his own authority. To be sure, by the end of the tenth century, Edward the Elder was not remembered fondly at the Old Minster: he was a 'greedy king'.[5]

A desire to clip the bishop of Winchester's wings may also have been one of the reasons behind the reorganisation of the southern English dioceses, which took place some time after 909. At a council presided over by Archbishop Plegmund of Canterbury, it was decided that the two great dioceses of Winchester and Sherborne should be subdivided into smaller units, the former into two dioceses (Winchester and Ramsbury) and the latter into three (Sherborne, Wells and Crediton). It is not clear whose idea this was, but it could not have been popular with the bishops of Sherborne and Winchester. Indeed, the reform seems to have taken place shortly after the deaths of Bishops Denewulf and Asser, in 908 and 909 respectively, and it would have suited Plegmund if he could consolidate his own position as head of the English Church at the expense of their successors. However, there were other obvious reasons for the shake-up, too. It was important to increase the number of bishops and (with them) centres of religious activity, so that pastoral provision across Wessex could be made more effective. So the original plan may have envisaged a bishop for every shire. The new dioceses were certainly designed to cover specific areas of the kingdom and line up to an extent with the established shire boundaries: Winchester in Hampshire, Surrey and the Isle of Wight; Ramsbury in Wiltshire and Berkshire; Sherborne in Dorset; Wells in Somerset; and Crediton in Devon.

The bishops were political figures, chosen by the king, and he expected them to preach loyalty and obedience to his regime and his dynasty as well as carry out their share of legal, administrative and even sometimes military duties in the regions to which they had been assigned. Much more explicitly than in previous reigns, the subdivision of the West Saxon dioceses by Edward the Elder signalled how important the bishops were as agents of royal government, whose task it was to spread and enforce the king's authority. Or, put slightly differently: 'Edward's kingship seems to epitomise the new hard-nosed monarchy of Wessex, determined to exploit all its resources, lay and ecclesiastical, for its own benefit'.[6]

Beyond Wessex itself, however, Edward and his successors did much less to shape the structures of the church. This was inevitable – they had fewer lands in these areas, so were politically weaker and less able to assert themselves. But it may also have been part of a deliberate strategy designed to avoid antagonising local elites whose cooperation was vital to the achievement of the southern kings' wider ambitions. Either way, the dioceses of English Mercia (principally Hereford and Worcester) remained untouched, and as Danish-occupied lands were conquered by Edward the Elder and Aethelflaed his sister, no new dioceses were created and no old ones were reestablished. To the extent that there was any episcopal control at all in the east midlands or East Anglia during the first half of the tenth century, it was exercised by the bishops of Dorchester and London, respectively, although a bishop of Elmham was once again in place by the mid-950s.

King Aethelstan, however, proved as keen as his father had been to assert direct control over the dioceses of Wessex. He appointed men close to him as bishops: two of the priests from his household, Aelfheah and Beornstan, became bishops of Wells in 926 and Winchester in 931, respectively, whilst the monk Cenwald was also attached to the royal household for at least a short time before becoming bishop of Worcester in 928 or 929. Another priest, Oda, who attended Aethlestan's court early in the reign, became bishop of Ramsbury by 928, and he was eventually made archbishop of Canterbury by King Edmund in 941. Oda was scrupulously and publicly loyal to Aethelstan and Edmund and worked hard for them; he was an ideal leader of the English Church in that regard. In 936 he led an embassy from the West Saxon court to that of Hugh, duke of the Franks, and he was almost certainly heavily involved in the drafting of Edmund's law codes, particularly the first one which dealt exclusively with ecclesiastical matters. His attitude to King Eadwig, however, is less clear. The archbishop suddenly became a much less frequent witness to royal charters in 957 and 958, the time when the people of Mercia and Northumbria abandoned Eadwig and took Edgar as their king instead. And Oda played an important role in the reputedly scandalous events which took place during Eadwig's coronation celebrations: it was at the archbishop's urgent request that Dunstan burst in on the king and his partners and reprimanded him for his sexual and moral misconduct. And according to the *Anglo-Saxon Chronicle*, Oda was responsible for separating the king and his wife, Aelfgifu, in 958 'because they were too closely related'.[7]

Aethelstan's conquests, meanwhile, brought what was left of the church in northern England at least nominally under his control, and there is some evidence to suggest that he at least tried to establish clearer institutional arrangements there. A charter survives (only in a spurious version, unfortunately) in which the king granted four subordinate (or 'suffragan') bishops to Archbishop Hrothweard of York.[8] It is tempting to link this initiative to the events of 927 when, the *Anglo-Saxon Chronicle* records, Aethelstan 'succeeded to the kingdom of the Northumbrians'.[9] But nothing else is known about it, and Hrothweard appears to have died in the early 930s. So any attempt to implement the scheme may have been frustrated by this and by the need to deal with the opposition which Aethelstan and his successors continued to face north of the Humber.

Hrothweard's successor at York, Archbishop Wulfstan I, survived for over two decades until the mid-950s, but during that time, he must have been hard-pressed to deal with the volatility of northern politics as viking warlords and English kings battled for control of the region. He almost certainly had to make significant concessions and compromises with whomever happened to be in charge at any one time in order to maintain any kind of position for himself. It is likely that the resources of the archbishopric were severely depleted as a result, and it is hard to see how even basic pastoral functions can have been satisfactorily carried out in the north before the political situation finally began to stabilise there after the death of Erik Bloodaxe in 954. Nevertheless, the situation was not straightforward even then. Archbishop Wulfstan was removed from his position at about this time, probably a result of his long-time closeness to the Danish regime, and by 959, Bishop Oscytel of Dorchester (d.971), a southerner, had been installed as archbishop of York. The signs are that he held both posts together; this was a massive task as well as a highly irregular arrangement. The diocese of Dorchester was enormous and unwieldy: it encompassed the old diocese of Leicester and covered the newly formed shires of Oxfordshire, Buckinghamshire, Hertfordshire, Bedfordshire, Cambridgeshire, Huntingdonshire, Northamptonshire, Leicestershire and, almost certainly, Nottinghamshire. In the early years of King Eadwig's reign, Oscytel had appeared regularly as a witness to his charters. But from 958 (like Archbishop Oda of Canterbury), he only witnessed Edgar's. Both Eadwig and Edgar gave Oscytel estates in Nottinghamshire: the former granted him Southwell, where a great minster church was soon built, in 956, and the latter granted him Sutton in 958. Both of these grants may have been designed to provide the Dorchester diocese with some much-needed funds and to strengthen the bishop's position in the extreme north of his diocese, but the estates eventually ended up belonging to the archbishopric of York as Nottinghamshire was brought under its authority, and this was probably Oscytel's doing. He acquired other properties, too, but by the time he died, there were still plenty of estates which the archbishopric had lost and which had not been recovered.[10]

Oscytel's appointment at York was an important moment, however, and did mark the start of the revival of the northern archbishopric. King Edgar now had a loyal archbishop north of the Humber, and Oscytel had important connections. He was friends with abbot Dunstan of Glastonbury (d.988), who in the late 950s was also bishop of London and Worcester and who would soon, in 960, become archbishop of Canterbury. And his distant kinsman was a certain Oswald (d.992). It was Oscytel who reputedly introduced Dunstan and Oswald, and it was then Dunstan who, after becoming archbishop of Canterbury, persuaded King Edgar to appoint Oswald to the vacant bishopric of Worcester. Oswald would eventually succeed Oscytel as archbishop of York late in 971 or early in 972. From these positions of power, Dunstan and Oswald would become two of the most famous and influential reformers of the English Church.

Monasticism and *realpolitik*

The heavy toll taken on the English Church by the viking invasions of the ninth century was described in Chapter 4.* King Alfred had attempted to revive Christianity in his kingdom with a dedicated programme of education, and the reorganisation of the southern English dioceses led by committed bishops in the early 900s was another way of trying to restore ecclesiastical power and influence. However, a different approach was adopted from the 950s onwards, when a concerted attempt was undertaken by England's secular and ecclesiastical leaders to establish monasteries as the dynamic force behind religious renewal. The reformers' nostalgic aim was to restore what they saw as the Golden Age of English monastic life, that described by Bede in the *Ecclesiastical History of the English People*. Bede's pioneers had all been monks, and many of them had become inspirational bishops or archbishops who had brought the Christian faith to a deprived and spiritually impoverished English nation. They had built monasteries and established communities which set an example of how the Christian life should be lived, and it was the intention of their tenth-century successors to emulate this and model the highest standards of Christian conduct and practice.

There were more recent models to emulate, too, however. The emperor Louis the Pious (814–40) had attempted to impose common practices and observances on all the monasteries of his empire. And even fresher in the memory were the efforts of great monasteries like Cluny in Burgundy, Gorze in Lorraine and Fleury on the banks of the river Loire, which had all been reformed in the first third of the tenth century. All three of these institutions, and Emperor Louis before them, had used as the basis of their reforms the guidelines for the conduct of monastic life written by St Benedict of Nursia (c.480–550) in the sixth century. The ideal monastery described in the so-called Benedictine Rule is fully communal, and the monks live in a single building or complex of buildings under the direction of an abbot elected by them. The monks were required to renounce all personal property, take vows of chastity and profess unquestioning obedience to the abbot.

* Above, pp. 98–9

The Rule stresses the importance of humility and obedience at the outset and then gives detailed instructions on how and in what way the monks' days were to be structured. Their main responsibility was the daily performance together of what Benedict called the *Opus Dei*, or the eight divine offices. Beginning before dawn with Matins and followed at prescribed times throughout the day by Lauds, Prime, Terce, Sext, Nones, Vespers and Compline, these services formed the spine of the monks' day. Other services (probably at least two Masses every day) and a daily meeting of the monastic community had to be fitted into the timetable, too. When they were not praying, the monks were either working manually or studying. Benedict also gave instruction on other practical matters – the monks were to sleep for eight hours during the winter and for six in the summer, for example. Only the sick could eat meat, and the monks otherwise were vegetarians. They could drink some wine with their meals, but if their monastery was in an area where wine was not produced, the monks were exhorted not to grumble.

The Benedictine Rule provided a framework for monastic observance, but it also left much unsaid. Its flexibility in matters of detail was one of the reasons for its enduring popularity throughout the middle ages, not least in England in the later tenth century where it was adopted eagerly by the leading proponents of reform as the most (and for some, the only) worthwhile version of the religious life. The seeds of this movement were sown during the reign of King Aethelstan, it began to grow under Edmund and Eadwig, and it flowered whilst Edgar was king. Its significance is emphasised by contemporary accounts of what happened and by contemporary biographies of the leading participants; their dominance of the conventional narrative needs to be borne in mind. Even so, this was a crucial moment in the religious history of England, but furthermore, the English reform of the 960s and 970s was special because 'it was court-driven: occasionally imposed by royal fiat, and always backed by strong royal encouragement'.[11] Indeed, because royal involvement was so intense and pervasive, the kings could exploit the reform programme for their own political purposes. By aiming to impose conformity and standardisation in one sphere of English life, the movement, it has been said, 'offered a blueprint for unity' which contributed significantly to the making of the English kingdom.[12]

Like his grandfather Alfred, Aethelstan was noted for his piety and took a personal interest in religion. He founded two religious houses (at Milton Abbas in Dorset and at Muchelney in Somerset), and he was a generous patron of others, most notably Malmesbury in Wiltshire, where he was eventually buried. He was an enthusiastic collector and distributor of religious relics, and he was a generous donor of religious manuscripts to churches, gospel books especially. In 934, on his way to Scotland, he visited the shrine of St Cuthbert at Chester-le-Street, and later, a list was drawn up of all the gifts he left for the saint which included vestments, books and a large estate at Wearmouth. This was an exercise in devotion, of course, but also in what might today be called 'soft power': it was designed to get St Cuthbert on Aethelstan's side, but also to create ties between the southern king and his newly acquired northern lands. In return for his gifts, the community at

Chester-le-Street would be expected to pray for the king and his family and preach the virtues of loyalty and obedience to their congregations.

Aethelstan also looked enthusiastically outside England in a wider attempt to cement his power and position. There was nothing new about foreign influence making its presence felt at the court of the West Saxon kings, of course. Aethelwulf and, most notably, Alfred had developed strong connections with the continent, and King Aethelstan revived this tradition. Several of his half-sisters made prestigious marriages abroad, in Burgundy, Brittany and Francia for example, but the most impressive of all was the match made in 929 between Eadgyth and Otto, who would succeed his father, Henry the Fowler, as duke of Saxony and king of Germany in 936. Aethelstan also gave refuge at his court to some sons of dispossessed foreign royals: Louis, son of his half-sister Eadgifu and Charles the Simple, king of the West Franks, Alain, the heir to the Breton throne and Hakon, the son of King Harald of Norway. There is no reason to doubt that Aethelstan genuinely wanted to help these young men, but they (like his powerful brothers-in-law) gave him diplomatic leverage across Europe. More relevantly here, they also increased the range and frequency of English contacts with foreign religious, cultural and intellectual trends. The men who acted as Aethelstan's envoys and ambassadors were often members of the clergy (Bishop Cenwald of Worcester led the deputation to Saxony in the late 920s, for example), and it is only reasonable to assume that they returned to England with new ideas and freshly inspired by the contacts they had made with the continental monasteries they had visited during their trips.

No doubt these links further encouraged Aethelstan to promote scholarship and learning at his court. Scholars from France, Germany, Italy and Ireland are known to have worked there, but many able young Englishmen, eager for a career in the church, did the same, and they must have been influenced deeply by the sophisticated and cosmopolitan culture they encountered. Most important among these youths were Dunstan and Aethelwold. Dunstan appears to have come from a wealthy Somerset family with links to Glastonbury Abbey and leading figures in the church; Aethelwold's origins are more obscure. But howsoever they arrived there, at the royal court, they would have met men like Archbishop Oda of Canterbury, Bishop Cenwald of Worcester and Bishop Aelfheah of Winchester (934–51). Bishop Aelfheah, in fact, may have been one of Dunstan's influential relations, and it was he who ordained Dunstan and Aethelwold as priests at the request of King Aethelstan. The crucial point here, though, is that all three of these bishops identified themselves explicitly as monks and had strong connections with monasteries on the continent which had already been reformed on strict Benedictine lines. Archbishop Oda, indeed, took his monastic vows at the monastery of St Benoît-sur-Loire at Fleury, where St Benedict's relics were preserved, and it was to Fleury that Oda sent his nephew Oswald to be trained as a monk. However, they were also men with practical experience of the political world, and it must have become clear to their apprentices soon enough that, if reform of the church was to be carried out successfully in England, monastic discipline was not enough: political muscle (the support of the king, in other words) would be needed, too.

The importance of royal support for the incipient reform movement was made clear soon after the death of King Aethelstan in 939. His successor, Edmund, initially welcomed Dunstan at court, but according to William of Malmesbury, who was writing in the twelfth century, the king was soon turned against him by jealous rivals, and Dunstan was driven out of the royal circle. Then, however, as the king was out hunting near Cheddar Gorge in Somerset, his horse nearly ran over a cliff, but as he was about to fall to his death, the king remembered his harsh treatment of Dunstan, repented and was saved. As a result, he made Dunstan abbot of Glastonbury.[13] In reality, of course, it is hard to know how seriously to take this miracle story. Dunstan certainly did take over at Glastonbury in the early 940s, however, and he was soon joined there by Aethelwold. During the next decade or so the abbey 'became both powerhouse and seedbed for a religious revival', as it developed into a centre where the principles of the Benedictine Rule were put into practice through rigorous regimes of prayer, study and work.[14] These principles were eventually exported from Glastonbury when Aethelwold became abbot of Abingdon in 954. When he arrived there, the church was staffed by secular priests, but Aethelwold transformed Abingdon into an exemplary Benedictine community. He was joined there by enthusiastic collaborators from London, Winchester and Glastonbury, all of whom took monastic vows, and one of them, Osgar, was sent to Fleury by Aethelwold to perfect his knowledge of the Benedictine Rule and bring it back to Oxfordshire. Royal patronage was again instrumental here, however. Aethelwold was installed at Abingdon at the insistence of King Eadred and his mother, Eadgifu, who wanted to stop Aethelwold leaving England to pursue his studies on the continent, and later the king gave the monastery a large estate of 100 hides. The young prince Edgar, the king's nephew, was also educated at Abingdon where Aethelwold himself was his tutor.

Eadred was an enthusiastic ally of Dunstan as well as Aethelwold. Dunstan, indeed, became one of the king's principal advisers, and as the witness lists to Eadred's charters show, he spent much of his time at court between 946 and 955. Eadred granted Dunstan lands and even remembered him and his church in his will where it was stated that 'Abbot Dunstan is to receive 200 pounds, and to keep it at Glastonbury for the people of Somerset and Devon'.[15] Dunstan's relations with King Eadwig, however, were far less harmonious. Within a few months of Eadwig's accession in November 955, Dunstan had been forced into exile. The evidence suggests that it was his disapproval of the king's relationship with a woman called Aethelgifu and her daughter Aelfgifu which turned Eadwig against him. Famously, Dunstan's biographer records how, on the day of the new king's coronation, Eadwig chose to spend his time in bed with these two women rather than attend to affairs of state. It was Dunstan who entered the king's chamber, forcibly pulled him away from temptation and marched him back to the coronation feast.[16] This is another story which cannot really be taken at face value, and Dunstan may have fallen out with Eadwig, not because the new king was dissolute, but because he favoured the claim to the throne of the Eadwig's younger brother, Edgar, who was already a firm supporter of Benedictine reform thanks to Aethelwold's teaching. In any event,

Dunstan's expulsion from court almost certainly arose out of less lurid circumstances than those his biographer described, and as a result of the more complex political considerations which were discussed in Chapter 5.*

Dunstan spent his exile in Ghent at the monastery of St Peter, which itself had been recently reformed. In 957, however, after two years away from England, he was recalled by Edgar who had just become king north of the Thames. In the following year, on the death of Bishop Cenwald, Dunstan was appointed bishop of Worcester, and shortly after that, he was given charge of the diocese of London, too. Ultimately, in 960, after Edgar had succeeded to the whole kingdom following Eadwig's death, Dunstan became archbishop of Canterbury, a position he held until he died in 988. Enthusiastic royal support obviously lay behind all these appointments (the incumbent archbishop of Canterbury, Byrhthelm, had been unceremoniously and quite scandalously removed by Edgar to make way for Dunstan), and the same goes for the promotion of King Edgar's old tutor, Aethelwold, to the diocese of Winchester in 963. By then, moreover, Oswald (the nephew of Archbishop Oda of Canterbury and kinsman of Archbishop Oscytel of York) had already been bishop of Worcester for two years. He had received a textbook monastic training at Fleury and brought the reforming zeal he had acquired there back to England with him. In 971 he would succeed Oscytel at York whilst retaining the diocese of Worcester at the same time.

By the early 960s, three of southern England's most important dioceses were in the hands of monks who were determined to use every means at their disposal to spread their reforming ideals across the rest of the kingdom. Backed by an enthusiastic royal ally, their plan was to impose their monastic vision on the English Church by appointing like-minded evangelists to other positions of authority, establishing new monasteries which would observe the Benedictine Rule and refounding as reformed communities others which had ceased properly to function for one reason or other during the previous century. Dunstan may have effectively started the process when he was still bishop of London: he was later credited with appointing a new abbot of the monastery of St Peter at Westminster (Westminster Abbey) and with providing a dozen monks to serve there in 959. But it was Bishop Aethelwold of Winchester who acted most decisively, and he remained the driving force behind the entire movement for the rest of his life. In 964, with royal and papal backing, and supported by a troop of armed men, he had the secular priests who staffed the Old and New Minsters expelled, and he replaced them with monks from his old monastery at Abingdon. Soon afterwards, the nunneries at Nunnaminster and Wilton were enclosed with walls to show that the bishop expected women to follow the same strict rules of conduct as men. Chertsey in Surrey was also reorganised as a monastery in 964, but Aethelwold was prepared to exert his influence beyond his diocesan boundaries. Milton Abbas in Dorset became a monastery, whilst in East Anglia, the area where the church had probably suffered most at viking hands,

* Above, pp. 123–4

the monasteries at Peterborough and Ely were refounded, and a new one was established at Thorney, all on Benedictine lines, between 964 and 971. These Fenland communities were to become 'three of the most influential houses in English monastic history'.[17]

Bishop Oswald of Worcester also established or helped to refound a number of monasteries, including Westbury on Trym and Winchcombe in Gloucestershire and Pershore in Worcestershire. But his most notable foundation was Ramsey Abbey in Cambridgeshire – partly because it was a monk of Ramsey, Byrhtferth who later wrote Oswald's biography and gave his own monastery a particularly prominent place in his hero's career, but also because of where it was, in the heart of the eastern Danelaw. Like Aethelwold's East Anglian monasteries, Ramsey was built to reinstate model forms of Christianity in a region which had been deprived of them by its pagan conquerors. Oswald also reintroduced monks at Worcester itself, although he appears to have done this less violently and more gradually that Aethelwold did at Winchester. He built the church of St Mary for the monks, right next to the cathedral church of St Peter, which continued to be served by secular clergy. The two groups worked together, although the monks probably came to play the dominant role in the community and eventually their church became recognised as the cathedral. However, after becoming archbishop of York in 971, there is nothing to suggest that Oswald tried to reform the community there.

As for Dunstan, evidence that he actively set about establishing or refounding monasteries is even harder to find. A later biographer, Osbern of Canterbury, who wrote in the twelfth century, stated that Dunstan founded five monasteries from his own lands.[18] Malmesbury may have been one of these, although at best it is likely that Dunstan endowed these houses with lands or money rather than established them from scratch. Most curiously, there is no sign that the archbishop made any attempt to install monks at his cathedral church (Christ Church) in Canterbury. However, the principles of the reform movement had first been articulated and fostered at Glastonbury when Dunstan was abbot there, and monks trained at Glastonbury would play leading roles in the English Church in the second half of the tenth century. Papal approval for Aethelwold's radicalism at Winchester was obtained by Dunstan, and there can be no doubt that he collaborated closely with his fellow bishops and the king when it came to the revival of monastic practice across England. At a great assembly held one Easter during the mid-960s, King Edgar is reputed to have ordered the foundation of more than forty new monasteries. And although precise numbers and chronologies are hard to establish, in the half-century or so after Dunstan's return from exile, over thirty monasteries were set up in England and at least five or six nunneries.[19]

But there was more to the reform programme than just establishing or reestablishing monasteries. They also needed like-minded leaders, clear rules and plentiful resources. As to the first of these, Oswald himself became abbot of Ramsey, although day-to-day business there was managed by a dean. Elsewhere, loyal disciples of the leading reformers were chosen to put principle into practice. Wulfsige, who became abbot of Westminster in 959, had previously been a monk at Glastonbury under Dunstan. Aethelwold's pupil from Glastonbury, Aethelgar, became abbot of the New Minster. The Old Minster monks Byrhtnoth and Godeman became the first abbots of Ely and Thorney, and Oswald's friend and former pupil from Fleury, Germanus, was installed as abbot of Winchcombe.

But even with such men in charge, it remained likely that, without clear, universally applicable guidelines to follow, the new communities would all soon be pursuing their own versions of the monastic life. To avert this danger, and to establish uniformity of practice, a great ecclesiastical council was held at Winchester some time between the mid-960s and the early 970s (the precise date is not clear). In attendance were all the English bishops, abbots and abbesses, along with representatives from the abbeys of Fleury and Ghent. The king addressed a letter to the council in which

> he urged all to be of one mind as regards monastic usage, to follow the holy and approved fathers and so, with their minds anchored firmly on the ordinances of the Rule, to avoid all dissension, lest differing ways of observing the customs of one Rule and one country should bring their holy conversation into disrepute.[20]

The result of the meeting was the document known as the *Regularis Concordia*. Its main purpose was to provide an up-to-date version of the Rule of St Benedict, which all of the English monasteries and nunneries would be required to observe. There was nothing particularly novel about the regime it prescribed, and the details, which were probably compiled by Bishop Aethelwold, were derived largely from existing English (probably Glastonbury) practice and foreign models, most notably the customs of Fleury and ultimately, of course, the Benedictine Rule itself. Monastic life was to revolve around the communal performance of the eight divine offices and other services. Arrangements for eating (no more than two meals a day), working and sleeping were also prescribed. Silence was to be observed unless speaking was absolutely necessary, and complete obedience to the abbot was expected. There were some concessions to English conditions: a fire was allowed in a special room during winter, and the monks could work inside rather than in the cloister when it was deemed too cold. And there were other peculiarly English features. The monks were required to take communion every day, for example, before which they had to give confession. But the *Regularis Concordia*'s distinctiveness can be seen mainly in its attitude to secular power. After every one of the daily offices except Prime, prayers were to be said by the monks and nuns for the king, queen and royal family. Abbots were to be chosen freely, but with the consent and advice of the king. Edgar, indeed, features in the document as the ultimate patron and protector of the English monasteries, while Queen Aelfthryth performed the same role as 'protectress and fearless guardian' of the nunneries, 'so that he himself helping the men and his consort helping the women there should be no cause for any breath of scandal'.[21]

Committed personnel and clear principles could not sustain a monastery or nunnery for long, however, if it lacked resources. The leading bishops lavished valuable gifts on their favoured foundations – religious books, gold and silver ornaments, vestments, as well as land. A list survives of 'the treasures which Bishop Aethelwold gave to the monastery which is called *Medeshamstede* [Peterborough]'. It includes a gospel book decorated in silver, three silver crosses, two silver candlesticks and three gold ones, a number of copes, stoles and other garments, curtains, seat covers, bells, cups and altar cloths. Aethelwold also gave the monastery twenty-one books, various estates and large amounts of produce.[22] But if the monasteries were to become self-sufficient and remain strong into the future, they needed landed endowments from the king, queen and nobility. Byrhtferth of Ramsey reported that it was the nobleman Aethelwine, the youngest son of Ealdorman Aethelstan Half-King, who promised Oswald 200 hides of land ('not counting gold and silver', Byrhtferth stressed) to build his church there. Aethelwine and his brother Aelfwold gave more estates to Ramsey later, as did other leading figures, such as Ealdorman Byrhtnoth of Essex, the tragic hero of the Battle of Maldon.[23] Women could be patrons of the new monasticism, too. In her will, Aelfgifu, who was probably the divorced wife of King Eadwig, left estates to the Old and New Minsters as well as other religious houses.[24] But there was another side to the reformed monasteries' growing wealth. Extensive building works must have been undertaken across southern England as new churches were built, old ones remodelled and monastic precincts created or enlarged. At Winchester the works carried out by Bishop Aethelwold to enclose the expanding monastic complex there and extend the Old Minster led to the closure of streets, the diversion of streams and the demolition of houses. This may have contributed to Winchester's development into 'one of the conspicuous centres of Christendom, politically and culturally', but it surely caused some anger and resentment, too, as residents were forced out of their homes or compelled to exchange their property or settle for cash.[25]

And on a wider scale than this, the reform movement had its contentious features. Large amounts of monastic land in southern England had fallen into secular ownership one way or another during the viking invasions. When these lands were restored to the churches which originally owned them, or given afresh to new or refounded monasteries, they had first to be taken back from their lay owners. This was bound to cause resentment amongst those families who saw their own local power and income diminish as the privileges and authority of the reformed monasteries increased. What is more, during the conquest of midland and eastern England by Edward the Elder and his successors, many former monastic estates had fallen into royal hands. This gave the kings a landed presence in areas where they previously had none. King Edgar's surviving charters strongly suggest that he was quite happy to endow monasteries (and, indeed, lay supporters) with these estates. Some of these documents, and indeed others which purport to be grants made by even earlier kings, may have been forged later by monasteries keen to add an official stamp of legality and legitimacy to their acquisition of these lands, but either way, the result of all this activity on the land market was the construction, during the third quarter of the tenth century, of a network of royalist religious communities across the southern and eastern Danelaw. Their reliance on royal backing and patronage and their professions of loyalty to the ruling dynasty had the effect of enhancing royal power and extending royal influence throughout Mercia and East Anglia. In other words, 'With the gradual reconquest of the Danelaw, . . . ex-monastic lands played a vital role in the defence and spread of the West Saxon hegemony'.[26]

King Edgar was certainly devout. He had been well-schooled by Aethelwold at Abingdon, and there is no reason to doubt that he was a sincere advocate of monastic reform. William of Malmesbury later recounted the tale of how dismayed the young prince Edgar had been when he arrived at Abingdon and found it ruined and neglected. He swore then and there that, 'if he should ever be king, he would restore this place and others like it to their original state'. And it was a pious and spiritually driven King Edgar who was applauded by Bishop Aethelwold himself for having the determination 'zealously to set monasteries in order widely through-out his kingdom'.[27] Nevertheless, it is hardly surprising, given its political benefits, that King Edgar was such an enthusiastic supporter of the programme. There were further advantages, too. The grateful reformers portrayed the king in their writings as the dynamic force behind the movement (in the *Regularis Concordia* and, later, the *Anglo-Saxon Chronicle*, it is Edgar who is credited with removing the secular clergy from Winchester, Chertsey and Milton and replacing them with monks, not Aethelwold), and any opposition to the reforming scheme or any disruption it caused are completely ignored by them.[28] The high-point of such image-making can be found in the elaborate and magnificent frontispiece to the charter (written in gold letters and in book form) issued by the king in 966 to commemorate the refoundation of the New Minster as a monastery two years earlier.[29] The top half of the illustration shows Christ in Majesty, one hand raised in blessing, another holding a book of judgement, surrounded by angels. Below him stands an enlarged figure of King Edgar, flanked by saints Mary and Peter, the patron saints of the monastery. The king is looking upwards at Christ with arms outstretched offering the golden charter to him. The ideological value of this image is hard to gauge because it was a one-off, and although it may have been on public display at the New Minster from time to time, not many people can have seen it or studied it closely. Those who did, however, must have been struck by the way it symbolised the interdependence of secular and ecclesiastical power. But within it, too, is embedded the notion that the best route to Heaven was through loyalty to a king who had a special and unique relationship with Christ. King Alfred would have approved of his great-grandson's piety, but he would also have appreciated Edgar's determination to derive political capital from it.

Reform and reality

The first three-quarters of the tenth century have conventionally been seen as a momentous period in the history of the English Church. First came the diocesan reorganisation of the early 900s, a scheme devised in part to install evangelising bishops who would give pastoral care to a deprived population and restore

Christianity's pre-viking dominance across southern England. Then, in the 920s and 930s, the first stirrings of a deeper cultural and intellectual transformation within religious circles, one influenced heavily by Carolingian models, have been detected by historians. These paved the way for the great monastic transformation spearheaded by Dunstan, Aethelwold and Oswald from the late 950s onwards.

But whilst there is certainly much to be said for this view of how events unfolded, there are some problems with it. First, there were obvious limits to what was achieved. Bishoprics were reshaped primarily in Wessex, and north of the Thames little was done. Second, it is doubtful whether King Aethlestan saw his court as the centre of a trailblazing revolution; indeed, his interest in saints' cults and relics shows how deeply conservative his own religious faith could be. And third, it is easy to fall into the trap set by those contemporaries who wrote about the progress of monastic reform and to regard it uncritically as the towering achievement of saintly monks and pious kings. It bears repeating that there is next to no trace of the new monasticism extending into the north of England, and even in the south, its impact was localised, largely restricted to the heartland of Wessex in and around Winchester and to parts of the west and the east midlands where the leading reformers were most strongly established. Plenty of unreformed minsters (probably hundreds) survived, too. Great communities like Wells and Chester-le-Street, for example, continued to be staffed by secular clergy and priests, and it has been suggested that the reformed communities may in the end have made up no more than 10 per cent of England's religious houses.[30]

Even the leaders of the movement had their limitations and differences, despite the impression their biographers tried to convey. Dunstan cannot have been an easy man to deal with. He was exiled from court in the 950s, he was prepared to succeed as archbishop of Canterbury in 960 after the outrageous treatment of his predecessor and he does not seem to have done very much actively to found or refound any monasteries himself. Aethelwold was clearly a zealot who believed that only the purest form of monastic life was acceptable, and his readiness to use violence to remove the secular clergy at Winchester in 964 is difficult to reconcile with his sanctity. Oswald was deeply concerned with his churches at Ramsey and Worcester, but even in his cathedral church, the speed and scale of the changes he imposed are both open to question, and he leased many of Worcester's estates to laymen, particularly members of his own family. Then, after he became archbishop of York in 971, he appears to have done little to establish monasteries there. In reality, once the veil of propaganda woven by the surviving sources is drawn aside, the monastic reform movement appears less coherent in its conception, less coordinated in its approach and more patchy in its geographical coverage than its contemporary admirers (most of whom were monks themselves) wanted later generations to believe. Forms of religious life in later Anglo-Saxon England remained diverse and varied. Meanwhile, by disrupting established patterns of landholding and local power structures, the reform movement's social and political consequences may have been just as profound as its religious ones, and much more troublesome.

Nevertheless, having said all this, there were significant achievements. The monasteries established or refounded in England during this period would play a major role in England's religious and spiritual life through the eleventh and twelfth centuries. They were responsible for producing an estimated 90 per cent of English bishops between 970 and 1066, for example, and all of the archbishops of Canterbury appointed between 988 and 1038 had previously been monks at Glastonbury. Meanwhile, at centres like Christ Church, Canterbury, Winchester Old Minster, Sherborne and Worcester, the cathedrals were actually run on monastic lines, with the bishop also serving as abbot or prior in charge of a community of monks. These so-called monastic cathedrals were uniquely English, and more were established after 1066; they would be a distinctive feature of the kingdom's ecclesiastical landscape for the rest of the middle ages. The English monasteries were also at the forefront of a flourishing in the visual arts and vernacular literature during this period, and some of the most important thinkers of the next generation were products of reformed Benedictinism, not least Wulfstan the Homilist and Aelfric of Eynsham. This network of monasteries 'existed as powerful influences on the neighbourhoods in southern England, and also on the royal and national scene. They represent elements of potential stability in a country still subject to pagan attack'.[31] In this context, however, their importance as collaborators with the king in a wider political programme cannot be ignored. All the English kings of the tenth century expected the church to give them ideological and political support; in return, they gave the church protection and a share of resources. So royal backing for ecclesiastical reform during this period was always self-interested to a significant degree. As the English kingdom was enlarged, and as the need to embed royal power in new areas grew more pressing, the king's bishops and abbots were as important as his ealdormen and thegns, and his dioceses were as important as his shires.

Notes

1 *EHD*, i nos.35 (II Aethelstan, 23), 41 (III Edgar, 5.2), 37 (VI Aethelstan, Prologue); Attenborough, *Laws*, pp. 142–3 (III Aethelstan, Prologue).
2 *VSO*, pp. 106–10; *ASC* 973.
3 Alan Thacker, 'Dynastic Monasteries and Family Cults: Edward the Elder's Sainted Kindred', in Higham and Hill (eds.), *Edward the Elder 899–924*, pp. 248–63, at p. 253.
4 *EHD*, i no.101.
5 S814; Rumble, *Property and Piety in Early Medieval Winchester*, V (v) (p. 118).
6 Thacker, 'Dynastic Monasteries', p. 254.
7 *EHD*, i no.234; *ASC* 958.
8 S401.
9 *ASC* 927.
10 Robertson, *Anglo-Saxon Charters*, no.LIV.
11 Blair, *The Church in Anglo-Saxon Society*, p. 350.
12 Levi Roach, *Aethelred the Unready* (New Haven, 2016), p. 40.
13 'Vita Dunstani' in M. Winterbottom and R.M. Thomson (ed.), *William of Malmesbury. Saints' Lives. Lives of Ss. Wulfstan, Dunstan, Patrick, Benignus and Indract* (Oxford, 2002), pp. 198–205.
14 H.R. Loyn, *The English Church 940–1154* (Harlow, 2000), p. 11.

15 *EHD*, i no.107.
16 *EHD*, i no.234.
17 Loyn, *English Church*, p. 18.
18 W. Stubbs (ed.), *Memorials of St. Dunstan* (London, 1874), p. 89.
19 *VSO*, pp.76–7 and n.120.
20 *RC*, pp. 2–3.
21 *RC*, pp. 1–2.
22 Robertson, *Anglo-Saxon Charters*, no.XXXIX.
23 *VSO*, pp.182–3 and n.51.
24 Whitelock, *Wills*, p. 120.
25 Loyn, *English Church*, p. 16.
26 Fleming, 'Monastic Lands', p. 265.
27 'Vita Dunstani', in Winterbottom and Thomson (eds.), *William of Malmesbury. Saints' Lives*, pp. 238–9; *EHD*, i no.238.
28 *RC*, p. 2; *ASC* 964.
29 See Campbell (ed.), *The Anglo-Saxons*, p. 187 for an excellent reproduction.
30 Blair, *The Church in Anglo-Saxon Society*, p. 351.
31 Loyn, *English Church*, p. 23.

PART III

The testing of a kingdom, 975–1042

9

THE EVENTS, 975–1042

975–979

When King Edgar died on 8 July 975, he was no more than thirty-two years old. It is likely that his death was sudden and a surprise, and it also appears to be the case that he left no clear plan for the succession. Edgar's eldest surviving son, Edward, was perhaps eleven or twelve when his father died. But Edward's legitimacy may have been an issue, and the identity of his mother is unclear. Scandalous stories circulating at the end of the eleventh century claimed that Edward was Edgar's son by a nun of Wilton Abbey, whom the king had seduced. More credible, though, is the view that Edward's mother was an ealdorman's daughter called Aethelflaed, although just how formal Edgar's relationship with her was remains open to question. Edgar's other surviving son, Aethelred, was born in around 968. He was the second son born to Edgar and Aelfthryth, whom Edgar had married by 964. Their first son, Edmund, died in 971 or 972. Aelfthryth was the daughter of an influential landholder (and subsequently ealdorman) in Devon, Ordgar. She had also been widowed before she married Edgar: her first husband had been Aethelwold, ealdorman of East Anglia, the eldest son of Aethelstan Half-King.

Neither Edward nor Aethelred was old enough to take charge of his own leadership campaign in 975, and so factions formed around them as the struggle for the succession played itself out. The groupings themselves are hard to delineate, but Aethelred's most active supporter was probably his mother, Aelfthryth. She may have been joined by Bishop Aethelwold of Winchester and the ealdormen of western Mercia and Essex, Aelfhere and Byrhtnoth. Edward, however, was backed by the archbishop of Canterbury, Dunstan, and another powerful ealdorman, Aethelwine of East Anglia. All sorts of considerations would have prompted these leading figures, and others like them, to choose their side. But in the short term at least, and probably by the autumn of 975, the arguments had been settled, deals had been struck, and Edward was crowned king. The events of his short reign are then obscure and elusive. Only three authentic royal charters survive, which makes any objective assessment of Edward's administration impossible. The narrative sources meanwhile hint at simmering tensions among the ruling elite of the kingdom, and there was a famine to deal with as well. Everything seems clouded, in fact, by what happened during the evening of 18 March 978. The *Anglo-Saxon Chronicle* records the events briefly, but more lurid detail is given in the *Life of St Oswald*. On that day the king had travelled to visit his half-brother and stepmother at Corfe in Dorset where the latter had estates. When Edward arrived at the gate of Aelfthryth's residence with his small entourage, he was met by her retainers, dragged from his horse and butchered to death. Edward's body was hurriedly taken away and buried without ceremony nearby, at 'the house of a certain churl'.[1] His corpse was retrieved almost a year later and reburied with the proper formalities at Shaftesbury Abbey. Soon the late king was being venerated as a martyr and a saint. As for his brother Aethelred, he was consecrated king by Archbishop Dunstan at Kingston upon Thames on 4 May 979.

DEBATE 6

Who killed Edward the Martyr?

Edward the Martyr, king of the English, was murdered at Corfe in Dorset on 18 March 978. According to Byrhtferth's *Life of St Oswald*, 'thegns who were ardent supporters of his [half-]brother' the atheling Aethelred, slew the king. Aethelred was staying with his mother (Edward's stepmother), Aelfthryth, and the killing took place as the king arrived to visit them. Beyond these basic details, the circumstances of the murder are quite unclear.[1] Some historians have suggested that it might simply have been the tragic outcome of an argument which got out of hand between the king and some of the noblemen around Aethelred. On that reckoning it was an unplanned accident. King Edmund had died in such a fashion in 946. Others have argued that the murder might have been a more carefully managed affair, plotted in advance. Aethelred himself was no more than twelve at the time, and perhaps as young as nine or ten, so it is hard to implicate him directly in what happened. However, Aethelred's backers would have hoped to profit from Edward's death and their own candidate's succession to the throne. There had been arguments about which of King Edgar's sons should succeed him on his death in 975. Factions formed around the two rival candidates; allegiances were determined by family and local connections and almost certainly intensified by personal rivalries at the top of English political society. Edward was eventually crowned king, but there were undoubtedly those who remained unhappy with his accession, and Edward's short reign was soon destabilised from within. As part of the so-called anti-monastic backlash, some monasteries which had been favoured by King Edgar as part of the Benedictine Reform Movement had their lands appropriated or recovered by opportunistic nobles vying with each other to establish and extend regional control and influence. There is some evidence, too, that the king himself was volatile and unpredictable. If he was, this could have added to the growing atmosphere of fractious insecurity. Such incipient chaos might have given Aethelred's supporters the justification they needed (in their own minds at least) for getting rid of the king, and within a few decades of the murder, it was Aethelred's mother, Aelfthryth, who was seen as the instigator of the plot. Nothing survives, of course, to link her personally with the murder. Nevertheless, there is no doubt that she stood to gain if her son took Edward's place on the throne. What is more, that the killing took place on her lands and that the perpetrators (whom she surely must have known) went unpunished, are certainly incriminating if not conclusive considerations. Edward was soon venerated as a martyr and saint, and King Aethelred in due course became the most enthusiastic promoter of his half-brother's cult, not least through gifts to Shaftesbury Abbey where Edward was eventually buried, and through his laws, which insisted on the observance of Edward's feast day throughout England on 18 March.[2] Such acts could be interpreted as signs of guilt on Aethelred's behalf; whether they were or not, however, the murder of Edward the Martyr cast a shadow over Aethelred's reign from the start. It has not really lifted since.

1 *VSO*, pp. 138–41, at pp. 138–9
2 S899; Robertson, *Laws*, pp. 84–5 (V Atr, 16).

979–991

Aethelred II's reputation as one of England's worst ever kings dominates any account or discussion of his reign. His name is synonymous with defeat, treachery, capitulation and national disgrace. Aethelred has been popularly known for centuries as 'the Unready', with all the implications of incompetence and ineptitude which this carries. However, it is necessary to point out straight away that *unraed*, the original Old English word from which this nickname (which was first attested in the twelfth century) was derived, actually means 'badly advised' rather than unprepared and forms the second half of a pun on Aethelred's name: 'Aethelred *unraed*' literally means 'Good advice the badly advised'. Having said that, there is no doubt that Aethelred's reign ended with a Danish conquest of England, but it is also very important to remember that most of the commonly received wisdom about the king is derived from a single source, the *Anglo-Saxon Chronicle*. The bulk of the surviving entries covering Aethelred's reign were written shortly after his death. As a result, they are imbued with the gloom-laden and keenly felt knowledge of recent Danish triumph and inevitable English disaster, and highly disparaging of the king and his regime. To be sure, some of the *Chronicle's* criticisms are fair, and serious mistakes were made. But there is other evidence which allows for a more balanced analysis of the policies pursued by Aethelred and his government. Surviving royal charters and law codes, along with coins and other texts, suggest that the king and his advisers presided over a sophisticated administration and a rich kingdom, one which held out reasonably well against the Vikings for most of the reign and which only succumbed to conquest when the weight of pressure created by generations of factional struggle and years of continuous warfare finally overwhelmed it.

Aethelred cannot have been more than eleven or twelve years old when his brother Edward was murdered. So when he became king in 979, and for the next few years at least, he was inevitably reliant on the help and advice of others. Initially these were mainly men (and his mother, of course) who had served Edgar, but increasingly as the 980s went on and members of this old guard died or retired from the political scene, a new generation of ambitious younger advisers took their place. And as the king himself grew older, he had an increasingly large say in who the people around him would be. It was also during this decade, probably in around 985, that Aethelred married for the first time. The identity of his first wife is uncertain, but she was probably Aelfgifu, a daughter of Ealdorman Thored of southern Northumbria. Whoever she was, she would bear the king at least six sons and perhaps five daughters. The main feature of this period, however, at least with the benefit of hindsight, was the resumption of viking raids on England. The *Anglo-Saxon Chronicle* notes that there were assaults on Southampton, and in Kent and Cheshire in 980. Devon, Cornwall and Dorset were attacked in 981 and 982; Devon suffered again in 988. These incidents were traumatic and devastating for the people affected, of course, but probably not seen at the time as more than local problems. That view seems to have changed by the end of 990.

In December of that year, a papal ambassador arrived at Aethelred's court. He had come to negotiate a treaty between the English king and Duke Richard I of Normandy (942–96). It seems likely that this treaty was needed by then because at least some of the viking raiders who had attacked England in the 980s had done so from Norman bases. The deal itself, which was ratified at Rouen on 1 March 991, included a mutual agreement not to assist each other's enemies, and although the Vikings are not specified, the English probably had them in mind.[2] The making of this treaty suggests that Aethelred's government was starting to take the viking threat more seriously, and events later in the year would have confirmed to them that they were right to do so. In August 991, after first ravaging Ipswich, a large viking fleet overcame an English army led by Ealdorman Byrhtnoth at Northey Island near Maldon in Essex. The *Anglo-Saxon Chronicle* simply records the event and Byrhtnoth's death, but the great Old English poem, *The Battle of*

Maldon, describes the battle which took place and the English defeat in heroic and glorious terms. The accuracy of the poem's account is questionable (it is a literary work not a historical one), but that it was written at all indicates just how large an impact this setback had on those who lived through it and what followed. In its own way, too, the *Chronicle* notes the significance of this moment. After the battle 'it was determined that tribute [Old English, *gafol*] should first be paid to the Danish men because of the great terror they were causing along the coast'. The amount handed over was £10,000.[3]

992–1005

The story of the next ten years, as told at least by the *Anglo-Saxon Chronicle*, is one of relentless viking attacks and repeated English failure. In 992, a plan to put together an English fleet and take on the Vikings at sea was foiled by the treachery of Ealdorman Aelfric of Hampshire, who betrayed the English to the enemy. In 993, there was further viking activity in northern England, in Lincolnshire and North-umbria, but the English army which gathered to challenge them disintegrated before battle commenced after its leaders had fled from the field. Another viking army was seen off when it attempted to attack London in 994, but this only led to it burning and ravaging in other parts of the south-east. Finally, the *Chronicle* says, 'they seized horses and rode as widely as they wished, and continued to do inde-scribable damage'. This prompted the king and his councillors to agree to more tribute being paid. The Vikings received at least £16,000 and perhaps as much as £22,000. They also agreed to end their campaigning and fight on the English side if more raiders arrived.[4]

According to the *Chronicle*, the viking army of 994 was led by Olaf Tryggvason and Swein Forkbeard, king of Denmark (987–1013). Olaf was later celebrated in Norse poetry and sagas as a great chieftain and adventurer who eventually became king of Norway (995–9), but it is hard to separate truth from fiction where he is concerned. He may have been one of the leaders of the viking fleet at Maldon in 991. The same goes for King Swein, but this is not certain either. Swein had seized control of Denmark from his father, King Harald Bluetooth, in the late 980s, but his position there was probably not completely secure by 994, and he may have seen England as a potential source of wealth with which to cement his rule at home. As yet, conquest was not on his agenda, but his appearance in England was ominous. The *Chronicle* records that Olaf Tryggvason promised not to return to England after he had taken his share of tribute in 994. Indeed, it may have been the English government's plan to send Olaf back to Scandinavia so that he could contest King Swein's supremacy there by seizing power in Norway. This strategy worked up to a point. Olaf forced his way on to the Norwegian throne soon after he left England, and Swein did not return until after he had defeated and killed Olaf in battle in 999.

The Vikings began raiding once again in 997 and continued for the next few years. In 997, Devon and Cornwall bore the brunt of the attacks, but they spread to

Hampshire, Sussex and Kent in 998 and 999. The English strategies employed to combat this proved embarrassingly unsuccessful. The armies which were raised to confront the Vikings habitually fled before or shortly after the fighting began: 'a flight was always instigated by some means', the *Chronicle* says in the annal for 998, 'and always the enemy had the victory in the end'. In 999, the troops from Kent who confronted the Vikings at Rochester began the encounter well, 'but, alas! they too soon turned and fled'. Meanwhile, attempts to raise a fleet to take on the Vikings at sea dragged on aimlessly 'and then in the end it effected nothing . . . except the oppression of the people and the waste of money and the encouragement of their enemies'.[5] It is important to remember that this account of these events was not written until after King Aethelred had died, probably some time between 1016 and 1023. The author's description is therefore infused with knowledge of what happened later in the reign, and should not be read uncritically. And as will be seen in the following chapters, the 990s saw considerable achievements in other areas, in the creation of new legislation, for example, and in the further development of the coinage system. Aethelred's administration was neither hapless nor inactive. The very fact that it could raise large amounts of tribute to pay the Vikings (whatever the merits of that approach) shows how well-organised it continued to be. Nevertheless, even if the *Chronicle* is guilty of exaggerating English failings, and even if the viking threat was being managed one way or another, that threat not been eliminated by end of the 990s.

There was a temporary respite from the fighting in 1000 when the enemy fleet spent that summer in Normandy. This of course implies that the agreement Aethelred had made with Duke Richard in 991 had broken down, and in the spring of 1002, something like it was revived when Emma, the sister of Duke Richard II of Normandy (996–1026), crossed the Channel to England and married the English king. The new queen was probably about twenty, and she assumed an English name after her marriage, Aelfgifu. This marriage took place after another year of intensive campaigning in England following the return of the Vikings. A further tribute (£24,000) was paid to them in 1002, too. This and the marriage to Emma were meant to bring the viking raids on the kingdom to an end, temporarily or otherwise. What Aethelred did next, however, sounds like it was radical and shocking. According to the *Chronicle*,

> the king ordered to be slain all the Danish men who were in England – this was done on St Brice's Day [13 November] – because the king had been informed that they would treacherously deprive him, and then all his councillors, of life, and possess the kingdom afterwards.

And later Norman accounts of the Danes' treatment at Aethelred's hands were even more graphic: 'He ordered women to be buried up to the waists and the nipples to be torn from their breasts by ferocious mastiffs set upon them. He also gave orders to crush little children against door posts'.[6] It is hard to take such descriptions at face value, not least because the *Chronicle*'s assertion about the scale of the atrocities seems too hard to accept. Viking invaders had begun settling in England during the last third of the ninth century. Their descendants were therefore well-established across large parts of eastern and northern England by the start of the eleventh. The idea that Aethelred wanted to slaughter all of these people in 1002 seems absurd, and when, two years later, one of the king's charters referred to the decree he had issued 'to the effect that all the Danes who had sprung up in this island, sprouting like cockle amongst the wheat, were to be destroyed by a most just extermination', it may have been more recent arrivals he had in mind.[7] In 994, following his truce with Olaf Tryggvason, some viking warriors had remained in England having agreed to fight for Aethelred as paid mercenaries. By 1002, however, it is possible that their loyalty was suspect and that the king wanted to remove them. One such defector could have been a certain Pallig, who joined the Vikings in Devon in 1001 'with the ships which he could collect, because he had deserted Aethelred in spite of all the pledges which he had given him. And the king had also made great gifts to him, in estates and gold and silver'.[8] But whoever the targets of Aethelred's decree in 1002 actually were, it is also unclear how many people were killed as a result of it. In the charter he issued in 1004 which renewed the privileges of St Frideswide's in Oxford, the king described how the church had been destroyed during the events of November 1002: some families of Danish descent had broken into the church to take refuge, only for the locals to then burn it down with the families still inside.[9] And recent archaeological excavations in Oxford and Dorset have uncovered mass graves containing the remains of more than eighty bodies between them. It has been suggested that those hurriedly and carelessly buried in these pits may have been killed on St Brice's Day; the Oxford victims could have been those killed at St Frideswide's.[10] But even if they were, how often such attacks were repeated across England at the end of 1002 remains uncertain.

None of these strategies, diplomatic, financial or punitive, halted the Vikings in England. Aethelred and Richard II soon quarrelled again, and the English king ordered his troops to 'go to Normandy in order to devastate the land by robbery and fire', capture the duke and bring him to England 'with his hands bound together behind his back'. Unfortunately, however, the English expedition ended in humiliating failure when a Norman force surprised and slaughtered it just after landing. Only a few survivors managed to make it back to England where they told the furious king about the 'ferocious' Norman men and, they noted, women, whom they had encountered in battle.[11] It is hard to explain why the relationship between the king and the duke had broken down so fundamentally. It is also impossible to know how such an episode might have affected the relationship between the English king and his Norman queen. Emma frequently witnessed her husband's charters after 1002, which suggests that she was influential at court. But events in south-western England in 1003 may not have helped the newlyweds and may also have rekindled Aethelred's frustration at continued Norman support for the viking raiders. Exeter had been part of the dower lands granted to Emma by the king at the time of her marriage. In 1003, according to the *Anglo-Saxon Chronicle*, the city was attacked 'on account of the French *ceorl* Hugh, whom the queen had appointed as her reeve'. John of Worcester was even more explicit: Exeter fell 'through the evil counsel, negligence and treachery of the Norman Earl, Hugh', he alleged.[12] Norman sources also mention (but fail to date) an agreement made between Swein Forkbeard and Richard II: the Danes would sell their plunder only in Normandy in return for a Norman promise to shelter Swein's wounded.[13] It was probably events such as this which convinced Aethelred that a pre-emptive strike into Normandy might be the only effective way of getting the Normans to take him seriously.

Back in England meanwhile, the Vikings were themselves active in western England during 1003 and under the command of Swein Forkbeard once again. They finished off the destruction of Exeter and then burnt down Wilton. According to the *Chronicle*, Ealdorman Aelfric of Hampshire was reluctant to take a joint *fyrd* from his own county and from Wiltshire into battle against the enemy, and so 'he feigned him sick, and began retching to vomit, and said that he was taken ill, and thus betrayed the people whom he should have led'.[14] In the following year, 1004, Swein transferred his attention to East Anglia. The East Anglian leader, Ulf-cytel, decided to pay him off, but, having taken the money, Swein proceeded to burn down Norwich anyway. This was too much for an outraged Ulfcytel and his followers who confronted the Danish army after it had also sacked Thetford. The East Anglians were defeated, but only after a fierce battle which they would have won, the *Anglo-Saxon Chronicle* claimed, if their army had been bigger: 'if their full strength had been there, the Danes would never have got back to their ships; as they themselves said that they never met worse fighting in England than Ulfcytel dealt to them'.[15]

1006–1012

By now, the strain on the English ruling elite was starting to tell. In its entry for 1006, the *Anglo-Saxon Chronicle* reports what appears to have been a purge of the king's councillors: 'Wulfgeat was deprived of all his property, and Wulfheah and Ufegeat were blinded and Ealdorman Ælfhelm killed'.[16] Aelfhelm had succeeded Thored as ealdorman of southern Northumbria in the early 990s, and Wulfheah and Ufegeat were his sons; Wulfgeat was a leading member of the royal house-hold. A century or so later, it was being explicitly alleged that Eadric Streona was behind these events.[17] Eadric ultimately came to be blamed for most of the disasters of Aethelred's reign, so such an accusation should be treated with caution without direct evidence to back it up; nevertheless, Eadric's rise to a position of power and influence over the king seems to have begun just after these events, so the coincidence cannot be ignored. He was soon married to Aethelred's daughter, Eadgyth.

There was worse to follow in the same year, first when Malcolm II, king of Scots (1005–34), penetrated deep into Northumbria. He got as far as Durham, where Uhtred, the son of the lord of Bamburgh, saw him off and displayed the heads of his defeated victims on the city walls. As a reward, Uhtred became ealdorman of the whole of Northumbria and was soon married to another of the king's daughters, Aelfgifu. Then, just as serious, in July 1006 what the *Anglo-Saxon Chronicle* called 'the great fleet' under the command of a certain Tostig arrived at Sandwich in Kent and began to ravage and burn in the south-east. Aethelred 'ordered the whole nation from Wessex and Mercia to be called out' in response, but, despite campaigning throughout the autumn, he and his troops were unable to put a stop to the viking attacks. When winter came, the English army went home, and the Vikings retired to the Isle of Wight. But they did not stay there for long, and by Christmas, they had begun cutting their way through Hampshire and Berkshire. By the early months of 1007, 'no one could think or conceive how to drive them from the country, or to defend this country from them, for they had cruelly left their mark on every shire of Wessex with their burning and their harrying'. The best Aethelred and his advisers could do was pay them yet more tribute, this time £36,000.[18] Prominent amongst those advisers by this point (and chief amongst them by 1010 or 1012) was Eadric. He was appointed ealdorman of Mercia in 1007, and he became the king's son-in-law at about the same time. Eadric would play a key role in the political and military events of the following decade or so, and he may already have begun to develop the reputation for wickedness and treachery which has never left him. By the late eleventh century, he was known as Eadric Streona ('the Grasper').

The payment of tribute in 1007 bought Aethelred some time, and he used this to construct a large fleet. The new ships all came to Sandwich in 1009 to patrol the coast and prevent another viking invasion. However, before they could begin to do this, an argument between two leading English magnates, Brihtric, Ealdorman Eadric's brother, and Wulfnoth. When Brihtric accused Wulfnoth of some unspecified offence, the latter responded by absconding with twenty of the new ships. Brihtric pursued him with eighty more ships, but his fleet was caught in a storm, thrown ashore and wrecked. Wulfnoth finished what the weather had begun by burning what was left of the smashed vessels. When the king heard what had happened, he and his advisers abandoned their plans and left the remainder of the new fleet to make its way back to London. The *Chronicle* notes with disgust at this point that 'the toil of all the nation' had come to nothing, although 'no better than this was the victory which all the English people had expected'.[19] But worse was to follow, as the self-inflicted disaster which had destroyed the fleet was followed almost immediately in August 1009 by the arrival in England of what the *Chronicle* referred to as 'the immense raiding army, which we called Thorkell's army', after its leader Thorkell the Tall. Quite what 'immense' meant in this context is hard to say: perhaps the army was 5,000–8,000 strong. What is clear, however, is that for the next three years Thorkell and his allies plundered and destroyed villages, towns and countryside across much of southern England. The annal for 1011 in the *Chronicle* lists the counties and regions they had overrun by then: hardly anywhere in Wessex, East Anglia, Kent, Essex and the eastern midlands had been unaffected. The ultimate catastrophe occurred when Canterbury, the kingdom's spiritual centre, was occupied in the autumn of 1011. Then, to add outrage to disaster, Archbishop Aelfheah was taken prisoner.

The arrival and conduct of Thorkell's army prompted a range of responses from Aethelred and his advisers. To judge from the *Chronicle's* account, however, English military efforts were ineffective ('when they were in the east, the English army was kept in the west, and when they were in the south, our army was in the north'), and the Vikings were able to roam around the kingdom more or less as they pleased.[20] There was some resistance, notably once again from the defiant Ulfcytel of East Anglia, whose army fought the Danes and was defeated at Ringmere, near Thetford in Norfolk, in 1010. But elsewhere there appears to have been little if any effective English challenge to Thorkell's army. The exception was London, which the Danes failed repeatedly to take thanks to the stout defensive efforts of the inhabitants. The success or otherwise of further strategies is harder to judge. According to a twelfth-century source, Aethelred asked Duke Richard II of Normandy for advice and assistance in 1009, and perhaps this was connected to the arrival of Thorkell's army in the same year.[21] More definitely, when the army landed in 1009 a law code (VII Aethelred) was issued which called for the implementation of a national programme of prayer and penance. It also ordered local communities to pay their share of a new tax (one penny per hide) which would be distributed 'for God's sake'.[22] And a new coinage bearing the image of the Lamb of God may also have been issued at this time as part of the same wide-ranging attempt to regain divine favour. King Alfred had seen the viking raids as God's punishment on his sinful people, and King Aethelred evidently viewed them in similar terms. In the end, though, the government, led by Eadric Streona, fell back on its established method of appeasement – the payment of tribute – and shortly after Easter 1012 £48,000 was handed over. It was whilst they were at Greenwich drunkenly celebrating the receipt of this money that the Vikings clubbed Archbishop Aelfheah of Canterbury to death 'with bones and ox-heads' from their feast and 'the back of an axe'. His refusal to pay a ransom appears to have sealed his fate.[23]

1013–1016

There is no evidence that Thorkell himself was involved in the murder of Archbishop Aelfheah. But it may have been partly as a result of this atrocity (and on a promise of food, clothing and further payment) that he agreed from this point on to serve Aethelred, with forty-five ships, whilst the rest of his army disbanded. Helpful though this addition to his forces must have been, however, it cannot have prepared Aethelred for the ultimately fatal blow which next struck his kingdom. After the invasions of 1006–7 and 1009–12, a third began in August 1013 when Swein Forkbeard sailed his fleet up the east coast from Kent, into the Humber estuary and along the river Trent, before establishing a base at Gainsborough in Lincolnshire. This time, unlike in 994 or 1003, the Danish king had come to conquer.

It may have been the news of Thorkell's deal with Aethelred that prompted Swein to return. Olaf Tryggvason had used English money to challenge Swein in Scandinavia in the late 990s, and the Danish king might have been concerned that Thorkell would eventually try something similar. So Swein's attack on England can be interpreted as a pre-emptive strike designed to protect his position in Denmark. Whatever his reasons for coming, however, according to the *Anglo-Saxon Chronicle*, whole swathes of northern and central England succumbed to Swein 'at once'. Amongst those who submitted were 'Earl Uhtred and all the Northumbrians' as well as the people of Lincolnshire, the Five Boroughs and 'all the Danish settlers north of Watling Street'.[24] He then moved south, leaving his son Cnut in charge of the fleet, and soon Oxford and Winchester had submitted, too. London, where Aethelred and Thorkell were holding out, once again resisted stoutly, but Swein's only response to this opposition was to move on and look for easier targets elsewhere. He went to Bath, the site of Edgar's coronation forty years before, where Ealdorman Aethelmaer of Devon submitted along with 'the western thegns', and then he returned north at which point, the *Chronicle* says, 'all the nation regarded him as full king'.[25] The Londoners then accepted what must have seemed inevitable and acknowledged Swein's victory. King Aethelred, meanwhile, had already sent Queen Emma and their two sons, Edward and Alfred, to Normandy, and after spending Christmas 1013 on the Isle of Wight, where presumably he weighed up his limited options, the English king joined them at Duke Richard's court.

Aethelred had abandoned his kingdom. Whether or not he planned to try and return is unclear, but a counter-attack would have been difficult given Swein's dominant position within England. Swein's sudden death in February 1014, however, gave Aethelred an unexpected chance quickly to recover his throne. The Danish army chose Cnut as Swein's successor, but Aethelred managed to negotiate a return to England for himself and his family. According to the *Chronicle*,

> all the councillors who were in England, ecclesiastical and lay, determined to send for King Aethelred, and they said that no lord was dearer to them than their natural lord, if he would govern them more justly than he had done before.

Aethelred sent his son Edward to handle the talks with the message that the king 'would be a gracious lord to them, and reform all the things which they all hated; and all the things that had been said and done against him should be forgiven, on condition that they all unanimously turned to him without treachery'. These comments strongly suggest how unpopular Aethelred had become by the time he had left England, and reveal the misgivings that his leading men had about his ability to rule well and justly. Nevertheless, a deal was struck, and in spring 1014 Aethelred 'came home to his own people and he was gladly received by them all'.[26]

Aethelred's return began well. He went north to Lincolnshire to confront Cnut and drove him out of the kingdom. This success came at a cost, however: before he left England, Cnut mutilated all of his English hostages, and Aethelred had to raise another £21,000 to pay Thorkell's fleet at Greenwich. What is more, it was not long before tensions within the English ruling elite resurfaced and put the kingdom in jeopardy once again. It is possible to interpret what happened in several equally valid ways, but the immediate cause of trouble may have been the death of Aethelred's eldest son, Aethelstan, in 1014, and the succession dispute which almost certainly ensued. It is not clear what plans, if any, Aethelred had made for the succession. His eldest surviving son now was Edmund, but there was no guarantee the he would be accepted as his father's successor. Aethelred also had two sons by his second marriage to Queen Emma, the athelings Edward and Alfred, and their claims to the throne could not be ignored. Edmund had powerful backers, but two of the most important, prominent thegns from the midlands called Sigeferth and Morcar, were murdered at a council meeting held at Oxford in early 1015. The property of the murdered men was then seized, and Sigeferth's widow was confined in the convent at Malmesbury in Wiltshire. The man responsible for this wicked outrage, at least as far as the *Anglo-Saxon Chronicle* was concerned, was Ealdorman Eadric of Mercia, who must have been instrumental in organising the return of the king and his family in the previous year. It may be that he had decided to throw his weight behind the younger athelings' claim to the throne and pre-empt any challenge to them by Edmund and his supporters. Alternatively, Edmund may have been already have been plotting to make a bid for the throne with his allies' help, and Eadric was simply trying to thwart them. Either way, Edmund's response to the death of Sigeferth and Morcar was decisive and provocative. In a clear act of defiance against his father and Ealdorman Eadric, he took Sigeferth's widow from the convent and married her himself. He then moved on into the midlands and took possession of all Sigerferth's estates as well as Morcar's: 'the people all submitted to him', the *Chronicle* says.[27]

As the prospect of an English civil war loomed in the late summer of 1015, Cnut returned to England and landed in Wessex. He rampaged across Dorset, Wiltshire and Somerset, and this common threat seemed likely for a brief moment to bring the quarrelling English factions together. Edmund came with an army from the north, and Ealdorman Eadric gathered a force in the south, but before they were able to confront Cnut, Edmund learned that Eadric planned to betray him and defect to the enemy. Sure enough, taking forty ships and the whole of Wessex with him, the ealdorman threw in his lot with the Danish side.

The events of 1016 are described in great detail in the *Anglo-Saxon Chronicle*. Attempts by Edmund and his father to take on Cnut and Eadric were initially unsuccessful, and by this time, Aethelred seems to have been falling regularly and seriously ill. Edmund fared better when he joined forces with Ealdorman Uhtred of Northumbria, his brother-in-law, who had made his peace with King Aethelred after the latter's return from exile in 1014. Between them they exerted some military pressure on Ealdorman Eadric in his midland strongholds, but when Cnut managed to seize York, Uhtred submitted to him, 'out of necessity' the *Chronicle* says. Uhtred's reward for this, however, was to be lured into a meeting with Cnut where he and his followers were treacherously murdered. Cnut's success in the north forced Edmund back to London where Aethelred was still based. After Easter 1016, as Cnut's forces were about to begin besieging the city, Aethelred died on St George's Day, 23 April: 'he had held his kingdom with great toil and difficulties as long as his life lasted', the *Chronicle* says.[28] Aethelred was buried at St Paul's in London. This was a break with customary royal practice (most English kings since Alfred the Great had been buried at Winchester or Glastonbury), but an appropriate one since by this point London had become 'the symbolic and actual centre of English resistance to the Scandinavian invasions'.[29]

The leading men who were in London at the time of Aethelred's death, along with the Londoners themselves, chose Edmund as their new king. They may have been a minority within the English ruling elite, however, as their peers outside London 'elected Cnut as their lord and king, and, coming to him at Southampton, renounced and repudiated all the descendants of King Aethelred and made peace with him and swore fealty to him'.[30] Over the next few months the struggle to rule the English kingdom was played out across southern England. Several battles were fought, including one at Penselwood in Dorset and another at Sherston in Wiltshire, but none was decisive. Edmund forced another Danish army to abandon its siege of London and then defeated it at Brentford, only for another Danish force to renew the siege and be repelled in its turn. Eventually, and after Ealdorman Eadric had changed sides once again, this time to support Edmund, English and Danish armies confronted each other at Ashingdon in Essex on 18 October 1016. During the battle, and true to form, Eadric fled with his troops, and this, in the view of the *Chronicle*, led directly to Cnut's victory, Edmund's defeat and the destruction of 'all the nobility of England'.[31]

There may have been another battle after Ashingdon, but whether there was or not, the two sides had fought each other to a standstill by the autumn of 1016. Edmund and Cnut met at Alney, an island in the river Severn near Deerhurst in Gloucestershire, and agreed to divide the kingdom in two – Cnut would take control in Mercia and (probably) the north whilst Edmund would rule below the river Thames in the old kingdom of Wessex. It is not clear whether this arrangement was designed to give temporary respite to the rival rulers and their armies, or whether it was supposed to be permanent. Either way, it did not last. Edmund died at London on 29 November 1016 and was buried beside his grandfather King Edgar at Glastonbury Abbey. It is most likely that Edmund died from the effects of wounds he had received in one of the many battles he had recently fought. He was known as Edmund 'Ironside' by the 1050s, 'because of his valour'. Later accounts, however, cannot resist suggesting that he was either poisoned or gruesomely murdered whilst he sat on the toilet.[32]

DEBATE 7

How 'unready' was Aethelred II?

In a league table of medieval English rulers, Aethelred II would appear close to the bottom, competing with John, Stephen, Edward II and Richard III and a few later contenders to avoid the wooden spoon reserved for 'England's worst ever monarch'. Certainly, and to the extent that such a thing exists, this remains the popular view of Aethelred the Unready. His nickname of course does him no favours, and although every historian who discusses Aethelred stresses that the epithet is a misleading corruption of the Old English word *unraed*, roughly meaning 'badly' or 'ill-advised', the mud has stuck pretty fast. Aethelred was poorly served by the sources from the start. The main account of his reign, in the *Anglo-Saxon Chronicle*, was written up immediately after the Danish conquest of England which took place between 1013 and 1016. Infused with the knowledge of defeat, it provides a sorrowful description of the English failure to withstand the viking invasions and a bitter commentary on the reasons for English defeat. Over the middle ages, Aethelred's reputation worsened, and during the eighteenth and nineteenth centuries, his alleged feebleness hardened into undeniable historical certainty. In the 1940s, as eminent an Anglo-Saxonist as Sir Frank Stenton could state without fear of contradiction that Aethelred 'was a king of singular incompetence'.[1] Subsequently, there have been several significant attempts to reassess Aethelred's reign and at least partially rehabilitate the king. Crucially, these have been based on much more than the evidence of the *Chronicle*: Simon Keynes in particular used Aethelred's charters (or diplomas) and coins to shed fresh light on the internal political dynamics of the period. He concluded that 'there was far more behind certain aspects of the reign than the alleged personal incompetence and bad character of the king himself'.[2] Emphasis has also been placed on England's sophisticated systems of central and local administration, the kingdom's wealth as demonstrated by its coinage, and the intellectual activities pursued most notably by Archbishop Wulfstan. The sheer length of the reign and the strengths of the Danish invaders have also been relied upon to support a more generous view of Aethelred's problems and achievements. Most recently, Levi Roach has gone further and put Aethelred's piety at the heart of his biography. Aethelred's actions on St Brice's Day in 1002, in 1006 when he purged his court, and over the last decade of his reign as he issued one penitential law code after another were designed to eradicate sin and purify society.[3] But resourceful and creative though such attempts were, they did not succeed in eliminating the viking threat, and ultimately this should be what matters most for the historian of Aethelred's reign. Ann Williams has rightly argued that 'The failures of Aethelred's kingship were political failures, an inability to control and direct the tensions and rivalries which arose between the royal councillors as they jockeyed for power'.[4] To have any chance of success, a king needed to manage his nobility effectively. He did this by the judicious use of patronage, the encouragement of consensus, the resolution of disputes and the threat of force. But he did it most of all by taking the lead in war and by motivating his leading men to join him in protecting his kingdom. Aethelred could neither dominate nor inspire his nobles, he showed little appetite for getting involved in the fight himself, and so inevitably his reign ended in military ruin. Whatever else was achieved between 978 and 1016, and however great the challenges facing the king were, Aethelred's failure to meet the basic requirements of kingship was his and his alone.

1 Stenton, *Anglo-Saxon England*, p. 395.
2 Keynes, *Diplomas*, p. 230.
3 Roach, *Aethelred the Unready*, pp. 322–5.
4 Williams, *Aethelred the Unready*, p. 149.

1016–1035

After Edmund's death, Cnut succeeded him as ruler of the whole English kingdom. His reign would last nearly twenty years and was important in many ways. However, it is very difficult, if not impossible, to give a full chronological description of it. The *Anglo-Saxon Chronicle's* account is patchy and thin, and other narrative sources, most importantly the *Encomium of Queen Emma* and pieces of Scandinavian poetry, are problematic for other reasons. Very few of Cnut's charters survive (about thirty-six in all, of which roughly half are definitely authentic), and only eight writs. Meanwhile his coins and law codes, which testify to the continuing strength of England's administrative structures, are in the end forms of propaganda, as are two remarkable letters which Cnut addressed to the English people in 1019–20 and 1027.

According to John of Worcester in the twelfth century, Cnut had to establish his right to succeed Edmund as king in Wessex. Edmund had left brothers and sons, but at a meeting in London, Cnut was assured by the English leaders present that they wanted to have him as their king. The claims of Edmund's male relatives were dismissed and, having clarified and legitimised his position, Cnut was probably crowned in London by Archbishop Lyfing of Canterbury early in 1017. He then proceeded to consolidate his power. First he divided the kingdom into four: he would rule Wessex directly himself, but control of East Anglia, Northumbria and Mercia was delegated respectively to Thorkell the Tall, Erik of Hlathir and Eadric Streona. The broader significance of this measure will be discussed in due course.* In retaining Thorkell, however, who had shown himself to be no great friend of the

---

* Below, p. 229
Below, p. 229

Danish kings, perhaps Cnut was accepting that he was too powerful to be ignored. Their relationship would be a rocky one – Thorkell was exiled from England by Cnut in 1021 but then put in charge of Denmark by him in 1023! In Eadric's case, too, the arrangement soon broke down. Perhaps Cnut had been trying to lure Eadric into a false sense of security from the start, because the notoriously unreliable ealdorman was killed on the king's orders at Christmas 1017. He was not the only Englishman whom Cnut distrusted, however, and other important ealdormen in Mercia and Wessex suffered the same fate as Eadric. Potential claimants to the throne were also dealt with: in the following summer Cnut exiled King Edmund's brother, Eadwig, and then he 'ordered [Emma] the widow of King Aethelred, Richard's daughter, to be fetched as his wife'.[33] Cnut was already in an established relationship with an English woman, Aelfgifu of Northampton, the daughter of Ealdorman Aelfhelm of southern Northumbria who had been murdered in 1006. They had two sons (Swein and Harold Harefoot), and the relationship continued in some form after Cnut married Emma. It may be that Cnut married Emma to protect himself against any threat from the two sons she had with Aethelred, Edward and Alfred. If Cnut could have his own children with her, the claims of her other sons would be undermined, and Emma would have to support her new children against her old ones. How willingly Emma herself entered into this marriage is unclear. As for Edward and Alfred, they spent the next two decades in exile in Normandy under the protection of their mother's relatives.

Cnut still needed to secure his position in other ways, however. In 1018 an enormous tribute of £72,000 (and another £10,500 from London) was paid to the king. The larger of these sums was the single heaviest levy imposed on the English people to that date, whilst it is hard to avoid the conclusion that the smaller one was designed to punish the Londoners for the staunch support they had given to Aethelred and Edmund. Cnut probably used some of this to pay off his troops and send most of them back to Denmark. But it may also have been an important moment symbolically as it implied the submission of the English people to him. It was followed by a meeting at Oxford at which 'the Danes and the English reached an agreement'. It is not clear what the terms of this agreement were, although it may have taken the form of an adapted version of one of Aethelred's law codes.* Certainly (as Chapters 11 and 12 will show),† Archbishop Wulfstan of York made an effort to inform the new king what was expected of him by his new subjects. But it is reasonable to think that, following the tribute payment, it was this meeting which finally set the seal on Cnut's acquisition of power.

In 1019, Cnut left England for Denmark, where he had become king following the death (probably in the same year or shortly before) of his brother Harald. From now on he had to try and rule not just a kingdom, but an empire which spanned the North Sea. He was back in England during the early 1020s and regularly thereafter,

---

* Below, pp. 217, 248
† Below, pp. 248, 267

but events in Denmark and Norway soon came to preoccupy him as much as, if not more than, those in England. He was frequently in Scandinavia (in 1019, 1022–3, 1025–6, 1027, 1028–9) and not just to keep a weather eye on affairs there. He came under increasing pressure from his neighbours in Norway and Sweden as the decade went on, and he may well have been defeated by them (the outcome was at best inconclusive) at the so-called Battle of the Holy River in 1026. These events are obscure, but the point is that, for the first time, England was being ruled by an absentee king, and this was bound to have an effect on the way the kingdom was governed. It was during Cnut's reign, for example, that the title of ealdorman was replaced by that of earl, and several men with this title rose to prominence in the 1020s and 1030s: Godwine had become earl of Wessex at the latest by 1023, whilst Leofric (by 1032) and Siward (by 1033) were witnessing royal charters as earl of Mercia and earl of Northumbria respectively.

Not all of Cnut's absences were in Scandinavia. He campaigned in Scotland at least once if not twice during his reign, but most spectacularly, in 1027 he made a pilgrimage to Rome where he attended the coronation of the emperor Conrad II (1027–39). Germany, where Conrad had been king since 1024, had a border with Denmark, and Cnut's daughter with Queen Emma, Gunnhild, was betrothed to Conrad's son, Henry, in 1035 and married him in 1036. So, pious reasons aside, Cnut may have made his journey to Rome to get Conrad's support for his struggles against the kings of Norway and Sweden, and perhaps against the duke of Normandy, too, who may have begun agitating on behalf of the athelings Edward and Alfred by this time. Duke Robert I of Normandy (1027–35) may have been married for a time to Cnut's sister, Estrith, but if he was, this did not prevent him, at some point during his reign, sending envoys to Cnut demanding that that the athelings be allowed to return to England from their Norman exile. Cnut rejected this request, and in response (according to later Norman sources), Robert prepared a fleet and set sail for England, only to have his invasion plans ruined by the weather. The truth behind this story is impossible to establish, but there is evidence from Norman charters of about this time, which Edward witnessed as 'king', which strongly suggests that he was regarded as the rightful ruler of England by his Norman cousins.[34] So Cnut, who was perhaps alarmed by the commitment shown by the Normans to the athelings' cause as well as 'seriously ill', then sent envoys to the ducal court announcing that he 'was willing to return half the kingdom of England to the sons of King Aethelred, and to settle peace for his lifetime'. Duke Robert, however, was unable to do anything about this offer before he departed on a pilgrimage to Jerusalem from which he never returned.[35]

In 1028 Cnut sailed to Norway with fifty ships 'and drove King Olaf from the land, and made good his claim to all that land'.[36] Olaf Haraldsson (he was revered as St Olaf after his death) may have been recruited by King Aethelred when the latter had returned to England in 1014. If so, he probably helped to force Cnut out of the kingdom at that point. He may then have used the money he was paid by Aethelred to launch a bid for the Norwegian throne when he returned to Scandinavia. Certainly he ruled Norway from about 1016 and was a constant thorn in Cnut's side during the following decade or so. But by 1028 Cnut was ready to challenge him and had the resources needed both to fund a fleet and bribe Olaf's men to desert him. Once Olaf was out of the way (he was killed by his own people in Norway in 1030, perhaps at the semi-mythical battle of Stiklestad), Cnut left Norway under the control of one of his trusted lieutenants, Hakon, Cnut's nephew and son of Erik Hlathir, and returned to England. But Hakon died soon after this and was in turn replaced as regent in Norway by Cnut's English consort, Aelfgifu of Northampton, and her son by Cnut, Swein. Cnut may also have decided by this time to put his eldest son by Queen Emma, Harthacnut, in charge of Denmark. Cnut was clearly eager to have his Scandinavian lands ruled directly by members of his family, but these arrangements remained fragile. In 1034, the unpopular Swein and Aelfgifu were forced out of Norway, and the ten-year old Magnus, son of St Olaf, was installed as king. Denmark under Harthacnut would soon come under pressure from the Norwegians, too. Within a few years of his death on 12 November 1035 at Shaftesbury, Cnut's Scandinavian empire had disintegrated. He was buried in England, at Winchester in the Old Minster.

1035–1042

On Cnut's death a power struggle erupted in England which had echoes of the one which had paralysed politics in 975. It almost certainly reflected deeper and long-standing rifts between different factions at the English court, as two of the late king's sons and their respective supporters vied for control of the English throne. The eldest candidate was Harold Harefoot, Cnut's surviving son by Aelfgifu of Northampton (although his enemies claimed that Harold had less distinguished parents). The younger was Harthacnut, Cnut's son by Emma. According to the *Anglo-Saxon Chronicle*, the English elite divided along regional lines:

> Earl Leofric [of Mercia] and almost all the thegns north of the Thames and the shipmen in London chose Harold to the regency of all England, for himself and for his brother Harthacnut, who was then in Denmark. And Earl Godwine [of Wessex] and all the chief men in Wessex opposed it as long as they could, but they could not contrive anything against it.

This apparent compromise may have paid lip service to the idea of some form of shared rule, with Harold acting as a caretaker or regent until his half-brother returned. But in practice there was little Harthacnut's supporters could do to protect his interests as long as he was still in Denmark tussling with King Magnus of Norway. In his continued absence, Harold appears to have consolidated his own position, and he was soon regarded as 'full king over England'.[37]

It was during this period of instability and discord that the athelings Edward and Alfred returned to England from Normandy. According to Norman sources written several decades later, Edward came back to England when he heard of Cnut's death, defeated an English army at Southampton but then went back to Normandy, having realised that he would get nowhere without a larger force behind him. More certainly, according to the *Anglo-Saxon Chronicle*, 'the innocent atheling Alfred, the son of King Aethelred' arrived in England in 1036 to see his mother, who was in Winchester. It sounds like Emma had decided to abandon her plans to make Harthacnut king and instead to throw her weight behind a challenge to the throne by one of the sons of her first marriage.[38] Infuriatingly, the sources conflict about what happened after Alfred's arrival. They all agree that he died horribly, but there is no consensus about how this happened or about who was responsible. Some claim that Earl Godwine (who had by this time decided to abandon his allegiance to Harthacnut and support Harold instead) forcibly prevented Alfred from seeing Emma, took him into captivity and killed or mutilated his companions. Alfred was then blinded and finally died under the care of the monks at Ely. Other accounts describe Alfred's death but do not mention Godwine by name; implicitly they blame King Harold.

Whoever was responsible for what happened to him, Alfred's death had little immediate impact on the course of English politics, and in 1037, Harold 'was chosen as king everywhere, and Harthacnut was deserted because he was too long in Denmark'. Queen Emma, moreover, was forced into exile in Flanders 'without any mercy to face the raging winter'.[39] This was almost certainly a reflection of Harold's anger at Emma's scheming on behalf of his half-brothers. Meanwhile, Harthacnut had made peace for the time being with Magnus of Norway and was able finally to turn his attention to England. There was little sign that he or Emma, whom he joined at Bruges in 1039, would be able to do anything about the situation there whilst Harold (apparently more and more secure) reigned, but obligingly, Harold died, suddenly and unexpectedly, on 17 March 1040 and was buried at Westminster. Harthacnut crossed to England and immediately on his arrival he had Harold's body 'dug up and thrown into the fen'. Earl Godwine, too, according to John of Worcester, had to buy Harthacnut's goodwill with a ship manned by eighty fully armed warriors; he was also required to swear that he had not played any part in the death of Alfred in 1036 and that the whole thing had been King Harold's idea. Harthacnut also imposed 'a very severe tax', and all those who had initially welcomed him soon began to lose their enthusiasm. Harold had raised heavy taxes, too, as had Cnut, but Harthacnut's appear to have been particularly onerous. In 1041, moreover, Harthacnut acquired a reputation as a brutal tyrant to add to that of a grasping exploiter when he ravaged Worcestershire after two of his tax collectors had been killed there. Things were only made worse for his subjects by inflation so bad that the *Chronicle* explicitly bemoaned the rising price of wheat.[40]

In this atmosphere of growing discontent, Edward atheling returned to England from Normandy once more. In 1041, however, unlike in 1036, he was welcome. Indeed, he must have been invited, and his mother was probably responsible for this. Emma and Harthacnut may have been trying to build a stronger base of support for the latter's regime. Harthacnut may also have wanted someone to act as his deputy in England whilst he dealt with affairs in Denmark, or he may already have been ill and planning to install Edward as his designated successor. Whatever the reasons for his return, however, Edward 'was sworn in as king; and he thus stayed at his brother's court as long as he lived'.[41] As it happened, this was not long. Harthacnut died in June 1042, 'standing at his drink' at the wedding celebrations for one of his prominent nobles. Nobody mourned him, it seems. According to the *Chronicle*, 'he did nothing worthy of a king as long as he ruled', and without any hesitation, even before Harthacnut had been buried next to his father in the Old Minster at Winchester, 'all the people received Edward as king, as was his natural right'.[42] England would be ruled by a descendant of Alfred the Great once again.

DEBATE 8

How rich was eleventh-century England?

There are two main pieces of evidence used by historians to discuss the wealth of late Anglo-Saxon England. One is Domesday Book, which was compiled in the late 1080s. It provides a highly detailed picture of an overwhelmingly agrarian society, but also one in which the number of towns was increasing as trade and industrial production grew. Given what Domesday Book reveals, the comments made by Henry of Huntingdon a few decades later come as no surprise: England was 'rich in deposits of metals, namely iron, tin and lead, and some silver, although this is less common', and enjoyed 'a wonderful abundance of fish and meat, of costly wool and milk, and of cattle without number'.[1] The second kind of evidence conventionally used to assess England's wealth at this time is the coinage. The Anglo-Saxon kings of the tenth century constructed a well-organised and tightly controlled system for the production and management of the coins issued in their name. The increase in the number of mints in England and their geographical spread have been taken as proof of ever-increasing royal power. However, it is the number of coins in circulation in England during this period which has been used as perhaps the most important indicator of England's overall wealth. Inevitably, though, the methods used by numismatists to calculate the size of the circulating currency are plagued with problems, and so there are disagreements about how great the volume of coins was and what the numbers (even if agreed) might mean. Estimates over the years have varied greatly from £50,000 in the early eleventh century to £120,000.[2] It does seem to be accepted, however, that there was a significant increase in the amount of silver pennies circulating in England either side of 1000. This appears to have been caused by a rapid expansion of England's export trade from the 960s onwards, which in turn had been stimulated by the discovery of large new deposits of silver in Germany. The main beneficiaries here were England's wool traders, who sent their fleeces to Flanders. As they prospered, so other parts of the economy were boosted too, and the amount of circulating coin in the kingdom increased further.[3] Nevertheless, although there were strikingly large amounts of silver entering and leaving England through trade or tribute at this time, more recent and admittedly very tentative estimates suggest that between 973 and 1042 the value of circulating coin in England may only have been something between £15,000 and £30,000, or 3.6 and 7.2 million pennies. If the population was, say, about two million, that equates (at the most) to just over three and a half pennies per head of population, hardly a king's ransom, especially when compared with later periods (the century after the Black Death, for example) when the much larger number of coins in circulation can be calculated more confidently and population levels were not very different.[4] And was England more prosperous than other parts of mainland Europe by 1042? The evidence from Germany and Flanders might suggest not. To be sure, England was appreciably richer in the eleventh century than it had been in the eighth, but whether it was 'exceptionally wealthy' is much less certain.[5]

1 *Henry of Huntingdon: Historia Anglorum: The History of the English People*, ed. D. Greenway (Oxford, 1996), pp. 10–11.
2 M. Allen, *Mints and Money in Medieval England* (Cambridge, 2012), pp. 318–19.
3 P. Sawyer, *The Wealth of Anglo-Saxon England* (Oxford, 2013), esp. ch.5 and Table 5.
4 M. Allen, 'The Volume of the English Currency, *c.*973–1158', in B. Cook and G. Williams (eds.), *Coinage and History in the North Sea World c.AD500–1250: Essays in Honour of Marion Archibald* (Leiden, 2006), pp. 487–523 at pp. 499–501; idem., *Mints and Money*, ch.10 *passim*.
5 Sawyer, *Wealth*, p. 1.

Notes

1 *ASC* 978; *VSO*, pp. 136–41, quote at p. 141.
2 *EHD*, i no.230.
3 *ASC* 991.
4 *ASC* 994; *EHD*, i no.42 (II Atr, 7.2).
5 *ASC* 998, 999.
6 *ASC* 1002; *WJGND*, ii pp. 14–17.
7 *EHD*, i no.127.
8 *ASC* 1001.
9 *EHD*, i no.127.
10 Roach, *Aethelred the Unready*, pp. 196–200.
11 *WJGND*, ii pp. 12–15.
12 *ASC* 1003; *JW*, ii pp. 454–5.
13 *WJGND*, ii 16–19.
14 *ASC* 1003.
15 *ASC* 1004.
16 *ASC* 1006.

17 *JW*, ii pp. 456–9.
18 *ASC* 1007.
19 *ASC* 1009.
20 *ASC* 1010.
21 Henry, *Archdeacon of Huntingdon: Historia Anglorum: The History of the English People*, ed. and trans. Diana Greenway (Oxford, 1996), pp. 344–5.
22 *EHD*, i no.45 (VII Atr, 4).
23 *ASC* 1012.
24 *ASC* 1013.
25 *ASC* 1013.
26 *ASC* 1014.
27 *ASC* 1015.
28 *ASC* 1016.
29 S. Keynes, 'The Burial of King Aethelred the Unready at St Paul's', in D. Roffe (ed.) *The English and their Legacy, 900–1200. Essays in Honour of Ann Williams* (Woodbridge, 2012), pp. 129–48, at p. 142.
30 *JW*, ii pp. 484–5.
31 *ASC* 1016.
32 *ASC* 1057; Henry of Huntingdon, *Historia Anglorum*, pp. 360–1; *WMGRA*, i pp. 318–19.
33 *ASC* 1017.
34 *WJGND*, ii pp. 76–9; R.A. Brown (ed.), *The Norman Conquest of England: Sources and Documents* (Woodbridge, repr.1998), nos.167, 168.
35 *WJGND*, ii pp. 78–9.
36 *ASC* 1028.
37 *ASC* 1035.
38 *WJGND*, ii pp. 104–7; *ASC* 1036.
39 *ASC* 1037.
40 *ASC* 1040, 1041; *JW*, ii pp. 530–3.
41 *ASC* 1041.
42 *ASC* 1040, 1042.

10

RULING THE KINGDOM, 975–1042

Whether they set out to do so or not, King Edgar and his tenth-century predecessors created a single English kingdom. That kingdom, or most of it at least by 975, was held together by a sophisticated and elaborate framework of government, administration, finance, military force, law and ideology. In the forty years or so after Edgar's death, however, the strength of this superstructure and the integrity of the new realm would be sternly tested, first by relentless warfare and then by foreign conquest. Recurring political crises and humiliating military disasters culminated in the downfall of the ruling dynasty and a Danish takeover of England. But although individuals came and went, the young English kingdom survived intact because the systems which supported it continued to function well and even impressively under the most extreme pressure. Resilient and robust, they enabled the kingdom to emerge stronger than ever from this traumatic period.

King and nobility

The English king was set apart from his subjects by his wealth, his prestige and his powers. He had more land and money than anyone else in his kingdom. He had a unique, divinely approved status which was regularly confirmed by special rituals and ceremonies. And there were certain things over which he as king had exclusive jurisdiction: laws which applied to the whole kingdom could only be issued by him, only he could raise taxation or armies on a national scale, only coins bearing his name and image were allowed to circulate. However, the king's riches, his mystique and his exceptional authority were not enough on their own to guarantee loyalty or ensure peace. National politics in this period was not just a matter of what the king wanted or commanded. It was the preserve of a few hundred rich and resourceful men, and the course of political events, the success of a reign and the stability of the English kingdom depended to a large extent on how well the king managed his relationships with them. An effective king collaborated with his great men in the exercise of power and gave them gifts for dutiful service, but if he excluded too many from the decision-making process, rewarded too few or simply acted insensitively or ineptly, gripes could ripen into grievances out of which, ultimately, resistance and opposition might grow. The king needed to be masterful but not heavy-handed, flexible but not arbitrary. He needed to inspire awe and respect, not suspicion and fear. This was a difficult enough task at the best of times, and it tested the skills of the ablest rulers. But in periods of national crisis, the bonds between a king and his great men would be stretched to breaking point and sometimes beyond.

A king had to dominate his leading subjects, but he needed their help to govern his kingdom, and he was expected actively to seek it out. In broad terms this was a commonplace of political discourse by the start of the eleventh century. In his *Institutes of Polity*, written between 1008 and 1014, Archbishop Wulfstan of York was relying on long-accepted principles when he encouraged the king frequently to look for wisdom with his council (*witan*) and take advice against violators of the law. In his view, 'There are eight columns which firmly support lawful king-ship', and 'good counsel' was one of these.[1] But there were clearly moments when the king needed more than just helpful advice from his great men. This was most evidently the case between the end of one reign and the start of another, as no man could hope to become king without sufficient support from those who mattered politically. There were still no fixed rules of succession in this period. It was gener-ally accepted that the new king should be a close male relative of the old one, but there was usually more than one such viable candidate. And even succession from one member of the royal family to another did not always happen: between 1013 and 1016 a new, Danish ruling dynasty imposed itself on the English kingdom by force. The death of every king between 975 and 1042 was immediately preceded or followed (and sometimes both) by a crisis of some kind. Some of these, after Edgar's death in 975 and Cnut's in 1035, for example, lasted for several years. The final years of Aethelred II's reign were dominated by the question of who should follow him as king. At other times, in 978 or 1042 for example, the new king took power more smoothly, but the circumstances in which they did so were far from straightforward.

At each of these moments of transition from one reign to the next, the English nobility played a key role. Following the sudden death of King Edgar in 975, an assembly of 'all the leading men of both orders' (secular lords and churchmen, that is) unanimously chose his son Edward as his successor and arranged for the lands reserved for the king's sons to be assigned exclusively to the rival claimant, his half-brother Aethelred.[2] Four years later, the *Anglo-Saxon Chronicle* says, Aethelred was consecrated 'with much rejoicing by the councillors of the English people'.[3] But the fourteen month gap between that event in May 979 and Edward's mur-der in March 978 must have been taken up with extensive negotiations between Aethelred's supporters and other who questioned his right to succeed. Aethelred himself was of course unable to pass on an intact kingdom to his son Edmund, and when he died, the English nobility split once again, those in London choosing

Edmund and those beyond the city choosing Cnut. Then when Edmund died shortly afterwards, another assembly at London swore its willingness to have Cnut as king. Further high-level divisions, this time regional ones, were apparent in 1035 when 'all the councillors' gathered at Oxford had to make a choice between Harold Harefoot and Harthacnut. Earl Leofric and the thegns of Mercia chose Harold (and eventually prevailed) whilst Earl Godwine and the 'chief men' of Wessex opted for Harthacnut. Finally, in 1042, 'all the people' who 'chose' Edward as king were almost certainly wealthy and influential ones.[4]

On some of these occasions (975, 978, 1035), the kingdom's greatest subjects (or at least the ones who came out on the winning side) were able in effect to choose the next king. On others (most obviously after Edmund's death in 1016), they may have had little choice but to go along with what the militarily dominant claimant demanded. There were times, however, when the leading Englishmen could exercise influence over a reigning or aspiring monarch and even impose on him their view of how he should rule. For the first part of his reign, for example, the young Aethelred II, who was no more than twelve when he became king, necessarily relied on councillors who had served his father. But even when he was a little more mature himself, and as some of the most influential members of the older generation left the political stage (Ealdorman Aelfhere died in 983, Bishop Aethelwold of Winchester in 984 and Archbishop Dunstan of Canterbury in 988, for example), it has been argued that Aethelred fell under the influence of advisers who took advantage of his relative youth to pursue their own interests.[5] And the nobility could impose itself on the king more formally, too. This happened most dramatically in 1014 when 'all the councillors who were in England, ecclesiastical and lay', invited Aethelred back to England and gave him the chance to resume power 'if he would govern them more justly than he did before'. In 1018, too, a meeting took place at Oxford at which the Danes and the English 'came to an agreement . . . about keeping King Edgar's law'.[6] In fact, the new king may have issued an adapted version of the law code Aethelred had issued at Enham in 1008.* Be that as it may, both this and the agreement of 1014 sound like pacts, by which the English agreed to accept Aethelred and then Cnut as king in return for their promises of good government and lawful rule. And something similar may have happened (there is some reasonably reliable twelfth-century evidence to suggest that it did) when Edward atheling returned to England from Normandy in 1041 to act as some kind of junior partner in Harthacnut's regime. He met with 'the thegns of all England', who advised him that he would be accepted as king 'only if he guarantee to them upon oath that the laws of Cnut and his sons should continue in his time with unshaken firmness'.[7] It has been suggested that the detailed undertakings Aethelred and Cnut gave in order to get the stamp of approval from their leading subjects, and the laws of Cnut which Edward agreed to observe, were those which had been incorporated into Cnut's second law code in 1020 or 1021. The relevant clauses

---

* Below, p. 248

offered relief from a range of royal abuses (heavy taxation, oppressive officials) and were made 'with the advice of my councillors'. These men could use the leverage they enjoyed at such delicate moments to strike bargains with the individuals who wanted to rule them; or, more precisely, 'to define a contractual relationship between ruler and political nation'.[8]

Of course, kings could seek to mould their nobility so that it was more compliant, trustworthy and reliable. King Aethelred tried to do this for several years after 984, when he was keen to distance himself from the surviving advisors of his youth (not least his mother who left court) and cultivate his own circle of favourites. But by the early 990s the king had come to regret the decisions he had made, not least his plundering of several important churches in order to patronise his new followers. In a remarkable charter from 993, Aethelred publicly reflected on some of the things that had gone wrong in recent years. He concluded that they had happened 'partly on account of the ignorance of my youth . . . and partly on account of the abhorrent greed of certain of those men who ought to administer my interest'.[9] Another change of personnel was clearly needed, and alongside his mother, those around the king for the next decade or so, such as Ealdorman Aethelweard of the Western Provinces, Abbot Aelfsige of the New Minster, Winchester, Abbot Wulfgar of Abingdon and Wulfstan, who was bishop of London until 1002 when he became archbishop of York, have been described as men 'of considerable calibre' who oversaw a period of relative prosperity for the kingdom.[10] After that, of course, from the early 1000s, the weight of events began to overwhelm the regime. Partly in an attempt to deal with this and start afresh, in 1005–6, there were drastic changes in the membership of Aethelred's court once again. Some leading figures were executed (Ealdorman Aelfhelm of southern Northumbria) or blinded (Aelfhelm's sons, Wulfheah and Ufegeat), whilst others simply left court.[11] Something dramatic had happened and the purge suggests a regime gripped with panic and paranoia as the viking attacks intensified. However, the only thing that can be said for certain about what happened is that out of the confusion emerged a new leading counsellor for the king, Eadric Streona.

It is certainly tempting to blame Aethelred's misfortunes from this point on his imprudent promotion of Eadric, who became ealdorman of Mercia in 1007 and chief adviser to the king by about 1010. He also married Aethelred's daughter, Eadgyth. However, the extent to which Eadric's rise caused the problems Aethelred faced or simply coincided with them is far from clear. Eadric clearly must bear some share of responsibility for the disasters which ultimately led to the Danish conquest of England, but for the chroniclers looking back on these calamities, he was a useful scapegoat, too. As for Cnut, he tried to assert himself over the English nobility most forcefully at the start of his reign when a purge of existing personnel appears to have taken place. Ealdorman Uhtred of Northumbria was murdered just before Cnut became king, and shortly after he succeeded to the whole kingdom, Ealdorman Eadric of Mercia suffered the same fate. At the same time, other ealdormen and their relatives were either killed, exiled or outlawed. Cnut was helped here by shifts which were already taking place by 1016 in the composition of the English elite. Many leading figures had died since the early 1000s, whether naturally, in battle or murdered. And there were other longer-term changes underway, too. In the second half of the tenth century, even at times of crisis (most notably in 957 and 975), arguments and differences within the English nobility had not developed into outright armed conflict. This was at least partly because, one way or another, the families in this group were bound closely together in a complex network of alliances, friendships and family relationships. However, the almost constant warfare in England since 1006 stretched and broke many of those marriage, kinship and personal ties to the extent that, by 1016, the English ruling class was arguably less cohesive, more fragmented and more vulnerable to attack than it had been for generations.

Historians have debated the extent to which these developments were speeded up as a result of the conquest of 1014–16, and how far the established aristocracy was replaced by a new one after that. On one side of the argument, it has been suggested that the upheaval which afflicted the upper levels of political and landed society either side of Cnut's accession was considerable, and that not only were individuals removed from the scene, but they and their families also suffered widespread loss of estates and offices: 'as a direct result of the viking wars, there was a major upheaval among the landholding class' which affected the highest levels of society as well as the rank-and-file thegns.[12] On the other side, by contrast, the view has been that the changes, whilst significant, were not transformative. For one thing, landholders with Scandinavian names had been settled in the north and east of England for several generations by Cnut's reign, so it is impossible to tell how many of them were newcomers after 1016. For another, not all of Cnut's new men were Danish: two of the most important, Earls Leofric of Mercia and Godwine of Wessex, had English roots. Furthermore, many of Cnut's followers simply went home after 1018, their pockets full of English silver, and were not interested in taking control of English lands. Having said that, Cnut did put men who were closely connected to him by blood or marriage in positions of authority at the beginning of his reign: earls Erik, Ulf and Eadric were the king's brothers-in-law, and other newcomers like Hrani, Eilaf and Erik's son Hakon became earls in Gloucestershire, Herefordshire and Worcestershire respectively. And even when the new English earls Godwine and Leofric rose to dominance in the later 1020s, they had few direct or deep connections with the old aristocracy. Nevertheless, wherever they settled, it has been argued, there is no reason to believe that new Scandinavian landowners were ever more than a minority within the established population. Or, put another way, 'while it is likely that Cnut's men had possessions in nearly every shire in England, it is clear that there was no replacement of native landowners by foreigners on the scale that followed 1066'.[13]

Other evidence appears to support the theory that the changes which affected landholding and political leadership after 1016 were not revolutionary. It has been calculated that at least 110 thegns witnessed Cnut's surviving charters. Forty of these had Scandinavian names, seventy English, but it is difficult to know how many of the former came from families of viking descent already established in England before 1016. Similarly, at least eighty thegns attested Aethelred's charters between 1005 and 1016, whilst at least eighty-two attested Cnut's from 1018 to 1026. About thirty-two of these men acted as witnesses across both periods. Such figures have led to the conclusion that, as far as the composition of the English nobility was concerned, there was 'more 'continuity' than none, and rather less than a lot' in the two decades either side of 1016.[14]

But although this reinforces the idea that the disruption brought about by the Danish invasion and conquest was not exactly cataclysmic, there was certainly less continuity in this regard than there had typically been between the reigns of the tenth-century English kings. And it cannot be doubted that, for one reason or another, the first twenty years of the eleventh century were traumatic ones for the English nobility, their dependants and followers, nor that, by the end of the 1020s, a new generation of leading nobles had emerged in England. Three of them soon stood out from the rest. Leofric was probably appointed earl of Mercia before 1030, although he does not appear with this title until 1032. His family had links with the pre-Danish regime (his father, Leofwine, had been an ealdorman in part of Mercia). Siward appears as earl of Northumbria for the first time in 1033. He may have been Danish, but this is not certain. And equally obscure were the origins of the greatest of these three, Earl Godwine of Wessex. He appears as earl in parts of Wessex as early as 1018, but he was acting as earl of the whole of Wessex from 1023. Godwine's father was probably the Wulfnoth whose flight from court in 1009 had led to the destruction of most of the new royal fleet shortly afterwards. Wulfnoth's actions may have brought him into the Danish camp and given God-wine the chance to make an impression there. But wherever they began, the careers of these new men were made by Cnut.

Whilst the ruling dynasty changed and the ruling class evolved either side of 1016, much about the way the kings routinely managed their leading subjects remained the same across the whole of this period. For example, Aethelred, Cnut and his sons kept in touch with their great men through the regular holding of assemblies. These gatherings would have been held probably four or five times a year, most of them on or around the time of major religious festivals (Christmas, Easter and Whitsun). As in the earlier part of the tenth century, they would have included significant ritualistic and ceremonial elements: crown-wearings may have taken place, whilst any processions or hymns of praise sung to the king would have been highly solemn, stage-managed set-pieces. But there would have been less formal times during these meetings, too: drinking, feasting and hunting would all have served to develop relationships and foster the growth of an aristocratic *esprit de corps*. In these ways, assemblies 'helped to maintain social harmony and political stability'.[15] But there was business to get on with at assemblies, too. Law codes were issued, disputes were arbitrated, grants of land were made, witnessed and recorded in charters, diplomatic affairs were discussed. In 991, for example, Aethelred's treaty with Duke Richard I of Normandy was made after the king had consulted 'all the loyal men of his kingdom and the councillors of both orders', and the decision which led to the St Brice's Day Massacre in 1002 was taken by the king 'with the counsel of my leading men and magnates'. Aethelred met with his *witan* to discuss England's defensive needs in 1010, and together they petitioned the Danes for peace in 1011.[16]

There are plenty of other similar examples which, taken together, suggest the extent to which Aethelred and his leading subjects were collectively involved in responding to the Danish attacks they faced. The assemblies were designed to encourage consensus on these matters and to build a united front with which to confront the invaders. This did not work in the end, of course, as the unremitting strains of warfare eventually snapped many of the bonds which kept the members of the English aristocracy together. But this blow to the system did not prevent Cnut and his sons using assemblies and relying on their own *witan* in the same way as their predecessors after 1016. He may have been the only realistic candidate to succeed to Edmund Ironside's share of the English kingdom following the latter's death, but it seems clear from the sources that Cnut still grounded his claim on the consent of those important men who assembled at London to debate the issues. Later, Cnut's second law code, which was issued during an assembly held at Winchester in 1020 or 1021, was made 'with the advice of my councillors'. When he accompanied the body of the martyred Archbishop Aelfheah of Canterbury on a ship across the Thames from St Paul's to Southwark in 1023, Cnut did so alongside 'the archbishop [of Canterbury] and the diocesan bishops, and the earls, and very many ecclesiastics and also lay-folk'. And when he wrote a letter to his English subjects on his way home from Rome in 1027, he addressed it to the two archbishops 'and to all the bishops and leading men, and to the whole race of the English'.[17] To be sure, the last two examples do not describe assemblies, but they do demonstrate the importance Cnut placed on associating his leading subjects with his own deeds and decisions.

Household government

In this period, 'the principal active mainspring of government remained the king, his Household and his Court in the full domestic sense of the term'.[18] The king himself was of course directly involved in the business and mechanics of government and administration: he was no mere figurehead and he needed to be active and vigorous. The most obvious way to do this in a routine fashion was by travelling around the kingdom. This allowed the king to monitor the running of his estates and collect what was due to him in food and rent. However, by the turn of the eleventh century, these matters were largely in the hands of the king's officials (his sheriffs and reeves), and the royal household remained itinerant partly just to keep it occupied. The logistics of travel, communications and transportation must have required a good deal of planning and taken up considerable amounts of time. But moving the court was also designed to give the political cycle a predictable rhythm and to emphasise the king's continuing authority at its centre. At Christmas, Easter and Whitsun, the household was probably resident for three or four weeks at a time at fixed and familiar locations (Gloucester, London and Winchester eventually became the favoured locations for these gatherings). It was at these times that the household would grow in size as it was joined by many of the great secular and ecclesiastical lords. Then its movements during the rest of the year would be dictated by a range of factors: the timing of other church festivals might push the court towards one religious centre or another, whilst the king's hunting preferences might pull it back to a particular royal estate. What is clear, however, is that Aethelred and Cnut rarely left southern England: they might travel north or east on military campaigns from time to time, but Oxfordshire (where Aethelred held several assemblies during his reign) was more or less as far as they got in the normal course of events. This signals an acceptance by them that 'hands on' rule over the whole of their expanded kingdom was impossible, but also a determination on their part to emphasise that their subjects were now expected routinely to visit and defer to them in the heartland of their power.

Wherever the king was in his kingdom, constantly around him were his servants and officials of various kinds, as well as members of his family. Some of them would have known the king intimately in one way or another, and their physical closeness to him potentially allowed these individuals to affect and in some ways determine the course of royal policy. The kind of sources which might cast light on such relationships (letters and diaries, for example) simply do not exist for this period, but there is no reason to doubt that the king discussed issues of all kinds informally with his closest friends and family members. Queens were expected to give private counsel to the king and to others who might be trying to involve the king in their business, and they might intercede with the king on behalf of petitioners who could not gain access to him directly. This gave the queens the opportunity to exercise significant amounts of influence and to build up their own networks of patronage, support and power. Some were more successful in doing this than others, however, and much depended on the nature of the personal relationship between the king and the queen. King Aethelred married his first wife some time in the mid-980s; her identity is uncertain, but she was probably Aelfgifu, the daughter of Thored, the ealdorman of southern Northumbria from about 975 until the early 990s. Her primary duty was to produce children, and in this she was very successful: Aelfgifu and Aethelred had six sons and perhaps five daughters. But the king must also have hoped that his wife's connections would help strengthen his own links with the north. Whether or not they did is quite unclear, and in this as well as other areas, there is no trace of Aelfgifu's wider influence. She did not witness any of her husband's charters in the later 980s or 990s, for example, and it has been suggested that she was simply overshadowed at court during most of these years by Aethelred's mother, Aelfthryth.[19] Aelfthryth was of course hugely influential at the start of Aethelred's reign (allegedly complicit, indeed, in the murder of Edward the Martyr in 975) and for several years thereafter. The royal charter witness lists suggest that she was then absent from court between about 984 and about 993, a victim perhaps of her son's desire to assert his independence. But from her return until her death in about 1000, she retained a position of significant authority there. In his will, Aethelred's eldest son, Aethelstan, who died in 1014, referred to 'Aelfthryth, my grandmother, who brought me up', whilst his mother is not mentioned at all throughout the entire document.[20] It is possible that Aelfthryth was responsible for overseeing the education and upbringing of the other royal children, too, in which case she would have been better-placed than perhaps anyone else to train the next generation of English rulers and influence their development.

Aelfthryth was almost certainly dead by the time Aethelred married for the second time in 1002. Indeed, it is possible that the marriage was delayed until the queen mother had passed away. What had become of Aelfgifu by this point is less clear, although she had probably died, too. The new queen was Emma, the daughter of Duke Richard I of Normandy and the sister of Duke Richard II. This was a diplomatic and political union, one designed to revive and reinforce the agreement the Normans had made with the English in 991 not to provide a safe haven for viking raiders in their harbours. How far the relationship between Aethelred and Emma developed beyond this functional level is hard to say. She had several children with him between about 1005 and 1013 (two sons, Edward and Alfred, and a daughter, Godgifu) and appears reasonably often as a witness to his charters. But there is no sign that these new arrivals were supposed to take precedence over their elder half-siblings as far as the succession was concerned (Aethelstan remained Aethelred's likely heir until his death in 1014), and no evidence of Emma acting independently by distributing patronage or supporting followers of her own. Her life during Aethelred's reign 'seems to be dominated by marriage and children', and whilst a twelfth-century chronicler who was deeply hostile to Aethelred may have overstated things when he claimed that the king 'was so offensive even to his own wife that he would hardly deign to let her sleep with him' and that he preferred 'tumbling with concubines', it is quite possible that Emma's personal relationship with Aethelred was never particularly good and that, as the military situation in England deteriorated over the course of their marriage, it only got worse.[21]

Emma's second marriage to Cnut in 1017 gave her a new lease of political life. The union made sense for husband and wife: Emma would retain her queenly status and her place at the top of English society, whilst Cnut would draw her on to his side and away from her children by Aethelred who might still have harboured claims to the English throne. Emma certainly seems to have been more of an active participant in politics and patronage during Cnut's reign. That she was eventually buried next to him at Winchester rather than at St Paul's beside Aethelred suggests that their relationship was a good one. When she witnessed his charters, which she did regularly, she was usually described as *Regina* (Queen), a public acknowledgement of her status which few of her predecessors had been given. She was involved in land purchases and other transactions, too, and the births of her son Harthacnut and her daughter Gunnhild (who married the future emperor Henry III) strengthened her position at the heart of the regime by giving her a new stake in the succession and a prestigious European connection. That position was not completely secure, however: Harthacnut was sent to govern Denmark, and it was Harold Hare-foot, Cnut's eldest son by his first wife, Aelfgifu of Northampton, who was in England and best-placed to take power when Cnut died in 1035. Emma would spend the next five years plotting and planning, sometimes in England and some-times in exile, trying to place one or other of her sons on the English throne. But when she was finally successful, her moment of triumph was short-lived. Harthac-nut died, despised and unmourned by his people, in 1042, and within a year of his accession in 1042, King Edward had effectively forced his mother into retirement. Nevertheless, this rather anti-climactic end to Emma's career (she died in 1052) should not be allowed to obscure the fact that, in one way or another, she played a central part in English affairs for over forty years. Few of her male contemporaries managed anything like that.

The queen would have had her own servants to meet her daily needs, just like the king. But the king's household, predictably enough, would have been much the larger of the two. Its size and composition would fluctuate and vary from time to time and according to circumstances. Many of the people within it would perform different functions at different times and essentially be on call to deal with what-ever needed to be done. However, there was probably a core of individuals more or less permanently in attendance on the king, and some of these at least would have had defined domestic, financial, administrative or military roles and responsibilities. King Eadred had left money to some of these men in his will in 956 – his *discthegn* (seneschal), *hraeglthegn* (chamberlain) and *biriele* (butler), as well as his *stigweard* (stew-ard) – but there were certainly more than this, and there is no doubt that Aethelred and Cnut had such servants resident in their households, too. Royal charters were often witnessed by them, and sometimes they are given Latinised versions of their Old English titles: *discifer* (seneschal), *camerarius* (chamberlain), *pincerna* (butler) and so on. More commonly, though, they are grouped together in the witness lists just after the ealdormen or earls and referred to individually as *minister* or collectively as *ministri*. This is probably just a Latin form of the English word 'thegn' and denotes men who had some kind of close personal connection with the king, 'and who as his personal officials may have exerted considerable influence on his decisions'.[22] Sometimes more than thirty *ministri* witnessed a charter, and regularly over a dozen did so. But more than this, the witness lists to Aethelred's charters show that dif-ferent groups of *ministri* were influential at different times during his reign; further evidence that factions and cliques played a large part in the politics of this period.

In sources from later in the eleventh century, some of the men who witnessed Cnut's charters as *ministri* were also referred to as 'stallers'. This is a rather contro-versial term, and it is not clear in the end whether Cnut introduced a new office with this name (there is no contemporary evidence for its use during his reign), or whether it was simply a new honorific title for a rich man who held an existing position of influence and authority close to the king. The bulk of the evidence about who the stallers were and what they did dates from the reign of Edward the Confessor, and even then it is hard to interpret conclusively.[23] Similar debates have surrounded the word 'housecarl' (from the Old Norse (probably) for 'house'

+ 'man/servant'), which came into use after 1016 as the name for a member of the king's military entourage. There was certainly nothing new about kings and other great men retaining armed warriors in their household. The hearth troop was a recognised and long-established part of aristocratic life, and it appears that the housecarls were on one level the latest manifestation of this. In 1035, as Harthacnut remained in Denmark, his mother Emma stayed in Winchester 'with the house-carls of her son the king' to protect her. But they also performed other, somewhat different roles, too, although they might still include the use of violence: in 1040 Harthacnut imposed a heavy tax and 'sent his housecarls throughout the provinces to extort the tribute', and when two of them were killed at Worcester, he sent five of his earls 'and almost all his housecarls with a great army' to ravage the city and its surroundings.[24] So the housecarls, as well as forming the elite corps of the king's army in wartime, could also enforce unpopular royal policies and punish those who did not obey the king's orders. However, there is still no reason to think that their predecessors did not carry out similar tasks and perform similar functions from time to time. They were there to do the king's bidding, whatever that was.

It is accepted by most historians, too, that the royal household continued to be the place where the bulk of the king's documents were produced during this period. Under Aethelred, certainly, it has been established with a reasonable degree of certainty that most of his charters were produced during assemblies held on royal estates by a centralised agency attached to the king's household.[25] With Cnut, however, the situation is less clear. Far fewer of his documents survive, and many are of dubious authenticity, so it is hard to generalise about practices during his reign. It has been argued, however, that a fair proportion of those documents were written by scribes acting for the recipient or beneficiary, not for the government, and that 'a royal writing office under Cnut is not conspicuous by its presence'.[26] But whether the documents were produced centrally or not, they were certainly developing in form during this period. By Aethelred's reign and perhaps even before, it had become common for the king to use another kind of document (*gewrit*) to issue orders and give instructions to his officials. Aethelred certainly, and Cnut probably, had a seal, and perhaps this was used to authenticate the 'writs' sent in this way. They become more and more common from the second quarter of the eleventh century, and the writing and sealing of writs may have been another job for specialised staff within the royal household. As writs came to be used more often from Cnut's reign onwards, a decline in charter production has been identified; however, the idea that the potentially multipurpose writ simply superseded the staid, old-fashioned charter has been dismissed.[27] They were different kinds of document which com-plemented each other. The charter was a solemn, often very long and elaborately worded address in Latin to future generations which set out the boundaries of an estate and the terms on which it was to be held, whereas the writs which survive from this period were much shorter documents than charters, written in English and almost exclusively concerned to notify contemporaries that the king had made a grant of land, that ownership of a particular estate had changed hands with the king's permission or that rights over specified lands had been conceded by the king. Writs were addressed to individuals (often the local bishop, earl or sheriff) and almost certainly designed to be read out quickly and easily to the assembled company at the shire court. As well as giving the king a convenient way of communicating with his officials, therefore, writs also provided him with another way of reminding the important men of the shire that, wherever the king himself might be, royal authority remained pervasive and present.

DEBATE 9

Where did Anglo-Saxon royal documents come from?

Historians of Anglo-Saxon England place great emphasis on the documents issued in the names of the kings they study, principally their charters (or diplomas) and (later in the period) their writs. What these documents say reveals a huge amount about royal patronage, the composition of the royal court and much else. The styles in which they were written are also crucial in illustrating levels of scholarship and how these were deployed in the service of ideas about kingship and authority. But how these documents were produced, where and by whom are all questions of great significance, too, not least because of what they imply about the increasing sophistication and complexity of royal government. It makes sense to assume that the documents issued in the king's name were produced by people close to him, and since the priests attached to his household were the only royal servants routinely able to read and write English and Latin, it is likely that they acted as scribes in addition to carrying out their normal spiritual functions. There is little doubt, for example, that the draftsman known as Aethelstan A, who produced a series of elaborate and sophisticated royal charters between 928 and 935, was a priest in the royal household, whilst the vast majority of royal charters surviving from Aethelred II's reign were produced by a central writing office of some kind. The most recent work on the subject has emphasised bluntly that 'it is absolutely clear that there can no longer be any serious argument about the existence of an Anglo-Saxon chancery in the tenth century. The evidence is as overwhelming as it is emphatic'.[1] However, it is also the case that plenty of royal documents were created, not by royal servants working in a royal chancery attached to the royal household, but by scribes working on behalf of those individuals or institutions receiving the lands or privileges granted to them by the king. A bishop or an abbot whose church was given lands might have the terms of the grant written up by his own scribes. This practice, indeed, seems to have been the conventional one until the later ninth century, at which point royal draftsmen in Wessex began to take a more active role in producing charters.

But even in the tenth and eleventh centuries, as kings assumed more control over their documents and centralised charter production became the norm, the system remained flexible. Many charters were issued during royal assemblies, for example, and there is no reason to doubt that those who drafted them on these occasions may either have been royal servants working with the beneficiaries or the latter's scribes working together with the king's officials on matters of style and detail. Other grants made by King Edgar may have been written up locally at monasteries such as Abingdon and Glastonbury (hence the stylistic differences between them), but always with centrally dictated guidelines in mind about things like the dating of the document, the form of the boundary clause or the king's title. So there was probably never a complete royal monopoly over charter production, and the system was adaptable. Nevertheless, there is every reason to believe that royal control over the system grew ever tighter and more systematic through the tenth and eleventh centuries. Military force, diplomacy and ritual all underpinned the development of royal power during this period, but so did a fledgling bureaucracy which embodied notions of power in writing.

1 Ben Snook, *The Anglo-Saxon Chancery: The History and Production of Anglo-Saxon Charters from Alfred to Edgar* (Woodbridge, 2015), p. 191.

Local government

By 975, most of southern and central England was already divided into the districts known as shires. These were the fundamental units of local administration in this period, used by the king and his officials as the basis for assessing and enforcing a whole range of military, financial, judicial and general administrative obligations. It has been suggested that the process of dividing the whole of England up to the river Tees into shires was completed in the fifty years either side of 1000.[28] Certainly, some shires appear by name for the first time in Aethelred's reign: Oxfordshire, Cambridgeshire, Hertfordshire, Buckinghamshire, Bedfordshire, Huntingdonshire, Northamptonshire, Lincolnshire and Nottinghamshire.[29] Other shires are not named until later in the eleventh century (Derbyshire, Leicestershire and Yorkshire), and although they were clearly functioning as administrative units by 1066, it is not obvious when they began to do so. So it is not certain by any means that the system of shires extended as far as, let alone beyond, the river Tees by 1042. At that date, indeed, it is safer to say that the English king remained more the overlord of Northumbria than the ruler of it. The region north of the river Tees (ancient Bernicia) had been ruled by the family of the lords of Bamburgh since the late ninth century. The king in the south can have had little if any influence over what happened there. The southern part of Northumbria, meanwhile, centred on York, had been enormously affected by Scandinavian invasion and settlement over the course of nearly 200 years. After the death of Erik Bloodaxe in 954, it would hardly have been surprising if the English kings had their doubts about the loyalty of this region, and they attempted to control it through a succession of earls appointed by the kings from the local nobility. This did not always work well. Ealdorman Thored disappears suddenly from the records in 992, and his successor, Aelfhelm, was murdered in 1006. When Swein Forkbeard arrived in northern England in 1013, the region submitted to him immediately. Sometimes, however, one ealdorman governed the whole of the north, from the Humber to the Scottish border. For example, King Aethelred rewarded Uhtred of Bamburgh for a great victory against the Scots by making him ealdorman of all Northumbria in 1006 and by making him his son-in-law (he married Aethelred's daughter, Aelfgifu). Uhtred later submitted to Swein in 1013 and to Cnut in 1016, but he probably had little choice, and between these two dates, he sided with Aethelred, married his daughter and fought alongside his new brother-in-law Edmund Ironside in Staffordshire, Cheshire and Shrewsbury against Eadric Streona. He was murdered in 1016 after having been summoned to Cnut's court. Uhtred was succeeded by Cnut's appointee, Erik of Hlathir. It may be that Erik was supposed to govern all of Northumbria (the *Chronicle* says he was made earl 'just as Uhtred had been'), but he disappears from the records in 1023, and in any event, the lords of Bamburgh retained their autonomy and power at the same time.[29] Uhtred's place was filled at Bamburgh first by his brother Eadulf and then by two of his sons. When Earl Siward, Erik's eventual successor in southern Northumbria, killed the last of these, another Eadulf, in 1041, he married the murdered man's niece and reunited the two parts of the earldom once again under his sole control. Even so, royal power beyond the Humber remained relatively weak, arguably more theoretical rather than real, and it was probably non-existent beyond the Tyne during this period. Even the great lords of Bamburgh struggled to hold their own against a resurgent King Malcolm II of Scots (d.1034), who inflicted a major defeat on the English at Carham-on-Tweed, between Kelso and Coldstream, in 1018. As a result of this, the Scottish kingdom was extended as far as the Tweed and into Cumbria, whilst Malcolm and his successors continued to covet lands even further south than this. King Cnut went to Scotland at least once (in 1031) and perhaps twice (there is some evidence of an earlier campaign in the mid-1020s), but he did little to reverse this situation. According to the *Chronicle*, in 1031, King Malcolm 'surrendered to him, and became his man, but he observed it but little time'.[31] By 1042, Northumbria had yet to be fully integrated into the English kingdom.

In the ninth century, every shire in Wessex had been under the control of an ealdorman. During the first half of the tenth century, as territories north of the Thames had also been divided into shires, some ealdormen, men like Aethelstan Half-King and Aelfhere of Mercia, had been put in charge of whole groups of shires at once and consequently become very powerful indeed. And still in the 990s, some ealdormen were controlling extensive areas. A royal charter of 997 was witnessed by Aethelweard, ealdorman of 'the western districts' (probably Devon, Dorset and Somerset; in other words, western Wessex), whilst Aelfric was ealdorman of 'the Winchester districts' (central Wessex). Others attested the same charter as ealdormen 'of the Northumbrian districts', 'of the east Saxons' and 'of the provinces of the Hwicce' (central Mercia).[32] Eadric Streona was ealdorman of Mercia from 1007, and his prominence from this point on in the events of Aethelred's reign suggests that he had very wide powers indeed. Nevertheless, it remains hard to determine the significance of what happened at the highest levels of local leadership, particularly under King Cnut. In 1017, he divided the English kingdom into four: 'Wessex for himself, East Anglia for Thorkell [the Tall], Mercia for Eadric [Streona] and Northumbria for Erik [of Hlathir]'.[33] But this arrangement did not last long: Eadric was murdered almost immediately, and there is no evidence that he was replaced in Mercia for a while. Thorkell was exiled in 1021, and what happened to East Anglia after that is not clear. Erik was probably Cnut's leading earl for two years after Thorkell left the kingdom, but his fate after 1023 is unknown, and from this point Godwine of Wessex, and then Leofric of Mercia and Siward of Northumbria, start to become more and more prominent.

These men were all called 'earl' (perhaps derived from *jarl*, Old Norse for a chieftain or high-ranking subject of the king) rather than 'ealdorman', and the latter term falls out of use during Cnut's reign. It is not clear whether this was anything more than just a change of title for the king's leading men, and firm conclusions are difficult to reach given that so little is known about many of Cnut's earls, let alone about how they carried out their roles. Much about what they did looks similar to what went before, but it is possible to suggest that, by the 1030s at least, they were controlling their regions more loosely than their predecessors. Like them, they presumably had some kind of general, supervisory authority over their assigned areas, but it seems unlikely that Godwine and Leofric exercised much direct, day to day power within them. If for no other reason, their earldoms were simply too large for one man to govern. At the local level of shire and hundred, routine duties were delegated more and more to the lower-ranking reeves. Such men had always been important in running the king's estates and carrying out other administrative, financial and judicial functions. There were particular types of reeve with responsibility for commercial centres (*burh*-reeves) and ports (port-reeves). But it is in Aethelred's reign that the most important reeve of all, the 'shire-reeve' or sheriff, appears for the first time: Wulfsige, who was sheriff of Kent in the 980s, is the earliest recorded holder of this title.[34] The sheriff was, or soon came to be, the king's personal representative in his shire, responsible for arranging the king's business and for running teams of other reeves to collect the money due to the king from his estates. The sheriff would also organise the shire court which met twice a year in the presence of the local bishop and ealdorman (or earl) and ensure that the hundred (or wapentake) courts were meeting regularly (once a month) and working well. He would also have the task of organising military forces. By 1066, the English shires were divided into at least 730 hundreds or wapentakes. They varied in size, largely depending on population density: shires with smaller hundreds (in southern England and East Anglia), tended to have larger populations. But however large or small they were, the hundreds/wapentakes were crucial components in an increasingly sophisticated administrative system. Not only did each one have its own monthly court attended by all the important people of the area, but they were used as the basis for assessing the various obligations (fiscal, military, policing) which local communities had to fulfil. They enforced royal authority, but they also reinforced it by making it a regular feature of everyday life.

By the end of this period, then, most of the English kingdom was made up of a network of territorial units (shires, hundreds/wapentakes) under the authority of royal officials (sheriffs) and their subordinates. The system was still developing, of course, and far from complete, but this consciously created uniformity of organisation and practice enabled the kings of England to rule the greater part of their kingdom (by wider eleventh-century standards at least) intensively and directly. They could mobilise armies and construct fleets, and they could raise apparently enormous amounts of tax regularly. This explains at least in part how Aethelred was able to hold on for as long as he did against repeated viking attacks, and it gave Cnut access to the resources which he needed to establish and construct his regime.

Military organisation

Some bold claims have been made for the military strength of late Anglo-Saxon England. For example:

> the more that becomes known about the ways in which English armies assembled and fought in this period the more it may become apparent that it saw the mobilisation of the country and its resources for war to an extent that was not to be repeated until the total wars of the twentieth century.[35]

Such a statement may seem extravagant on the face of things, given that the kingdom was invaded and decisively conquered twice during the eleventh century, first by the Danes in 1014–16 and then by the Normans in 1066. Nevertheless, it is worth remembering that the English, despite serious defeats and setbacks, withstood twenty years of Danish attacks before the final catastrophe of King Swein's invasion and that the Battle of Hastings was the third pitched battle fought in less than a month by many of the men who died there. It was not the English military system that was at fault in the eleventh century: it was the extraordinary amount of pressure placed upon it that eventually led to its collapse.

At the heart of the king's forces remained the few hundred experienced, professional warriors who between them constituted the armed element within the royal household (the hearth troop), and the personal armed followings of the great men who accompanied the king on campaign, fought alongside him in battle or garrisoned important strongpoints in times of crisis. They would serve out of a sense of duty and personal loyalty to their leader and in the hope of reward, either financial or in the form of land. It has already been mentioned that, under King Cnut, these men were often called housecarls, but this was almost certainly just a different name for the same kind of fighting men who had been retained for centuries in the entourages of powerful lords. It was the king's principal duty to protect his kingdom, and he would have been expected to set an example by fighting courageously himself. Here certainly, Aethelred's record was not a distinguished one. The army he called out from Wessex and Mercia in 1006 did more harm than good, and little if anything to stop the Vikings rampaging across southern England. And when in 1009 Aethelred did come close to engaging Thorkell the Tall in battle, Ealdorman Eadric managed somehow to disrupt and ruin the plan. Aethelred's greatest personal military success came after his return to England from Normandy in 1014, when his campaigning in Lincolnshire forced Cnut out of the kingdom. But this only provided a temporary respite, and when Cnut returned to England in 1015–16, Aethelred was ill and unable to campaign. The English military effort by then was in the hands of Edmund Ironside, whose reputation rests on his impressive but ultimately fruitless military exploits during this short period. He fought several battles against the Danes in 1016 before finally being defeated by Cnut at Ashingdon.

It was more common during Aethelred's reign for the Vikings to be challenged by armies raised locally rather than centrally. It was the *fyrd* of Essex, led by Ealdorman Byrhtnoth and his personal retainers, which was defeated at Maldon in 991, a Kentish army was defeated in 999, 'an immense army' from Devon and Somerset was overcome in 1001, and 'a great English army' from Wiltshire and Hampshire was let down by its cowardly leader, Ealdorman Aelfric, in 1003. Other local leaders led their men more bravely, even if in the end the outcome was the same. Ulfcytel of East Anglia made a great name for himself when he took on the Danes in 1004 and 1010. He was eventually killed at the battle of Ashingdon in 1016 along with many other leading English noblemen. But in these local encounters, below the level of the leaders and their own military followers, it is hard to know for sure how the armies were composed and how the troops were recruited. The three 'common burdens' of bridge work, fortress work and service in the *fyrd* were probably still imposed on landholders, and it has been suggested on the strength of later evidence that, by this time, contingents were being raised on the basis of one man for every five hides of land.[36*] How well-trained and equipped such men were is another matter, and the use of *ad hoc* levies raised by local officials or ealdorman as and when they were needed is more reminiscent of what had happened in the English kingdoms during the 860s and 870s than it is of the great campaigns of the early tenth century.

Perhaps the prolonged period of peace under King Edgar had in some way sapped the efficiency and effectiveness of the system which Alfred the Great and his successors had created. London staunchly resisted a series of Danish attacks, and the city was eventually able to make its own deal with Cnut in 1016. But there is little sign of other towns putting up similar opposition to the Danes, and no compelling evidence that the *burhs* built by Alfred, Edward the Elder and Aethelflaed were performing any useful military function by the early 1000s. Excavations at some sites, such as Cricklade in Wiltshire, Wareham and Christchurch in Dorset and at Hereford, have shown that new stone walls were built at some point to reinforce the

* Above, pp. 132–3

existing defences, but although it is tempting to associate this kind of construction with the wars of Aethelred's reign, it is impossible to date precisely. The English naval response to the Danish attacks after 975 was also ineffectual. King Edgar is reputed to have had an enormous fleet at his disposal, and to have used it to circumnavigate his kingdom every year. By the 990s, however, it seems that the king's ships were in no fit state to do anything like this. In 992 Aethelred ordered that 'all the ships that were of any use'[37] should gather at London. In 999 a plan to take on the Danes off the Kentish coast was frustrated by delays, whilst in the following year the king's ships set out to meet him in Cumbria but for some reason failed to do so. And most disastrously, of course, when Aethelred did manage to construct a sizeable fleet in 1008–9, most of it was destroyed before it got anywhere near the enemy because of a quarrel between two of the king's advisers.

It must have been setbacks like this which encouraged Aethelred to use mercenary troops. He persuaded Olaf Tryggvason to enter his service with some of his troops in 994, and Thorkell the Tall did the same after 1012 with forty-five of his ships and their crews of *lithsmen* ('fleet men') after having spent three years fighting against the English. Thorkell received a huge payment of tribute (£48,000) and disbanded most of his army, then fought with Aethelred against Swein of Denmark and was with the king during Swein's first attempt to besiege London in 1013. Neither of Aethelred's Danish recruits proved reliable in the long term, however. It may have been concerns about the wavering loyalty of Olaf's men which prompted Aethelred to order the St Brice's Day Massacre in 1002, and Thorkell eventually sided with Cnut and was rewarded by him when he was put in charge of East Anglia in 1017. As for Cnut's use of ships, he kept forty from his own fleet in service with paid professional crews after he became king, and it was probably these along with a few others which he used when he set sail for Norway with fifty ships in 1028. The *lithsmen* were obviously a group with influence, however. In 1035 it was not just Earl Leofric and the thegns north of the Thames who sided with Harold Harefoot following the death of Cnut; 'the shipmen in London' did so too.[38]

Royal finance

Warfare was a costly business, as was maintaining the peace. No English king would even have the chance to make a success of his reign without ready and frequent access to large amounts of cash. Much of this came from the king's lands. Most of these were in the southern and central regions of England, which were low-lying and used for arable cultivation. The farming of wheat in these areas was more profitable than the growth of hardier crops such as oats and rye and the pastoral farming which was prevalent on the generally higher pastures, moors and mountains of the north. Eleventh-century yields were much lower than modern ones, but in a normal year, England produced more grain than it needed to feed its population, and where arable farming was impossible, thousands of sheep and cattle (small and thin ones, admittedly, compared with later periods) grazed on good-quality grass land and produced meat, milk, cheese, hides and, above all, wool. Other natural resources were available, too: tin from Cornwall, lead (even silver) from Cumbria and iron ore from the Forest of Dean, for example. Extensive parts of the king's lands would have been leased out in return for rent, payable in cash, foodstuffs or services. Surplus produce from the lands the king kept under his own control could be sold by his agents at local markets. There were limits to how much income the king could derive from his lands, however, and the amounts must have varied over time. In an overwhelmingly agrarian age, all the peoples of northern Europe were vulnerable in the same way to the inconsistencies of the weather and the inevitability of disease. Technology was basic, as was scientific understanding of the climate and animal husbandry. The means to avert or compensate for disaster were simply not available; poor harvests, famine and sickness amongst livestock and people were common. According to the *Anglo-Saxon Chronicle*, for example, it was 'the great famine throughout England, such that no man ever remembered one so cruel', which forced the viking army then in the kingdom to return to Denmark in 1005, and in 1046–7, 'there was no one alive who could remember so hard a winter as that was, both for pestilence and murrain'.[39]

So whilst the king's lands provided him with food and funds, they were not sufficient on their own to meet his financial needs. He made money from the operation of the legal system (fines and penalties), but more from his power to regulate internal and foreign trade. There is no doubt that, stimulated by the discovery of new silver deposits in Germany in the 960s and the resultant influx of much of that silver into England, English trade with the continent increased significantly in the late tenth century, and the English economy boomed. Merchants paid tolls on the goods they imported, for example, and trading communities might pay lump sums for the privilege of being exempt from such dues. Much trading activity could only take place at designated royal centres with royal officials overseeing the transactions. There was a developing export business, particularly with Scandinavian traders, who would have exchanged their furs and ivories at these trading centres for English wheat and cloth; with Flanders where the developing cloth trade was greedy for English wool, and with southern Europe where leather, silk, spices and gold might be found. All of this presupposes the existence in England of an infrastructure of transport and communications, as well as developing agricultural techniques in the countryside and artisanal technologies in urban centres. And whilst the claim that 'the most important economic developments before the Industrial Revolution took place in the later Anglo-Saxon period' is a startling one, eleventh-century England was certainly thriving.[40]

Increasing prosperity, of course, exposed England to covetous opportunists abroad, and it is no surprise that economic revival coincided with the resumption of viking attacks on the kingdom. To manage these, new fiscal devices were developed. Aethelred's use of Scandinavian mercenaries has already been mentioned, and the sum of £21,000 which the *Anglo-Saxon Chronicle* says he paid to Thorkell the Tall in 1014 was raised using a new form of taxation, the *heregeld* ('army-tax'), later more popularly known as *geld* or Danegeld. This may have been paid for the first time two years earlier, in 1012: there is no direct evidence of this (the payment of £48,000 which was made in that year was a conventional payment of tribute), but when the *heregeld* was temporarily suspended in 1051, the *Anglo-Saxon Chronicle* recorded that it had been in use for thirty-nine years.[41] Be that as it may, the *heregeld* was imposed regularly for the rest of this period, perhaps annually, and was used by Aethelred, Cnut and his sons to pay for the foreign forces, particularly the ships and their crews, which they retained to keep themselves in power. When the *Anglo-Saxon Chronicle* recorded the death of Harold Harefoot in 1040, it noted that, in his time, 'sixteen ships were paid for at eight marks to each rowlock [each crewman, probably], just as had been done in King Cnut's time'. This means that the forty ships kept in service by Cnut in 1018 would have cost nearly £14,000 per year, a significant sum. So it is fair to assume that one of the things which made Harold's successor, Harthacnut, so unpopular was his order that 'sixty-two ships should be paid for' at the same rate. And in 1041, the *Chronicle* records that the 'army-tax' of £21,099 pounds was paid, 'and later 11,048 were paid for thirty-two ships'.[42] These sums were paid by landowners, the scale of whose individual liabilities were determined by the number of hides for which their lands were assessed, whilst the actual sum they paid was fixed at a specified amount per hide (perhaps usually twelve pence, although this amount did vary) and collected by the king's local officials at particular times each year. This must have made the *heregeld* a controversial and contentious political issue, a burdensome imposition at the best of times, but also a tool open to abuse by an unscrupulous king.

These large payments of *heregeld* need to be distinguished from the enormous sums of *gafol* ('tribute') paid by the English to their viking enemies during this period. There was nothing new about this kind of payment – Scandinavian invaders had been receiving pay-offs from one beleaguered English kingdom or another since the ninth century. But the amounts paid by Aethelred and then Cnut at the start of his reign were, on the face of it, huge: £10,000 in 991, £16,000 (or £22,000, according to a treaty drawn up at the time[43]) in 994, £24,000 in 1002, £36,000 in 1007, £48,000 in 1012 and £72,000 in 1018. Some historians have been reluctant to take these enormous figures at face value.[44] Certainly they increase in suspiciously precise multiples of twelve from 1002 onwards, and there are inevitably many questions about the practicalities which must have been involved in assessing and collecting such amounts so frequently. Unlike *heregeld*, tributes were occasional, irregular payments and therefore raised as and when they were required. Individual shires were probably assessed for the payment of a particular amount, with these assessments then being apportioned (possibly at a meeting of the shire court) between the hundreds or wapentakes. Individual landholders would then (perhaps at the hundred court) be allocated their shares to pay. It may be that they had to contribute in some fixed, pre-assessed way (so much per hide), but the bulk of the responsibility probably fell on the richest individuals and institutions (churches and monasteries) who could sell or lease land quickly, raise the prices of their surplus produce or delve into their reserves of stored treasure and cash. There is evidence which supports the view that churches in particular were placed under severe financial strain by the need to find money to pay off the Vikings, and it may have been harassed landholders like this who were responsible for charging the very high prices for wheat which the *Anglo-Saxon Chronicle* complained of in 1040.[45] There is evidence, too, that if a landowner could not pay his share, someone else could offer to do it for him and gain title to their lands as a result. And in the last resort, compliance could be secured by force, as it was when Harthacnut sent a small army to Worcestershire to avenge the killing of two of his tax collectors there in 1041. So finding the money was anything but optional, and the *geld* 'was a fiscal engine of elemental strength'.[46] Even if complaints about levels of taxation were exaggerated, and even if the figures in the *Chronicle* were massaged to a degree, a massive administrative effort must have been involved in raising tribute and *heregeld* anything like as often as the sources suggest. This provides further reason for thinking that the kings of this period had at their disposal an extensive set of written records concerning their kingdom which has now been lost. It is also further proof of the complexity and sophistication of eleventh-century English government. Paradoxically, of course, it was the kingdom's wealth and the ability to tap it so often which made England such an attractive target for invaders.

Linked to the king's wealth and England's system of taxation was the coinage. There was usually only one coin in circulation during this period, the silver penny, and it has been estimated (albeit using problematic methods) that 132 million of these were struck during Aethelred's reign and 83 million during Cnut's. Peak production may have been reached between 1017 and 1023, when perhaps as many as 47 million coins were minted.[46] But it is not just the number of coins produced that was impressive. By 1016, the regular payment of tribute and its removal from the kingdom by invaders returning home had led to a shortage of silver in England, and under Cnut, the weight of the silver penny was reduced. Despite this, the number of coins in circulation in England after 1016 may have continued to increase until 1066, and the English coinage remained superior to any other in north-west Europe in terms of its silver content whilst the system for administering was as well-developed as any other and probably more so. The minting of coins was a royal monopoly. Dies were made in London during the early part of Aethelred's reign, although this part of the process appears to have become more regionalised by the end of it and during Cnut's. Silver pennies of standard design (image and title of the king on one side, name and location of the moneyer on the other) were then produced by some sixty or seventy mints, staffed by royally licensed moneyers, located across southern and central England (the only northern mint was at York). The pennies were of relatively high value in themselves, and they could be cut into halves (halfpennies) or quarters (farthings) to provide smaller change. During Edward the Confessor's reign, there were probably more coins circulating in England than at any other time during the eleventh century. England's prosperity continued to be both a blessing and (as the events of 1066 would show) a curse.

The high quality and geographical spread of the coinage are important indicators of how far royal power was acknowledged across the kingdom, and the king's image and title on the coins were visible manifestations of royal power. Under Aethelred, however, the imagery on his coins took on an even greater significance. The earliest type of coin issued during his reign, around 980, depicted the Hand of God coming out of a cloud with the Greek letters Alpha and Omega, which symbolised Christ, on either side. Perhaps these coins were designed to show divine approval for Aethelred's rule after the reign's violent start. Later coins introduced around the turn of the century were more conventional and showed the king helmeted and ready for war, but in the so-called *Agnus Dei* type the king's portrait was replaced with an image of the Lamb of God, whilst on the other side there was a dove, the symbol of the Holy Spirit. It is not known for certain when this coinage was first issued, but it may have been in 1009 when the government implemented a whole series of spiritual measures, including the payment of a penitential tax, in an attempt to regain heavenly favour in the face of continued Danish attacks.

But the importance of the coinage to the king was more than symbolic. He made money from it, too. Local moneyers would pay to acquire their centrally struck dies or for the right to make their own, and at least every six years during the early eleventh century, and every three from 1036, a new coinage was issued, at which time weights and designs might be altered. Cnut issued three coinage types during his reign, and it has been suggested that they might have circulated in turn from 1017–23, 1023–29 and 1029–36.[48] Only coins of the current type were legal tender; so when the designs changed, old coins had to be brought to the mints and exchanged for new ones. For this privilege, people might pay as much as fifteen per cent of the value of their old coins. Some of this would be kept by the moneyer, but the bulk (effectively a tax on wealth) would be pocketed by the king. The importance to the king of retaining his monopoly over coin production was repeatedly emphasised in Aethelred's legislation: in one regulation, it was declared that moneyers who carried on their business in woods or other such places (that is, secretively and outside the official system) would be executed, unless the king decided to show them mercy, whilst in another, it was provided that any moneyer accused of striking false coins would be put to the triple ordeal. If found guilty, he would be killed.[49]

A kingdom worth fighting for

The kingdom of England was a prize worth winning and keeping by the early eleventh century. Its wealth made it a tempting target for greedy would-be conquerors, and the coverage and uniformity of its governmental systems made that wealth relatively easy to extract by whomever was in charge. In addition, however, those same systems allowed for much more by this time than the collection of money, and they enabled the rulers of England 'routinely to monitor, constrain and direct significant aspects of the behaviour of even quite ordinary people throughout the area from the Channel to the Tees'.[50] This administrative apparatus could function effectively under the strain of prolonged warfare during Aethelred's reign, it coped perfectly well during Cnut's when the king himself was absent for long periods, and it was tough enough to withstand entire changes of ruling dynasty in 1016 and 1042. The mechanisms and instruments of English executive power, forged and fashioned into shape over the previous century and a half, had allowed a single English kingdom to develop and remain stable. They also guaranteed that, whatever challenges it faced in the future, that kingdom would endure and grow stronger still.

DEBATE 10

Was England a nation-state by 1042?

'It may seem extravagant to describe early England as a 'nation-state'. Nevertheless it is unavoidable'.[1] The idea that the kingdom of England was the richest and most mature political entity in eleventh-century western Europe is now a commonplace in writing about this period. And certainly, there is much to support this view. There was a well-developed sense of English identity by 1042 which bound rulers and ruled together; the English Church, its bishops, priests and monasteries, bolstered and legitimised secular might. But it was around the king that political power crystallised and from him that it spread. The king's ultimate and supreme authority, gilded by elaborate and regular rituals, was recognised from Cornwall to Northumbria and confirmed by oaths of loyalty to him taken by all adult males. A robust administrative framework underpinned this strength: a network of (by 1000) thirty-two counties or shires, each subdivided into hundreds (in southern England) or wapentakes (in much of the Danelaw). Shires and hundreds had their own courts which met regularly, kept the peace and settled disputes. They were presided over by royal appointees (sheriffs and earls), who effectively governed their shires and earldoms for the king and executed his orders, increasingly given in the form of short, written, sealed commands known as writs. This administrative structure also enabled the king to collect revenues quickly and regularly, both from his own lands across the kingdom, but also from the jewel in England's fiscal crown, the land tax called the *geld*. Domesday Book, compiled in about 1087, shows that virtually every village and estate in England was liable for this tax. Much of it was collected in kind, but also in coins, and nowhere in Europe had a better coinage system than England. Since the reign of King Edgar (959–975), England had used a single uniform coinage. The design of the coins, their weight and silver content were all standardised. This facilitated trade, but it also raised money for the king. The images on the coins (in themselves powerful transmitters of royal authority) were changed every few years, and only coins of the current type were legal tender. When old coins were exchanged for new ones, the king's officials took their share for the royal coffers. There were limits to the precociousness of the Anglo-Saxon state, though. Northern England south of the rivers Tees and Ribble had not been divided into shires by 1042, and elsewhere local variations in law and custom remained significant. What is more, a developed political organisation could be a problem. England, for all its governmental ripeness, was comprehensively conquered twice in the eleventh century, and arguably it was the very sophistication of the kingdom's systems which, once in foreign hands, made this possible. Moreover, 'The structures of Anglo-Saxon monarchy might be strong, yet individual kings weak, as a result of personal inability and political circumstance'.[2] This was the case, catastrophically, with Aethelred II. So to be sure, England had many of the characteristics of a nation-state by 1042, but perhaps this only made the kingdom more vulnerable.

---

1 James Campbell, 'The United Kingdom of England: The Anglo-Saxon Achievement', in A. Grant and K.J. Stringer (eds.), *The Making of English History* (London, 1995), pp. 31–47, repr. in idem, *The Anglo-Saxon State* (London, 2000), pp. 31–53, at p. 32.
2 David Carpenter, *The Struggle for Mastery: Britain 1066–1284* (London, 2003), p. 67.

Notes

1 M. Swanton (ed. and trans.), *Anglo-Saxon Prose* (London, 1993), p. 189. The other seven 'columns' were truth, patience, liberality, formidableness, helpfulness, moderation and righteousness.
2 *EHD*, i no.123.
3 *ASC* 978.
4 *ASC* 1035, 1042.
5 Keynes, *Diplomas*, pp. 176–86.
6 *ASC* 1014; *JW*, ii pp. 504–5. *ASC* 1018 says 'according to Edgar's law'.
7 J.R. Maddicott, 'Edward the Confessor's Return to England in 1041', *EHR* 119 (2004), pp.650–66; quote at p. 650..
8 Maddicott, 'Edward the Confessor's Return to England', p. 666; P. Stafford, 'The Laws of Cnut and the History of Anglo-Saxon Royal Promises', *Anglo-Saxon England* 10 (1982), pp. 173–90.
9 S876.
10 Keynes, *Diplomas*, p. 189.
11 *ASC* 1006.
12 K. Mack, 'Changing Thegns: Cnut's Conquest and the English Aristocracy', *Albion* 16 (1984), pp. 375–87, at p. 377; Fleming, *Kings and Lords in Conquest England*, ch.2.
13 Lawson, *Cnut*, pp. 159–60.
14 S. Keynes, 'Cnut's Earls', in Rumble (ed.) *The Reign of Cnut*, p. 79.
15 Maddicott, *Origins of the English Parliament*, p. 55.
16 *EHD*, i nos.230, 127; *ASC* 1010, 1011.
17 *EHD*, i no.49 (p. 455) (II Cnut: Secular, Prologue); *ASC* 1023; *EHD*, i no.53 (p. 476).
18 Loyn, *Governance of Anglo-Saxon England*, p. 95.
19 A. Williams, *Aethelred the Unready: The Ill-Counselled King* (London, 2003), p. 28.
20 *EHD*, i no.129 (p. 596).
21 P. Stafford, *Queen Emma & Queen Edith: Queenship and Women's Power in Eleventh-Century England* (Oxford, 1997), p. 221; *WMGRA*, i pp. 276–7.
22 Keynes, *Diplomas*, p. 161.
23 K. Mack, 'The Stallers: Administrative Innovation in the Reign of Edward the Confessor', *Journal of Medieval History* 12 (1986), pp. 123–34.
24 *ASC* 1035; *JW*, ii pp. 532–3.
25 Keynes, *Diplomas*, ch.3.
26 Lawson, *Cnut*, pp. 66–71, Appendix III, at p. 219.
27 Keynes, *Diplomas*, pp. 140–5.
28 Williams, *Kingship and Government*, pp. 109–10.
29 *ASC* 1010, 1011, 1016.

30 *ASC* 1016.
31 *ASC* 1027 (a misdating for 1031).
32 S891.
33 *ASC* 1017.
34 S1458.
35 M.K. Lawson, *The Battle of Hastings, 1066* (Stroud, 2002), p. 160.
36 Williams, *Conquest and Government*, p. 121.
37 *ASC* 992.
38 *ASC* 1035.
39 *ASC* 1005, 1046.
40 James Campbell, 'Norwich', in M.D. Lobel (ed.), *The Atlas of Historic Towns*, ii vols (London, 1975), i p. 1.
41 *ASC* 1014, 1012, 1052.
42 *ASC* 1040, 1041.
43 *EHD*, i no.42 (II Atr, 7.2).
44 Compare John Gillingham, '"The Most Precious Jewel in the English Crown": Levels of Danegeld and Heregeld in the Early Eleventh Century', *EHR* 104 (1989), pp. 373–84 and idem, 'Chronicles and Coins as Evidence for Levels of Tribute and Taxation in Late Tenth- and Early Eleventh-Century England', *EHR* (105), pp. 939–50, with M.K. Lawson, '"Those Stories Look True": Levels of Taxation in the Reigns of Aethelred II and Cnut', *EHR* 104 (1989), pp. 385–406 and idem, 'Danegeld and Heregeld Once More', *EHR* (105), pp. 951–61.
45 Williams, *Aethelred the Unready*, p. 229 n.15; *ASC* 1040.
46 *JW*, ii p. 532–3; Richard Fletcher, *Bloodfeud. Murder and Revenge in Anglo-Saxon England* (London, 2003), p. 100.
47 K. Jonsson, 'The Coinage of Cnut', in Rumble (ed.), *The Reign of Cnut*, Table 11.8 at p. 218. The table is based on calculations in D.M. Metcalf, 'Continuity and Change in English Monetary History, *c.*973–1086. Part 2', *British Numismatic Journal*, 51 (1982), pp. 52–90. For comments on his methodology, see M. Allen, *Mints and Money in Medieval England* (Cambridge, 2012), pp. 318–19; Sawyer, *Wealth of Anglo-Saxon England*, pp. 116–19.
48 Lawson, *Cnut*, p. 180.
49 *EHD*, i no.43 (III Atr, 8, 16).
50 Molyneaux, *Formation*, p. 11.

11

THE KINGS AND THE LAW, 975–1042

The sheer amount of royal law-making during this period is enough to make it stand out above any which preceded it. Many of the concerns which had preoccupied their predecessors (crime, community responsibilities, the rights of the church) also feature prominently in the legislation of Aethelred and Cnut. However, there were differences as well. Entire law codes under Aethelred were designed to address the spiritual and moral failings of his subjects at a time of national crisis, whilst Cnut's laws were issued as part of a campaign to justify and legitimise the very seizure of power which Aethelred's reforms had failed to prevent. So once again, these lengthy, detailed and multiple royal pronouncements may reveal more about the thoughts and fears of those who wrote and compiled them than they do about how the legal system actually worked in early eleventh-century England. For this kind of information, it is case reports which matter. These show that there were still limits to the king's control of the justice system and that local vested interests (powerful landholders, mainly) continued to manipulate legal disputes in their own interests. Nevertheless, these reports also demonstrate that there was in place by this time an evolving network of courts which were beginning collectively to articulate an emphasis on consistent practice, procedure and even principle. And even more significantly, the most important of these tribunals were decidedly and unambiguously *royal* courts supervised by *royal* officials. Undoubtedly, the king's power was still unevenly distributed across England by 1042, but, steadily enough, his courts were making it a routine reality for more and more of his people.

Aethelred's laws

At least ten and perhaps as many as twelve law codes (or fragments of codes) survive in the name of Aethelred II – more than for any other Anglo-Saxon king. This much law-making is not really explained away by the length of Aethelred's reign, because the codes were issued more or less in two separate bursts of legislative activity, the first between about 993 and 997 and the second between about 1008 and 1014. The numbers given to these texts by modern historians is, as usual, no guide to the order in which they were produced. However, it seems right to say that the first of these two periods saw the making of the codes known as I–IV Aethelred, whilst during the second, V–X Aethelred were probably all produced. The early codes were overwhelmingly secular in their concerns, whilst the later ones were preoccupied with moral, spiritual and ecclesiastical matters. The two groups will be discussed in turn, as will the reasons for the differences between them.

The early codes

It is no great surprise that Aethelred did not begin issuing laws until the 990s. At the start of that decade the king was approaching his mid-twenties, but he was still under the influence of many of the councillors who had seen him through his adolescence; men who, the king was soon to recall, had not always influenced him for the better. There had been a change of guard around the king by about 993, however, and from then and through the next decade his advisers were much more experienced, reputable and capable than those who had earlier led him astray.* What is more, of course, England was on a war footing throughout the 990s. The Vikings had started raiding again in the previous decade, but the threat had increased significantly after their victory at Maldon in Essex in 991, and in 994, an army led by Olaf Tryggvason and King Swein Forkbeard of Denmark had caused havoc in south-eastern England. The code known as II Aethelred was a direct response to the events of 994. It was a treaty setting out the terms agreed between Aethelred and the viking army and, in broad terms, an attempt to prevent further fighting. It established 'a general peace' and set the amount of tribute payable to the Vikings at £22,000. Then, in return for food, the Vikings agreed to help the English against other raiding fleets and join forces with Aethelred against regions which sheltered enemy troops. Traders coming to England in ships were to be protected, and levels of compensation were set for Englishmen killed by Danes and *vice versa*.[1]

The rest of Aethelred's early legislation is rather less easy to date and summarise. All of it (and II Aethelred as well) survives only in collections from the twelfth century, and it is often impossible to know how the texts came to acquire the form they have in those sources. In 997 a royal assembly was held at Wantage in Berkshire, and it may be that III Aethelred, which was definitely issued there at some point and is sometimes known as 'the Wantage Code', was produced at that time. The purpose of the Wantage Code was to extend legislation already issued at Woodstock (I Aethelred) to former viking-controlled lands in the north-east midlands. So it must have been produced after the Woodstock enactment, but perhaps not very long after. As for IV Aethelred, that is actually a composite text made up

---

* Above, p. 218

of pieces probably from several other documents. It begins with what appears to be a set of replies to an enquiry concerning the regulations and legal customs of the city and port of London (hence the document is sometimes known as the 'Institutes of London'), but later it contains a long section on the coinage system which may have been part of another set of laws which has now been lost. Only I Aethelred, it seems, survives in anything like its original and official form.

I Aethelred had typically traditional royal concerns at its heart, most notably the need to preserve order and reinforce communal obligations. Interestingly, however, it explicitly states that its contents were 'according to English law' (*aefter Engla lada*, in Old English), the first such expression in any Anglo-Saxon code.[2] First, it declared in words almost identical to those which opened Edgar's Andover code, 'that every free man shall have a trustworthy surety who shall hold him to the performance of every legal duty, if he has been charged'. It reinforced this shortly afterwards with another statement of principle: 'And every lord shall be personally responsible as surety for the men of his own household'.[3] Meanwhile it proceeded to outline what should happen, and what a lord should do if it was one of his followers who had been charged. On one level, Aethelred was simply restating the importance of the lordship bond. However, he did so at great length and in a way which showed him trying to incorporate the lord's obligations into the structure of royal justice. So, if a lord's follower was accused, the lord was required to support him in the hundred court, but if he escaped, the lord would have to pay the man's *wergild* to the king, and if it was found that the lord had advised the man to flee, the lord's own *wergild* would be payable.[4]

There was more thoroughly detailed legislation in IV Aethelred concerning the coinage. It followed hard upon King Edgar's overhaul of the monetary system at the end of his reign, but it has been described as 'the most sophisticated discussion of the subject in the Anglo-Saxon corpus'.[5] The prevention of unauthorised minting and the circulation of defective coins were its main concerns. Forging coin dies, making poor-quality coins out of good ones and using sub-standard coins in markets were all offences which the king's officials were enjoined to stamp out. It concludes: 'And the coinage is to be maintained by all at the standard which I lay down in your instructions, in accordance with the decision at which we have all arrived'.[6] And the sustained quality of Aethelred's coinage throughout his reign suggests that they took him at his word. It is the exhaustive and comprehensive treatment of subjects like the coinage in IV Aethelred and the system of surety in I Aethelred which have led one historian to argue that 'English legislation had seldom before been so thoroughly planned' and another to state that the 990s saw 'some of the finest legislation ever produced by the Anglo-Saxon kings'.[7]

But if the style and content of English royal legislation were evolving by the 990s, so were its areas of interest. As was seen in Chapter 7,* Edgar's *Wihtbordesstan*

* Above, pp. 159–60

code had allowed those areas of central and northern England previously controlled by the Vikings to have their own laws and customs as long as they accepted and acknowledged the overall authority of the English king. III Aethelred attempted to go further and begin speeding up the process of assimilation. The Wantage code was aimed primarily at the Five Boroughs of the north-east midlands (Lincoln, Stamford, Nottingham, Derby and Leicester), and the king may have seen dealing with these established centres as a way to start spreading his laws to the rest of the north. It is notable if nothing else for the amount of Scandinavian terminology and vocabulary it contains: established local practices and customs were not simply swept away and some of its clauses may have been added by those responsible for its implementation. But at the same time, the king emphasised his ultimate power. The purpose of issuing the code, he said was 'in order that his peace may remain as firm as it best was in the days of his ancestors'.[8] And not only that, the enactment stipulated harsher punishments for some offences in the Five Boroughs than in other legislation which already applied to southern England. Under the coinage provisions in IV Aethelred, for example, forgers were subject to the ordeal, and only those 'who carry on their business in woods or work in other such places' or who imported defective coins would be executed. At Wantage, however, it was declared that all forgers would undergo the triple ordeal and, if found guilty, would be executed.[9] It is a little difficult to explain these variations: different punishments for the same offence in different parts of the kingdom might not help the 'drive towards unity' which III Aethelred might otherwise represent. To be sure, it was 'a text where royal resolutions were fused with local measures and practices', but whether it successfully accomplished Aethelred's aim of bringing the disparate parts of his extended kingdom closer together is another matter.[10]

The later codes

The law codes which historians refer to as V–X Aethelred are today associated with one individual who, experts agree, almost certainly wrote large parts of them. Wulfstan became bishop of London in 996, and little is known about his life before then. In 1002 he was promoted to the sees of Worcester and York, and he held both together until 1016 when he either resigned or delegated authority at Worcester. He died in 1023. Wulfstan's reputation rests on his writings, which are sometimes easily attributable to him because they carry his pen-name *lupus* (Latin for 'wolf'), but more usually because of their idiosyncratic and distinctive prose style. His works ranged widely, from government and administration (*The Institutes of Polity*) to estate management. But he is best known for his sermons. At least twenty-two and perhaps more than thirty of Wulfstan's sermons or 'homilies' (he is sometimes known as Wulfstan the Homilist) survive, and this is probably only a small proportion of those he originally wrote. They contain discussions of the Christian life, beliefs, rituals and prayers. Some were written for specific occasions, such as the ones for 'Dedication of a church' or 'Consecration of a bishop', and the best-known of all was the *Sermo Lupi ad Anglos* ('The Sermon of the Wolf to the English'), an awful warning about the link between English moral failure and the viking attacks of 1014. They are all deeply scholarly, based on mainstream and more obscure sources from the recent past or much earlier. And they are all intensely concerned with the need to follow God's law as set out by scripture and clarified by later authorities: chastity for priests and self-restraint for the laity; festivals and fast days were to be observed; the poor and weak should be provided for. Wulfstan was a religious and a social conservative: God had assigned a position and a function to every individual, and their duty was to fulfil their given role. It was the job of the church and the secular government to enforce the performance of these obligations, because if they were ignored or defied, the God-given order and shape of society would start to crumble and eventually collapse. The viking attacks of the early 1000s were clear evidence for Wulfstan that the English people were in a state of moral crisis and that the English kingdom was under existential attack. The only way of rescuing the situation was through penance and reformed behaviour, which, once again, it was the task of the ecclesiastical and political establishment to enforce. Despite, or perhaps because of, their apocalyptic content, Wulfstan's writings certainly struck a contemporary chord: the large number of copies of his work, as well as the considerable number of other texts which contain bits of Wulfstan's prose, testify to his influence and popularity.

Wulfstan's abilities must have been clear to his contemporaries and particularly to the king by 996, when he appears as bishop of London. After that he regularly witnessed Aethelred's charters and remained at the king's right hand for the rest of the reign. In 1008 he drafted his version of the laws that the king had issued at Enham in Hampshire (V/VI and probably X Aethelred), and he did the same again at Bath in 1009 (VII Aethelred) and in 1014 (VIII Aethelred). It is impossible to be sure why Wulfstan became interested in royal legislation, but he obviously saw it as a means of spreading the same kind of messages, this time with the king's backing, which he preached in his sermons. More specifically, his particular preoccupations may have been intensified by the turn of the millennium when, according to some, Christ's Second Coming and the Last Judgement would occur. And although the new century eventually began without an apocalypse, the viking attacks of the early 1000s and other events such as the great famine of 1005 can only have strengthened Wulfstan's view that things were going from bad to worse and that active intervention was required to salvage the situation. V Aethelred is clear from the start about what was most important:

> First, namely, that we all shall love and honour one God and zealously hold one Christian faith and entirely cast off every heathen practice; and we all [the *witan*] have confirmed both with word and with pledge that we will hold one Christian faith under the rule of one king.[11]

It then proceeds to outline some other principles, but all with a decidedly religious emphasis on moderation and mercy. So 'peace and friendship are to be rightly maintained in both religious and secular concerns within this country', and 'Christian men are not to be condemned to death for all too small offences', so that 'God's handiwork and his own purchase which he paid for so dearly is not to be destroyed for small offences'. Following this come provisions concerning members of the clergy which essentially exhort them to behave properly and in line with their duties. Of course, priests should be chaste, and 'every Christian man is zealously to avoid illegal intercourse, and duly keep the laws of the Church'.[12] The church should receive its tithes and other dues; feast days and fast days are to be observed; there should be no trading on Sundays and no ordeals or oath-taking on religious festivals. The overall message of the code is summed up by two of its later clauses. First:

> every Christian man is to do what is needful for him; heed zealously his Christian duties, and form the habit of frequent confession, and freely confess his sins and willingly atone for them as directed.

and second:

> God's law henceforth is to be eagerly loved by word and deed; then God will at once become gracious to this nation.[13]

Until the very end when it addresses more conventional matters such as deserting the royal army and plotting against the king's life, the decrees in the code fail to specify any punishments, and they read more like notes for one of Wulfstan's sermons than the kind of royal legislation which had typically been produced during the tenth century. Indeed, it is quite possible that Wulfstan himself did preach the content of this and later codes to his congregations and that he expected other bishops to do something similar. This raises an important issue about the surviving texts of Aethelred's later codes: they might be accurate records of what the king and his councillors ordered, but it is more likely that they are Wulfstan's rewritten version of those pronouncements. They might even be a record of Wulfstan's preaching which was turned into royal legislation in some form. The Latin version of V Aethelred describes how the bishops at Enham met together and deliberated on their own before getting permission from the king to preach on various matters to the large crowds which had assembled. This meant that 'Wulfstan could quite legitimately publicise his preaching as the decrees of the *witan*', which in turn 'raises considerable doubts whether they were really the means by which Aethelred's government implemented its decisions'.[14]

Nevertheless, there is no reason to think that Wulfstan's codes entirely misrepresent what the king and his councillors wanted. At the very least, they express an anxiety about England's plight between 1008 and 1014 which must have been shared by all members of the political and religious establishment. The laws issued at Bath in 1009 (VII Aethelred), which coincide with the arrival in England of Thorkell the Tall, do the same. This legislation survives in two versions, one in Old English and the other (which was written up after 1066) in Latin. The former begins by asserting that 'All of us have need eagerly to labour that we may obtain God's mercy and his compassion and that we may be able through his help to withstand our enemies'. It then goes on to order the whole nation to fast 'for three days on bread and herbs and water' at the following Michaelmas (29 September), every man was to go barefoot to church and give confession. A tax of one penny was to be taken from every hide and redistributed as charity along with the food which would have been eaten but for the fast. Special masses and psalms were to be sung, tithes and other church dues were to be paid, and 'all in common, ecclesiastics and laymen, are to turn eagerly to God and to deserve his mercy'.[15]

The decrees issued at Bath, along with those produced in the previous year at Enham 'lay down a programme for the spiritual and moral purification of the kingdom' at a time of crisis.[16] And that Wulfstan's worries were shared by the king seems clear from the issue of the special *Agnus Dei* coinage at around this time. Unusually, there was no image of the king on these coins, something which could not have happened without royal permission. Instead, on one side of the coin was an image of the Lamb of God carrying a long cross, whilst on the other a dove representing the Holy Spirit was depicted. It has been argued that this coin could have been issued to coincide with the publication of the Enham legislation. The assembly there was held at Pentecost, the feast which commemorated the moment when Christ's apostles received the Holy Spirit and began to preach, and the place-name 'Enham' seems to mean something like 'place were lambs are bred'. Numismatists prefer to date the *Agnus Dei* coinage to 1009, however, in which case its production may have been ordered at Enham. This in turn means that it may have been minted at the same time as the penitential tax was ordered at Bath.[17] Either way, codes and coins together show the ecclesiastical and secular elites working together in a concerted attempt to reform standards of behaviour and impose moral standards.

If nothing else, King Aethelred would have been happy with how the Enham code finished and the Bath code began. In 1008 the instruction was:

> And let us loyally support one royal lord, and all together defend our lives and our land, as well as we ever can, and pray Almighty God from our inmost heart for his help.

And in 1009:

> In the first place one God shall be loved and honoured above all, and all men shall show obedience to their king in accordance with the best traditions of their ancestors, and cooperate with him in defending his kingdom.[18]

The virtues of loyalty and obedience to the king again take a central place in royal legislation, although it is hard to know how seriously Aethelred's subjects took these exhortations as the problems in England continued to worsen. It would not be long, of course, before Aethelred and his family found themselves in exile in Normandy, after England had seemingly fallen to Swein Forkbeard's invasion of

1013. And even when the king was recalled after Swein's death in 1014, there are clear hints of how far he would have to go in order to recover the trust and allegiance of his people. Aethelred had to agree to 'govern them more justly than he did before ... and reform all the things which they all hated', and it is quite possible that the final set of surviving laws issued in his name (VIII Aethelred) were one of the results of this process (almost certainly overseen by Archbishop Wulfstan) of negotiation and reconciliation.[19] It deals with familiar themes: church dues, the proper observance of fasts and feasts and charitable obligations, for example. It also addresses the problem of offences committed by clergy and what should happen to those who commit offences within the boundaries of a church and violate its rights of sanctuary. The king's officials were given the job of protecting the church and upholding its rights. The picture painted by VIII Aethelred is a rather lurid one of a church staffed by villains which is under attack from outside predators. This may not be how things really were, but Wulfstan's anxieties about the collapse of morality and social order are clear: 'we eagerly direct and lovingly pray that men in every order will lead the life which belongs to them'; 'let us love God with our inmost heart and heed God's laws as well as ever we can'; 'let us zealously honour the true Christian religion and utterly despise all Christian practices'. This time, the final clause sounds a little hollow, even desperate: 'And let us loyally support one royal lord, and let each of our friends love the next with true fidelity and support him rightly'.[20]

The content of VIII Aethelred is exclusively ecclesiastical and almost certainly reflects Archbishop Wulfstan's priorities rather than the king's, even if the latter did assent to its publication. Aethelred had to keep his leading lay subjects happy, too, and it has been suggested that secular legislation was issued in 1014 in a separate code alongside VIII Aethelred and that this eventually found its way into Cnut's laws. There is certainly one section in the code now designated II Cnut which has a distinctly generous tone and where the emphasis 'was no longer on what the subject should do for authority but on what authority could do for its subjects'. And it begins: 'Now this is the mitigation by which I wish to protect all the people from what they were hitherto oppressed with all too greatly', which sounds like just the sort of thing Aethelred might have said on his return to England in 1014.[21] It deals with a range of matters including extortion by royal officials, the rights of widows, protection of the heirs of those who die intestate, abuses of lordship and more. But one clause may have resonated with Aethelred more than any other:

> the man, who in his cowardice deserts his lord or his comrades, whether it is on an expedition by sea or on one on land, is to forfeit all that he owns and his own life; and the lord is to succeed to the possessions and to the land which he previously gave him.[22]

After more than a century of sustained royal law-making, it remained the case that loyalty, whether to the king, a lord, a family, a neighbourhood or (Wulfstan would have said) God's law was seen as the virtuous foundation on which Anglo-Saxon society rested. The last decade and a half of Aethelred's reign had shown all too clearly what happened when that foundation was undermined.

Cnut's laws

1018

Cnut's reign began ominously. He was crowned in London by the archbishop of Canterbury early in 1017, but by the end of that year, Ealdorman Eadric Streona had been killed on the king's orders, and other important ealdormen in Mercia and Wessex would soon suffer the same fate. During 1018, Cnut exiled the late King Edmund's brother, Eadwig, and he married Emma of Normandy when he was already in an established relationship with an English woman, Aelfgifu of North-ampton. So by the time an enormous tribute of £72,000 (and another £10,500 from London) was paid to the king in the same year, elements within the English elite, not least Archbishop Wulfstan of York, may well have felt troubled about the aggressive approach the new regime was adopting. And the meeting which took place at Oxford during 1018, at which 'the Danes and the English reached an agreement according to Edgar's law', could well have been held to deal with such concerns.[23] It is not in the end clear what was agreed at Oxford. However, it is at least tempting to imagine Wulfstan briefing Cnut about what was expected of an English king, and there is a record of sorts which hints at the kinds of discussion the new king and his advisers might have had.[24] The single surviving copy begins: 'This is the ordinance which the councillors determined and devised according to many good precedents'. And it continues:

> the councillors determined that above all things they would love King Cnut with due loyalty and zealously observe Edgar's laws. And they agreed that they would, with God's help, investigate further at leisure what was necessary for the nation, as best they could.

So a general statement of loyalty was followed, first, by a reference to 'Edgar's laws' as representing a period of prosperity and stability before the upheavals of the previous two decades, and second, by an undertaking to revisit 'what was necessary for the nation' in due course. Specific laws then followed the opening statement. Most of these were taken from the Enham code of 1008 (V/VI Aethelred), with bits and pieces from Edgar's legislation. But, rather improvised as the selection was (and it was 'beyond dispute Wulfstan's work'), it acted as a stop-gap and served to steady the English ship of state. The old and new guards now had some time during which they could think more calmly about what to do next. The text of 1018 (it does not have a number like a normal law code) 'represents a provisional statement of the aspects of the previous regime that the archbishop considered fundamental . . . while foreshadowing the infinitely fuller promulgation that these and everything else would be given a couple of years later'.[25]

Cnut I/II

By the end of 1020 or 1021, the king and his advisers had made their decisions about 'what was necessary for the nation', and at Christmas in one of those years, while the court was assembled at Winchester, the law codes known as I and II Cnut were issued. Together they make up 'the fullest single record of Anglo-Saxon law'.[26] I Cnut is entirely ecclesiastical, and many of its provisions were taken more or less word for word from previous enactments. It drew heavily on the text of the 1018 Oxford agreement which, as has been said already, was itself derived largely from VI Aethelred and some of Edgar's legislation. Its areas of concern were therefore conventional: the payment of church dues, the behaviour of clergymen, the observance of religious festivals, standards of good Christian conduct and so on. Much of it, especially towards the end, reads like the headings for different parts of a sermon rather than laws as such: 'We desire and we pray, for the love of God, that every Christian man should readily understand what is for his own good', for example, or

> And very zealously we enjoin upon all Christian men that ever, from their inmost hearts, they love God and zealously uphold the true Christian faith, and eagerly obey their spiritual teachers, and frequently and often ponder over and inquire into the precepts and laws of God for their own advantage.

But this tone and approach is only to be expected from a text written by Archbishop Wulfstan.[27] As for II Cnut, most of that also amounts to a collection and codification of already existing laws, and exhaustive efforts have been made by historians to reveal the origins of what it contains.[28] It begins in terms which echo earlier pronouncements by Aethelred and his predecessors:

1   The first provision is, that I desire that justice be promoted and every injustice zealously suppressed, that every illegality be rooted up and eradicated from this land with the utmost diligence, and the law of God promoted
    1.1 And henceforth all men, both poor and rich, shall be regarded as entitled to the benefit of the law, and just decisions shall be pronounced on their behalf.[29]

Later, it more or less repeats word for word Edgar's legislation on the holding of the shire and borough courts, and the sections of the code on the coinage and the punishment of forgers largely restate existing rules as well.[30] But there is at least some sense of development in Cnut's great code. Where Aethelred had declared, for example, that 'every free man shall have a trustworthy surety who shall hold him to the performance of every legal duty', Cnut ordered that every free man over the age of twelve had to belong to a tithing. And whilst previous kings had regularly legislated about the need for commercial transactions to be publicly witnessed, Cnut went a little further: 'no one is to buy anything worth more than four pence, neither livestock nor other goods, unless he has the trustworthy witness of four men, whether it is in the borough or in the country'.[31] So II Cnut is not entirely derivative. Indeed, it also contains some provisions of its own which do not appear to be based on earlier texts (although other sources may have been used which are now lost). For example, 'the rights which the king possesses over all men in Wessex', as well as in Mercia and the Danelaw, are listed. And there is an important statement of principle 'that every man over twelve years of age is to give an oath that he will not be a thief or accessory to a theft'.[32] Such concerns (asserting royal authority across a newly expanded kingdom and preventing stealing) were not new, of course. But it is just possible that, phrased as they are, they might represent the will of the new king himself.

It has been said that I and II Cnut together 'deserve to rank among the most sophisticated legislative statements of post-Roman Europe'.[33] However, impressive though they are in their coverage and detail, there are many problems with them which should always be borne in mind. They may reflect the mind and will of the king to some unknowable extent, but it is much more likely they represent the priorities of Archbishop Wulfstan and so 'are likely to contain only measures which the archbishop found acceptable'. It has been suggested further that they may give 'a somewhat optimistic view' of Cnut's regime by toning down any emphasis on harsh punishments, leaving out anything which sounded oppressive and showing Cnut in as favourable a light as possible.[34] The king would certainly have been happy to go along with this way of being presented and to have himself associated directly with the English kings of the recent past. But Cnut was a Dane who probably spoke only basic English, knew little of his kingdom's customs and spent much of his reign abroad. So whether or not he had any interest in the specifics of the codes issued in his name, or in the actual workings of the legal system over which he presided, is another matter. And even if he did, 'codifying the law did not necessarily fill the bill of those who had to live and enforce it'.[35]

Law in action

The first part of the law code issued by Aethelred II at Woodstock (I Aethelred) is long and detailed. Indeed, it is 'one of the bulkiest single-issue laws in the Anglo-Saxon corpus'.[36] It sets out to ensure that all men of a certain status had their own surety (a lord or another man), whose job it was to guarantee their good conduct and answer for it if they fell short of the expected standard in any way. The code starts with a statement of principle: 'every free man shall have a trustworthy surety who shall hold him to the performance of every legal duty, if he has been accused'.[37] There then follow separate provisions designed to cater for a range of contingencies, and it is worth focusing on some of these here to see how royal legislators attempted to address one particularly important issue.

The first thing to establish was whether the accused man was of free status or not. If he was not (and was therefore a slave), he would be subjected straight away to an ordeal of some kind (the code does not specify which one). Then, if found guilty of a first offence, he would be branded; but if this was not a first offence, he would be executed. However, the provision is mainly concerned with free men and their sureties. If a free man was detained peacefully, his reputation immediately came into play. If the accused's reputation was bad, he would go straight to the triple ordeal. However, he could try and establish his good reputation with the assistance of oath-helpers chosen by his surety. If they were unwilling to swear an oath, the accused would still be put to the triple ordeal. However, if they were prepared to swear, the accused then had a choice. He could opt to abide by their oaths in the hope that they would be enough to establish his innocence. Or, if he was concerned that the oath-helpers might not be as supportive as this, or that the weight of their testimony was not great enough to clear him, he could elect instead to undergo the single ordeal. One way or the other, either through oath-helpers or the ordeal, guilt or innocence would be established. As for punishment, the accused would be executed if this was not his first offence. But if it was, and if he held bookland, he would pay fines to the king. If he was not a holder of bookland, he would be ordered to pay compensation to the accuser and his own *wergild* to his lord.

The code also tried to establish what should happen if the accused fled to avoid the charges. In that case, his surety was liable to pay the value of his goods to the accuser and the *wergild* of the accused to the latter's lord (if the lord was not himself the surety). But if the lord was the surety, a second principle became relevant: 'every lord shall be personally responsible as surety for the men of his own household'.[38] He would pay the accused's *wergild* to the king if the former escaped. Furthermore, if it was alleged that the lord had actually aided the escape, he was required to clear himself of the accusation with oath-helpers. If he was successful, he received the accuser's *wergild*, but if he failed, he had to pay his own *wergild* to the king and the accused was outlawed.

A close reading of this clause reveals a central authority grappling to address a significant and pressing issue in hard-headed, practical ways. But in the end, there is little to show Aethelred's provisions working in practice, despite the fact that at least a quarter, and perhaps a third, of surviving Anglo-Saxon lawsuits date from his reign. Kings continued to hear some cases themselves, and not necessarily in a formal way. Harold Harefoot was 'lying in Oxford very ill and despairing of his life' when a claim was brought before him by the monks of Christ Church, Canterbury.[39] The claim concerned the king's own allegedly wrongful seizure of property, so it might not be typical. Nevertheless, by this point late in the period, it is likely that the king only tended to get personally involved in cases which concerned him and his rights or in the most serious disputes, where allegations of disloyalty or treason were concerned, for example, or where those close to the king were involved. 'And no one is to have any jurisdiction over a king's thegn except the king himself', one of Aethelred's laws declared.[40]

A good illustration of the king's court in action is provided by the case of Ealdorman Aelfric of Mercia who in 985, the *Anglo-Saxon Chronicle* records, 'was driven out of the land'. Aelfric was only exiled, however, after a formal legal process, that is 'by the unanimous legal counsel and most just judgement of bishops, ealdormen and all magnates of this realm at the royal vill called Cirencester'.[41] There were also other ways for the king's influence to make itself felt. Aethelred asserted that he was entitled to any fine imposed on a holder of bookland, and Cnut claimed exclusive jurisdiction for himself (or in practice his officials) over a whole range of criminal cases in Wessex, Mercia and the Danelaw.[42] Nevertheless, the king's authority over the system of justice could still be challenged, and he did not always find it easy to enforce his will. Some time in the late 980s, a certain Wulfbald seized his stepmother's lands following the death of his father.[43] The king twice ordered him to return what he had taken, but Wulfbald ignored him each time, and on both occasions, he was fined the amount of his *wergild*. Wulfbald then took possession of another estate belonging to one of his kinsmen, and when the king commanded him twice more to return that one, he did nothing yet again and was fined for the third and fourth times. A 'great meeting' was then held at London at which Aethelred's councillors assigned to the king all Wulfbald's property 'and himself likewise as the king desires, either to remain alive or be condemned to death'. Wulfbald soon died anyway, but his widow then picked up where her husband had left off and took matters even further. She and her son killed a king's thegn (who was also Wulfbald's cousin) and fifteen of his companions, as a result of which all of Wulfbald's property was for the second time assigned to the king at another council meeting. Clearly the king and his advisers had found themselves embroiled in a nasty dispute over family property, and the seeming disregard for royal authority displayed by Wulfbald and his widow is strikingly blatant. Having said that, the king's interest in the case was persistent and he did end up in possession of Wulfbald's property (the record of the case is contained in a royal charter in which Aethelred grants some of it to his mother). So ultimately royal decisions were enforced, and the king's justice prevailed.

By Cnut's reign, the network of courts below the level of the king's own was firmly in place and well-established. The shire court was supposed to meet twice a year (King Edgar had stipulated this first and Cnut followed him) and probably dealt with the most serious crimes and the more high-profile land disputes.[44] One of these arose some time between 990 and 992 when Wynflaed and Leofwine quarrelled over two estates at Hagbourne and Bradfield in Berkshire.[45] Leofwine appears to have been in possession of the estates, but Wynflaed claimed they were rightfully hers because she had exchanged them for an estate at Datchet in Buckinghamshire with a certain Aelfric. Wynflaed was able to produce an impressive group of witnesses to back up this claim, including the archbishop of Canterbury and the king's mother, Aelfthryth. But Leofwine refused to accept this hefty evidence and successfully insisted that the case should be heard in the Berkshire shire court. There, with sealed orders from the king to decide the case justly, Wynflaed was able to establish her claim with the help of another large team of influential witnesses. Leofwine was then advised not to swear an oath of his own because, if he did so unsuccessfully and failed to prove his own title to the lands, the consequences for him would be more serious than if he did what he eventually chose to do, namely hand over the estates to Wynflaed without contesting her claim. Wynflaed was then told 'to produce all his [Leofwine's] father's gold and silver that she had', but Leofwine for his part demanded an oath from her 'that all his property was there'. Wynflaed claimed she was unable to do this and at this point in the proceedings the record ends leaving, as usual, many unanswered questions. The basis of Wynflaed's victory, for example, is not clear: it may be that it was the sheer weight of evidence (that is, the number of prominent people) on her side that made the difference. It would also be interesting to know what, if anything, the king said about the case in the sealed document he sent to the court. At the very least, however, this example shows how the king could still directly intervene in a case whether he heard it himself or not.

By contrast, another case which was heard in the Herefordshire shire court, suggests that legal technicalities and procedures were sometimes less important than raw power and influence. Some time during Cnut's reign, a man called Edwin attended the shire meeting and sued his own mother for the recovery of a piece of land she was holding. A prominent local landholder, Thurkil the White, stood up and said that he would represent the mother as 'it was for him to do so, if he knew the case'. So Thurkil and three nominated thegns rode out to visit the woman. Angrily and loudly, she denied that she had any land which belonged to her son and promptly summoned her kinswoman, Leofflaed, and nominated her as the sole beneficiary of her estate, money and belongings after her death. It is at this point in the record that it becomes clear why Thurkil thought it was 'for him' to pursue the case: Leofflaed was his wife! On returning to the shire court, Thurkil asked for his wife's new rights to be acknowledged, and so they were. The rather flimsy nature of the mother's defence seems not to have been an issue here. Thurkil was an important man, and those presiding over the court were important men, too: they included the local bishop, one of Cnut's earls, the sheriff and 'all the thegns of Herefordshire'.[46] It is no great surprise that they sided with one of their own number on this occasion.

As for the hundred court, The Hundred Ordinance had ordered that it should meet every four weeks, and Aethelred had extended this principle (if it was not already in operation there) to the wapentakes of the Five Boroughs and beyond.[47] The number of references to the hundred court in II Cnut suggest that, by the 1020s, it was the busiest and most commonly used court: 'no one shall appeal to the king, unless he fails to obtain justice within his hundred', Cnut declared, echoing similar provisions by previous kings.[48] Less grave crimes (perhaps those which did not involve the death penalty) were probably heard there, as well as certain land cases. In Edgar's reign, for example, abbot Byrhtnoth of Ely had bought 200 acres at nearby Witchford, a transaction witnessed by the whole hundred. In the disturbances after Edgar's death the vendor annulled the agreement, claiming he had acted under compulsion and had many times desired to return the money he had received. Ealdorman Aethelwine then came to Ely and heard the plea 'with the whole hundred in the churchyard at the northern gate of the monastery', and there brought the case to an end with the abbot having to pay another thirty shillings to the vendor, making a total purchase price of twelve pounds.[49] The involvement of the local ealdorman probably made this meeting of the hundred untypical, and the bare record of the case probably conceals a good deal of wrangling and negotiation behind the scenes. However, witnessing transactions and resolving disputes arising from them was part of the hundred's routine business. But it was also the hundred's job to supervise local peacekeeping arrangements by keeping tithings fully manned:

> And it is our will that every free man . . . be brought, if he is over twelve years old, into a hundred or tithing; otherwise he is not to be entitled to any rights of free men.[50]

To be sure, in the pauses between official business, local people could make connections, exchange gossip and information and do deals: they were significant local gatherings which served to tie neighbourhoods, kindreds and lords' followings together. Ultimately, however, the courts of shire and hundred were designed to preserve social order, protect property and transmit royal power. Presided over by the king's nominated representatives, the local bishop and ealdorman in the shire court and a royal reeve in the hundred, they channelled the distribution of centralised authority.

But whilst the system of courts was continuing to evolve by the end of this period, there was evidently still room for allegations to be heard in less formal or institutionalised ways. In the early 970s, a servant from the household of a man called Flodoald was arrested by Eadric, the king's reeve at Calne in Wiltshire. The crime is not specified in the record, but the penalty if found guilty was death. The servant was held in chains whilst waiting for his owner's arrival, after which he would undergo the ordeal and carry a red-hot iron bar. When Flodoald arrived, his concern about the damage to his reputation this case might cause prompted him to offer the reeve a whole pound of silver, as well as the servant himself, if he would drop the charges. The servant was also supported by his own friends and family. Deaf to their pleas, however, Eadric pressed ahead and forced the accused slave

> to carry in his bare hand a searing piece of iron of considerable size glowing red-hot from much coal. When the man . . . took it hesitantly in hand, at once a huge burn filled the entire palm of his scorched hand.

His hand was sealed up in the usual way for three days, but when it was uncovered 'his very enemies judged the man innocent, and his ill-wishers declared him unimpaired'.[51] The gaps in this account are very striking. It is far from clear how the servant came to be suspected: if an accusation was made against him, there is no record of the accuser. There is also no mention of a priest being involved in the ordeal, and Athelstan's laws (or any laws) about the procedure to be followed on such an occasion do not appear to have featured in the proceedings. What is more, there is nothing to show that the servant was brought before any kind of court prior to the ordeal. Taken at face value, the account suggests that Eadric the reeve was solely responsible for suspecting and arresting the servant and for deciding how he should be dealt with. Interestingly, however, this may be exactly what was supposed to happen given what the opening clause of Aethelred's Woodstock code said about the treatment of accused slaves: a finding of guilt at the ordeal should be punished by death for anything other than a first offence.[52]* Even so, it is fair to say that the purpose of this account was not to tell future generations about how the ordeal or the courts worked, so it may simply have skated over such details. Rather it was designed to reinforce the saintly credentials of St Swithun, who interceded to heal the servant after Flodoald and his companions had prayed for his help. Nevertheless, the prominence of the king's reeve at the heart of the case is another reminder of how pervasive royal control of one kind or another over the system of justice was becoming by this point.

But whilst some kinds of cases, most notably involving theft and serious violence, were increasingly seen in this period as matters to be dealt with by the king and his officials, there were still limits to what they could achieve. So local communities continued to bear much of the responsibility for routine law enforcement, albeit within a developing framework of ultimately royal supervision. The behaviour of individuals could be monitored and (to an extent) controlled through the use of systems designed to enforce communal responsibilities for good behaviour. Tithings were first mentioned during the reign of Aethelstan,† but by Cnut's reign, it was settled law that every free man over the age of twelve should belong to a hundred and a tithing if he wished to be entitled to defend himself in court and have his *wergild* paid if he was killed: 'otherwise he shall not be entitled to any of the rights of a freeman'. Additionally, every man over the age of twelve was required by Cnut's laws to swear that he would not be a thief or a thief's accomplice.[53] Local people were expected to pursue thieves by raising the hue and cry and then to seize them so that they could be tried. If someone heard the hue but failed to respond to it, they could be fined 'for insubordination to the king'. In ways like this, 'Kings sought to channel self-help, and to regulate it, in order to prevent abuse and perhaps in order to limit the escalation of disputes'.[54]

The payment of compensation by guilty parties to the victims of crime or their families was also designed to bring quarrels formally to an end and prevent grievances flaring up again in the future. But compensation was, in theory at least, a private matter between the parties; punishment, by contrast, was inflicted on the wrongdoer by the appropriate authority. Increasingly by 1042, this was the king. By the early eleventh century, certain offences were categorised as *botleas*, that is offences for which no compensation could be paid. Presumably this meant that they were so serious that only more stringent penalties would do, and it is possible to see in these offences the origins of 'royal pleas' or 'pleas of the crown', that is serious criminal cases over which the king and his courts had assumed exclusive jurisdiction by the twelfth century. One such offence, according to Aethelred's laws, was a breach of the peace which the king 'establishes in person', whilst Cnut's laws specified other *botleas* as 'assaults upon houses, arson, theft which cannot be disproved, murder which cannot be denied, and treachery towards a man's lord'.[55]

---

* Above, p. 250
† Above, pp. 167–8

The last offence encompassed treason as well, whilst someone guilty of 'theft which cannot be disproved' was probably caught in the act or at least in possession of the stolen goods. As for 'murder which cannot be denied', such a phrase implies that there were other kinds of homicide which did not justify execution. A lesser physical punishment might be imposed in such a case, and perhaps even a fine or loss of lands. For certain offences someone could be placed outside the protection of the law altogether, just as someone who managed to flee rather than face trial and possible punishment might also be declared an outlaw. In such cases, the outlaw lost his property: if it was bookland, it was forfeited to the king. Cnut's laws also stipulated which fines the king was entitled to collect for various offences committed in Wessex, Mercia and the Danelaw.[56] For the king, controlling the system of justice meant profit as well as power.

The roots of the common law

It is inevitably very hard if not impossible to gauge how successful the Anglo-Saxon kings were when it came to preserving order and containing crime. Nevertheless, it is clear that by the end of this period, they claimed an increasingly exclusive right to declare what the laws were, supervise their enforcement, punish wrongdoers and profit from the sanctions they imposed. To be sure, these were still very early days in the creation of what ultimately became 'the English common law', but the existence of a strong central authority which was acknowledged across the kingdom as the ultimate source of justice was a vital prerequisite for any such later development. Even so, as far as the evidence allows for any conclusions about this period at all, much everyday legal procedure appear to have remained improvised and extempore. The laws and legal principles used were still based to a large degree on local, time-honoured custom rather than the pronouncements of the king. And, if the surviving reports of actual cases are representative to any degree, laws as such often featured only indirectly when it came to deciding guilt or innocence, right or wrong. Large amounts of discretionary power to decide how, where and when accusations and disputes should be dealt with rested in the hands of those with the job of preserving order, prosecuting crime and enforcing rights over property. Prominent among these men were members of the clergy, most notably bishops, who had a substantial role to play in the administration of secular justice. So England was not yet a kingdom governed by a set of uniform and consistent written laws by 1042; nor was its legal system managed by a group of trained, professional lawyers. Nonetheless, the issuing of royal legislation was a regular and frequent event from the 990s onwards. If nothing else, this further embedded the principle that the king was the ultimate judge and law-giver in the kingdom. Meanwhile, the outline of a functioning and extensive network of royal courts, so dimly visible in 950, was slowly coming into focus, in southern England at least, by 1042. These courts of shire and hundred would evolve and be supplemented by other courts in years to come, but they would underpin England's legal system for the rest of the middle ages. And at the same time as royal jurisdiction over criminal and civil disputes expanded, later kings would also develop the ideas first nurtured by their Anglo-Saxon predecessors about oaths of loyalty to the king, crime as treason and communal duties carried out under royal supervision to extend and deepen their own power. The tree of English justice would grow famously strong and its branches would eventually cover much of the world. But its roots lay deep in the Anglo-Saxon soil.

Notes

1   *EHD*, i no.42 (II Atr).
2   Robertson, *Laws*, p. 52 (I Atr, Prologue).
3   Robertson, *Laws*, pp. 52–5 (I Atr, 1, 1.10); *EHD*, i no.41 (III Edgar, 6).
4   Robertson, *Laws*, pp. 52–5 (I Atr, 1.2, 1.7–9a).
5   Wormald, *MEL*, i p. 328.
6   Robertson, *Laws*, pp. 75–9 (IV Atr, 5–9, quote at 9.3).
7   Wormald, *MEL*, i p. 325; Keynes, *Diplomas*, p. 196.
8   *EHD*, i no.43 (III Atr, 1).
9   Robertson, *Laws*, pp. 74–7 (IV Atr, 5, 7); *EHD*, i no.43 (III Atr, 8).
10   Williams, *Aethelred the Unready*, p. 58; Wormald, *MEL*, i p. 329.
11   *EHD*, i no.44 (V Atr, 1).
12   *EHD*, i no.44 (V Atr, 1.2, 3, 3.1, 10).
13   *EHD*, i no.44 (V Atr, 22, 26).
14   Lawson, 'Archbishop Wulfstan and the Homiletic Element', pp. 150–1; idem, *Cnut*, p. 62.
15   *EHD*, i no.45 (VII Atr, OE, Prologue, 1, 2, 7). Original versions and translations of this and the Latin text are at Robertson, *Laws*, pp. 108–17.
16   Williams, *Aethelred the Unready*, p. 94.
17   Lawson, 'Archbishop Wulfstan and the Homiletic Element', pp. 152–4; idem, *Cnut*, pp. 62–3.
18   *EHD*, i no.44 (V Atr, 35); Robertson, *Laws*, pp. 108–9 (VII Atr, Lat, 1).
19   *ASC* 1014.
20   *EHD*, i no.46 (VIII Atr, 31, 43.1, 44, 44.1).
21   Wormald, *MEL*, i pp. 361–2; *EHD*, i no.50 (II Cnut, 69).
22   *EHD*, i no.50 (II Cnut, 77).
23   *ASC* 1018; *JW*, ii pp. 504–5 ('an agreement about keeping Edgar's law').
24   *EHD*, i no.47.
25   Wormald, *MEL*, i p. 346; A. Kennedy, 'Cnut's Law Code of 1018', *ANS* 11 (1983), pp. 57–81.
26   Wormald, *MEL*, i p. 345.
27   Robertson, *Laws*, pp. 168–9, 170–1 (I Cnut, 18, 21).
28   Wormald, *MEL*, i pp. 356–60 (this deals with the sources for I Cnut, too); Lawson, 'Archbishop Wulfstan and the Homiletic Element', p. 158 n.99.
29   Robertson, *Laws*, pp. 174–5 (II Cnut, 1–1.1); compare Robertson, *Laws*, pp. 94–5 (VI Atr, 8).
30   Robertson, *Laws*, pp. 178–9, 182–3; *EHD*, i no.50 (II Cnut, 8, 18); compare *EHD*, i no.35 (II Aethelstan, 14–14.1); Robertson, *Laws*, pp. 28–9, 74–5, 100–1 (III Edgar, 8; IV Atr, 5.3; VI Atr, 32).
31   Robertson, *Laws*, pp. 52–3 (I Atr, 1); *EHD*, i no.50 (II Cnut, 20, 24); compare, for example, *EHD*, i no.41 (IV Edgar, 6–6.2).
32   *EHD*, i no.50 (II Cnut, 12, 14, 15, 21).
33   Wormald, *MEL*, i p. 365.
34   Lawson, *Cnut*, p. 188; idem, 'Archbishop Wulfstan and the Homiletic Element', p. 159.
35   Wormald, *MEL*, i p. 366.
36   Robertson, *Laws*, pp. 52–5 (I Atr, 1).

37 Robertson, *Laws*, p. 53 (I Atr, 1).
38 Robertson, *Laws*, pp. 54–5 (I Atr, 1.10).
39 S1467; Robertson, *Anglo-Saxon Charters*, no.XCI.
40 *EHD*, i no.43 (III Atr, 11).
41 *ASC* 985.
42 Robertson, *Laws*, 54–5; *EHD*, i no.49 (I Atr, 1.14; II Cnut, 12, 14, 15).
43 S877; Robertson, *Anglo-Saxon Charters*, no.LXIII; *EHD*, i no.120.
44 *EHD*, i no.40 (III Edgar, 5.1); Robertson, *Laws*, pp. 182–3 (II Cnut, 18).
45 Robertson, *Anglo-Saxon Charters*, no.LXVI; Wormald, *MEL*, i pp. 151–3.
46 S1462; *EHD*, i no.135; Robertson, *Anglo-Saxon Charters*, no.LXXVIII.
47 *EHD*, i nos.39, 40, 43 (I Edgar, 1; III Edgar, 5.1; III Aethelred, 3.1).
48 Robertson, *Laws*, pp. 182–3 (II Cnut, 17–18).
49 J. Fairweather (trans), *Liber Eliensis. A History of the Isle of Ely from the Seventh Century to the Twelfth* (Woodbridge, 2005), p. 115.
50 *EHD*, i no.49 (II Cnut, 20); Robertson, *Laws*, pp. 184–5.
51 The case is described and discussed in Hudson, *Laws*, pp. 68–9.
52 Robertson, *Laws*, pp. 54–5 (I Atr, 2).
53 Robertson, *Laws*, pp. 184–5 (II Cnut, 20,21).
54 Robertson, *Laws*, pp. 188–9 (II Cnut, 29.1); Hudson, *Laws*, p. 172.
55 Robertson, *Laws*, pp. 64–5, 206–7 (III Atr, 1, II Cnut, 64).
56 Robertson, *Laws*, pp. 180–1 (II Cnut, 12–15).

12

THE KINGS AND THE CHURCH, 975–1042

This was a traumatic period for the newly created English kingdom, as the last few chapters have shown. The murder of King Edward the Martyr in 978 was followed by the return of the Vikings to English shores from the late 980s, the failures of King Aethelred and, ultimately, Danish conquest in 1013–16. Peace and stability only began to return to England in the 1020s and 1030s, but there was uncertainty about the course of political events once more after the death of Cnut in 1035. Of course, as Chapter 10 explained, there was a large amount of institutional continuity across this period, and the governmental systems and administrative mechanisms which had evolved in the first three-quarters of the tenth century proved remarkably resilient and robust, even as the strains on them intensified either side of 1000. Nevertheless, this was indeed a turbulent and challenging time for the English king and his subjects, and in all of these events and developments, for good or ill, the English Church and the kingdom's leading churchmen played a central role.

All churches great and small

By the start of the eleventh century, there were seventeen English dioceses in all, from Cornwall in the far south-west to Durham, where the community at Chester-le-Street moved in 995, in the far north. Some of them were much bigger than others (the largest diocese of all in purely territorial terms was Dorchester and the smallest was Rochester), but the bishops were, for the most part, rich men with extensive estates to administer. Having said this, not all of them were equally well-off: whilst the archbishop of Canterbury and the bishop of Winchester were enormously wealthy, for example, the archbishop of York was much less so. Within each diocese, moreover, there were other centres of religious authority and power. The

Benedictine Reform Movement of the late tenth century had established or reestablished monasteries and nunneries across much of England south of the Humber.
These, even more than the cathedrals, controlled sizeable amounts of territory, large
numbers of people and considerable amounts of cash. There were also still hundreds of unreformed minsters, staffed by secular (that is, non-monastic) clergy who
ministered to their surrounding populations; but also by this time an increasingly
common sight in the countryside would have been small churches established by
local landowners and manned by individual priests. As yet, these were intended
just to meet the spiritual needs of the lord and his tenants, but they would grow in
importance over the next century and ultimately replace the minsters as the main
providers of pastoral care. Their emergence from the late tenth century onwards
marks the beginnings of England's parish system. The main point here, however, is
that the churches of eleventh-century England, the cathedrals, monasteries, minsters and even the humble wooden structures erected next to the houses of local
lords, were ever-present reminders to the population of the power of religion. The
men who ran these places and managed their resources were immensely important,
and it is hardly surprising that the kings of this period appointed them where they
could and regarded them as essential collaborators in the development of their own
royal power and prestige.

The church and royal power

Leading churchmen continued to play the same roles in government and administration during this period as they had before it. Despite the disruption caused by
the viking attacks under King Aethelred, for example, there is no reason to doubt
that bishops continued to preside over the shire courts during his reign and after
it. Indeed, it is likely that their local administrative responsibilities (raising money,
recruiting troops, preserving order generally) grew as the mood of national crisis
deepened. Some even played a military role at moments of particular peril: in 992
Bishop Aescwig of Dorchester and Bishop Aelfstan of London (or Rochester; there
were two bishops with that name at the time and the record does not make it clear
which one it means) were appointed by the king, along with two leading ealdormen, to lead his fleet and 'to try if they could entrap the Danish army anywhere at
sea', and in 1016, Bishop Eadnoth of Dorchester and abbot Wulfsige of Ramsey
were both killed at the battle of Ashingdon.[1]

At the centre of affairs, however, the church's primary duty remained the same:
in return for the protection he swore to give it, the king was crowned and anointed
and given his unique, divinely approved status. This was not always straightforward.
After Edgar's death in 975, Archbishop Dunstan of Canterbury had to decide which
of the late king's sons he should support, and something similar happened after
Cnut's death in 1035. One story (admittedly from a partisan source) describes how
Archbishop Aethelnoth refused to cooperate when Harold Harefoot demanded
that he should consecrate him king and hand over the crown and sceptre. Aethelnoth reportedly said that he would not consecrate anyone other than a son of

Queen Emma, and he forbade all the bishops from participating in a consecration. Whether he or the archbishop of York eventually crowned Harold in 1037 is not clear.[2] In normal circumstances, however, following the coronation, the leading clergy counselled the king as members of his *witan*, attended his assemblies and witnessed his charters. They advised him on political, diplomatic, military and legal matters, and they were responsible in some cases for much of the tone and direction of royal policy. The death of Bishop Aethelwold of Winchester in 984 prompted King Aethelred to describe him in a charter as someone 'whose industry and pastoral care administered not only to my interest but also to that of all inhabitants of this country, the common people as well as the leading men'.[3] Later in Aethelred's reign, the royal charter witness lists suggest that men such as Archbishop Sigeric of Canterbury (990–4), who was credited by the *Anglo-Saxon Chronicle* with responsibility for suggesting the first payment of tribute to the Vikings in 991, abbot Aelfweard of Glastonbury (d.1009) and abbot Wulfgar of Abingdon (990–1016) were particularly influential. The last of these was referred to in another charter by the king as 'friendly to me with complete devotion'.[4] But perhaps the most important figure of all in this context was Archbishop Wulfstan of York. His contribution to the legislation of Aethelred and Cnut was described in Chapter 11,[*] and his commitment, first, to preserving Aethelred's regime and, second, to entrenching Cnut's, cannot be underestimated.

Aethelred II and the church

975–978: the anti-monastic backlash

The English Church was not always a focus for stability or political harmony during the tenth century. After King Edgar's death in 975, the ecclesiastical reforms he had supported, most notably the reestablishment and reform of Benedictine monasticism, came under threat. Elements among the English nobility allegedly seized the opportunity presented by the end of Edgar's strong, domineering rule and attempted to regain lands and privileges which they had lost to the monasteries favoured by the late king. In doing so, they were helped by the newly uncertain political situation. Edgar had left two sons by different wives, Edward and Aethelred, and both had a claim to the throne. Edward was the elder of the two (he was about thirteen and Aethelred was no more than nine), but neither was old enough to rule on their own account and so factions developed around them. Aethelred's mother Aelfthryth was probably his most enthusiastic supporter, but he also appears to have been backed by Bishop Aethelwold of Winchester as well as the most senior ealdorman, Aelfhere of western Mercia. For his part, Edward was favoured by another leading ealdorman, Aethelwine of East Anglia, and, crucially, by Archbishop Dunstan of Canterbury, who crowned him king, and

---

* Above, pp. 243–50

Archbishop Oswald of York. This was not, therefore, a simple case of one faction straining to sustain the reform movement whilst another tried to undermine it. Clearly, there were leading supporters of reform on both sides, as well as individuals who are known to have taken back, or simply taken, monastic lands. For example, the *Anglo-Saxon Chronicle* (which is supported by the account of Byrhtferth of Ramsey in his *Life* of St Oswald) singles out the actions of Ealdorman Aelfhere and describes him as one of the many 'adversaries of God . . . [who] broke God's law and hindered the monastic life, and destroyed monasteries and dispersed the monks and put to flight the servants of God, whom King Edgar had ordered the holy bishop Aethelwold to institute'.[5] How unscrupulous or widespread such conduct actually was, however, is harder to say. Its effects in most cases, moreover, were only temporary and did not hinder the development of the monasteries. It may be that landholders like Aelfhere were, in their view at least, only recovering lands which they should never have lost in the first place, and which they had only given away after being put under pressure by King Edgar. After Edgar's death, for example, the monastery at Abingdon was deprived of lands which had been granted to it by the late king, but whether they were taken illegally was clearly a moot point. When King Aethelred referred to this event later in his reign, he was unsure about it: the lands had been 'withdrawn by force, by the decree and order of all the leading men . . . Whether they did this thing justly or unjustly, they themselves may know'.[6]

Without doubt, however, the years immediately following Edgar's death were anxious ones for the reformed English monasteries. And to be sure the atmosphere of political uncertainty which characterised the late 970s allowed hitherto suppressed resentments at the way the monastic reform movement had interfered with established patterns of religious patronage and local power to rise to the surface. Nevertheless, such anti-monastic feeling as existed after 975 was at most a symptom of political instability and not an existential threat to the reform programme itself. Its cause lay in long-standing regional rivalries among England's leading families and in their determination to further their own ambitions by controlling the new king, whoever he was.

979–993: the badly advised king

Later writers who looked back on Aethelred's reign with hindsight saw the start of its many troubles in the murder of King Edward in March 978 by his half-brother's supporters. Aethelred was not installed as king for over a year after the killing (he was consecrated at Kingston upon Thames by the two archbishops, Dunstan and Oswald, in May 979), and viking raids on England resumed soon after that, in 980. But whether Aethelred and those who had negotiated his path to the throne immediately saw this as divine punishment for their indirect involvement in the slaying of the late king is less clear. In these early stages of the reign, indeed, probably the most pressing concern for Aethelred (who was still no more than thirteen at the start of the new decade) and his advisers was to bring the feuding English nobility together, stabilise central government and local administration and return to some kind of business as usual. It is hard to identify the contribution of particular individuals here, but Archbishop Dunstan of Canterbury, Archbishop Oswald of York and Bishop Aethelwold of Winchester must surely have played a significant role at the heart of national affairs along with the king's leading lay counsellors. In other words, the teenage Aethelred was surrounded by a generation of people who had served his father. And it is hardly surprising that he became increasingly frustrated with this situation as he grew older and that he eventually reacted against it. The king's mother Aelfthryth, who regularly appeared as a witness to her son's charters in the early 980s, disappears from the witness lists in the second half of the decade, for example, and the death of Bishop Aethelwold in 984 was another important event in this context. Followed as it was by Dunstan's death in 988 and Oswald's in 992, as the king matured he was gradually deprived of the eminent and experienced voices which these and other influential figures provided. The gaps they left around the king were filled with men of Aethelred's own choosing, but the indications are that the newcomers had a less than positive influence on him and took advantage of his patronage during these years to secure church lands for themselves: Abingdon Abbey, the Old Minster at Winchester and the diocese of Rochester all suffered in this way. In 986, indeed, the *Anglo-Saxon Chronicle* records how Aethelred 'laid waste the diocese of Rochester'. Later evidence corroborates this and alleges that the king had acted so violently because he had given an estate belonging to the bishop of Rochester to one of his own followers only for the bishop to evict him.[7]

993–1005: remorse and reform

Aethelred's charters suggest that most of those who benefited from his change of direction after 984 were laymen. He still had bishops around him, but their influence on the king and his policies during these years appears to have been negligible. It is almost as if Aethelred, in a conscious rejection of his father's way of doing things, had deliberately decided to work without high-level ecclesiastical advice. But if this was the case, by the early 990s, he had begun to regret his actions. The defeat and death of Ealdorman Byrhtnoth of Essex at Maldon in 991 was deeply shocking, and there were further demoralising Danish attacks through the rest of the 990s. As the military pressure mounted, the king issued a series of charters in which he expressed his regrets about the way his recent advisers had abused their position and exploited his inexperience. In one from 993, which granted privileges to Abingdon Abbey, he confessed that 'the ignorance of my youth' had been to blame, along with 'the abhorrent greed of certain of those men who ought to administer to my interest'. The king also acknowledged that his misdeeds began only after the death of Bishop Aethelwold, a clear sign of how strong his influence at court had been and how much it had been missed. In several other charters, from 995, 997, 998 and (probably) 999, Aethelred restored estates to the dioceses of Rochester and Winchester and to the abbey of Abingdon in similarly remorseful terms.[8] His mother began witnessing charters again from the early 990s, and a new group of royal advisers emerged at the same time. Ealdorman Aethelweard of the Western Provinces was the senior layman, but once again leading churchmen began to play a prominent role in royal affairs. The king's charters show that the archbishops of Canterbury, the bishops of Winchester and London and the abbots of Glastonbury, Abingdon and the New Minster, Winchester were all regular attenders at court, and it has been suggested that, whatever later accounts of the reign said, the 990s and early 1000s can be seen 'as a period when the internal affairs of Aethelred's kingdom prospered, under the guidance of the king acting with the assistance and advice of a group of distinguished ecclesiastics and laymen'.[9] The reformed coinage system was functioning well and Aethelred's early legislation reflected favourably on strong and sophisticated systems of central and local government. Certainly, the church itself did much better out of its newly reestablished good relations with the king than it had in the late 980s: numerous royal charters of this period granted estates and privileges to monasteries across southern England as the reforming spirit of King Edgar's reign was revived at the highest level of government.

Nevertheless, it would be unwise to push the view of internal prosperity and success during these years too far. The record of military failure in the *Anglo-Saxon Chronicle* cannot be ignored, even if it was written later and bitterly. The expressions of remorse for previous misdeeds in the king's charters hint at a regime concerned that its unpurged sins would provoke divine anger and punishment, as does the development from the 990s at Shaftesbury of a martyr's cult around the remains of Aethelred's recently murdered half-brother, Edward. And an event such as the St Brice's Day Massacre in 1002, whatever actually happened, reveals the king's frustration at least, even his desperation, at his inability to deal conclusively with the Danish threat. It would be fascinating to know what part, if any, his ecclesiastical advisers played in coming up with this notorious plan.

1006–1016: penance and purification

The famine which struck England in 1005 was a harbinger of much worse to come. The arrival of 'the great fleet' in 1006 was followed in 1009–12 by the ferocious invasion of 'the immense raiding army' under Thorkell the Tall, and then by the conquest of Swein Forkbeard in 1013–14. As for the royal government, it was hampered and undermined by in-fighting and murderous rivalries, and its efforts to deal with the viking attacks using military and financial means all failed. The kingdom's religious leaders responded to this ongoing catastrophe by interpreting it as a punishment imposed by God on a sinful people. Atonement and penance on a national scale were therefore essential. The various pieces of legislation conceived and drafted by Archbishop Wulfstan of York between 1008 and 1014 (principally V, VI, VII and VIII Aethelred) were discussed in detail in Chapter 11.* Together they made up a programme for the spiritual purification and moral cleansing of

---

* Above, pp. 243–8

the English kingdom and its people, a programme which, as Wulfstan's *Sermo Lupi ad Anglos* also made clear, could only be implemented successfully if secular and ecclesiastical authorities worked together to enforce God's laws on earth. The *Sermo* was probably written shortly after Swein Forkbeard's death in February 1014, and it is very likely that, at the same time, Wulfstan played a leading role in the *witan's* decision to recall Aethelred from his Norman exile and reinstate him as king. This was a matter of negotiation, of course, and Aethelred was allowed to return by his subjects only 'if he would govern them more justly than he did before'. The concessions he made to the church are probably contained in the provisions of VIII Aethelred, whilst what remains of his deal with the lay aristocracy may be covered in the closing parts of II Cnut.[10] It is an irony, of course, that 'The new beginning which Aethelred promised in 1014, and which his kingdom's resilience permitted, was in the event fulfilled by the rule of a conqueror'.[11]

Cnut and the English Church

From the middle of the ninth century until the Danish conquest of 1013–16, the kings of Wessex and (later) England had all come from the same family. Not all of them had succeeded peacefully or easily, but the extent of dynastic continuity from Aethelwulf to Aethelred II was still remarkable and contributed in no small way to the success (in some cases) and the survival (in others) of the southern kings. This unbroken line of related rulers came to an end in 1014 with the triumph of Swein Forkbeard, and when his son Cnut succeeded him only two years later in 1016, he lacked the pedigree and lineage which had done so much to bolster his predecessors' regimes. There were other issues, too, which made Cnut's situation particularly difficult. The new king was a Christian and had probably been baptised as a child. But Christianity had only been officially adopted in Denmark in the 960s when Cnut's grandfather, Harald Bluetooth (d.*c.*987), converted, and the attitude of Cnut's father, Swein, towards the new religion seems to have been somewhat ambivalent at times. So, in 1016 there may have been some in England who quietly wondered, fairly or not, about the strength of the new king's Christian credentials, and their doubts would have been compounded by the presence of men around Cnut, or amongst the rank and file of his army, who probably held fast to their traditional pagan beliefs. And, what is more, that army, led by the king or by those associated with him, had been responsible for devastating much of the English countryside and many of its churches during the recent campaigns. Few among the English ecclesiastical elite would either have forgotten or forgiven the sacking of Canterbury by viking troops in 1011 and the murder of Archbishop Aelfheah in the following year. And, for example, the monks of Ramsey Abbey surely regarded with suspicion if not outright hostility a foreign warlord who had killed their abbot in battle in 1016. Cnut must have had some way to go before he convinced his new subjects that he was a good friend of the church.

One way Cnut tried to overcome these problems was by cultivating an image of himself as deeply devout. His piety is usually described by historians as 'ostentatious' or 'extravagant', and it was certainly orchestrated to make as large a public impact as possible. He went on pilgrimage, for example, and was keen to make sure everyone knew about it. He is reported to have visited the shrine of St Cuthbert at Durham, going so far as to walk the last five miles barefoot. And in 1027, Cnut travelled to Rome. In a letter he wrote to his subjects describing his trip, he stressed the pious reasons for having gone, how well-received he had been by the pope and how successful he had been in negotiating a reduction in the tolls and fees to be paid by English pilgrims and merchants who would make the same journey in the future.[12] Back in England, the king also gave lavish and generous gifts to individual churches: lands, gold crosses, holy relics and magnificent reliquaries to house them, gospel books decorated with precious metals and jewels. On one occasion the king is reported to have left his own crown on the head of a crucifix in the Old Minster, Winchester – a rich gift, to be sure, but also a clear attempt by Cnut to identify himself with another king, the suffering Christ. Even the most famous story of all about Cnut, how he used his inability to turn back the waves as a demonstration of the limits of earthly power, can also be interpreted as a public display of piety on his part.[13] And in the so-called *Liber vitae*, a volume consisting largely of lists of benefactors to the New Minster at Winchester, there is a contemporary depiction of Cnut and Queen Emma giving an enormous gold cross to the church. As the king puts the cross on the altar, an angel places a crown on his head and points upwards towards the seated figure of Christ, once again explicitly connecting the earthly and heavenly rulers. The echoes in this image of the way King Edgar was depicted in his charter refounding the New Minster in 966 cannot be overlooked, however.* Cnut was imitating a great king in an effort to be seen as one himself.[14]

It seems certain that, behind the king, there were clergymen advising him on the best way to present himself as a good Christian ruler. Gift-giving, acts of humility, pilgrimages – all were undertaken with at least some sincerity on the king's part (although the true depth of his convictions is hard to gauge), but also for hardheaded political reasons: 'Like many an earlier barbarian ruler he sought the prestige which ecclesiastical recognition and approval could alone confer'.[15] But beyond helping him to develop a reputation for personal piety, Cnut needed the church to assist him more formally and officially in his search for legitimacy and validation. However, given the undeveloped state of ecclesiastical institutions in Denmark, he was not in a position to bring in clergymen from his homeland to do this. And anyway, if Cnut could rely on existing structures and personnel in England, he would be able to present himself as a force for continuity and stability. One way or another, 'In matters of religion he was largely obliged to play an English game, with English men, and by English rules'.[16]

Cnut's position was far from secure as 1016 drew to a close. Edmund Ironside had died in November, but he had left brothers and sons. Meanwhile, the two sons King Aethelred had with Emma were in exile in Normandy, there was a large Danish army still in England which needed to be demobilised, and the loyalty of the

---

* Above, p. 186

surviving English nobility was far from certain. The attitude of the leading English churchmen to the new regime was therefore crucial, and from the start they seem to have backed it and done their best to sustain it. Precise details of what happened at the beginning of the reign are hard to pin down, but in the twelfth century, John of Worcester described how Cnut summoned the leading English clergy and lay-men to London. There he asked those who had been present when the kingdom was split between him and Edmund after the battle of Ashingdon to confirm the details of the deal which they had struck. In particular, Cnut wanted confirmation that Edmund's male relations had no claim to succeed him in Wessex, and it was agreed that this was the case. The chronicler alleges that this was a lie told by selfish men hoping to profit from the new king's generosity. It is just as likely, however, that the English leaders were being pragmatic and signalling the need for the fighting to end. Either way, it is most likely that Cnut was crowned at this point or shortly afterwards, probably by Archbishop Lyfing of Canterbury. Just as important as this event, though, were those which took place in 1018 at Oxford where, according to the *Anglo-Saxon Chronicle*, 'the Danes and the English reached an agreement'. This was discussed in Chapter 11,* but it is worth dwelling on certain aspects of it once more here. The brief surviving record of the Oxford meeting tellingly announces that 'In the first place, the councillors determined that above all things they would ever honour one God and steadfastly hold one Christian faith, and would love King Cnut with due loyalty and zealously observe Edgar's laws', and it ends with an injunction 'diligently to avoid every heathen practice'.[17] That Edgar's laws were important at the start of Cnut's reign is made clear once more in a letter sent by the king to his English subjects from Denmark in 1019–20: 'it is my will that all the nation, ecclesiastical and lay, shall steadfastly observe Edgar's laws, which all men have chosen and sworn at Oxford'.[18] And one of the surviving texts of the *Chronicle* ('D') also records that the Oxford agreement was made 'according to Edgar's law', an addition which was retained by John of Worcester, albeit in a modified form, when he wrote his version of the *Chronicle* in the twelfth century. This, along with other specifically East Midlands references in the 'D' text, has led to a strong belief amongst historians that this version of the *Chronicle*, and consequently the unique mention of 'Edgar's law' in its entry for 1018, had its origins in Worcester.[19] This is important because the bishop of Worcester until at least 1016 (as well as being the archbishop of York) was Wulfstan, and he has been seen as 'beyond dispute' the prime mover behind what happened at Oxford and the author of the agreement made there.[20] Wulfstan clearly went to considerable lengths in 1018 in order to establish a legal and religious basis for the new regime which was acceptable to the English and the Danes alike. 'Edgar's laws' probably had more symbolic than actual value: the reference to them denoted continuity and stability at a time when established norms of conduct and behaviour must have looked seriously threatened. But Cnut had to be a model Christian king as well, just as Edgar had been.

* Above, p. 248

It was a brazenly opportunistic thing to do, but, thanks to Archbishop Wulfstan, Aethelred's long, troubled reign was deliberately overlooked in 1018: Cnut was Edgar's heir. And until his death in 1023, Wulfstan continued to exert his influence over royal policy. As Chapter 11 showed,* Cnut's surviving law codes were certainly compiled by him. I Cnut dealt with entirely ecclesiastical matters, but its announcement that dates had been fixed for the feast days of Edward the Martyr and Dunstan was particularly significant in an ideological sense: Cnut was again being associated with the rightful line of English kings (that is, not Aethelred, whose supporters had murdered Edward) and, through Dunstan, with spiritual reform and renewal.[21] But it is also tempting to find the archbishop at work moulding Cnut's image in other ways. The *Anglo-Saxon Chronicle* highlights the leading role played by Wulfstan in 1020 when Cnut had a church consecrated on the site of his victory at Ashingdon.[22] This was not crude triumphalism; rather, as a memorial to all the men (English and Danes) who had been killed there, it was a further attempt at reconciliation, one almost certainly orchestrated by the leading churchman of the day.

Other ostensibly pious acts by Cnut have also been explained by historians in more political terms. In June 1023, the body of Archbishop Aelfheah of Canterbury, who had been killed by the Danes in 1012, was taken from London to Canterbury. It has been suggested that this was part of a plan by the king, first, to remove a symbol of resistance to his regime in London, where opposition may have been gathering around the figure of the martyred archbishop, and second, to cultivate better relations with England's most important church. Miracles had already been reported at Aelfheah's tomb at St Paul's in London, so 'the acquisition of the remains of the most recent archiepiscopal saint was a great coup for the cathedral community' at Canterbury.[23] At the same time, Cnut is reported to have given other prestigious relics and valuable estates to Christ Church, and the fact that he had allowed the cathedral monks to take one of their own number, Aethelnoth, as their archbishop in 1020 shows how eager he was to make amends for the actions of his fellow Scandinavians in 1011–12 and secure the support of the archbishop, his church and his city.

Finally in this context, two of William of Malmesbury's stories about Cnut and his English predecessors are worth mentioning. One of King Edgar's daughters, Edith, had been a nun at Wilton. She died in the later 980s, and by the early eleventh century, she was being revered as a saint. King Aethelred had encouraged the development of her cult but, according to William of Malmesbury, when Cnut visited her shrine, he declared with 'barbaric crudity' that no child of a king as lustful and tyrannical as Edgar could possibly be regarded as saintly. Then, on her tomb being opened, Edith raised herself up causing the king to collapse in an unconscious heap. William claimed that Cnut did not like English saints because he was a foreigner.[24] This was not completely fair, and the story itself cannot be literally true. Nevertheless, it does hint at the problems which might have been caused

* Above, pp. 248–50.

by a new king from a different culture whose attitude towards the English way of doing things may naturally have been rather rough and ready. Cnut later built a fine golden shrine to house Edith's remains, however, so he had clearly been converted to her virtues by someone and then done the politically sensible thing by generously honouring the royal saint. William's account of Cnut's visit to Glastonbury (probably in 1032) is also revealing. He went there on the anniversary of Edmund Ironside's death (30 November) to place a cloak decorated with peacock feathers on his old adversary's tomb. The peacock was a symbol in Christian iconography of the resurrection of the flesh, so Cnut was clearly expressing his hope for Edmund's salvation. But William also describes how Cnut used to refer to Edmund as his brother, and this may have been a deliberate attempt to remind his subjects of the agreement the two men had made about the division of England and the position of Edmund's heirs after the battle of Ashingdon. Put simply, 'Favouring Edmund, stressing their brotherhood, and bringing their treaty to the fore diminished the extent to which Cnut looked a usurper'.[25] It is not clear whose idea it had been to construct Edith's shrine at Wilton or to visit Edmund's tomb at Glastonbury, but looking down on these events from above, Archbishop Wulfstan would surely have approved.

Out of the frying pan . . .

In this period, particularly between about 1000 and 1025, the English Church did much more than provide its usual ideological and material backing for the royal regime. As the kingdom was confronted with the possibility and then the reality of foreign, perhaps even pagan, conquest, English defeat was seen as a sure sign of moral and spiritual failure. Leading churchmen used the means available to them to defend Christianity itself, as only Christian morality and Christian standards of behaviour could bond the layers of society together once again: a return to good orthodox practice and the importance of atonement and penance were emphasised repeatedly in royal legislation and sermons. Put bluntly, what was at stake for contemporary religious thinkers in the last decade of Aethelred's reign was not just the future of a particular ruling family, but the eternal salvation of the English people. Of course, Armageddon did not in the end follow the accession of Cnut, and from that point, the church's job was a different one – to mould the new king into an archetypal Christian monarch who could take up the reins of government and rebuild a cohesive, integrated and, above all, God-fearing community. And indeed, by 1042, stability had returned and the dangers seemed to have passed; even a further change of dynasty in that year may have been seen by the ecclesiastical authorities as promising more than it threatened. Another revolution would soon overwhelm the English Church, of course, and after 1066, its personnel would be decimated and its buildings destroyed. But memories are resilient and harder to suppress: to be sure, much of the Anglo-Saxon Church was dismantled and reconstructed by the Normans, but they could not completely obliterate its history or ruin its reputation, and enough survived to produce from the twelfth century onwards distinctively English forms of Christian life and worship. One thing did remain constant throughout all this turmoil, though: the Norman kings would need and expect the support of the church just as much as their Anglo-Saxon predecessors had done. Religious rhetoric, theory and imagery legitimised royal authority, whilst the legal, administrative and sometimes even military roles performed by clergymen underpinned royal power. This mutually supportive relationship between the English king and his church had been most strongly forged in the ninth and tenth centuries, and it would remain an indispensable cornerstone of political and religious life in the kingdom of England for the rest of the middle ages.

Notes

1 *ASC* 992, 1016.
2 *Encomium Emmae Reginae*, ed. A. Campbell (repr. Cambridge, 1998), pp. 41–2.
3 S876.
4 *ASC* 991; S937.
5 *ASC* 975; *VSO*, pp. 122–7.
6 *EHD*, i no.123.
7 *ASC* 986; *WMGRA*, i pp. 270–1; Roach, *Aethelred the Unready*, pp. 102–4.
8 S876, 885, 891, 893, 937.
9 Keynes, *Diplomas*, p. 193.
10 *ASC* 1014; (II Cnut, 69–83).
11 Wormald, *MEL*, i p. 464.
12 Symeon of Durham, *Libellus de exordio atque procursu istius, hoc est Dunelmensis, ecclesie* ('Tract on the Origins and Progress of this Church of Durham'), ed. and trans. David Rollason (Oxford, 2000), pp. 166–9; *EHD*, i no.53.
13 For the crown story, see Lawson, *Cnut*, p. 125. For the earliest version of the waves legend, see *Henry of Huntingdon: Historia Anglorum*, ed. Greenway, pp. 366–9.
14 The *Liber vitae* image is reproduced in Campell (ed.), *The Anglo-Saxons*, p. 208.
15 Brooks, *Early History*, p. 287.
16 Lawson, *Cnut*, p. 122.
17 *ASC* 1018; *EHD*, i no.47.
18 *EHD*, i no.48 (Cnut 1020, 13).
19 *ASC* 1018; *JW*, ii pp. 504–5: 'English and Danes came to an agreement at Oxford about keeping Edgar's law'.
20 Wormald, *MEL* i p. 346.
21 Robertson, *Laws*, pp. 168–9 (I Cnut, 17.1).
22 *ASC* 1020.
23 Brooks, *Early History*, p. 292.
24 William of Malmesbury, *The Deeds of the Bishops of England (Gesta Pontificum Anglorum)*, trans. D. Preest (Woodbridge, 2002), p. 127.
25 *WMGRA*, i pp. 330–3; Lawson, *Cnut*, p. 130.

GLOSSARY OF TERMS

Words in italics within an entry are themselves explained at the appropriate point in the Glossary.

Angelcynn   Old English for 'English people', and a direct translation of the Latin term *gens Anglorum*, which was most famously used by Bede in the title of his *Historia ecclesiastica gentis Anglorum*. The word is first recorded in Mercia in the 850s, but it was adopted notably by Alfred the Great in his vernacular translations, and occasionally by the *Anglo-Saxon Chronicle*, to denote a people with a shared, Christian past living under West Saxon rule.

Anglo-Saxon Chronicle   The principal narrative source for English history until the mid-twelfth century. Originally compiled in Wessex in the late ninth century, this so-called common stock was copied and circulated thereafter. No original text of the common stock survives, and the *Chronicle* now exists in eight different versions, labelled from A to H by historians. These were compiled at various dates in various places, and some cover a much wider timespan and contain much more information than others.

appeal   An accusation, usually of violence or theft, brought in a court by one individual against another.

archdiocese   A *diocese* under the authority of an archbishop. There were two archdioceses in England, Canterbury and York.

atheling   A royal prince deemed 'throne-worthy', that is, with a realistic claim to be king.

Benedictine monasteries   Monastic communities which followed the Rule for the conduct of monastic life composed by St Benedict of Nursia (d.*c*.547). The establishment or revival of such monasteries was a central aim of the tenth-century monastic reform movement in England. The central text of this programme, which prescribed uniform practices for the monks and nuns of the reformed monasteries, was the *Regularis Concordia*, published *c*.973.

boc   See *charter, bookland*.

bookland   Land conveyed by a *boc*. Usually this formality gave the landholder special privileges, such as immunity from customary services (for example, paying *feorm* to the king), with the exception of the *common burdens*, and the holder was entitled to bequeath the land to anyone he chose. It should be distinguished from *folkland*.

Burghal Hidage   See *burh*.

burh (i) Old English word for a fortified site, many of which were established by Alfred the Great and his immediate successors, and listed in the document known as the *Burghal Hidage*; (ii) more broadly, and by the later tenth century, an urban settlement, usually with a market and a mint.

Carolingian The name given by historians to the dynasty which ruled the Franks from 751 until the last Carolingian king of the West Franks died in 987. The dynasty's name is derived from the Latinised name of Charles ('Carolus') Martel (d.741), the father of the first Carolingian king of the Franks, Pepin the Short (d.768).

ceorl An ordinary free peasant.

charter A document giving or transferring rights over a defined estate. The most formal type of charter is referred to by historians as a *diploma* and by contemporaries as a *boc*. In Anglo-Saxon England, the formal parts of a charter were written in Latin whilst the precise description of the estate being conveyed or privileged (the boundary clause) was typically written in English.

common burdens The three military obligations (in Latin, *trinoda necessitas*) due from all holders of *bookland*, namely the maintenance of bridges and fortifications and service in the *fyrd*. First introduced in eighth-century Mercia, they were then adopted more widely across England and formed the basis of the kingdom's defensive system up to and beyond the Norman Conquest.

county See *shire*.

Danegeld See *heregeld*.

Danelaw (i) In legal terms, an area of England (roughly Yorkshire, East Anglia and the eastern and central midlands) distinguishable from those parts subject to Mercian or West Saxon law; (ii) more loosely, those regions of England conquered and settled by Scandinavian invaders from the later ninth century onwards.

diocese The area under the authority of a bishop.

diploma See *charter*.

ealdorman The senior royal official (the Old English word literally means 'elder man') in a shire or group of shires, probably from the late eighth century onwards. Appointed by the king, ealdormen had military, financial, judicial and wider administrative responsibilities to carry out on his behalf.

earl From the reign of Cnut onwards, the title of ealdorman was replaced by that of earl, although earls are occasionally mentioned in the sources before 1016. Most of Cnut's earls appear to have been, broadly speaking, ealdorman by a different name and the change in title does not appear to have denoted a change in function. The title may have been an Anglicised version of the Old Norse *jarl*.

feorm The rent in kind owed to the king or another lord by those who lived on his estates. It was payable in fixed amounts of food, drink and livestock, probably collected at specified times of the year, and used to feed the lord's itinerant household as it travelled around his lands. Over time, arrangements such as this were increasingly replaced with payments in cash.

feud A legal state of affairs in which individuals or groups within a community were in conflict with each other because of wrongs done by one side to the other. Feuds could be settled by acts of private vengeance, by negotiation and/or the payment of compensation. The law codes of this period regularly attempted to control and regulate the way feuds operated and limit the violence they might provoke. A feud might also be referred to by historians as a *vendetta*.

folkland Land subject to all the customary burdens and inalienable outside the holder's kindred. To be distinguished from *bookland*.

frankpledge See *tithing*.

fyrd The Old English word for a military expedition, it is more commonly used to describe an army of some kind, whether raised locally and led by an *ealdorman*, or nationally and led by the king. Service in the *fyrd* was one of the *common burdens*.

gafol The Old English word for the monetary *tribute* paid by English rulers to viking invaders, particularly during the reign of Aethelred II.

geld See *heregeld*.

hearth troop The military component of a lord's *household*, made up of the armed followers who spent most time in his company.

heregeld An annual tax imposed on landholders at a specified but variable number of *pennies* per *hide*. It was raised for the first time in *c*.1012 to pay Scandinavian mercenaries led by Thorkell the Tall. It was often known later as *Danegeld*, or just *geld*, and should not be confused with *gafol*.

hide Derived from the Old English word for a domestic household, it eventually came to mean a unit of land (perhaps 120 acres) on the basis of which tax (e.g. *heregeld*) and other public obligations were calculated.

housecarl Derived from the Old Norse *húskarl*, the word literally means 'house man' or 'man of the household'. In England after 1016, it was used to describe the warriors in the king's *household*, although they performed non-military duties, too.

household The group of people which served a lord, travelled with him and met his regular domestic administrative, financial and military needs. The royal household was the biggest of all.

hundred The administrative subdivision of a *shire*, with its own *hundred court* which met every two weeks from the late tenth century. In most parts of midland and northern England (Yorkshire, Lincolnshire, Nottinghamshire, Derbyshire and Leicestershire), the equivalent subdivisions were called *wapentakes* not hundreds.

hundred court See *hundred*.

king's thegn See *thegn*.

mancus A gold coin worth thirty silver pennies.

minster Spelt *mynster* in Old English and referred to as a *monasterium* in Latin, a church staffed by a community of clergy who might or might not be monks.

mint An official centre of coin production, where a group of *moneyers*, licenced by the king, would produce the latest issue of the royal coinage.

moneyer An official licenced by the king to make *pennies* at a *mint*.

oath A solemn vow, often made on holy relics. Oaths were particularly important in formal legal proceedings.

oath-helping When someone was involved in a legal dispute, *oaths* could be taken by his or her supporters in order to support their case or affirm their innocence and good character.

ordeal A trial in which judgement about guilt or innocence was based on evidence of divine intervention. It usually took the form of *trial by water* or *trial by hot iron*.

parish The territorial subdivision of a *diocese*, under the authority of priest resident in a parish church. The development of a parochial system in England got underway meaningfully in the tenth and eleventh centuries, but the process was still not complete by 1066.

penny The silver penny was the only coin in regular circulation during this period. 'Denarius' in Latin, there were 12 in a *shilling* and 240 in a *pound*.

pound A unit of currency used only for accounting purposes. There were 240 *pennies* in a pound.

province In ecclesiastical terms, a collection of *dioceses* under the authority of an archbishop. There were two provinces in England: Canterbury (south of the Humber estuary) and York (north of the Humber).

reeve   Originally an official responsible for the everyday management of a lord's estates, the reeves' role (particularly that of the royal reeves) later developed to encompass wide-ranging judicial, military and fiscal duties in their localities. They feature prominently as executive officers in royal law codes from the early tenth century onwards and the first reference to a 'shire-reeve' (*sheriff*) dates from Aethelred II's reign.

regular clergy   Clergy (usually monks) living in a community and following a rule (Latin, 'regula') which set out in detail how they should live and work. The most widely followed rule in the middle ages was the Rule of St Benedict: see *Benedictine monasteries*.

Regularis Concordia   See *Benedictine monasteries*.

Rule   See *regular clergy*.

secular canons   Clergy living communally and serving in a cathedral or minster, but not following a monastic rule.

secular clergy   Clergy not belonging to a religious (monastic) order.

sheriff   From the late tenth century, the principal officer of royal government in the *shire*. Each *shire* had a sheriff appointed by the king. He had major financial, judicial and policing responsibilities. See also *reeve*.

shilling   A unit of currency used only for accounting purposes. There were twelve *pennies* in a shilling and twenty shillings in a *pound*.

shire   A large and more or less defined expanse of territory, and the principal unit of local government in England by the eleventh century, although not all of the kingdom had been divided into shires by 1042. Every shire was under the authority of a *sheriff* and had its own *shire court*, which met usually every six months. The word *county* is virtually synonymous.

shire court   See *shire*.

slave   A peasant who was legally unfree and the property of a lord. Slaves could be bought and sold and had no legal standing of their own.

synod   A church council.

tithe   The tenth of agricultural produce or income paid annually by landholders to the church. Aethelstan's first law code made the payment of tithes compulsory.

tithing   A group of ten or twelve males over the age of twelve who swore to keep the king's peace and guarantee the good behaviour of the others in their group. All adult males of unfree status were supposed to be in such a group. It might also be referred to as the system of *frankpledge*.

trial by hot iron   An *ordeal* in which the accused in a trial carried a hot piece of iron, guilt or innocence being revealed by the extent to which God had allowed the hand to heal after a specified period.

trial by water   An *ordeal* in which the accused in a trial was immersed in a pool of water. Having been blessed by a priest beforehand, it was believed that the water would reject the guilty and that he or she would therefore float rather than sink.

tribute   A payment (in cash or kind) owed to a lord, or a victorious enemy, whose superiority had been accepted by a group or an individual. See also *gafol*.

thegn   Old English meaning 'one who serves', the term denotes a substantial landholder and man of influence and standing in his locality. He would be expected to undertake various administrative and military duties, and some thegns (*king's thegns*) might acquire important positions in the royal household. Their importance to the ordered functioning of local society is clear from the frequency with which the law codes of the tenth and eleventh centuries refer to their functions and responsibilities.

vendetta   See *feud*.

wapentake   See *hundred*.

wergild   Old English meaning literally 'man-price', this was originally the amount of money fixed by law and payable by the perpetrator or his kin to the relatives of someone who had been unlawfully killed. All classes of society (men and women) except slaves had a wergild, and the amount was determined by social status. The king's wergild was the highest of all. It later came to be used as the fine for various offences and the value of a person's oath in legal proceedings.

witan   Literally, the 'wise men' who advised the king. The membership of this group was not fixed, and neither were its meeting-times and places, but routinely it would meet several times a year and be made up of the greatest lay and ecclesiastical landholders. The king was expected to consult them on important political, military, legal and diplomatic matters, whilst at times of national crisis (between reigns, for example, when a new king had to be chosen) the *witan* had great political power in its own right.

writ   A brief document (much shorter and less formal than a *charter*), written in the vernacular and carrying an impression of the royal seal, which took the form of an address by the king to the recipient, perhaps the local *sheriff* or bishop. The earliest surviving writs date from the eleventh century and most are concerned with the transfer of property rights or the granting of privileges over land. They were probably designed to be read out and publicised at the *shire* or *hundred court*.

SUGGESTIONS FOR FURTHER READING

This is not a comprehensive bibliography; far from it. Rather it is a selection of some of the more important and accessible works on this period, which interested readers might want to look at next. Those works contain their own much longer lists of suggestions about where even more specialised treatments can be found. I have also referred over the course of the book to some works which do not appear here. Full details of those are contained in the citations themselves.

Primary sources

Collections

The most valuable and comprehensive collection of translated primary sources for this period is *English Historical Documents i, c.500–1042*, trans. D. Whitelock, 2nd edn (London, 1979). *English Historical Documents ii, 1042–1189*, ed. D.C. Douglas and G.W. Greenaway, 2nd edn (London, 1981), contains some useful material relating to the end of the period covered by this book, as does *The Norman Conquest of England: Sources and Documents*, ed. R.A. Brown (Woodbridge, 1984). Old, but still helpful, is *Select English Historical Documents of the Ninth and Tenth Centuries*, ed. and trans. F.E. Harmer (Cambridge, 1914). Together these provide a good selection of administrative and legal sources (charters, writs, law codes), as well as letters, sermons and more literary texts. They also contain extracts from many of the principal narrative sources, in particular (in the case of the *EHD* volumes), full translations of the *Anglo-Saxon Chronicle*. Essential for the reign of King Alfred, and for the events surrounding it, is the compendium of sources, including Alfred's Treaty with Guthrum, his will, the Burghal Hidage and extracts from the king's translations, contained in *Alfred the Great. Asser's Life of King Alfred and Other Contemporary Sources*, trans. S. Keynes and M. Lapidge (London, 1983). The editors' Introduction and their detailed Notes on the texts are also indispensable resources.

Narrative and biographies

The *Anglo-Saxon Chronicle* is the single most important narrative source for English history during this period. In my view, the best single-volume edition of it is *The Anglo-Saxon Chronicle: A Revised Translation*, ed. and trans. D. Whitelock, D.C. Douglas, and S.I. Tucker (New Brunswick, 1961). A Latin version (down to 975) of the *ASC* written by Ealdorman Aethelweard complements the original in numerous important ways: *The Chronicle of Aethelweard*, ed. and trans. A. Campbell (Edinburgh, 1962).

Other relevant narrative accounts were written abroad after the Anglo-Saxon period had ended. For example, *The Gesta Normannorum Ducum of William of Jumièges, Orderic Vitalis and Robert of Torigni*, vol. ii, ed. and trans. E.M.C. Van Houts (Oxford, 1995) has much of, admittedly skewed, interest to say about English affairs from the reign of Aethelred onwards. Other English writers, too, although working in the twelfth century, frequently had things to say about the events discussed here. The most notable of their works include: *The Chronicle of John of Worcester*, ii, ed. R.R. Darlington and P. McGurk, trans. J. Bray and P. McGurk (Oxford, 1995), and William of Malmesbury's *Gesta Regum Anglorum: The History of the English Kings*, 2 vols, ed. and trans. R.A.B. Mynors, R.M. Thomson and M. Winterbottom (Oxford, 1998–9). The latter is a particularly important, if problematic, source for the reign of Aethelstan. Meanwhile, writing at roughly the same time, Henry, archdeacon of Huntingdon was the first to tell some famous stories, not least the one about Cnut and the waves: *Historia Anglorum: The History of the English People*, ed. D.E. Greenway (Oxford, 1996), a condensed version of which is contained in *Henry of Huntingdon: The History of the English People: 1000–1154*, trans. D.E. Greenway (Oxford, 2002).

A modern English translation of Asser's *Life of Alfred* is contained in K&L, pp. 67–110. The debate surrounding the *Life's* authenticity and its complex manuscript history are both outlined at ibid., pp. 48–58 and 223–5. The same issues are explored in greater detail in S. Keynes, 'On the authenticity of Asser's *Life of King Alfred*', *Journal of Ecclesiastical History*, 47 (1996), pp. 529–51. Patrick Wormald's entry on Asser in the *ODNB* is brief but powerful. There are no other royal biographies from this period, and saints fared better than kings in this regard. Near-contemporary accounts were written of the lives of all the leaders of the Benedictine Reform Movement. There are extracts from some of these in *EHD*, i nos.234–6. For Dunstan, the earliest account of his life is *The Life of St Dunstan* by the author known only as B, in *The Early Lives of St Dunstan*, ed. and trans. M. Winterbottom and M. Lapidge (Oxford, 2012), pp. 1–109. William of Malmesbury's biography of Dunstan's is also now available in a modern translation: 'Vita Dunstani' in *William of Malmesbury, Saints' Lives. Lives of Ss. Wulfstan, Dunstan, Patrick, Benignus and Indract*, ed. M. Winterbottom and R.M. Thomson (Oxford, 2002), pp. 198–205. For Aethelwold, see *Wulfstan of Winchester. The Life of St Aethelwold*, ed. and trans. M. Lapidge and M. Winterbottom (Oxford, 1991), pp. 1–69. And for Oswald, there survives *The Life of St Oswald* by Byrhtferth of Ramsey in *Byrhtferth of Ramsey. The Lives of St Oswald and St Ecgwine*, ed. M. Lapidge (Oxford, 2009), pp. 1–203. For the principal document of the reform movement, see *Regularis Concordia*, ed. and trans. T. Symons (London, 1953).

Charters, Wills, Writs and Laws

Anglo-Saxon Charters, ed. and trans. A.J. Robertson, 2nd edn (Cambridge, 1956) is an indispensable collection. But the main resource here is *Anglo-Saxon Charters: An Annotated List and Bibliography*, ed. P.H. Sawyer (London, 1968); revised by S. Kelly and R. Rushforth *et al* online at <http://esawyer.org.uk/> ('The Electronic Sawyer'). The relevance of the documents contained in *Anglo-Saxon Wills*, ed. and trans. D. Whitelock (Cambridge, 1930), and *Anglo-Saxon Writs*, ed. F.E. Harmer (Manchester, 1952; reprinted Stamford, 1989), is obvious. The standard collection of Anglo-Saxon laws for over a century has been *Die Gesetze der Angelsachsen*, ed. F. Liebermann, 3 vols, (Halle, 1903–16). However, more accessible and user-friendly, if a little old-fashioned in their presentation, are *The Laws of the Earliest English Kings*, ed. and trans. F.L. Attenborough (Cambridge, 1922), and *The Laws of the Kings of England from Edmund to Henry I*, ed. and trans. A.J. Robertson (Cambridge, 1925).

General works

For the Anglo-Saxon age generally, two works, although both rather old by now, remain fundamental: F.M. Stenton, *Anglo-Saxon England*, 3rd edn (Oxford, 1971), originally published in 1943, is arguably still the most important book ever written about this period, whilst J. Campbell (ed), *The Anglo-Saxons* (Oxford, 1982) contains a set of stimulating and illuminating essays (as well as many lavish illustrations) on all aspects of pre-conquest England. A more recent general work, also well-illustrated, is *The Anglo-Saxon World*, ed. N.J. Higham and M.J. Ryan (New Haven, 2013). P. Stafford, *Unification and Conquest. A Political and Social History of England in the Tenth and Eleventh Centuries* (London, 1989) gives a thorough and thoughtful analysis of the main developments, as does Ann Williams, *Kingship and Government in Pre-Conquest England, c.500–1066* (Basingstoke, 1999), chs.6–10. B. Yorke, *Wessex in the Early Middle Ages* (Leicester, 1995), chs.3 and 5–7, and D. Rollason, *Northumbria, 500–1100: Creation and Destruction of a Kingdom* (Cambridge, 2003), especially chs.6–7, view what happened from different ends of England. The final phase of the period covered by this book is also dealt with in stimulating if idiosyncratic fashion by W. Kapelle, *The Norman Conquest of the North. The Region and its Transformation, 1000–1135* (Croom Helm, 1979), ch.1. Two essays by Simon Keynes also provide valuable outlines: 'England, 700–900', in *The New Cambridge Medieval History II, c.700–c.900*, ed. R. McKitterick (Cambridge, 1995), pp. 18–42, and 'England, c.900–1016', in *The New Cambridge Medieval History III, c.900–c.1024*, ed. T. Reuter (Cambridge, 1999), pp. 456–84. For a freshly non-political overview, by contrast, which concentrates on the significance of material culture, see R. Fleming, *Britain after Rome: The Fall and Rise, 400–1070* (London, 2010), especially chs.8–12. *The Wiley-Blackwell Encyclopedia of Anglo-Saxon England*, ed. M. Lapidge, J. Blair, S. Keynes and D. Scragg, 2nd edn (Oxford, 2013), is a treasure-house of useful information and perceptive explanation arranged alphabetically.

H.R. Loyn, *The Governance of Anglo-Saxon England 500–1087* (Stanford, 1984), deals with the development of English government before, during and beyond the period covered by this book. P. Stafford, 'Kings, Kingship and Kingdoms' in *From the Viking to the Normans*, ed. W. Davies (Oxford, 2003), pp. 11–39, also offers a stimulating review. Two more recent books on this subject, however, have already become very influential: J.R. Maddicott, *The Origins of the English Parliament, 924–1327* (Oxford, 2010), especially Ch.1 in this context, and George Molyneaux, *The Formation of the English Kingdom in the Tenth Century* (Oxford, 2015). But the works of James Campbell must take centre-stage here: it is thanks in large part to him that the relative sophistication and strength of late Anglo-Saxon government and administration has been recognised. Among his more important essays are: 'The Late Anglo-Saxon State: A Maximum View', *Proceedings of the British Academy*, 87 (1994), pp. 39–65; 'Some Agents and Agencies of the Late Anglo-Saxon State', in J.C. Holt (ed), *Domesday Studies: Papers Read at the Novocentenary*

Conference of the Royal Historical Society and the Institute of British Geographers, Winchester, 1986 (Woodbridge, 1987), pp. 201–18; and 'The United Kingdom of England: The Anglo-Saxon Achievement' in Uniting the Kingdom: The Making of British History, ed. A. Grant and K.J. Stringer (London, 1985). All three of these were reprinted in J. Campbell, The Anglo-Saxon State (London, 2000). Another of his key essays, 'Observations on English Government from the Tenth to the Twelfth Centuries', Transactions of the Royal Historical Society, 5th series, 25 (1975), pp. 39–54, was reprinted in J. Campbell, Essays in Anglo-Saxon History (London, 1986).

The standard introduction to developments in the law during this period is now J. Hudson, The Oxford History of the Laws of England. Volume II: 871–1216 (Oxford, 2012), Part I. But it is the pioneering, if sometimes difficult, work of Patrick Wormald which has had by far the greatest influence. To his The Making of English Law: King Alfred to the Twelfth Century, i, Legislation and its Limits (Oxford, 1998), can be added his 'Papers Preparatory to The Making of English Law: King Alfred to the Twelfth Century, ii, From God's Law to Common Law', ed. S. Baxter and J.G.H. Hudson (London, 2014), online at <http://early englishlaws.ac.uk/reference/wormald/>. Wormald's essay 'Lex Scripta and Verbum Regis: Legislation and Germanic Kingship from Euric to Cnut', in Early Medieval Kingship, ed. P.H. Sawyer and I.N. Wood (Leeds, 1977), pp. 105–38, reprinted in his Legal Culture in the Early Medieval West. Law as Text, Image and Experience (London, 1999), is also seminal.

There are several very important introductions to and overviews of the Anglo-Saxon Church, all of which deal to some extent with its role in government. The dominant one is J. Blair, The Church in Anglo-Saxon Society (Oxford, 2005). Chs.6–8 apply most obviously here, although they are challenging for non-specialists. The most recent general study is A.E. Redgate, Religion, Politics and Society in Britain, 800–1066 (Abingdon, 2014). H.R. Loyn, The English Church, 940–1154 (Harlow, 2005), begins its account with the Benedictine Reform Movement, whilst N. Brooks, The Early History of the Church of Canterbury: Christ Church from 597 to 1066 (Leicester, 1984) covers much more than its title suggests.

The best overview of the economies of Britain in the Middle Ages is C. Dyer, Making a Living in the Middle Ages: The Peoples of Britain 850–1520 (2002). The first two chapters are most relevant here. A shorter but interesting presentation of some of the main themes is David Griffiths, 'Exchange, Trade and Urbanisation', in From the Vikings to the Normans, ed. Davies, pp. 73–104. P.H. Sawyer, The Wealth of Anglo-Saxon England (Oxford, 2013) is now required reading on the English economy generally and more specifically on the English coinage. For further introductory reading on the coinage, see P. Grierson and M. Blackburn, Medieval European Coinage I. The Early Middle Ages (Cambridge, 1986), ch.10, which covers the period up to 924, and the essays in Kings, Currency and Alliances: History and Coinage of Southern England in the Ninth Century, ed. M. Blackburn and D.N. Dumville (Woodbridge, 1998). Martin Allen, Mints and Money in Medieval England (Cambridge, 2012), ch.1, provides a good over view of the main issues from c.973 onwards.

Discussions of the Vikings feature in most of the general works cited above and in many of the more specialised ones referred to below. Beyond these, H.R. Loyn, The Vikings in Britain (London, 1977), is still an effective discussion of the viking impact on Britain. There are also good, short overviews by Simon Keynes, 'The Vikings in England, c.790–1016', in The Oxford Illustrated History of the Vikings, ed. P. Sawyer (Oxford, 1997), and by Barbara E. Crawford, 'The Vikings', in From the Vikings to the Normans, ed. Davies, pp. 41–71. Another, which covers the first part of this period, is Simon Coupland, 'The Vikings in Francia and Anglo-Saxon England to 911', in New Cambridge Medieval History II, ed. McKitterick, pp. 190–201. J. Haywood, The Penguin Historical Atlas of the Vikings (London, 1995), is invaluable. For wider-angle views, there are excellent sections on the Vikings in A.P. Smyth, Warlords and Holy Men: Scotland AD 80–1000 (London, 1984), ch.5, and

D. Ó Cróinín, *Early Medieval Ireland, 400–1200*, 2nd edn (Abingdon, 2017), ch.10. An important recent discussion, which argues that the dominant West Saxon sources may have had an interest in downplaying the scale and importance of the earliest raids because they took place outside Wessex, is Clare Downham, 'The Earliest Viking Activity in England', *EHR* 132 (2017), pp. 1–12.

The English response to the Vikings naturally brings up the subject of military organisation. The most thorough handling of this is R. Abels, *Lordship and Military Obligation in Anglo-Saxon England* (London, 1988). See also N. Brooks, 'The Development of Military Obligations in Eighth- and Ninth-Century England', in *England Before the Conquest. Studies in Primary Sources Presented to Dorothy Whitelock*, ed. P. Clemoes and K. Hughes (Cambridge, 1971), pp. 69–84, and idem, 'England in the Ninth Century: The Crucible of Defeat', *Transactions of the Royal Historical Society*, 5th series, 29 (1979), pp. 1–20. There is a very strong and positive assessment of the military capabilities of late Anglo-Saxon England in M.K. Lawson, *The Battle of Hastings, 1066* (Stroud, 2002), ch.4.

On royal women, P. Stafford, 'The King's Wife in Wessex, 800–1066', *Past and Present* 91 (1981), pp. 3–27, and idem, *Queen Emma and Queen Edith. Queenship and Women's Power in Eleventh-Century England* (Oxford, 1997), are now standard texts. In addition, her *Queens, Concubines and Dowagers. The King's Wife in the Early Middle Ages* (London, 1983) ranges widely over its subject from the sixth to the eleventh century but has much of particular relevance to say about this period, as does J.L. Nelson, 'Medieval Queenship', in *Women in Medieval Western European Culture*, ed. L. Mitchell (New York, 1998). For the roles and position of women more generally, see Stafford, *Unification and Conquest*, ch.10.

Janet Nelson's work on the importance of high-status ritual in early medieval society has been deeply influential. Most of her essays and articles are now available together in *Politics and Ritual in Early Medieval Europe* (London, 1986), in which chs.12 and 15–16 on inauguration rites and English coronation *ordines* have been of particular use here. Levi Roach, *Kingship and Consent in Anglo-Saxon England, 871–978: Assemblies and the State in the Early Middle Ages* (Cambridge, 2013), especially ch.8, provides a recent discussion of this area.

Finally here, almost anyone of any importance in British history during this period will be the subject of an entry in the *Oxford Dictionary of National Biography*, ed. H.C.G. Matthew, B. Harrison *et al* (Oxford, 1992 onwards). This is an extraordinary and immensely helpful resource, both in its printed and its online forms (www.oxforddnb.com/). Written by leading specialists, the essays are scholarly, informed and digestible. I will single out some, but by no means all, of the most important as they apply here.

Introduction

Most of the areas discussed in general terms in the Introduction (government, the economy, military organisation) are dealt with in works referred to above and below. A brief but insightful guide to rural life and social structure, albeit only in Wessex, is available in Yorke, *Wessex in the Early Middle Ages*, ch.6, whilst another with some overlapping and some different concerns is provided by Robin Fleming, 'Lords and Labour', in *From the Vikings to the Normans*, ed. Davies, pp. 107–37. As for general developments in the rest of Britain outside England, there is a good summary in Donnchadh Ó Corráin, 'Ireland, Scotland and Wales, c.700 to the early eleventh century', in *New Cambridge Medieval History II*, ed. McKitterick pp. 43–63. On the individual parts of the British Isles, several books on Scotland are particularly helpful in casting a non-English light on the affairs of northern England: A.A.M. Duncan, *Scotland: The Making of the Kingdom* (Edinburgh,

1975), especially chs.4 and 5; Smyth, *Warlords and Holy Men*, chs.6 and 7; and Alex Woolf, *From Pictland to Alba, 789–1070* (Edinburgh, 2007). On Wales, W. Davies, *Wales in the Early Middle Ages* (Leicester, 1982), remains essential, whilst T.M. Charles-Edwards, *Wales and the Britons, 350–1064* (Oxford, 2013), is the latest survey. Part III is most relevant here. Further west, Ó Cróinín, *Early Medieval Ireland* is an excellent introduction. As for continental Europe and the Carolingians, a series of accessible entry-points to a vast amount of scholarship is provided by several contributions to *New Cambridge Medieval History II*, ed. McKitterick, namely: R. McKitterick, 'England and the Continent', pp. 64–84; P. Fouracre, 'Frankish Gaul to 814', pp. 85–109; J.L. Nelson, 'The Frankish kingdoms, 814–898: the West', pp. 110–41; J.J. Contreni, 'The Carolingian renaissance: education and literary culture', pp. 709–57. Also valuable is G. Brown, 'Introduction: the Carolingian Renaissance', in *Carolingian Culture: Emulation and Innovation* (Cambridge, 1994), ed. R. McKitterick, pp. 1–51.

The starting-point for any discussion of Englishness or English national identity before 1066 is Bede, *Ecclesiastical History of the English People*, ed. and trans. B. Colgrave and R.A.B. Mynors (Oxford, 1969). There is an enormous amount of scholarly literature on Bede, but P. Wormald, 'The Age of Bede and Aethelbald', in *The Anglo-Saxons*, ed. Campbell, pp. 70–100, is a good place to start. Another of Wormald's essays is also of particular relevance here: 'Bede, the *Bretwaldas* and the Origins of the *Gens Anglorum*', in *Ideal and Reality in Frankish and Anglo-Saxon Society: Studies Presented to J.M. Wallace-Hadrill*, ed. P. Wormald, D. Bullough and R. Collins (Oxford, 1983), pp. 99–129. A second ground-breaking essay on this topic is Sarah Foot, 'The Making of *Angelcynn*: English Identity before the Norman Conquest', *Transactions of the Royal Historical Society*, 6th series, 6 (1996), pp. 25–49. Her entry on 'English People' in *The Wiley-Blackwell Encyclopedia of Anglo-Saxon England*, ed. Lapidge *et al*, is also full of valuable insight. There is an excellent overview of all the issues and debates concerning notions of pre-conquest Englishness in Hugh M. Thomas, *The English and the Normans: Ethnic Hostility, Assimilation, and Identity 1066–c.1220* (Oxford, 2003), ch.2.

Chapter 1: The events, 796–899

Because the available source material is so scanty, there are no full-scale modern biographies available for any Anglo-Saxon king before Alfred the Great. The shorter ones in *ODNB* plug the gap admirably, whilst the course of events and a sense of the main developments can be put together from the general works referred to above. The Introduction to K&L, pp. 11–44 is also very helpful here, as are Williams, *Kingship and Government*, ch.6, and P. Wormald, 'The Ninth Century', in *The Anglo-Saxons*, ed. Campbell, pp. 132–57. Together these do much more than just recount what happened. As for Alfred, of the many accounts of his life and achievements, Patrick Wormald's entry on him in the *ODNB* is essential reading in all respects. Two other biographies I prefer are: R. Abels, *Alfred the Great: War, Kingship and Culture in Anglo-Saxon England* (Harlow, 1998), for its good sense and reliability, and A.P. Smyth, *Alfred the Great* (Oxford, 1995), for its thoroughness and its readiness to challenge received wisdom, particularly on the authenticity of Asser's *Life of Alfred*.

Chapter 2: Ruling the kingdoms, 796–899

Inevitably given the nature and amount of evidence which has survived, most of the specialist work in this area has concentrated on Wessex and the reign of King Alfred. Roach,

Kingship and Consent, attempts to cast its net more widely but is mainly concerned with the tenth century. Yorke, *Wessex in the Early Middle Ages*, pp. 94–123, provides a short but solid foundation. As for Alfred, *Alfred the Great: Papers from the Eleventh-Centenary Conferences*, ed. T. Reuter (Aldershot, 2003), contains numerous important studies, several of which are referred to below, whilst thought-provoking and sometimes very complex ideas about aspects of Alfred's reign, particularly his translations, can be found in D. Pratt, *The Political Thought of King Alfred the Great* (Cambridge, 2007).

Two studies of government and administration which repay careful study are N. Brooks, 'Alfredian Government: the West Saxon Inheritance', in *Alfred the Great*, ed. Reuter, pp. 153–73, and S. Keynes, 'The Power of the Written Word: Alfredian England, 871–99', in *ibid*, pp. 175–97. Important discussions of Alfred's coinage are R.H.M. Dolley and C.E. Blunt, 'The Coinage of Alfred the Great, 871–99', in *Anglo-Saxon Coins. Studies Presented to F.M. Stenton*, ed. R.H.M. Dolley (London, 1961), pp. 77–95; S. Keynes, 'King Alfred and the Mercians', *Kings, Currency and Alliances*, ed. Blackburn and Dumville, pp. 1–45, and M. Blackburn, 'Alfred's Coinage Reforms in Context', in *Alfred the Great*, ed. Reuter, pp. 199–215.

On Alfred's *burhs* and his relationship with London, see the picture essay by P. Wormald in *The Anglo-Saxons*, ed. Campbell, pp. 152–3; Abels, *Alfred the Great*, ch.6; Pratt, *Political Thought*, ch.6; N. Brooks, 'The Administrative Background to the Burghal Hidage', in *The Defence of Wessex: the Burghal Hidage and Anglo-Saxon Fortifications*, ed. D. Hill, as well as A.R. Rumble (Manchester, 1996), pp. 128–50; D. Hill, 'The Origin of King Alfred's Urban Policies', in *Alfred the Great*, ed. Reuter, pp. 19–33; and D. Keene, 'Alfred and London', in *ibid*, pp. 235–49.

Much has been written about Alfred's interest in learning and his literacy programme. For entry-level discussions, see Abels, *Alfred the Great*, ch.7, and K&L, pp. 23–41. Two *ODNB* entries are also clear and helpful: Patrick Wormald's on Asser and Michael Lapidge's short essay on 'Scholars at King Alfred's Court', both of which point towards further entries about other important figures. More ambitious readers should eventually go on to look at Pratt, *Political Thought*, Part II, and some of the essays by Janet Nelson reprinted in her *Rulers and Ruling Families in Early Medieval Europe. Alfred, Charles the Bald and Others* (Aldershot, 1999), in particular nos.I, II and IV.

On 'The Kingdom of the Anglo-Saxons' created by King Alfred and inherited by his successors, see S. Keynes, 'King Alfred and the Mercians', in *Kings, Currency and Alliances*, ed. Blackburn and Dumville, at pp. 34–9; and idem., 'Edward, king of the Anglo-Saxons', in *Edward the Elder, 899–924*, ed. N.J. Higham and D.H. Hill (London, 2001), pp. 40–66, at pp. 57–62.

Chapter 3: The kings and the law, 796–899

Hudson, *History of the Laws*, chs.2–4, contain much of relevance here, although his account ranges across the period from 871–1066. Early English law-making is discussed in *MEL*, i pp. 93–108. Successively more detailed treatments of Alfred's Laws and *Domboc* are covered in turn in K&L, pp. 163–70, 303–11; Abels, *Alfred the Great*, pp. 274–84; *MEL*, i pp. 265–85, 416–29; and Pratt, *Political Thought*, ch.11.

Chapter 4: The kings and the church, 796–899

There are sections of Redgate, *Religion, Politics and Society* which deal in passing with this period; most pertinent here are chs.3–5 and 10. Yorke, *Wessex in the Early Middle Ages*, pp. 192–203, and Brooks, *Early History*, ch.7, also add to the picture, although they only deal with southern England. A major recent study of English monasticism before the Benedictine Reform of the tenth century is Sarah Foot, *Monastic Life in Anglo-Saxon England, c.600–900* (Cambridge, 2006), whilst those with a grounding in the basic developments could move on eventually to the relevant parts of Blair, *The Church in Anglo-Saxon Society*. Chs.2–5, deal with the period up to 850 whilst chs.6–8 move on from there.

Chapter 5: The events, 899–975

E. John, 'The Age of Edgar', in *The Anglo-Saxons*, ed. Campbell, pp. 160–91 is a good place to start, as is Stafford, *Unification and Conquest*, chs.2–3. There are no modern biographies of any of the kings of this period (or of Aethelflaed, Lady of the Mercians), apart from Aethelstan. Very useful profiles are in *ODNB*. However, there are two immensely helpful collections of essays, one about Edward the Elder, *Edward the Elder*, ed. Higham and Hill, and another about Edgar: *Edgar, King of the English, 959–975. New Interpretations*, ed. Donald Scragg (Woodbridge, 2008). Amongst many important contributions to these volumes, there are two outstanding ones by Simon Keynes: in the first, his 'Edward, king of the Anglo-Saxons', at pp. 40–66, and in the second, his 'Edgar, *rex admirabilis*', at pp. 3–59. Framed between Edward and Edgar, Aethelstan is the subject of one of the best books written about Anglo-Saxon England: Sarah Foot, *Aethelstan. The First King of England* (New Haven, 2011). Her *ODNB* entry on Aethelstan is in many respects an abridged version of this. Michael Wood's work on Aethelstan has done much to remind students of the reign's importance and distinctiveness. Two of his pieces stand out: 'The Making of King Aethelstan's Empire: an English Charlemagne', in *Ideal and Reality*, ed. Wormald, Bullough and Collins, pp. 250–72, and 'The Lost Life of King Athelstan', in his own collection, *In Search of England. Journeys into the English Past* (London, 1999), pp. 149–68.

Chapter 6: Ruling the kingdom, 899–975

Williams, *Kingship and Government*, ch.7; Yorke, *Wessex in the Early Middle Ages*, pp. 123–32; and Stafford, *Unification and Conquest*, ch.8, give short, helpful overviews. The most important recent contributions to studies of English government in the tenth century are Roach, *Kingship and Consent*, Molyneaux, *The Formation of the English Kingdom*, especially ch.4, and B. Snook, *The Anglo-Saxon Chancery. The History, Language and Production of Anglo-Saxon Charters from Alfred to Edgar* (Woodbridge, 2015).

On individual reigns, all the contributions in *Edward the Elder*, ed. Higham and Hill, are valuable in different ways. Particularly here, though, I would recommend S. Keynes, 'Edward, king of the Anglo-Saxons', pp. 40–66; S. Lyon, 'The Coinage of Edward the Elder', pp. 67–78; and D. Hill, 'The shiring of Mercia – again', pp. 144–59. For Aethelstan, Foot, *Aethelstan*, ch.5, is essential, as is Maddicott, *The Origins of the English Parliament*, ch.1 (particularly on Aethelstan's councils). As for Edgar, these essays from *Edgar, King of the English*, ed. Scragg, are the most relevant in this context: S. Keynes, 'Edgar, *rex admirabilis*', pp. 3–59, and H. Pagan, 'The Pre-Reform Coinage of Edgar', pp. 192–207. For more on the coinage specifically, see H.M. Dolley and D.M. Metcalf, 'The Reform of the English Coinage under Eadgar', in *Anglo-Saxon Coins*, ed. Dolley and Blunt, pp. 136–68, and C.E. Blunt, B.H.I.H. Stewart, C.S.S. Lyon, *Coinage in Tenth-Century England from Edward the Elder to Edgar's Reform* (Oxford, 1989).

Chapter 7: The kings and the law, 899–975

For passing observations, see Hudson, *History of the Laws*, chs.2–4, and for a general overview, see *MEL*, i pp. 430–49. Edward the Elder's law codes are considered in *ibid*, pp. 286–90; Aethelstan's are discussed in *ibid*, ii pp. 290–308, and Foot, *Aethelstan*, pp. 136–48. There are also important points made about Aethelstan's laws in D. Pratt, 'Written Law and the Communication of Authority in Tenth-Century England', in *England and the Continent in the Tenth Century: Studies in Honour of Wilhelm Levison (1876–1947)*, ed. D. Rollason, C. Leyser and H. Williams (Turnhout, 2010), pp. 331–50. The legislation of Edmund and Edgar is covered by *MEL*, i pp. 308–12, 313–20.

Chapter 8: The kings and the church, 899–975

Redgate, *Religion, Politics and Society*, chs.3–5, 10, is still relevant here, as is Stafford, *Unification and Conquest*, ch.11. On Edward the Elder's relationship with Winchester and reorganisation of Wessex's diocesan structure, see A.R. Rumble, 'Edward the Elder and the churches of Winchester and Wessex', in *Edward the Elder*, ed. Higham and Hill, pp. 230–47. On Aethelstan and the church, see Foot, *Aethelstan*, ch.4, especially pp. 95–9, 117–26.

In many ways, the best starting-point for a study of the Benedictine Reform Movement in England remains D. Knowles, *The Monastic Order in England*, 2nd edn (Cambridge, 1963), ch.III. There are other short, accessible introductions by E. John in *The Anglo-Saxons*, ed. Campbell, pp. 181–9; Loyn, *The English Church*, ch.1; and Yorke, *Wessex in the Early Middle Ages*, pp. 203–25. Mechtild Gretsch in *ODNB* on 'Benedictine reformers' is also very useful and leads on to other relevant entries. A brief but incisive view is provided in Blair, *The Church in Anglo-Saxon Society*, pp. 350–4. Four volumes of essays have greatly enriched these basic accounts. First, *Tenth-Century Studies*, ed. D. Parsons (London and Chichester, 1975). I would recommend in particular D.A. Bullough, 'The Continental Background of the Reform', pp. 20–36. Second, *Bishop Aethelwold: His Career and Influence*, ed. B. Yorke (Woodbridge, 1988). Yorke's own essay, 'Aethelwold and the Politics of the Tenth Century', pp. 65–88, stands out. Third, *St. Dunstan: his Life, Times and Cult*, ed. N. Ramsay, N. Sparks and T. Tatton-Brown, (Woodbridge, 1992), in which N. Brooks, 'The Career of Dunstan', pp. 1–23, complements his earlier analysis: idem, *Early History*, pp. 243–50. Fourth, *St Oswald of Worcester: Life and Influence*, ed. N. Brooks and C. Cubitt (Leicester, 1996). D. Bullough, 'St Oswald: monk, bishop and archbishop', pp. 1–22, is an excellent summary of its subject's career.

Chapter 9: The events, 975–1042

There are good digests of the most important events and developments in E. John, 'The Return of the Vikings', in *The Anglo-Saxons*, ed. Campbell, pp. 192–213, and in Stafford, *Unification and Conquest*, ch.3. Aethelred and Cnut have been far better served by biographers than most of their predecessors. In addition to the *ODNB* entries on Aethelred and Cnut by Simon Keynes and M.K. Lawson respectively and the framework of events during Aethelred's reign provided in S. Keynes, *The Diplomas of King Aethelred 'the Unready', 978–1016* (Cambridge, 1980), ch.4, there are several full, modern profiles of both kings, including Ryan Lavelle, *Aethelred II: King of the English*, 2nd edn. (Stroud, 2008), Ann Williams, *Aethelred the Unready. The Ill-Counselled King* (London, 2003), and M.K. Lawson, *Cnut: The Danes in England in the Early Eleventh Century* (London, 1993).

The most up to date accounts of the reigns, however, are Levi Roach, *Aethelred the Unready* (New Haven, 2016), and Timothy Bolton, *Cnut the Great* (New Haven, 2017). Useful collections of essays have also been published about these two rulers: on Aethelred, *Ethelred the Unready: papers from the Millenary Conference*, ed. D. Hill (London, 1978), and *The Battle of Maldon AD 991*, ed. D. Scragg, and on Cnut, *The Reign of Cnut. King of England, Denmark and Norway*, ed. Alexander R. Rumble (Leicester, 1994). But, whilst not a book for the beginner, perhaps the most important work on either king and a ground-breaking one across the field of Anglo-Saxon studies, is Keynes, *Diplomas*. For the reigns of Kings Harold I and Harthacnut, *ODNB* provides short, sound introductions. Events in northern England during the century before 1066 are analysed in enlightening ways in Richard Fletcher, *Bloodfeud. Murder and Revenge in Anglo-Saxon England* (London, 2002) and Kapelle, *Norman Conquest of the North*, ch.1.

Chapter 10: Ruling the kingdom, 975–1042

The most important book on Aethelred's government remains Keynes, *Diplomas*, particularly ch.3, although more straightforward introductions are given in Williams, *Kingship and Government*, chs.9 and 10; Yorke, *Wessex in the Early Middle Ages*, pp. 132–48; and Stafford, *Unification and Conquest*, ch.8. For discussions of Cnut's government, see Lawson, *Cnut*; ch.5, Bolton, *Cnut the Great*, chs.3 and 6; S. Keynes, 'Cnut's earls', pp. 43–88; and K. Jonsson, 'The coinage of Cnut', pp. 193–230. The last two of these are both in *The Reign of Cnut*, ed. Rumble. Stafford, *Queen Emma and Queen Edith*, analyses the relationship between Queen Emma and her two royal husbands in expert depth.

Chapter 11: The kings and the law, 975–1042

Once again, Hudson, *History of the Laws*, chs.2–4, offers the most stable foundation. There is also a general overview in *MEL*, i pp. 449–65. The legislation of Aethelred and Cnut is discussed in passing in all the general biographies, although Roach, *Aethelred the Unready*, pp. 225–35, and Lawson, *Cnut*, pp. 59–65, 188–91, discusses their kings' laws in more dedicated detail. K. Lawson, 'Archbishop Wulfstan and the homiletic element in the laws of Aethelred and Cnut', *EHR* 107 (1992), pp. 565–86, reprinted in *The Reign of Cnut*, ed. Rumble, is also illuminating. For Aethelred's law-making, see also *MEL*, i pp. 320–45, and ibid, pp. 345–66 for Cnut's.

Chapter 12: The kings and the church, 975–1042

Parts of Redgate, *Religion, Politics and Society* are again pertinent here, as are Loyn, *The English Church*, pp. 24–54, Yorke, *Wessex in the Early Middle Ages*, pp. 225–39, and Stafford, *Unification and Conquest*, ch.11. Aethelred's spirituality and piety, and his relationship with Archbishop Wulfstan, are discussed periodically in Roach, *Aethelred the Unready*: see, in particular, pp. 153–67, 225–35. Lawson, *Cnut*, ch.4, tackles that king's relationship with the church, whilst Patrick Wormald's entry on Wulfstan in *ODNB* is a very illuminating survey of his career. The relevant parts of Blair, *The Church in Anglo-Saxon Society*, chs.6–8, deal in passing with this period and beyond.

Online resources

ODNB, the online version: www.oxforddnb.com/

MEL, ii, ed. S. Baxter and J.G.H. Hudson, a collection of Wormald, 'Papers Preparatory': http://earlyenglishlaws.ac.uk/reference/wormald/

The Electronic Sawyer, ed. S. Kelly, R. Rushforth *et al*, a revised and searchable version of Sawyer (ed), *Anglo-Saxon Charters*: www.esawyer.org.uk/

Online resources

INDEX

Note: Entries in **bold** are also defined in the Glossary of Terms

Aberdeen (Scotland) 117
Abingdon (Oxon.), abbey 98, 103, 181,
    182, 186, 227, 262, 263, 264; abbot of
    (*see* Aethelwold; Wulfgar)
Aclea, battle 22
Aelfflaed, daughter of king Offa 2
Aelfflaed, wife of king Edward the Elder 115
Aelfgifu, daughter of king Aethelred II 201,
    222, 223, 228
Aelfgifu, first wife of king Aethelred II 196
Aelfgifu, half-sister of king Aethelstan 117
Aelfgifu, wife of king Eadwig 123, 135,
    176; her will 185
Aelfgifu/Emma, queen *see* Emma
Aelfgifu of Northampton, first wife of king
    Cnut 208, 210, 224, 248
Aelfheah, archbishop of Canterbury and saint,
    murder 202, 265; translation 221, 268
Aelfheah, bishop of Wells and
    Winchester 176
Aelfheah, ealdorman of Hampshire 164
Aelfhelm, archbishop of Canterbury 115
Aelfhelm, ealdorman of southern
    Northumbria 200, 208, 218, 228
Aelfhere, ealdorman of Mercia 126, 144,
    154, 193, 217, 228, 261, 262
Aelfric, ealdorman of Hampshire 197, 200
Aelfric, ealdorman of Mercia 251
Aelfric, ealdorman of the Winchester
    districts 228–9, 231
Aelfric, treasurer of king Alfred 47

Aelfric of Eynsham, abbot and scholar 188
Aelfsige, abbot of the New Minster,
    Winchester 218
Aelfsige, litigant 163
Aelfstan, bishop of London/Rochester 260
Aelfthryth, daughter of king Alfred 66, 113
Aelfthryth, queen 134–5, 193, 222–3, 252,
    261, 263; in *Regularis Concordia* 184; role
    in murder of king Edward the Martyr
    194–5, 222
Aelfweard, abbot of Glastonbury 261
Aelfweard, son of king Edward the Elder
    115, 116, 129
Aelfwold, son of Aethelstan Half-King 185
Aelfwyn, daughter of Aethelflaed and
    Aethelred 114, 129, 131, 135
Aelle, king of Northumbria 25, 40
Aescwig, bishop of Dorchester 260
Aethelbald, king of Mercia 2, 5
Aethelbald, king of Wessex 22, 42; death
    and burial 24; marries step-mother Judith
    24, 113; rebels against king Aethelwulf
    23–4, 41, 43, 56
Aethelberht, king of East Anglia 2
Aethelberht, king of Kent 9; Laws 5, 77,
    78, 80, 84
Aethelberht, king of Wessex 24; death and
    burial 24; as sub-king of Kent 23–4, 41,
    42, 56
Aethelflaed, lady of the Mercians 21, 33,
    46, 64, 115, 116, 142, 170, 176, 231;

campaigns of 917–18 112; death 113, 131; relationship with Edward the Elder 111, 114, 129, 131

Aethelflaed, wife (?), of king Edgar 193

Aethelflaed, wife of king Edmund 135

Aethelgar, abbot of the New Minster, Winchester 184

Aethelheard, archbishop of Canterbury 96

Aethelhelm, ealdorman of Wiltshire 51

Aethelhelm Higa, litigant 87–9

Aethelmaer, ealdorman of Devon 203

Aethelmund, ealdorman of Mercia 121

Aethelnoth, archbishop of Canterbury 260, 268

Aethelnoth, ealdorman of Somerset 51, 58

Aethelred, archbishop of Canterbury 45, 58, 103–4

Aethelred, ealdorman of Mercia 33, 34, 35, 46, 49, 64, 72, 114, 115, 129, 131, 135; death 111, 131

Aethelred, king of Mercia 2

Aethelred I, king of Northumbria 2, 17

Aethelred I, king of Wessex 56–7, 109; alliance with Mercia 25; campaigns against Vikings 26, 45; death and burial 26, 45; events of reign 24–6

Aethelred II (the Unready), king of the English 120, 208, 211, 216, 218, 228, 229, 233, 236, 238, 259, 260, 266, 268, 269, 273, 274; administration and government 198, 220–1, 222, 224, 225, 226, 227, 229–30, 235–6, 253; and the church 261–5, 268; early life and murder of king Edward the Martyr 193–5, 196, 216, 222, 262, 268; events of reign 195–205 *passim;* (builds fleet 201; death 205; marriages 196, 222–3; relations with Normandy 196, 199–200, 202, 208, 223; return in 1014 203, 209, 217, 265); law and justice (Laws 208, 217, 236, 240–8, 251, 252, 255, 265); penitential emphasis after 1008 244–8 (*see also* law codes); reputation 21, 196, 198 (Debate 206–7); *see also Anglo-Saxon Chronicle;* coins; Emma; London; St. Brice's Day Massacre

Aethelstan, king of the English 122, 128, 133, 134, 147, 149, 150, 160; becomes king of the English 116, 129; early life in Mercia 115–16, 129; relationship with Winchester 116

Aethelstan, king of the English, administration: charters 136, 137, 138–9; coins 145–7; foreign contacts 117, 138, 180; formation of shires and hundreds 142–3, 167; as king of the Anglo-Saxons 137; as *Rex totius Britanniae* 134, 137; use of assemblies 139–40; wears crown 132, 141

Aethelstan, king of the English, events of reign 115–19 *passim; Brunanburh* campaign 118, 119–20; childlessness 120, 130; death and burial 118–19, 181; implicated in death of half-brother Edwin 116; posthumous reputation 119; Scottish campaign 117, 121 (*see also* naval warfare); submissions and campaigns of 927 116–17, 131–2 (*see also* Cornwall, Welsh

Aethelstan, king of the English, law and justice: Laws 144, 145, 153, 154, 155, 156–7, 158, 159, 162, 165, 166, 168, 274 (*see also* law codes, ordeal)

Aethelstan, king of the English, piety and the church 176–7, 179 (*see also* Cuthbert); support for monasticism 179, 180

Aethelstan, son of king Aethelred II 204, 223; his will 223

Aethelstan, sub-king of Kent 21–2, 23, 54

Aethelstan A, scribe 136, 226

Aethelstan/Guthrum, Viking *see* Guthrum

Aethelstan Half-King, ealdorman of East Anglia 185, 193, 228

Aethelstan of Sunbury, litigant 163–4

Aethelswith, daughter of king Aethelwulf of Wessex, marries king Burgred of Mercia 22, 46

Aethelweard, ealdorman of the western provinces and chronicler 121, 144, 218, 228, 264; on the 890s 34, 36, 62, 109; on *Brunanburh* 118, 119; on early 900s 110, 111; on king Aethelstan 119; on king Alfred 69, 73; on king Eadwig 124

Aethelweard, son of king Alfred 66

Aethelwine, ealdorman of East Anglia 144, 154, 185, 193, 253, 261

Aethelwold, bishop of Winchester and saint 124, 173, 180, 186, 193, 217, 261, 262, 263; contribution to monastic reform 182–5, 187; expels secular clergy from Old and New Minsters, Winchester 125; at Glastonbury and Abingdon 181, 186; tutors prince Edgar 125, 181, 182, 186

Aethelwold, ealdorman of East Anglia 135, 144, 193

Aethelwold, nephew of king Alfred, revolts against Edward the Elder 42, 43, 109–10, 129, 130

Aethelwulf, ealdorman of Berkshire 26, 53–4

Aethelwulf, king of Wessex 4, 41, 43, 44, 48, 51, 55, 109, 180, 265; burial 24, 174; events of reign 21–4 (*see also* Welsh); fights Vikings and allies with Mercia 22; loses power to son Aethelbald 23–4; marriages 23, 44–5, 46, 113; relations with archbishop of Canterbury 97–8; as sub-king of Kent 19, 21, 41, 56, 97; visits Rome 22–3, 81; will 23, 42, 45, 56, 103, 104

Aetheredeshid see Queenhithe

Aidan, saint 8, 92

Aire, river 122

Alain, Breton prince 180

Alcuin of York, scholar 9

Aldwych (London) 6, 61

Alfred, son of king Aethelred II 203, 204, 208, 209, 223; death 210–11

Alfred the Great, king of Wessex and the Anglo-Saxons 13, 23, 24, 33, 41, 52, 81, 90, 95, 98, 114, 115, 142, 148, 160, 186, 202, 212; early campaigns against Vikings 25–6; early life: 25; marriage to Ealhswith 25, 46, 51; with Osburh his mother 65; visits Rome twice 22, 81

Alfred the Great, king of Wessex and the Anglo-Saxons, achievements and reputation: 54–5, 69, 73–4, 90, 130; and *Anglo-Saxon Chronicle* 20, 70–2, 73 (*see also* English people); Debate 73–4; legendary stories about 30

Alfred the Great, king of Wessex and the Anglo-Saxons, administration: charters 57, 71; coins 28, 71–2, 146; divides annual income in two 50; organisation of household and servants 47, 135–6 (see also *discthegn, hraeglthegn*); resistance to policies 57–8, 62–3

Alfred the Great, king of Wessex and the Anglo-Saxons, events of reign: 27–36 *passim*; becomes king 26, 42, 55–7; candle clock 100; campaigns of 890s 34–6; death and burial 36, 43, 109, 145, 174, 205; develops Winchester 174; Edington campaign and battle 30–1, 33, 53, 55, 59, 70, 72; extends authority over English Mercia and establishes 'kingdom of the Anglo-Saxons' 33, 72, 128–9; fights at sea 32, 54, 60; flees Vikings and goes into hiding 29–30, 54, 58; illnesses 36, 57, 70, 100, 123; links with King Ceolwulf II of Mercia 28; pays Vikings 27, 110; will 45, 49–50, 56, 100, 109, 147 (*see also* lands); 'restores' London 32–3, 48, 61 (*see also* London);

tomb 89; treaty with Guthrum 33, 70, 72, 104, 112, 169

Alfred the Great, king of Wessex and the Anglo-Saxons, law and justice: *Domboc see* law codes; loyalty oath 85–6, 102, 157–8, 169; personal involvement 82, 163 (in Helmstan's case 87–9); *see also* courts

Alfred the Great, king of Wessex and the Anglo-Saxons, military reforms: 55, 59–64 *passim*; builds *burhs* 60–4, 102, 131, 145, 231, 272; builds ships 60 (*see also* naval warfare); reorganizes *fyrd* 59–60, 61, 132

Alfred the Great, king of Wessex and the Anglo-Saxons, relations with Church: 99–105 *passim*, 172; founds monastery at Athelney and nunnery at Shaftesbury 50, 100; harsh policies 102–4 (see also *bishops*); personal piety 99–101, 102, 179

Alfred the Great, king of Wessex and the Anglo-Saxons, revival of literacy and learning: 51–2, 64–72 *passim*, 178; establishes court school 66–7, 71; importance of 'wisdom' 65–6, 67, 68, 69, 82, 83, 84; other motives 65–9, 101; personal love of learning 65; Preface to *Pastoral Care* 64, 65–6, 67, 70, 101; Preface to *Consolation of Philosophy* 67; Preface to *Dialogues* 101; recruits foreign scholars 45, 66, 101, 180; success of plans 69, 155 (*see also* Asser, Augustine, Boethius, Gregory I, Grimbald, John the Old Saxon, *Pastoral Care*, Plegmund, Psalms, Werferth); targets officials 51–2, 67, 68, 82; translations 20, 47, 64, 65, 67–8, 69, 73, 101, 102, 271

Aller (Somerset) 31

Alney (Glos.) 205

Alresford (Hants.) 103

Amesbury (Wilts.) 139

Andover (Hants.) 162; *see also* law codes

Angelcynn 12, 70, 72, 271; and *Anglo-Saxon Chronicle* 70–1

Angles 12, 32, 71, 118

Anglesey (Wales) 126

Anglo-Saxon Chronicle 4, 13, 18–27 *passim*, 32, 40, 42, 43, 46, 50, 53, 54, 55, 58, 98, 109, 110–26 *passim*, 131–2, 138, 142, 149, 160, 169, 176, 177, 194, 211, 228, 233, 234, 251, 261, 262, 271; on 890s 34–6, 52, 59–62; on Aethelwold's revolt 109–10; on battle of Maldon 196–7; *Bretwalda* 13, 19; on *Brunanburh* 118, 119; Debate 20–1; on events of 878 29–31

passim, 57; on king Aethelred II 196,
198–9, 200–5 *passim*, 206, 216, 263, 264;
on king Alfred 72; on king Cnut 207,
267, 268; on king Edgar 125–6, 134, 174,
186; on kings Harold I and Harthacnut
210–12 *passim*, 234, 235; production
and purpose 18, 70–1, 73; *see also* Alfred;
Angelcynn; Asser; Mercian Register
Anglo-Saxons 4, 170; conversion to
Christianity 9, 13, 92; kingdom of 72,
84, 111, 112, 113, 128, 129; kings (*see*
Aethelstan; Alfred; Edward the Elder)
Annals of Ulster 118, 119
Anwend, Viking 28
Appledore (Kent) 34
aristocracy, English *see* nobility
armies *see* military organisation
Arnulf, king of the East Franks 33
Ashdown (Berks.), battle 26, 57
Ashingdon (Essex), battle 119, 205, 231,
260, 267, 269
assemblies, royal 21, 45, 56, 81, 82, 95,
156, 157, 160, 162, 172, 183, 221, 222,
241, 261; development in tenth century
137–42; purpose 45, 149, 150, 220–1,
225; role in royal succession 216–17;
see also Aethelstan; charters; crown-
wearings; Edward the Elder; ritual; *witan*
Asser, bishop of Sherborne and biographer
of king Alfred 25, 26, 27, 29–34 *passim*,
42, 45, 47, 51, 52, 54, 58, 60, 66–7,
101, 109, 174; on Aethelbald's revolt
23–4, 43; on Alfred and London 32;
on Alfred as judge 82, 163; on Alfred's
household 50; on Alfred's officials 62–3,
66–7, 69, 82; on Ceolwulf II 27, 71;
death 175; on Edington 30–1, 53; given
lands and honours by king Alfred 101;
Life of Alfred 34, 70, 71, 73 (intended
audience (*see* Welsh); links with *Anglo-
Saxon Chronicle* 20, 34); portrayal of
Alfred 57, 65, 68–9, 70, 99–100, 104;
on queenship in Wessex 46; recruited by
king Alfred 66
atheling, meaning 41, 271
Athelney (Somerset) 30, 31, 54; monastery
founded by king Alfred 50, 100
Augustine of Canterbury, saint 5, 78, 92
Augustine of Hippo, saint, author of
Soliloquies 67
Avars 9
Avon, river 110

Bakewell (Derbys.) 113, 131
Baldred, king of Kent 19

Baldwin II, count of Flanders 113
Baltic, sea 37
Bamburgh (Northumberland) 1, 114; lords
of 28, 116, 149, 201, 227, 228 (*see also*
Eadulf; Ealdred; Oswulf)
Banwell (Som.), monastery 101
Basing (Hants.), battle 26
Bath (Som.) 203, 244, 245, 246; *see also*
Edgar
Battle of Maldon, poem 185, 196–7
Beadricesworth see Bury St. Edmund's
Bede, historian 2, 4, 8, 21, 44, 66, 67,
78, 94; conversion of Anglo-Saxons to
Christianity 12–13, 92, 178; notions of
English identity 13, 70–1; notions of
imperium over England 5, 19, 271
Bedford (Beds.) 29, 33, 72, 111, 112, 131
Bedfordshire 177, 227
Benedictine reform movement *see*
monasticism
Benedictine Rule 178–9, 181, 182, 184, 274
Benedict of Nursia, saint 102, 178–9,
180, 271
Benfleet (Essex) 32, 35
Beorhtric, king of Wessex 2, 18, 41, 46
Beornstan, bishop of Winchester 176
Beornwulf, king of Mercia 17, 18, 19, 48,
95, 97
Beornwulf, town-reeve of Winchester 52
Berhtwulf, king of Mercia 22
Berkshire 1, 22, 175, 201, 241; *fyrd* 26,
53–4; shire court 252
Bernicia, kingdom 1, 28, 123, 149
Bertha, wife of king Aethelberht of Kent 9
bishops 92–3, 98–9, 160, 175, 178, 184,
186–7, 259, 261, 263; importance
to king Alfred 67, 101–3; role in
government and legal system 95–6, 102,
139, 154–5, 172–3, 176, 221, 237, 245,
251, 256, 260
Boethius, author of *Consolation of Philosophy*
47, 67, 69
Bohemia (Czech Republic) 9
bookland 5, 7–8, 48, 51, 53, 54, 102,
109, 132, 141, 251, 252, 256, 271, 272
botleas 255–6
Boulogne (France) 33–4
Bradfield (Berks.) 252
Bredy (Dor.) 61
Brentford (Middx) 205
Bretwalda/Brytenwalda 13, 19
Bridgnorth (Shrops.) 35, 111, 131
Brihtferth, ealdorman of Essex 163–4
Brihtric, thegn 201
Brihtwold, abbot of Reculver 5

Brinsworth (Yorks.) 119

Bristol Channel 9, 111

Britons 2, 13, 117, 118, 148, 159

Brittany (France) 111, 180

Bromborough (Ches.) 120

Bromswold (Cambs.) 119

Bruges (Belgium) 211

Brunanburh, battle 21, 118, 132; Debate 119–20

Brycheiniog (Wales) 8

Buckingham (Bucks.) 61, 111, 112, 117, 131, 139

Buckinghamshire 117, 227

Burghal Hidage 60–2, 174, 271, 272; *see also burhs*

Burgred, king of Mercia, alliance with Wessex and marriage 22, 25, 46; flees Mercia 27, 28, 58

burhs 231, 272; built by Edward the Elder and Aethelflaed 111–13, 131, 142; *burh*-reeve/town-reeve 52, 229; courts 143, 144, 145, 162; king Alfred's reforms 60–4; mints 145; *see also* Burghal Hidage; economy

Burnswark (Scotland) 119

Bury St. Edmund's (Suff.) 26

Buttington (Wales) 35, 51, 62

Byrhtferth of Ramsey, monk and author of *Life* of St. Oswald 183, 185, 194, 262

Byrhthelm, archbishop of Canterbury 182

Byrhtnoth, abbot of Ely 184, 253; *see also* lawsuits

Byrhtnoth, ealdorman of Essex 185, 193, 196, 231, 263

Caithness (Scotland) 117

Calne (Wilts.) 254

Cambridge (Cambs.) 28, 145

Cambridgeshire 110, 112, 183, 227

Canterbury (Kent) 7, 10, 25; archbishop 44, 95, 221, 248, 252, 259, 264 (*see also* Aelfheah; Aelfhelm; Aethelheard; Aethelnoth; Aethelred; Augustine; Byrhthelm; Ceolnoth; Dunstan; Hadrian; Lyfing; Oda; Plegmund; Sigeric; Theodore of Tarsus; Wulfhelm; Wulfred); cathedral (Christ Church) 188, 268; diocese 93, 271; ecclesiastical province 92, 273; relations with Mercia and Wessex 96–8; sacked by Vikings 22, 202, 265

Carham-on-Tweed (Scotland), battle 228

Carhampton (Som.) 20, 22

Carlisle (Cumb.) 123

Carolingian Empire *see* Charlemagne

Carolingian Renaissance, importance of writing in law and government 81, 84; *see also* Charlemagne

Carolingians 9; influence on England 7, 23, 24, 44–5, 64, 81, 84, 138, 187, 272; *see also* Charlemagne

Castleford (Yorks.) 122

Cedd, bishop of the East Saxons 94

Cenred, father of king Ine 3

Cenwald, bishop of Worcester 176, 180, 182

Cenwulf, king of Mercia 17–18, 96–7

Ceolnoth, archbishop of Canterbury 97–8

Ceolwulf I, king of Mercia 17, 43–4

Ceolwulf II, king of Mercia 27–8, 29, 33, 71

ceorl 11, 200, 272; *wergild* 12, 87; *see also* peasantry

Charlemagne, emperor 2, 18, 23, 64; administrative and cultural reforms ('Carolingian Renaissance') 7; conquests and imperial coronation ('Carolingian Empire') 9–10, 144

Charles Martel 272

Charles the Bald, king of the West Franks 23, 60

Charles the Simple, king of the West Franks 113, 118, 138, 180

charters, royal 4–5, 40, 113, 123, 124, 132, 134, 194, 196, 206, 207, 219–20, 224, 264; Debate 226–7; issued at assemblies 45, 96, 138–9, 141, 172, 225; production 136–7; *see also* diplomas; household; individual kings; New Minster; writs

Cheddar (Somerset) 139, 181

Chelsea (London) 63; ecclesiastical council (synod) 97

Chertsey (Sy.), abbey 182, 186

Cheshire 55, 99, 114, 118, 120, 196, 228

Chester (Ches.) 25, 35, 111, 114, 115, 126, 131, 133, 134, 145, 148, 170

Chester-le-Street (Northd.) 98, 117, 179–80

Chichester (Sus.) 35, 61

Chippenham (Wilts.) 29, 31, 57, 58

Chirbury (Shrops.) 131

Chisbury (Wilts.) 61

Christ Church, Canterbury *see* Canterbury

Christchurch (Dor.) 231

Church, English chs.4, 8, 12 *passim*; impact of viking raids 66, 98–9; in pre-viking England: 91–5; relationship with kings 95–8; *see also* bishops; councils; household; minsters; monasticism; parishes; *Regularis Concordia*

Church, English, under king Alfred:
65–6, 99–104, 172; role in law and
government 68, 102
Church, English, 899–975: diocesan
reorganisation 175–6, 186–7; influence
and treatment in law codes 160–1;
monastic reform see monasticism; role in
law and government 172–4, 186
Church, English, 975–1042: influence
on law codes 243–50; role in law and
government 237, 256, 260–9
Cirencester (Glos.) 31, 251
Clofesho, ecclesiastical councils 95, 96
Cluny (France), abbey 178
Cnut, king of England and Denmark 211,
222, 228, 230, 231, 234, 253; becoming
king 203–5; before events of reign 207–10
passim; campaigns in Scandinavia 208–9;
death and burial 210, 216, 224, 259,
260; marriages 208, 210, 223–4; Oxford
pact of 1018 208, 217, 267–8; purge
and appointments of 1016–17 207–8,
218–19, 229, 232; sources for reign
207; visits Rome 209; see also Aelfgifu of
Northampton, Emma; coinage; nobility
Cnut, king of England and Denmark,
administration: charters 225; earls under
229, 272; use of assemblies 221–2
Cnut, king of England and Denmark, law
and justice: laws 240, 247, 248–50, 252,
255, 256, 261; see also law codes
Cnut, king of England and Denmark, piety
and the Church 265–9; story of the
waves 266; and St. Edith 268–9; visits
Edmund Ironside's tomb 268
coins and coinage 40, 44, 49, 114, 166, 237;
Debate 212–13; in king Cnut's reign
207, 235–6, 249; king Edgar's reforms
125, 126, 146–7, 148, 150; Mercia/
Wessex monetary alliance 25–6, 28, 71;
royal control 147, 215; in tenth century
145–6, 159; under king Aethelred II 196,
198, 206, 235–6, 242, 243, 264 (Agnus
Dei ('Lamb of God') type 202, 236, 246);
under king Aethelstan 132, 141; under
king Alfred 71–2; under king Eadwig
124; see also burhs; law codes; mancus;
mints; moneyers
Colchester (Essex) 112, 139
Coldstream (Scotland) 228
Colne estuary (Essex) 35
Colyton (Devon) 143, 157
common burdens 8, 53, 54, 62, 231,
271, 272, 273
Congresbury (Som.), monsastery 101

Connacht (Ireland) 8
Conrad II, emperor 209
consecration, royal 23, 41, 43, 44, 95,
97, 115, 116, 121–2, 126, 129, 133–4,
173, 194, 216, 260–1, 262; Frankish
influence on 44, 46
Consolation of Philosophy see Alfred; Boethius
Constantine II, king of Scots 114, 119, 121,
131; relations with king Aethelstan 117–18
Corbridge (Northd.), battles 114
Corfe (Dor.) 194
Cornwall 1, 18, 20, 98, 147, 159, 196, 197,
232, 237; conquered by Aethelstan 117,
131, 132; diocese 259
coronation 18, 95, 97, 123, 129, 134, 140,
148, 173, 174, 176, 181, 203, 209, 261;
oath 140, 160, 161, 173; ordo 44, 129;
see also crown; crown-wearings; Edgar;
ritual
Corpus Iuris Civilis 78
councils, ecclesiastical 92, 93, 95, 96, 97,
125, 160, 175, 184, 274; see also Chelsea;
Clofesho; Croft; Hertford; Winchester
courts 11, 78, 80–1, 90, 143–4, 145, 158;
899–975 161–3, 165, 169; 975–1042
229–30, 237, 240, 249, 252, 254, 255,
256, 260; in king Alfred's Wessex 82–3;
see also burhs; hundred court; king's
court; shire court
Crediton, diocese 175
Cricklade (Wilts.) 110, 231
Croft (Lincs.), ecclesiastical council 97
crown, royal 44, 109, 132, 140, 141, 266;
see also Aethelstan; coronation; crown-
wearings
crown-wearings 140–1, 174, 220; see also
crown
Cumbria 99, 133, 228, 232, 233
Cuthbert, saint, visits king Alfred 30; shrine
visited by kings Aethelstan and Cnut
179, 266
Cuthred, sub-king of Kent 17, 96

Dalriada, kingdom 8
danegeld see heregeld
Danelaw 31, 112, 131, 183, 185–6, 237;
Debate 169–70; in law codes 159–60,
250, 252, 256, 272
Danes see Vikings
Danube, river 9
Datchet (Bucks.) 252
Davenport (Ches.) 114
David, Old Testament king of Israel 81
Dee, river 134
Deerhurst (Glos.) 205

Deira, kingdom 1, 28

Denewulf, bishop of Winchester 103–4, 174, 175

Denmark 36, 197, 203, 208, 209, 210, 211, 224, 225, 233, 265, 266, 267; kings (*see* Harald I Bluetooth; Harald II; Swein Forkbeard)

Deormod, steward of king Alfred 47

Derby (Derbys.) 29, 112, 113, 131, 170, 243; *see also* Five Boroughs

Derbyshire 19, 27, 227, 273

Derwent, river 113

Devil's Dyke (Cambs.) 110

Devon 1, 29, 35, 58, 103, 143, 157, 175, 181, 193, 196, 197, 199, 228; ealdorman (*see* Aethelmaer); *fyrd* 29, 231

Dialogues see Alfred; Gregory I

diplomas, royal 4, 6, 136, 206, 272; *see also* charters

discthegn (king Alfred's seneschal) 136

Domboc (law code of king Alfred) *see* Alfred

Domesday Book 170, 212, 237

Donald, king of Strathclyde 131

Dorchester (Dor.): bishop 52, 176 (*see also* Aescwig; Eadnoth; Oscytel); diocese 177, 259

Dore (Derbys.) 19

Dorset 26, 29, 103, 109, 175, 179, 182, 194, 196, 199, 204, 205, 228, 231

Dover (Kent) 26, 98

Dublin (Ireland) 114, 118, 119, 120, 121; *see also* Olaf Guthfrithson

Dumfriesshire (Scotland) 118

Dumnonia, kingdom 1

Dunnottar (Scotland) 117

Dunstan, bishop of Worcester, bishop of London, archbishop of Canterbury and saint 180, 268; as abbot of Glastonbury 121, 181, 184; contribution to monastic reform 182, 183, 187; death 217, 263; relationship with king Aethelred II 194, 217, 262, 263; relationship with king Eadwig 123–4, 176, 181–2; relationship with king Edgar 125, 140, 164, 173, 178, 182; relationship with king Edward the Martyr 193, 260, 261

Dunwich, bishop 92, 98; diocese 93

Durham (Northd.) 201, 259, 266; *see also* Symeon of Durham

Dyfed (Wales) 8

Dyle, river 33

Eadberht Praen 17, 96

Eadburh, daughter of king Offa, marries king Beorhtric of Wessex 2, 18, 46

Eadgifu, daughter of king Edward the Elder 113, 118, 138, 180

Eadgifu, wife of king Edward the Elder 115, 120, 134–5, 181

Eadgyth, daughter of king Aethelred II 200, 218

Eadgyth, half-sister of king Aethelstan 117, 138, 180

Eadhild, half-sister of king Aethelstan 117, 138

Eadnoth, bishop of Dorchester 260

Eadred, king of the English 115, 130, 133, 134, 139, 140, 143, 149, 163; death and burial 123, 124, 129, 130, 164; events of reign 121–3 *passim*; support for monastic reform 181; will 135–6, 224

Eadric, ealdorman of Wessex 144

Eadric, king of Kent, Laws 77, 80

Eadric, king's reeve 254

Eadric Streona, ealdorman of Mercia, in king Aethelred II's reign 200, 201, 202, 204, 205, 218, 228, 231; in king Cnut's reign 207–8, 219, 229, 248

Eadulf, lord of Bamburgh 228

Eadulf, son of Eadulf, lord of Bamburgh 228

Eadwig, king of the English 133, 134, 135, 148, 177, 179, 185; charters 123, 124; coins 124; death and burial 124; division of kingdom with Edgar 124, 130, 176; events of reign 123–4 *passim*; image and reputation 124; relationship with abbot Dunstan 123–4, 181–2

Eadwig, son of king Aethelred II 208

Eadwulf, king's thegn 52

ealdormen 11, 52, 67, 68, 69, 79, 85, 135, 139, 188, 224, 253; disappearance of title 209, 229; origins and duties 50–1, 80, 82, 86, 144, 154, 162, 163, 172, 173, 228–9, 254, 272; role in military organisation 53–4, 59, 132, 142, 231, 272

Ealdred, lord of Bamburgh 114, 131

Ealhferth, bishop of Winchester 103

Ealhhere, ealdorman of Kent 54

Ealhmund, king of Kent (?), 18

Ealhswith, wife of king Alfred 25, 46; death and burial 174

Eamont (Cumb.) 116, 117, 131

Eanred, king of Northumbria 18

Eardwulf, king of Northumbria 17–18, 43

earls/earldoms 118, 122, 221, 224, 225, 228, 237, 272; under king Cnut 219, 229

East Anglia 9, 10, 12, 32, 33, 34, 35, 54, 59, 89, 93, 110, 112, 130, 145, 207, 229,

232, 272; kingdom 1, 2, 18, 25, 27, 50,
58; church in 98, 99, 176, 182–3, 186;
conquered and settled by Vikings 26,
31, 55, 56, 169, 200, 202; ealdormen
(*see* Aethelstan Half-King; Aethelwine;
Aethelwold); kings (*see* Aethelberht;
Edmund); *see also* Ulfcytel
East Saxons, kingdom *see* Essex
Ecclesiastical History of the English People see
Bede
Ecgberht, king of Wessex 13, 22, 41–2,
44, 48, 109, 174; death and burial 20,
21; events of reign 18–20; relations with
archbishop of Canterbury 97–8
Ecgberht I, king of Northumbria 25, 28
Ecgberht II, king of Northumbria 28
Ecgferth, landholder 164
Ecgfrith, king of Mercia 41, 43
Ecgwulf, marshal of king Alfred 47
Ecgwynn, wife of Edward the Elder 115
economy, English 49, 63, 232–3; Debate
212–13; towns and *burhs* 6, 10, 63–4,
145, 158–9, 170, 212; trade and trading
6–7, 26, 49, 82, 94, 146, 158–9, 212–13,
233, 237, 241; *see also emporia; wics*
Eddisbury (Ches.) 111, 131
Edgar the Peaceable, king of the English
121, 172, 196, 231, 253; as king of
Mercia 123–4, 130, 176; as king of
Northumbria 124, 176; tutored by
Aethelwold 181, 186
Edgar the Peaceable, king of the English,
administration: charters and titles 134,
137, 139, 185, 227; coinage reforms
146–7, 148, 237, 242; formation of shires,
hundreds and courts 143, 161–2, 169, 252
Edgar the Peaceable, king of the English,
and Church: in Foundation Charter of
New Minster 186, 266; political benefits
of support 185–6; in *Regularis Concordia*
184; role in monastic reform 125, 179,
182, 183, 186, 195, 262, 264
Edgar the Peaceable, king of the
English, events of reign 123–6 *passim*;
becomes king of the English 124;
circumnavigations of Britain 126,
133, 150, 232 (*see also* naval warfare);
coronation at Bath and events of 973 21,
126, 133–4, 140, 148, 173, 203; death
and burial 126, 194, 205, 216, 261, 260;
marriages 135, 193, 261; and northern
England 148–9, 177–8
Edgar the Peaceable, king of the English,
image and reputation 125–6, 136, 215;
significance of reign 128, 149–50

Edgar the Peaceable, king of the English,
law and justice: laws 143, 144, 145, 153,
154, 158–63 *passim*, 167–9 *passim*, 173,
242–3, 249 (importance in 1018 217,
242, 248, 267–8; role in Aethelstan's
case 164; *see also* law codes)
Edington (Wilts.), battle 30–1, 33, 53, 55,
59, 72, 119
Edith, daughter of king Edgar and saint *see*
Cnut
Edmund, king of East Anglia, death and
veneration 26, 98
Edmund, king of the English 115, 118,
119, 123, 134, 135; events of reign
120–1 *passim* (murder and burial 121,
126, 130, 194; reconquers northern
England 120–1, 122, 133); law and
justice (Laws 141, 143, 153, 155–6, 157,
160, 161, 163, 167, 168, 176 (*see also*
law codes)); role in monastic reform 176,
179, 181
Edmund, son of king Edgar 193
Edmund Ironside, king of England 204,
207, 208, 216–17, 221, 228, 231, 248,
266, 267; events of reign 205; tomb (*see*
Cnut)
Edward the Confessor, king of England
204, 223, 224, 235; exile in Normandy
203, 208, 209; returns to England and
becomes king 203, 210–11, 211–12, 217
Edward the Elder, king of the Anglo-
Saxons 21, 61, 120, 128, 148, 153, 170,
172, 185; in king Alfred's reign 34, 64,
66
Edward the Elder, king of the Anglo-
Saxons, administration: charters and
assemblies 136, 138; coinage 145–6;
formation of shires 142
Edward the Elder, king of the Anglo-
Saxons, events of reign 109–15 *passim*;
Aethelwold's revolt 41, 42, 109–10, 129,
130; builds *burhs* 111–14 *passim*, 131,
142, 231; 'coronation' 43, 109; death
and burial 115, 116, 117; fights Bretons
111; founds New Minster, Winchester
174 (relations with Winchester 175–6);
marriages 134–5; pays Vikings 110;
submissions of 917 112; takes control of
Mercia 113 (*see also* Strathclyde), 131,
147 (political relations with Mercia 129)
Edward the Elder, king of the Anglo-
Saxons, law and justice: ;aws 82–3, 85,
86, 144–5, 154, 155, 157, 158, 159,
163, 165, 166, 167; in Helmstan's case
87–9; *see also* law codes

Edward the Martyr, king of the English, events of reign 193–4, 261–2 *passim*; cult 194, 264, 268; Debate 194–5; murder and burial 194, 196, 216, 222, 259, 262

Edwin, king of Northumbria 4, 44

Edwin, son of Edward the Elder 115–16

Egbert's Stone (Som./Wilts.) 30, 53, 70

Eilaf, earl of Herefordshire 219

Ellendun (Wroughton, Wilts.), battle 18, 119

Elmham (Norf.), diocese 93, 98, 176

Ely (Cambs.), abbey 98, 183, 211, 253; abbot (*see* Byrhtnoth)

Emma/Aelfgifu, queen 261; following Cnut's death 211, 224, 225; relations with Aethelred II 198, 199–200, 203, 204, 223, 266; relations with Cnut 208, 209, 210, 223, 248, 266; *see also Encomium of Queen Emma*

emporia 6, 49

Encomium of Queen Emma 207

English Mercia *see* Mercia

Englefield (Berks.) 26, 54

English people 10–13; and king Alfred 70–1; *see also Angelcynn;* Bede

Enham (Hants.) 217, 244, 245, 246, 248

Eoforwic (York, Yorks.) 6, 49

Eorcenwold, bishop 3

Erik Bloodaxe, viking ruler of York 122, 133; death 122–3, 126, 177, 228

Erik Hlathir, earl of Northumbria 207, 210, 219, 228, 229

Essex 21, 23, 34, 35, 42, 51, 56, 110, 111, 112, 131, 196, 205, 231, 241, 263; ealdorman 52 (*see also* Byrhtnoth)

estates, royal *see* lands

Evesham (Worcs.) 98

Exeter (Dev.), 26, 29, 35, 57, 117, 131, 145, 154, 155, 156; monastery 101

Farndon (Ches.) 114–15

Farnham (Sy.) 34

Faversham (Kent) 156, 168

feasting, royal 7, 8, 44, 52, 134, 135, 140, 141, 181, 220

feorm 48, 271, 272

feud 77, 82, 272; in *Domboc* 86, 87; in tenth century 141, 161, 166–7

Finland 37

Firth of Forth 1

Five Boroughs 111, 112, 113, 121, 170, 203, 243, 253; *see also* Derby; Leicester; Lincoln; Nottingham; Stamford

Flanders (Belgium) 66, 116, 118, 211, 212, 213, 233; count (*see* Baldwin II)

Fleury (France), abbey 178, 180, 181, 182, 184

Flodoald, litigant *see* lawsuits

folkland 48, 271, 272

Fonthill (Wilts.) 87–9; *see also* lawsuits

Forest of Dean (Glos.) 233

France 9, 50, 118, 180

Francia 18, 37, 46, 79, 81, 138, 180

frankpledge *see* tithings

Frome (Som.) 123

Fulco, archbishop of Rheims 98–9, 100–1

Fulham (London) 31

fyrd 53–4, 142, 272; in king Aethelred II's reign 231; king Alfred's reforms 59–60, 61, 132; meaning 52, 273

gafol, meaning 197, 273, 274; distinguished from *heregeld* 234; *see also* tribute

Gainsborough (Lincs.) 203

geld *see* heregeld

genealogies, royal 4, 6, 40, 42

Germanus, abbot of Winchcombe 184

Germany 9, 146, 180, 209, 212, 213

Gewisse 1

gift-giving/gifts, royal 3–4, 23, 40, 43, 44, 47, 48, 49, 52, 123, 141, 149, 179, 195, 199, 216, 266

Glastonbury (Som.), abbey 121, 126, 180, 181, 183, 184, 205, 227, 269; abbot 264; monks 137, 188

Gloucester (Glos.) 33, 72, 118, 222; St. Oswald's Priory 110–11

Gloucestershire 18, 111, 121, 183, 205, 219

Godeman, abbot of Thorney 184

Godgifu, daughter of king Aethelred II 223

Godwine, earl of Wessex 209, 210, 211, 217, 219, 220, 229

Gorze (France), abbey 178

Gothfrith, Viking 126

government, central: 796–899 43–50 *passim* (*see also* assemblies; household; ritual; *witan*); 899–975 134–42 *passim* (*see also* assemblies; charters; household; ritual); 975–1042 215–26 *passim* (*see also* assemblies; charters; housecarls; household; nobility; stallers; *witan;* writs); in pre-viking England 2–7; *see also* crown-wearings; hearth troop; kings/ kingship; wealth

government, local: 796–899 50–2 *passim* (*see also* ealdormen; reeves; shires); 899–975 142–5 *passim* (*see also* ealdormen; English Mercia; hundred court; hundreds; reeves; shire court; shires; wapentakes); 975–1042: 227–30 *passim* (*see also* earls; ealdormen; hundreds; shires; wapentakes)

Grately Code *see* law codes

Great Army/great heathen army *see* Vikings

Greenwich (London) 202, 204

Gregory I 'the Great', pope, sends missionaries to England 9, 13, 92; *Dialogues* 68, 100, 102; *Pastoral Care* 65, 67, 70, 101

Grimbald, monk and scholar 66; tomb and miracles 174–5

Gunnhild, daughter of king Cnut 209, 223

Guthfrith, king of Northumbria 28, 36

Guthfrith, Viking 116

Guthrum/Aethelstan, Viking 26, 28, 57, 58; defeat at Edington and baptism 31, 59, 99; treaty with Alfred 33, 70, 72, 104, 112, 169

Gwynedd (Wales) 8

Hadrian, archbishop of Canterbury 66

Haedde, bishop 3

Hagbourne (Berks.) 252

Hakon, earl of Worcestershire 210, 219

Hakon, Norwegian prince 180

Halfdan, Viking 25, 28

Hampshire 1, 26, 30, 103, 141, 156, 175, 198, 201, 244; ealdorman 52 (*see also* Aelfheah; Aelfric); *fyrd* 53, 59, 70, 231

Hamwic (Southampton, Hants.) 6, 10, 49, 54

Harald I Bluetooth, king of Denmark 197, 265

Harald II, king of Denmark 208

Harald Fairhair, king of Norway 122, 180

Harold I Harefoot, king of England 208, 210–11, 217, 232, 234, 251, 260

Harthacnut, king of England 210–12, 217, 223, 224, 225, 234, 235

Harz mountains (Germany) 146

Hastein, Viking 34, 35

Hastings (Sus.) 61; battle 230

hearth troop *see* household

Helmstan, king's thegn *see* lawsuits

Hengest, legendary warrior 4

Henry I (the Fowler), king of the East Franks 117, 138, 180

Henry III, emperor 223

Henry of Huntingdon, chronicler 21, 212

Hereford (Heref.) 116, 117, 131, 231; diocese 93, 176

Herefordshire 111, 219, 253; shire court 253

heregeld 233, 235, 272, 273; also called *geld*/Danegeld 233, 273; distinguished from *gafol* 234

Hertford (Herts.) 35, 111, 131; ecclesiastical council 92

Hertfordshire 177, 227

Hexham (Northd.), bishop/diocese 93, 98

hide, meaning 6, 61, 148, 234, 273

Hingston Down (Corn.), battle 20

Hlothere, king of Kent 5; Laws 77

Holme (Cambs.), battle 110

Holy River (Sweden), battle 209

horse-thegn *see* Wulfric

housecarls *see* household, royal

household, royal 3–4, 40, 46–7, 49–50, 51, 95, 132, 134–5, 142, 149, 176, 221–6, 274; hearth troop 7, 52, 58, 132, 225, 230, 273; housecarls 225, 230; king Alfred's 47, 50; king Eadred's 135–6; production of documents 136–7, 225–7

hraeglthegn (king Alfred's chamberlain) 136

Hrani, earl of Gloucestershire 219

Hrotheweard, archbishop of York 177

Hugh, duke of the Franks 117, 138, 176

Hugh, reeve of queen Emma 200

Humber, estuary 2, 10, 13, 19, 49, 92, 98, 112, 113, 117, 130, 131, 149, 159, 177, 178, 202, 228, 260, 273

hundred court 143, 144, 162, 164, 165, 167, 229, 234, 237, 242, 253–4, 256, 273; origins 145, 163

Hundred Ordinance (I Edgar) *see* law codes

hundreds/wapentakes 132, 133, 143, 148, 150, 158, 167, 229, 230, 234, 237, 253–4, 255, 273, 274; *see also* hundred court; Hundred Ordinance

hunting, royal 52, 136, 181, 220, 222

Huntingdon (Cambs.) 112, 119; *see also* Henry of Huntingdon

Hwicce, kingdom 2, 229

income, royal *see* wealth

Ine, king of Wessex, Laws 3, 5, 7, 52, 77, 80, 81, 83, 84, 155

Institutes of London *see* law codes

Institutes of Polity 216, 243

Iona (Scotland), abbey 8

Ipswich (Suff.) 7, 10, 170, 196

Ireland 8, 9, 13, 25, 50, 92, 111, 114, 116, 119, 180

Irish Sea 1, 9, 119

Isle of Man, ruler 134

Isle of Wight (Hants.) 2, 6, 175, 201, 203

Italy 9, 180

Ivarr the Boneless, Viking 25, 114, 116

John VIII, pope 103, 104

John of Worcester, chronicler 21, 121, 124, 133, 134, 136, 150, 161, 200, 207, 211, 267

John the Old Saxon, monk and scholar 66
Judith, queen of Wessex, consecrated 23,
  44, 46; marries king Aethelbald 24, 113;
  marries king Aethelwulf 23, 44–5, 113
Judoc, saint 174
justice *see* law
Justinian, emperor 78
Jutes 12

Kelso (Scotland) 228
Kempsford (Glos.) 18
Kenneth II, king of Scots 126, 134
Kent 1, 12, 17, 19, 20, 24, 27, 34, 42,
  54, 62, 70, 101, 109, 110, 112, 156,
  196, 198, 201, 202, 231, 232; church
  in 95–8, 103; ealdormen (*see* Ealhhere;
  Sigehelm); kings/kingdom 2, 4, 6, 18,
  21, 22, 48, 51, 92 (*see also* Aethelberht;
  Baldred; Eadric; Ealhmund; Hlothere;
  Wihtred); sub-kings (*see* Aethelbert;
  Aethelstan; Aethelwulf; Cuthred)); Laws
  77, 79, 80, 81, 155, 167–8; sheriff (*see*
  Wulfsige)
Kent, William, architect 73
Keynes, Simon, historian 206
king's court 81, 82, 161–2, 251
kings/kingship, in pre-viking England 2–8;
  expectations and requirements 43–6,
  57, 81, 84, 207, 215–18; Frankish/
  Carolingian influence 138; itinerant
  nature 47, 136, 221; succession criteria
  40–3, 129, 216; *see also* assemblies;
  charters; Church; coins and coinage;
  consecration; coronation; crown;
  crown-wearing; feasting; genealogies;
  gift-giving; government; hearth troop;
  household; hunting; individual kings by
  name; king's court; lands; naval warfare;
  nobility; ritual
king's thegns *see* thegns
Kingston upon Thames (Sy.) 21, 41, 97,
  109, 115, 116, 122, 194, 262
kin/kinship 77, 78, 80, 142, 165, 219, 167;
  in *Domboc* 85, 86

Lake District 126
Lancashire 1, 99
landholding 10, 11, 104, 187, 219–20;
  see also bookland; folkland
lands, royal 3, 4, 44, 48–9, 51, 52, 104,
  139, 144, 145, 147–8, 149, 150, 176,
  216, 221, 225, 229, 232–3, 237, 272;
  in king Alfred's will 49–50, 100, 109;
  see also feorm; vills
Langandene 56

law, systems of, in pre-viking England
  5, ch.3 *passim* (development by 899,
  89–90), ch.7 *passim* (development by
  975 168–9), ch.11 *passim* (strengths
  and limitations by 1042 256–7); *see also*
  bishops, *botleas*, Church, courts, *Domboc*,
  feud, hundred court, king's court,
  kinship, law codes, lawsuits, lordship,
  oath-helping, oaths, ordeal, reeves, shire
  court, tithings, *wergild*
law codes 5, 77–80, 155–61, 240–50;
  authorship (*see* Wulfstan II); purpose 5,
  78, 84–5, 155, 243–4, 250
law codes, *Domboc* (king Alfred's law code)
  83–7 *passim*, 88, 71, 77, 78, 82, 153;
  contents 85–7, 167; form and purpose
  83–4; in king Edward the Elder's reign
  145, 154, 157 (*see also* feud, kinship, law,
  lordship, *wergild*)
law codes, other: I Edward 154, 158,
  165, 166; II Edward 155, 157, 163;
  I Aethelstan (Ordinance on Charities)
  154, 160; II Aethelstan (Grately Code)
  141, 145, 146, 156, 158, 165, 166, 168,
  173; III Aethelstan 155, 167, 168; IV
  Aethelstan (Thunderfield Code) 156, 157;
  V Aethelstan 154, 155, 156; VI Aethelstan
  143, 154–5, 167, 168; I Edmund 160; II
  Edmund 155, 161; III Edmund (Colyton
  Code) 157; I Edgar (Hundred Ordinance)
  143, 144, 162, 167, 253; II Edgar 154,
  160; III Edgar (Andover Code) 162;
  IV Edgar (*Wihtbordestan* Code) 154,
  159, 160, 143, 149, 242–3; I Aethelred
  (Woodstock Code) 241, 242; II Aethelred
  241; III Aethelred (Wantage Code) 241,
  243; IV Aethelred (Institutes of London)
  241–2 (coinage in 242, 243); V Aethelred
  244–5, 246, 248; VI Aethelred 244,
  246, 248; VII Aethelred 244, 245–6;
  VIII Aethelred 244, 247; X Aethelred
  244; 1018 code 217, 248, 249, 267; I
  Cnut 249; II Cnut 247, 249–50; *see also*
  Church, Danelaw
Laws of Henry I 133
lawsuits 80, 251; Aethelstan's case 163–4;
  Byrhtnoth's case 253; Edwin's case 253;
  Flodoald's case 254; Helmstan's case
  ('The Fonthill Letter') 87–9, 161 (*see also*
  Alfred); Wulfbald's case 252; Wynflaed's
  case 252–3; *see also* oaths; ordeal
Lea, river 33, 35, 72
Leicester (Leics.) 29, 112, 113, 120, 131,
  170, 243; diocese 93, 98, 177; *see also*
  Five Boroughs

Leicestershire 142, 227, 273
Leinster (Ireland) 8
Leo III, pope 9
Leofa, murderer 121
Leofric, earl of Mercia 209, 210, 217, 219, 220, 229, 232
Leofwine, ealdorman of Mercia 220
Leofwine, litigant 252
Liber Regulae Pastoralis see Pastoral Care
Lichfield (Staffs.), diocese 93, 96
Lincoln (Lincs.) 26, 29, 113, 170, 243; *see also* Five Boroughs
Lincolnshire 2, 27, 93, 97, 110, 169, 197, 203, 204, 227, 231, 273
Lindisfarne (Northd.) 9, 19; bishop 93; monks 98
Lindsey (Lincs.), kingdom 2; diocese 93, 98
lithsmen 232
Loire, river 60, 178, 180
Lombards (Italy), kingdom of 9
London 7, 10, 22, 25, 27, 29, 35, 92, 111, 146, 168, 181, 208, 210, 216–17, 221, 222, 248, 267, 268; bishop/diocese 93, 176, 264 (*see also* Aelfstan; Dunstan; Wulfstan II); in king Aethelred II's reign 197, 201, 202, 203, 205, 207, 231, 232, 235, 252; and king Alfred 32, 33, 48, 61, 64, 72; *see also* Aldwych; Institutes of London; *Lundenwic*
lordship 77, 133, 168, 242; in *Domboc* 86
Louis, brother of king Rudolf II of Burgundy 117
Louis IV, king of the West Franks 118, 138, 180
Louis the Pious, emperor 7, 178
Louvain (France) 33
Ludeca, king of Mercia 19
Lundenwic (Aldwych, London) 6, 49, 61
Lyfing, archbishop of Canterbury 207, 267

Maccus, killer of Erik Bloodaxe 123
Maccus, Viking 126
Magnus, king of Norway 210, 211
Malcolm, king of Strathclyde 134
Malcolm I, king of Scots 121
Malcolm II, king of Scots 201, 228
Maldon (Essex) 112, 131; battle 185, 196–7, 231, 241, 263; *see also Battle of Maldon*
Malmesbury (Wilts.), abbey 119, 179, 183, 204; *see also* William of Malmesbury
Manchester (Lancs.) 113, 131
mancus, meaning 103, 136, 164, 273
Medeshamstede see Peterborough

Mercia 35, 36, 55, 58, 70, 80, 84, 93, 101, 110, 120, 135, 139, 144, 159, 186, 201, 231, 250, 252, 256, 271, 272
Mercia, kingdom: 1–2, 5, 6, 7, 17–19, 40, 41, 89; alliance with Wessex 22, 25, 28, 45, 46, 54, 71
Mercia, coinage 25–6, 49, 71–2; and church in Kent 96–8; conquered by Vikings 27–8, 29, 31, 57, 169; kings (*see* Aethelbald, Aethelred, Aethelstan, Beornwulf, Burgred, Cenwulf, Ceolwulf I, Ceolwulf II, Ecgfrith, Ludeca, Offa, Wiglaf, Wulfhere); *see also* queens and queenship
Mercia, English Mercia 33, 36, 64, 71, 72, 111, 130, 147, 176 (division into shires 142–3); ealdorman 50–1, 62, 248 (*see also* Aelfhere, Aelfric, Aethelmund, Aethelred, Eadric Streona, Leofwine); earl (*see* Leofric); under king Cnut 207, 208, 229; overrun by king Edmund 121, 133; relationship with Wessex 110–16 *passim*, 128–9, 131; resistance to rule from Wessex 114; separated from Wessex in 924 115–16; separated from Wessex in 957 123–4; separated from Wessex in 1016 205; *see also* Aethelflaed, Mercian Register
Mercian Register 112, 113, 114, 129
Meretun, battle 26
Mersea Island (Essex) 35
Mersey, river and estuary 111, 113
military organisation, before king Alfred 7–8, 52–4; from 899–975 130–4; king Alfred's reforms 59–64; after king Edgar 230–2; *see also* Burghal Hidage; *burhs*; common burdens; ealdormen; *fyrd*; hearth troop; housecarls; naval warfare; reeves; thegns; weapons
Milton Abbas (Dor.), abbey 179, 182
Milton Regis (Kent) 34
ministri see thegns
Minster in Thanet (Kent) 97, 98
minsters 93–5, 97, 98, 99, 103, 104, 187, 260; *see also* monasticism; Ripon; Southwell; Whitby; Wimborne
mints 7, 63, 71–2, 145, 147, 212, 235, 236; *see also* coins; moneyers
missionaries 5, 8, 9, 13, 78, 92, 94
monastic cathedrals 188
monasticism 93; anti-monastic backlash 261–2; contentious features 185–6; extent and limits of reform 186–8; reform in tenth century 125, 178–86, 259–60; *see also* Aethelstan; Aethelwold;

Benedictine Rule; Dunstan; Eadred;
  Edgar; Edmund; minsters; monastic
  cathedrals; Oswald
moneyers 145, 146, 147, 159, 166, 235,
  236, 273; *see also* mints
Montgomery (Wales) 35
Moors in Spain 9
Morcar, northern thegn 204
Moses, Old Testament prophet 78, 84
Muchelney (Som.), abbey 179
Munster (Ireland) 8

naval warfare 32, 54; king Aethelred
  II's fleet 197, 198, 201, 220; king
  Aethelstan's Scottish expedition 117;
  king Alfred's reforms 60; king Edgar's
  fleet 126, 133, 232; *see also lithsmen;*
  shipsokes
New Minster, Winchester 115, 124,
  174–5, 182, 184, 185, 186, 218, 264,
  266; Foundation Charter 137, 186;
  see also Edward the Elder
nobility, English 69, 185, 205, 207,
  215–21, 261, 263, 267; changes under
  Cnut 218–20; role in royal succession
  42, 45, 56, 216–17; in *witan* 3, 137–8
Norfolk 1, 202
Normandy (France) 198, 199–200, 203,
  208, 210, 211, 217, 231, 246, 266; dukes
  (*see* Richard I; Richard II; Robert I)
Northampton (Northants.) 29, 112, 120;
  see also Aelfgifu of Northampton
Northamptonshire 177, 227
Northey Island (Essex) 196
North Sea 208
Northumbria 6, 9, 10, 12, 19, 35, 36, 40,
  80, 89, 93, 110, 113, 114, 139, 148,
  169, 201, 203, 207, 237; conquered
  by Aethelstan 116, 117, 130, 131;
  conquered by Eadred 122, 133;
  conquered by Edmund 120–1, 133;
  ealdormen (*see* Aethelhelm; Oslac;
  Oswulf; Thored; Uhtred); earls (*see*
  Erik Hlathir; Siward); incorporated
  into English kingdom 123, 130, 148–9,
  227; ruled by Edgar 124, 176; kingdom
  (conquered and settled by Vikings
  25, 28, 31, 34, 56; kings (*see* Aelle;
  Aethelred I; Eanred; Eardwulf; Ecgberht
  I; Ecgberht II; Edwin; Guthfrith;
  Osberht; Oswald; Oswy; Ricsige;
  Sigeferth)
Norway 36, 209–10, 232; kings (*see* Harald
  Fairhair; Magnus; Olaf I; Olaf II)
Norwich (Norf.) 145, 170, 200

Nottingham (Notts.) 25, 29, 45, 54, 57,
  113, 131, 139, 145, 170, 243; *see also*
  Five Boroughs
Nottinghamshire 177, 227, 273
Nunnaminster (St Mary's Abbey,
  Winchester) 174, 182

oath-helping/oath-helpers 79, 165,
  251, 273
oaths 27, 29, 34, 122, 140, 273; in king
  Alfred's *Domboc* 85, 87; in legal system 11,
  78–9, 88, 165–6, 251; loyalty 44, 168,
  237, 257; *see also* coronation; oath-helping
Oda, bishop of Ramsbury and archbishop
  of Canterbury 123, 160, 173, 176, 177,
  180, 182
Odda, ealdorman of Devon 58
Offa, king of Mercia 2, 10, 17, 18, 19, 41,
  43, 44, 46, 78, 84, 91, 96; coinage 7
Offa's Dyke 6, 8, 72
Olaf I Tryggvason, king of Norway 197,
  199, 203, 232, 241
Olaf II Haraldsson, king of Norway and
  saint 209, 210
Olaf Guthfrithson, viking ruler of Dublin
  and York 118, 119, 120–1
Olaf Sihtricson, viking ruler of York 116,
  121, 122, 133
Old Minster, Winchester 100, 103–4, 123,
  137, 174, 175, 184, 185, 188, 210, 212,
  263, 266; expulsion of secular clergy
  125, 182
Old Testament 13, 78, 81, 84
Ordal 166
ordeal 79, 157, 161, 236, 243, 245, 250–1,
  273, 274; in Flodoald's case 254–5; in
  king Aethelstan's reign 166, 173
Ordgar, ealdorman of Devon 135, 193
Ordinance on Charities (I Aethelstan) *see*
  law codes
Ordlaf, ealdorman of Wiltshire 87–9
Orosius's *History against the Pagans* 67
Osberht, king of Northumbria 25
Osbern of Canterbury, biographer of
  Dunstan 183
Osburh, wife of king Aethelwulf of Wessex
  23; with son Alfred 65
Oscetel, Viking 28
Oscytel, bishop of Dorchester and
  archbishop of York 177–8, 182
Osgar, monk 181
Oslac, ealdorman of Northumbria 149, 159
Osric, ealdorman of Hampshire 53
Oswald, bishop of Worcester, archbishop
  of York and saint 125, 140, 178,

180, 182, 183, 184, 185, 262, 263;
contribution to monastic reform 183,
187; *Life* (*see* Byrhtferth)
Oswald, king of Northumbria and saint 8,
110; *see also* Gloucester
Oswulf, lord of Bamburgh and ealdorman
of Northumbria 123, 149
Oswy, king of Northumbria 92
Otto I, emperor 117, 138, 180
Ottonians 141; *see also* Henry I; Otto I
Ouse, river 33, 72, 110
Owain, king of Strathclyde 118, 119
Oxford (Oxon.) 61, 72, 73, 111, 203,
204, 208, 217, 248, 249, 251, 267; pact
of 1018 (*see* Cnut; Wulfstan II); St.
Frideswide's church 199
Oxfordshire 1, 103, 177, 181, 222, 227

Pallig, Viking 199
papacy *see* popes
parishes 94, 260, 273
Parret, river 62
Pastoral Care 65–6, 67, 70, 101; *see also*
Alfred; Gregory I
Paulinus, bishop of York 92
Peak District (Derbys.) 6, 113
peasantry 11–12, 148; *see also* ceorl; slaves
Pecsaetna 6
Pennines 123
Penrith (Cumb.) 116, 131
Penselwood (Som./Dor.) 30, 205
Peterborough (Cambs.), abbey 94, 98,
183, 185
Picts 8
Plegmund, archbishop of Canterbury 64,
66, 101, 175
Pontefract (Yorks.) 122
popes 18, 44, 58, 97, 103, 266; annual
tribute 51; role in conversion of Anglo-
Saxons 9, 13, 92; *see also* Gregory I; John
VIII; Leo III; Rome
population 47, 229; English 11, 213;
Scandinavian 37; Wessex 62
Powys (Wales) 8
Psalms/Psalter 65, 66, 67, 100, 246
Pucklechurch (Glos.) 121

Queenhithe/*Aetheredeshid* (London) 64
queens and queenship, in Wessex 23; contrast
between Mercia and Wessex 46; in tenth
century 134–5, 184, 185, 222, 224; *see also*
Aelfthryth; Ealhswith; Emma; Judith

Ragnall, viking ruler of York 113, 114, 131
Ragnall Guthfrithson, viking ruler of
York 121

Ragnar Lothbrok, Viking 25
Ramsbury, diocese 175; bishop (*see* Oda)
Ramsey (Cambs.), abbey 183, 185, 187,
265; *see also* Byrhtferth; Wulfsige
Reading (Berks.) 26, 27
Reculver (Kent), abbey 97; *see also*
Brihtwold
reeves, royal 48, 69, 140, 168, 200; *burh-*
reeve (*see burhs*); importance in local
government and justice 51, 67, 68, 82,
83, 85, 89, 143, 144–5, 148, 154–5,
157, 158, 160, 163, 221, 229, 254–5,
274; role in military organisation 51, 53,
132; shire-reeves (*see* sheriffs)
Regularis Concordia 125, 126, 184, 186,
271, 274
Repton (Derbys.) 27, 28, 54
Ribble, river 237
Richard I, duke of Normandy 196, 198,
208, 221, 223
Richard II, duke of Normandy 198, 199,
200, 202, 203
Ricsige, king of Northumbria 28
Ringmere (Norf.) 202
Ripon (Yorks.), bishop 92; minster 122
ritual, royal 4, 40, 46, 129, 215, 227, 237;
at assemblies 44, 126, 140, 141, 174,
220; *see also* consecration; coronation;
crown; crown-wearings
Roach, Levi, historian 206
Robert I, duke of Normandy 209
Rochester (Kent) 7, 32, 198; bishop 52, 92
(*see also* Aelfstan); diocese 93, 259, 263
Roger of Wendover, chronicler 122–3
Rother, river 34
Romans/Roman Empire 5, 10, 61, 78,
81, 92
Rome (Italy) 5, 9, 13, 51, 78, 92; visits by
English kings 18, 22–3, 27, 28, 41, 43,
56, 81, 209, 221, 266
Rouen (France) 196
Rudolf II, king of Burgundy 117
Rule of St. Benedict see Benedictine Rule
Runcorn (Ches.) 111, 131
Russia 37

St. Albans (Herts.) 122
St. Brice's Day Massacre 198, 199, 206,
221, 232, 264
St. Paul's Cathedral (London) 205, 221,
223, 268
St. Peter's, Ghent (Belgium), abbey 182, 184
St. Swithun 255
Sandwich (Kent) 22, 54, 201
Saxons 12, 32, 69
Saxony (Germany), duchy 9, 146, 180

Scotland 8, 114, 117, 119, 121, 132, 139, 141, 179, 209, 228
Scots 117, 118, 119, 228; king/kingdom 113, 116, 132, 133, 228; *see also* Constantine II; Kenneth II; Malcolm I; Malcolm II
Seine, river 35, 60
Selsey (Sus.), diocese 93
Selwood, forest (Som./Dor./Wilts.) 62
Sermo Lupi ad Anglos (Sermon of the Wolf to the English) *see* Wulfstan II
Severn, river/estuary 35, 62, 111, 205
Shaftesbury (Dor.) 210; abbey 194, 195, 264; nunnery founded by king Alfred 50, 100
Sheppey (Kent) 20, 22, 98
Sherborne (Dor.) 24, 188; bishop (*see* Asser); diocese 93, 174, 175
sheriffs 167, 221, 226, 230, 237, 274, 275; first appearance 229
Sherston (Wilts.) 205
shipsokes 133
shire court 143–4, 164–5, 173, 226, 229–30, 234, 237, 249, 252–4, 256, 261, 274, 275; early development 162–3
shires 133, 144, 188, 234, 237, 272, 274; development 142–3, 148, 150, 162–3, 177, 227, 228, 229, 230; origins 51, 142; shire-reeves (*see* sheriffs); *see also* shire court
Shoebury (Essex) 35
Shrewsbury (Shrops.) 228
Sigeferth, king of Northumbria 36
Sigeferth, northern thegn 204
Sigehelm, ealdorman of Kent 135
Sigeric, archbishop of Canterbury 261
Sigewulf, cup-bearer of king Alfred 47
Sihtric, viking ruler of York 114, 116, 121, 131
Sittingbourne (Kent) 34
Siward, earl of Northumbria 209, 220, 228, 229
slaves/slavery 11, 12, 79, 156, 168, 250, 254–5, 274, 275
Solomon, Old Testament king of Israel 81, 83
Somerset 1, 20, 29, 30, 31, 51, 58, 98, 101, 123, 139, 175, 179, 180, 181, 204, 228; ealdorman 35, 62 (*see also* Aethelnoth); *fyrd* 53, 59, 70, 231
Southampton (Hants.) 6, 196, 205, 210
South Saxons, kingdom 1, 2, 19, 22
Southwark (London) 221
Southwell minster (Notts.) 177
Spain 9
Stafford (Staffs.) 111, 131

Staffordshire 99, 228
Stainmore (Cumb.) 123, 126
stallers 224
Stamford (Lincs.) 29, 112, 113, 170, 243; *see also* Five Boroughs
Steepholme, island 111
Stenton, Sir Frank, historian 206
Steyning (Sx.) 24
Stiklestad (Norway), battle 210
Stowe (Bucks.) 73
Strathclyde, kingdom 8, 121, 126; king/ruler 116 (*see also* Donald; Malcolm; Owain); submit to Edward the Elder 113; Welsh 119
succession, royal *see* assemblies; kings/kingship; nobility; *witan*
Suffolk 1
Sunbury (Middx.) 163–4
Surrey 19, 21, 22, 23, 42, 51, 56, 97, 109, 112, 156, 175, 182
Sussex 1, 21, 23, 24, 35, 42, 51, 52, 56, 198
Sutton (Notts.) 177
Sutton Hoo (Suff.) 9
Sweden 36, 209
Swein, son of king Cnut 208, 210
Swein Forkbeard, king of Denmark 197, 200, 241, 265; invasion of 1013–14 202–3, 228, 230, 232, 246–7, 264
Swinbeorg 56
Symeon of Durham, chronicler 116, 117, 122
synods *see* councils; Whitby

Tamar, river 117
Tamworth (Staffs.) 54, 111, 113, 116, 120, 131
Tanshelf (Yorks.) 122
taxation 50, 215, 218, 233, 235; *see also gafol; heregeld*; tribute
Tees, river 1, 28, 80, 123, 128, 147, 148, 149, 150, 159, 227, 236, 237
Tempsford (Beds.) 112
Tettenhall (Staffs.), battle 110, 111, 130
Thames, river 1, 2, 6, 10, 18, 22, 24, 32, 33, 34, 35, 49, 62, 72, 93, 110, 124, 130, 136, 139, 182, 187, 205, 210, 221, 228, 232
Thanet (Kent) 22, 126
thegns 4, 11, 12, 67, 85, 155, 172, 188, 194, 203, 204, 210, 217, 219, 220, 232, 253, 274; described as *ministri* 224; king's thegns 11, 27, 52, 71, 87, 136, 139, 224, 251, 252, 273 (*see also discthegn; horse-thegn; hraeglthegn*); role in military organisation 50, 53, 58, 62; *wergild* 12
Thelwall (Ches.) 113, 131

Theodore of Tarsus, archbishop of
Canterbury 66, 92–3
Thetford (Norf.) 26, 200, 202
Thored, ealdorman of southern
Northumbria 196, 200, 222, 228
Thored, Viking 126
Thorkell the Tall, viking leader and earl of
East Anglia 201–4 passim, 207–8, 229,
231, 232, 233, 245, 264, 273
Thorney (Cambs.), abbey 98, 183, 184
Thunderfield (Sy.) 156, 157; see also law
codes
Thurkil the White, thegn 253
Thurwif, slave 163–4
tithes 10, 93, 154, 160, 173, 245, 246, 274
tithings 167, 168, 169, 249, 254, 255,
272, 274
Torksey (Lincs.) 27
Tostig, Viking 201
Towcester (Northants.) 112
towns see burhs; economy; emporia; wics
trade see economy
Trent, river 2, 113, 203
Tribal Hidage 6
tribute 2, 4, 6, 11, 40, 51, 57, 103, 117,
149, 160, 197, 213, 225, 248, 274; first
paid to Vikings 197, 261; paid by king
Aethelred II 197, 198, 201, 202, 208,
232, 234–5, 241; see also gafol
Tyne, river 28, 80, 114, 228

Ubba, Viking 25
Ufegeat, northern thegn 200, 218
Uhtred, ealdorman of Northumbria 201,
203, 204–5, 218, 228
Uhtred of Bamburgh 131
Ulf, earl under Cnut 219
Ulfcytel, East Anglian warrior 200, 202, 231

vendetta see feud
Viken (Norway) 37
Viking, meaning 36–7; campaigns of 890s
34–6; conquer England 197–205 passim;
Debates 36–7, 169–70; defeated by king
Alfred 29–30; defeats in tenth century
110–23 passim; impact of raids in ninth
century 48–9, 66, 98–9, 101; reasons
for raids 37; resumption of raids 196–7;
see also Danelaw
vills, royal 48, 54, 139

Wales 8, 19, 29, 35, 70, 111, 117, 126,
134, 139, 141; see also Welsh
Wallingford (Oxon.) 61, 63, 174
Wantage Code see law codes

wapentakes see hundreds
Wardour (Wilts.) 87, 88
Wareham (Dor.) 29, 54, 57, 61, 63, 231
Warwick (Warks.) 33, 111, 131
Warwickshire 142
Watling Street 33, 72, 112, 203
wealth, royal 6–7, 48–50, 147–8, 232–6;
see also coins; economy; gafol; heregeld;
lands; taxation
weapons and weaponry 3, 11, 47, 48,
52–3, 79, 85, 87, 111, 149
Wednesfield (Staffs.) 110
Wells, diocese 187; bishop (see Aelfheah);
diocese 175
Welsh 6, 8, 46, 52, 62, 66, 126, 132;
intended audience for Asser's Life of
Alfred 70; submit to king Aethelstan
116–17; submit to king Aethelwulf 22;
see also Strathclyde; Wales
Welshpool (Wales) 35
Werferth, bishop of Worcester 64, 66;
translates Dialogues of Gregory I 68, 100,
101–2
wergild 12, 79–80, 89, 164, 167, 242, 251,
252, 255, 275; in Domboc 86–7
Wessex 3, 12, 13, 31, 40, 58, 66, 70, 79,
110, 114, 130, 139, 201, 204, 208,
210, 217, 226, 229, 231, 248; church
in 96–8, 99–105 passim, 175–6, 187
(importance of Winchester 174–5);
coinage (see coins and coinage);
ealdorman (see Eadric); earl (see
Godwine); invaded by Vikings 22,
24–5, 26–7, 28–9, 32, 34–6, 52, 54,
55, 56, 57, 103; kingdom 1, 2, 17, 50,
128, 173, 205; kings (see Aethelbald;
Aethelberht; Aethelred I; Aethelwulf;
Alfred; Beorhtric; Ecgberht; Ine);
law and justice ch.3 passim, 252, 256;
military organisation 59–64; queens
(see Asser; queens and queenship);
relationship with Mercia 22, 25, 28, 45,
46, 71, 72, 115–16, 129, 131; rise in
ninth century 18–20, 21, 32–3; royal
wealth 147–8; shires of 51, 142, 144,
163, 201; succession in 22, 23–4, 41–3,
56, 115–16, 124, 148, 207, 228, 267
(dynastic stability 265)
Westbury on Trym (Glos.), abbey 183
Westminster Abbey (London) 182; abbot
(see Wulfsige)
Westmoreland 126
West Saxons, kingdom see Wessex
Whitby (Yorks.) minster 94, 98; synod 92
wics 6, 10

Wiglaf, king of Mercia 19, 22, 97
Wigningamere 112
Wihtbordestan Code (IV Edgar) *see* law codes
Wihtgara 6
Wihtred, king of Kent 77
Wilfrid, saint 122
William of Malmesbury, chronicler 21; on
   king Aethelstan 115, 116–17; on king
   Eadwig 124; on king Edgar 186; on king
   Edmund 181; on king Edward the Elder
   114–15
Williams, Ann, historian 206
Wilton (Wilts.) 200; abbey 193, 268, 269;
   battle 27
Wiltshire 27, 30, 51, 58, 87, 89, 110, 139,
   175, 179, 204, 254; ealdorman 35, 62
   (*see also* Aethelhelm; Wulfhere); *fyrd* 18,
   53, 59, 70, 200, 231
Wimborne (Dor.), minster 26, 109
Winchcombe (Glos.), abbey 183, 184;
   abbot (*see* Germanus)
Winchester (Hants.) 21, 24, 36, 52, 63,
   89, 139, 146, 181, 187, 203, 211, 222,
   223, 225, 249; bishop/bishopric 49, 92,
   93, 175–6, 259, 264 (*see also* Aelfheah;
   Aethelwold; Beornstan; Denewulf;
   Ealhferth); in Burghal Hidage 61–2;
   council 125, 184; development in
   tenth century 174–5, 185; ealdorman
   of the Winchester districts (*see* Aelfric);
   monks 186; resistance to king Aethelstan
   116, 119; *see also* New Minster;
   Nunnaminster; Old Minster
Wirral peninsula (Ches.)
witan 3, 40, 43, 57, 58, 244, 245, 265, 275;
   business 4, 42, 44, 45–6, 56, 137–8,
   141, 160, 172, 216, 221; composition 3,
   95, 172, 261
Witchford (Cambs.) 253
Witham (Essex) 111, 112, 131
Wolverhampton (Staffs.) 110
Woodstock (Oxon.) 241, 250, 254; *see also*
   law codes
Worcester (Worcs.) 225, 267; diocese 93,
   176 (bishops (*see* Cenwald; Dunstan;
   Oswald; Werferth; Wulfstan II));
   monastery 187, 188 (monks 137); *see also*
   John of Worcester
Worcestershire 131, 211, 219, 235

Worr, ealdorman 18
writs 207, 237, 275; compared with
   charters 225–6
Wroughton (Wilts.), battle *see Ellendun*
Wulfbald, litigant *see* lawsuits
Wulfgar, abbot of Abingdon 218, 261
Wulfgeat, thegn 200
Wulfheah, northern thegn 200
Wulfhelm, archbishop of Canterbury
   141, 160
Wulfhere, ealdorman of Wiltshire, deserts
   king Alfred 45, 58, 85
Wulfhere, king of Mercia 2, 6
Wulfnoth, thegn 201, 220
Wulfred, archbishop of Canterbury 96–7
Wulfric, horse-thegn 52
Wulfsige, abbot of Ramsey 260
Wulfsige, abbot of Westminster 183–4
Wulfsige, sheriff of Kent 229
Wulfstan, litigant 163
Wulfstan I, archbishop of York 121,
   122, 177
Wulfstan II (*lupus*/the Homilist), bishop
   of London, Worcester and archbishop
   of York 188, 206, 218, 269; author of
   law codes 244–6, 247–8, 248–50, 261,
   264–5; influence on king Cnut 208, 248
   (Oxford pact of 1018 248, 267–8); *Sermo
   Lupi ad Anglos* 243–4, 265; writings 216,
   243 (*see also Institutes of Polity*)
Wye, river 117
Wynflaed, litigant *see* lawsuits

Yaxley (Cambs.) 163
York (Yorks.) 6, 7, 10, 25, 28, 43, 51,
   113, 114, 116, 119, 120–1, 122, 123,
   130, 139, 145, 149, 170, 205, 227,
   235; archbishop 259, 261 (*see also*
   Hrothweard; Oscytel; Oswald;
   Wulfstan I; Wulfstan II); archbishopric/
   archdiocese 93, 125, 177, 271; bishop/
   bishopric 93 (*see also* Paulinus);
   ecclesiastical province 92, 273; viking
   rulers 135, 149 (*see also* Erik Bloodaxe;
   Olaf Guthfrithson; Olaf Sihtricson;
   Ragnall; Ragnall Guthfrithson); *see also*
   Alcuin; *Eoforwic*
Yorkshire 1, 80, 94, 98, 99, 118, 169,
   272, 273